The Psychology of Personnel Selection

This engaging and thought-provoking text introduces the main techniques, theories, research and debates in personnel selection, helping students and practitioners to identify the major predictors of job performance as well as the most suitable methods for assessing them. Tomas Chamorro-Premuzic and Adrian Furnham provide a comprehensive, critical and up-to-date review of the constructs we use in assessing people – intelligence, personality, creativity, leadership and talent – and explore how these help us to predict differences in individuals' performance. Covering selection techniques such as interviews, references, biographical data, judgement tests and academic performance, *The Psychology of Personnel Selection* provides a lively discussion of both the theory behind the use of such techniques and the evidence for their usefulness and validity. *The Psychology of Personnel Selection* is essential reading for students of psychology, business studies, management and human resources, as well as for anyone involved in selection and assessment at work.

TOMAS CHAMORRO-PREMUZIC is a senior lecturer at Goldsmiths, research fellow at UCL, and visiting professor at NYU in London. He is a world-renowned expert in personality, intelligence and psychometrics, and makes frequent media appearances providing psychological expertise on these issues.

ADRIAN FURNHAM is Professor of Psychology at UCL. He is also a consultant on organisational behaviour and management, and a writer and broadcaster. His columns have appeared in management magazines such as *Mastering Management* and *Human Resources*, as well as the *Financial Times*, *Sunday Times* and *Daily Telegraph*.

The Psychology of Personnel Selection

Tomas Chamorro-Premuzic

Adrian Furnham

CAMBRIDGE
UNIVERSITY PRESS

CAMBRIDGE UNIVERSITY PRESS
Cambridge, New York, Melbourne, Madrid, Cape Town, Singapore, São Paulo, Delhi, Dubai, Tokyo

Cambridge University Press
The Edinburgh Building, Cambridge CB2 8RU, UK

Published in the United States of America by Cambridge University Press, New York

www.cambridge.org
Information on this title: www.cambridge.org/9780521687874

First published 2010

Printed in the United Kingdom at the University Press, Cambridge

A catalogue record for this publication is available from the British Library

Library of Congress Cataloguing in Publication data
Chamorro-Premuzic, Tomas.
The psychology of personnel selection / Tomas Chamorro-Premuzic, Adrian Furnham.
    p.   cm.
Includes bibliographical references and index.
ISBN 978-0-521-86829-7 (hardback) – ISBN 978-0-521-68787-4 (pbk.)
1. Employee selection.   2. Employees – Recruiting.   I. Furnham, Adrian.   II. Title.
HF5549.5.S38C45   2010
658.3′112019 – dc22   2009032958

ISBN 978-0-521-86829-7 Hardback
ISBN 978-0-521-68787-4 Paperback

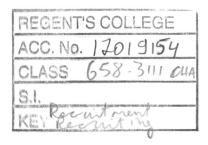

For my father, in the hope that he survives this and many later editions
– TC-P

For Alison, who is particularly talented at personnel selection
– AF

Contents

Boxes

Figures

Tables

Prologue and acknowledgements

If it weren't for the fact that nobody really asked us to do it (and we say this with due apologies to our commissioning editor), writing this book was a bit like doing any other job: its success can be measured in various forms, namely (a) whether it sells well, (b) whether people enjoy it and (c) whether it is somehow useful to others. We have actually tried to address each of these three areas, thus hoping that some of you (perhaps the wealthier public, comprising consultants and businesspeople) will *buy* it, others (perhaps the poorer audience, comprising students, including those wishing to enter the wealthier world of consultancy and business) would *read* it and others (maybe fellow academics in need of a quick quote) would *cite* it. However, given that nobody asked us to do this, we can only regard this book as a hobby, and the main aim of any hobby is that one enjoys doing it and learns something from it. In that sense, this book is already a great success, but we have to admit that with the readers' and buyers' contribution it could be even greater.

We would like to thank Andrew Peart and Cambridge University Press for tolerating the late delivery of our manuscript without putting any pressure at all (wisely knowing that it would make no difference whatsoever). Andrew's proactivity and enthusiasm is living proof to one of the *leitmotivs* of this book, namely that you have to hire the right people for the right job.

Tomas Chamorro-Premuzic
Adrian Furnham
London

PART 1

Methods of personnel selection

1 Early, unscientific methods

1.1   Introduction

Since the beginning of time, individuals have had to make 'people deci-sions': who to marry, to employ, to fight. In recent decades, sociobiology and evolutionary psychology have suggested that many of these apparently (quasi-logical) decisions are based on powerful people markers that we respond to, but are unaware that we are doing so. We assess people on a daily basis. There is, however, in every culture, a rich and interesting history of the techniques groups have favoured in making people decisions. Many of these techniques have quietly passed into history but others remain in use despite being rigorously tested and found wanting.

It appears that there have always been schools of thought with their ingenious methods that assess and reveal the 'true nature' of individuals, specifically their qualities, abilities, traits and motives. It is patently obvious that people are com-plex, capricious and quixotic. They are difficult to actually read, to understand and therefore to predict. Neither their virtues or values nor their potential for disaster are easily apparent. People are deceptive, both in the impression management and self-delusional sense. Some are self-aware: they know their strengths, limitations, even what really motivates them; they may even be able to report their condition. Many others are not.

Charlatans, snake-oil salesmen and their ilk find easy pickings among those who feel they need to evaluate or assess others for work purposes. The odd thing is that many of these disproved, pre-scientific, worthless and misleading systems still exist. They have advocates who still ply their trade despite lack of evidence that their systems actually work in the sense of providing reliable and valid assessments (see Section 2.6 and Figure 2.7 for an explanation of the technical meaning of 'reliability' and 'validity', which are the two main psychometric requirements that accurate instruments ought to fulfil). We shall consider some of these. These are essentially pre-scientific methods that pre-date the beginning of the twentieth century. Most have been thoroughly investigated and shown to be both unreliable and invalid. That is, there is ample evidence to suggest it is very unwise to use these methods in selection. However, they continue to be used. One reason for this is that scientific methods are often based on more common sense than these pre-scientific, counterintuitive approaches are. Ironically, counterintuitive methods and approaches have wider appeal than simple, logical methods. In that sense employers and companies are fooled by non-qualified consultants because, like Oscar Wilde, they 'believe anything as long as it is incredible'. Some of these discredited but still used methods are reviewed in this chapter.

This book attempts a comprehensive, critical and up-to-date review of the different methods used to assess people. It covers all the well-known and well-used techniques, looking at both theory and evidence for their usefulness, validity and efficacy. However, because it has been wisely pointed that that those who do not know their history are compelled to repeat it, we believe it important to look critically at some of the earlier, 'pre-scientific' methods which remain in use.

The interesting question is why some of these techniques remain in use despite the overwhelming evidence that they are invalid. French organisations still use graphological analysis of potential employees. Astrology is widely practised and almost every newspaper contains some sort of 'star readings', presumably because people consult them and act upon them. Whilst classic phrenology has almost completely disappeared, it has been argued that the current enthusiasm for PET and MSRI scanning is really no more than a form of electrical phrenology.

Over the years there have been two types of research investigation into earlier and largely discredited methods. The first has been attempts to investigate validity claims by examining concurrent, construct, discriminant, but mainly the *predictive* validity of these tests. Most of these investigations have shown that claims made by the methods are essentially false. The second topic of interest has essentially been why, if the technqieues are demonstrably invalid, do people continue to use them. We will review both of these research traditions in this chapter.

1.2   Graphology

Graphology is the study and analysis of handwriting, and has been used for centuries as an aid in personnel selection. The use of graphology is still prevalent in Europe, where estimates for the percentage of organisations using the technique range from 38 per cent (Shackleton & Newell, 1994) to 93 per cent (Bruchon-Schweitzer & Ferrieux, 1991). In the United States, graphology gained some acceptance in many corporate workplaces during the late 1980s and early 1990s (Davey, 1989; Edwards & Armitage, 1992). In Europe, the French lead the way in the use of graphologists (Furnham, 2004); this is in line with a strong psychodynamic tradition in France, particularly compared to the UK.

Part of the appeal of graphology is that people cannot supposedly fake their 'real' personality because they are unaware of how they project it. This assumption applies not only to graphology but also to psychodynamic techniques in general (e.g., projective tests and the currently in-vogue implicit association tests). The problem is that since interpretation is subjective, different 'raters' (even when they are clinical experts) end up making different interpretations, making

Figure 1.1 *Graphology: what does this say about the candidate's motivation?*

graphology untestable at best, and unreliable at worst. There also appear to be different schools of psychology which interpret specific aspects of handwriting differently.

Although it is difficult to assess how many organisations currently use graphology – or when and why they use it – it does appear that hiring decisions regarding a large number of job applicants around the world are determined, in part at least, by handwriting. Some organisations are happy to boast of their usage of graphology, while others often keep it quiet for fear perhaps of ridicule or perhaps because they believe they have an efficient but hidden means to evaluate candidates' suitability.

Although studies of the relationship between handwriting and character or personality date back to the seventeenth century, it was not until the late nineteenth century that the foundations of modern graphology were laid by the French abbot Jean-Hippolyte Michon (1872). Michon claimed he was able to discern the particular features of handwriting that writers with similar personalities had in common. Thus he developed an inventory of about 100 graphological features or 'fixed signs', such as a particular way of crossing the *t* or dotting the *i*, which were associated with certain types of personality.

A few decades later, Jean Crepieux-Jamin (1909) further developed this research, and claimed to have found further associations between particular features of handwriting and personality traits. The result was additional features which, when analysed in combination, were believed to indicate different personality traits. Inevitably, however, this process of matching particular features of handwriting with particular types of personality began to produce conflicting results: the associations found by one graphologist would often contradict those found by others (Hartford, 1973). This remains the case today with different schools of thought emphasising the 'meaning' of particular letters. Interinterpreter reliability is nearly always unacceptably low. Further validity is preconditioned on reliability of 'diagnosis'. It is hard for unreliable measures to be valid.

Table 1.1 *Two factors underlying graphological scoring (adapted from Furnham et al., 2003)*

	Dimensions	Details
Size of handwriting	.84	
Width of handwriting	.84	
Pressure of handwriting	.48	
Slant of handwriting	.37	
Use of bottom loops	.36	
Crossed *t*'s (quantity)		.87
T-crosses (type)		.82
I's dotted (quantity)		.49
Connectedness		.40
Percentage of page used		.35

Note: Loadings <.35 not shown.

Later, the German school of graphology under Ludwig Klages (1917, 1930) took a different approach to the subject. This favoured a more intuitive, theoretical psychology of expressive behaviour. It is probably this approach to handwriting that has had the greatest influence, and Klages is held in high esteem by most contemporary graphologists (Lewinson, 1986).

Contemporary graphologists still use these 'insights' to determine personality characteristics of individuals through analysis of their handwriting. For example, a predominance of strokes to the right is said to indicate 'goal-directed' people, whereas a predominance of left movements indicates concern with the self. Other information about personality can be 'gleaned' from the interpretation of letter formation, zones representing different spheres of the human psyche and so on (for a review, see Greasley, 2000). Furnham, Chamorro-Premuzic and Callahan (2003) factor analysed fourteen graphological criteria and found they were reduced to two fundamental areas: *dimension* of writing (size, width, slant) and *details* (connections, loops, etc.) (see Table 1.1). However, these variables were unrelated to established (and validated) personality inventories.

Eysenck and Gudjonsson (1986) suggested that there appear to be two different basic approaches to the assessment of both handwriting and personality, namely holistic vs analytic. This gives four basic types of analysis. *Holistic analysis of handwriting*: this is basically impressionistic, because the graphologist, using his or her experience and insight, offers a general description of the kind of personality he or she believes the handwriting discloses. *Analytic analysis of handwriting*: this uses measurements of the constituents of the handwriting, such as slant, pressure, etc., which are then converted into personality assessment on the basis of a formula of code. *Holistic analysis of personality*: this is also impressionistic, and may be done after an interview, when a trained psychologist offers a personality description on the basis of his or her questions, observations and intuitions. *Analytical analysis of personality*: this involves the application of psychometrically assessed, reliable and valid personality tests (questionnaires, physiological responses to a person, and the various grade scores obtained).

This classification suggests quite different approaches to the evaluation of the validity of graphological analysis in the prediction of personality. Holistic matching is the impressionistic interpretation of writing matched with an impressionistic account of personality. Holistic correlation is the impressionistic interpretation of writing correlated with a quantitative assessment of personality, while analytic matching involves the measurement of the constituents of the handwriting matched with an impressionistic account of personality. Analytic correlation is the measurement of the constituents of handwriting correlated with a quantitative assessment of personality.

1.2.1 Scientific evidence for graphology

Early studies appeared to provide *some* support for this form of personality assessment (Allport & Vernon, 1933; Hull & Montgomery, 1919). Some more recent studies have also claimed to have found evidence that graphologists can recognise certain personality traits from handwriting samples (Linton, Epstein & Hartford, 1962; Nevo, 1988; Oosthuizen, 1990). There are also many articles in professional journals and serious newspapers advocating graphology through evidence involving personal experience (Lavell, 1994; Watson, 1993).

However, when studies are carefully selected in terms of their methodological veracity, then the evidence is *overwhelmingly negative* (Eysenck & Gudjonsson, 1986; Neter & Ben-Shakhar, 1989; Tett & Palmer, 1997).

Furnham (1988) listed the conclusions drawn from six studies conducted in the 1970s and 1980s:

(1) 'It was concluded that the analyst could not accurately predict personality from handwriting.' This was based on a study by Vestewig, Santee and Moss (1976) from Wright State University, who asked six handwriting experts to rate 48 specimens of handwriting on fifteen personal variables.
(2) 'No evidence was found for the validity of graphological signs.' This is from Lester, McLaughlin and Nosal (1977), who used sixteen graphological signs of Extraversion to try to predict from handwriting samples the Extraversion of 109 subjects whose personality test scores were known.
(3) 'Thus, the results did not support the claim that the three handwriting measures were valid indicators of Extraversion.' This is based on the study by Rosenthal and Lines (1978), who attempted to correlate three graphological indices with the Extraversion scores of 58 students.
(4) 'There is thus little support here for the validity of graphological analysis.' This was based on a study by Eysenck and Gudjonsson (1986), who employed

a professional graphologist to analyse handwriting from 99 subjects and then fill out personality questionnaires as she thought would have been done by the respondents.

(5) 'The graphologist did not perform significantly better than a chance model.' This was the conclusion of Ben-Shakhar and colleagues (1986) at the Hebrew University, who asked graphologists to judge the profession, out of eight possibilities, of 40 successful professionals.

(6) 'Although the literature on the topic suffers from significant methodological negligence, the general trend of findings is to suggest that graphology is not a viable assessment method.' This conclusion comes from Klimoski and Rafael (1983), based at Ohio State University, after a careful review of the literature. Yet many of these studies could be criticised methodologically in terms of measurement of both personality and graphology.

Furnham and Gunter (1987) investigated the 'trait' method of graphology, which attempts to predict specific personality traits from individual features of handwriting. Participants completed the Eysenck Personality Questionnaire (EPQ) and copied a passage of test in their own handwriting. The writing samples were coded on thirteen handwriting-feature dimensions (size, slant and so on) that graphologists report to be diagnostic of personality traits. Only chance-level correlations were observed between writing features and EPQ scores. Similarly, Bayne and O'Neill (1988) asked graphologists to estimate people's Myers-Briggs type (Extravert–Introvert, Sensing–Intuition, Thinking–Feeling, Judging–Perceiving) from handwriting samples. Though highly confident in their judgements, none of the graphologists' appraisals accurately predicted the profile of the writers.

In a meta-analysis (a review of many studies in an area that provides a quantitative estimate of the average statistical relationship among the examined variables) of over 200 studies assessing the validity of graphological inferences, Dean (1992) found only a small effect size for inferring personality from handwriting and noted that the inclusion of studies with methodological shortcomings may have inflated the effect-size estimate. The liberal estimated effect size of 0.12 for inferring personality from neutral-content scripts (scripts with fixed content not under the control of the writer) is *not nearly large enough to be of any practical value* and would be too small to be perceptible. Thus, even a small, real effect cannot account for the magnitude of handwriting–personality relationships reported by graphologists.

Furthermore, gender, socioeconomic status and degree of literacy – all predictable from handwriting – may predict some personality traits. Thus, any weak ability of graphology to predict personality may be merely based on gender or socioeconomic status information assessed from handwriting. Graphological accuracy attributable to these variables is of dubious value because simpler, more reliable methods for assessing them are available.

1.2.2 Graphology and job performance

Graphological assessments for personnel selection focus on desired traits such as determination, sales drive and honesty. Given its apparent lack of validity for predicting personality, it would be surprising if graphology proved to be a valid predictor of job performance. Indeed, the results of research investigating the validity of graphology for predicting job performance has generally been negative (Kravitz et al., 1996; Rafaeli & Klimoski, 1983).

Ben-Shakar and colleagues (1986) used two empirical studies to test the validity of graphological predictions. In one study, bank employees were rated by graphologists on several job-relevant traits. A linear model developed for the study outperformed the graphologists. In the second study, the professions of forty successful professionals were judged. The graphologists did not perform significantly better than a chance model. The results of both studies led to the conclusion that, when analysing spontaneously produced text, graphologists and non-graphologists *achieve similar validities.*

In a meta-analytic review of seventeen studies, Neter and Ben-Shakhar (1989) found that graphologists performed no better than did non-graphologists in predicting job performance. When handwriting samples were autobiographical, the two groups achieved modest accuracy in prediction. When the content of the scripts was neutral (that is, identical for all writers), neither group was able to draw valid inferences about job performance. Thus, belief in the validity of graphology, as it is currently used to predict job performance, *lacks empirical support.*

As a necessary condition for valid inference, the reliability of predictions based on graphology must first be established (Goldberg, 1986). However, reliability of graphological prediction has its own precondition: handwriting features must first be reliably encoded. This precondition appears to be met; the mean agreement between different judges measuring objective handwriting features (such as slant or slope) is high, and the mean agreement about subjective handwriting features (like rhythm) is still respectable (Dean, 1992).

But agreement about what these features signify is less impressive. In studies reviewed by Dean (1992), the mean agreement of interpretations made by graphologists was $r = 0.42$. Even lay judges exhibit some agreement in their naive interpretations, with a reliability ($r = 0.30$), only slightly lower than that of the graphologists. Measuring graphological features can be made reasonably precise. The error is in suggesting that graphology is systematically related to things like individual ability, motivation and personality. Further, the theory of how, when or why a person's abilities or personality shapes their handwriting (or indeed vice-versa) is unclear. How or why should handwriting as opposed to many other activities be such a good marker of personality? This obvious question is never answered.

Why, then, does graphology persist? Ben-Shakhar and colleagues (1986, p. 176) have pointed out that graphology 'seems to have the right kind of properties for reflecting personality'. Both personality and handwriting differ from person to person, and it might be expected that one offers insight into the other. Unlike other pseudosciences like astrology, graphology provides a sample of actual expressive behaviour from which to infer personality (Ben-Shakhar, 1989). That is, handwriting bears many features that graphologists use to predict personality, including characteristics that the writer would prefer not to disclose or perhaps is not even conscious of possessing.

Moreover, many of the purported relationships between handwriting and personality appear almost intuitive. For example, small handwriting is believed to imply modesty and large handwriting implies egotism. In many examples like this, the empirical relationships between handwriting features and personality traits identified by graphologists closely parallel *semantic associations* between words used to describe handwriting features (for example, *regular* rhythm) and personality traits (for example, *reliable*).

Research by Chapman and Chapman (1967) suggests that where semantic relationships such as these exist, the intuitive statistician may infer non-existent or illusory correlations in the direction dictated by semantic association. For example, Chapman and Chapman (1967) presented naive judges with a set of Draw-a-person (DAP) drawings, along with contrived symptom statements about the patient who provided the drawing. The DAP is a projective test in which patients are asked to draw a person, and from those drawings clinicians make inferences about their underlying psychopathology.

Chapman and Chapman (1967) found that, although symptom statements were uncorrelated with features of the drawing, naive participants perceived illusory correlations between the same semantically related pairs of drawing features and clinical symptoms that clinicians believed to be related. For example, like clinicians, naive participants perceived drawing a big head as correlated with concerns about intelligence and elaboration of the eyes as correlated with paranoia.

This has been confirmed by a careful study by King and Koehler (2000), who showed that illusory correlations in graphological evidence was rife. They also concluded that this *may partially account for continued use of graphology despite overwhelming evidence against its predictive validities* (p. 336).

This is an example of what is known as the 'confirmation bias' (Nickerson, 1998). When a person is inspecting some evidence in a search of systematic relationships, semantic association is likely to guide the formulation of hypotheses about what goes with what, producing a kind of expectation. Other potential relationships may not be considered and hence not detected even if they are consistent with the observed evidence.

In other words, graphology persists because when we examine evidence in the light of semantically determined hypotheses, ambiguous aspects of the evidence are interpreted in a manner consistent with the hypothesised relationship. Driver, Buckley and Frink (1996) asked 'should we write off graphology?' as a selection technique. Their answer was 'yes'. They note *'the overwhelming results of well-controlled empirical studies have been that the technique has not demonstrated acceptable validity . . . (and that) while the procedure may have an intuitive appeal, graphology should not be used in a selection context'* (p. 76).

Recent reviews of the literature have by and large supported previous reviews on the low validity of graphological analyses and their potential harm for personnel selection. This is true even for reviews that assessed evidence provided by graphological societies in different countries (Simner & Goffin, 2003).

1.3 Physiognomy and body build

Physiognomy is the study of inferring personal attributes, such as personality traits, through physical traits. In simple terms, this implies that a person's outer appearance (head and body shape) reflects their character or personality; thus body shape or facial features would reveal psychological aspects of the person (just like graphology is meant to do). For example, wider faces and levels of aggression are both positively affected by testosterone levels during puberty and would therefore co-vary (physiognomic readings are largely based on interpreting faces or the bony structure of the skull, on which soft tissues lie).

This belief has an exceptionally long history, dating back to ancient Greece. Both Aristotle and Plato made frequent reference to theories of this sort, and the ancient Greeks more generally believed that physical beauty was linked with moral goodness. Nor was this a particularly European phenomenon: examples of Chinese physiognomy show that this 'science' was practised in parts of Asia.

Most contemporary attempts at providing a scientific account for physiognomy can be dated back to the eighteenth century, when Johann Caspar Lavater published his *Essays on Physiognomy* (1775–8). Lavater's ideas on physiognomy, and in particular the divination of a person's character from his *facial* features, were based on the writings of the Italian Giambattista Della Porta, the French physiognomist Barthélemy Coclès, and the English philosopher and physician Sir Thomas Browne. For all three, it was possible to discern inner qualities of an individual from the outer appearance of his or her face: morphology reflects psychology. The idea was that a person's temperament influenced both his or her facial appearance and character, and it was thus possible to infer one from the other. Thus active people develop different body shapes than lazy people.

For example, Della Porta used woodcuts of animals to illustrate human characteristics, what Magli (1989) refers to as 'Zoological Physiognomics'. This element of physiognomy relied on a prior anthropomorphic physiognomy of a certain animal then being applied to humans (for example, representing someone as lion-like, or courageous). A related method for divining the character of a person during this period was that of metoposcopy, or the interpretation of

Extreme desespoir.
Eufferfte Verzweiflung.

Colere meslée de Crainte.
Zorn mit Forcht vermischt.

Figure 1.2 *Physiognomical interpretations of character*

facial wrinkles (especially those on the forehead). Girolamo Cardano worked out about 800 facial figures, each associated with astrological signs and qualities of temperament and character. He declared that one could tell by the lines on her face which woman is an adulteress and which has a hatred of lewdness!

While Lavater's ideas were not original, they were unique in their popularity and influence. By 1810, there were a total of fifty-five editions of Lavater's *Essays on Physiognomy*, variously priced to suit all pockets (Graham, 1961). Moreover, physiognomy had an important influence on nineteenth-century Victorian art and literature. For example, physiognomy appears in the work of many of the major nineteenth-century novelists, including Charles Dickens, Balzac and Charlotte Brontë. More generally, nineteenth-century physiognomy offered the possibility of assuaging fears about the 'other' – the characterisation of others based on their outer appearance proved to be an important tool in legitimising nationalism and colonialism (Gould, 1981).

At the beginning of the twentieth century, physiognomy enjoyed renewed popularity, this time taking on a more 'scientific' nature. Various vocational institutes used physiognomy as one of their main tools in assessing candidates, while others put physiognomy to more dubious use. Cesare Lombroso's *Criminal Anthropology* (1895), for example, claimed that murderers have prominent jaws and pickpockets have long hands and scanty beards.

Yet others developed the idea of 'personology', a New Age variation of physiognomy which holds that outward appearance (especially the face) is the key to a person's predominant temper and character (Whiteside, 1974). According to personology, there is a 'scientific' connection between genetics and behaviour, and genetics and physical appearance. Therefore, personologists conclude, there must be a connection between behaviour and physical appearance. This led some personologists to argue that there are sixty-eight behavioural traits, which a trained observer can identify with sight, measurement or touch. There are five 'trait areas' and the placement of each trait into an area develops from its location and relationship to a corresponding area in the brain. However, everything we know about the development and plasticity of the brain does not support these notions (Gould, 1981).

Whatever we might believe about physiognomy and personology, it is clear that many people make inferences about others based on appearance. There is an extensive literature on lookism, which will be considered shortly. Hassin and Trope (2000) argue that there are four reasons to assume that the face and physiognomy play an important role in social cognition:

1. The face is almost always seen whenever an interaction takes place. Thus the face always represents information that is available and is hard to neglect for any judgements.
2. Until quite recently in human evolution, facial features (unlike facial or behavioural expressions) could not be willfully altered.
3. The structure of the face is relatively stable (except in extreme conditions, such as accidents or surgery).
4. There are areas in the human brain specialised for face perception and processing.

Considerable experimental evidence suggests that people can and do infer personality traits from faces (Secord, 1965; Strich & Secord, 1965; Zebrowitz-McArthur & Berry, 1987). Taken as a whole, this research shows that the process of inferring traits from faces is highly reliable. That is, different judges tend to infer similar traits from given faces. Some studies have shown that this interjudge agreement is cross-cultural, thus suggesting that the cognitive work of reading traits from faces has some universal characteristics (Zebrowitz-McArthur & Berry, 1987).

However, the picture that emerges regarding the *validity* of physiognomic judgements is more ambiguous. Early studies that attempted to answer this question concluded that there was *no significant correlation* between facial features or physiognomic inference and the traits individuals actually possess (Cohen, 1973). In a later review of the literature on physiognomic inferences, Alley (1988) reached a similar conclusion.

More recent research suggests that face-based impressions may *sometimes* be valid (Berry, 1991; Zebrowitz, Voinescu & Collins, 1996). Berry (1990) asked students to report their impressions of their classmates (after one, five and nine weeks of the semester had elapsed), and used these impressions as the criterion with which she compared independent evaluations of the classmates' photographs. She found significant correlations between peer and photographs on three dimensions: power, warmth and honesty.

Recent studies of what has been called *lookism* have noted that features associated with an individual's physical attractiveness (face, body shape) can have a great influence on their employment opportunities (Swami & Furnham, 2008). One of the most widely researched settings of weight-based discrimination is in the workplace, where overweight individuals are vulnerable to stigmatising attitudes and anti-fat bias (Phul & Brownell, 2003). The literature points to prejudice and inequity for overweight and obese individuals, often even before the interview process begins.

Experimental studies have typically investigated hiring decisions by manipulating perceptions of employee weight, either through written descriptions or photographs. One study of job applicants for sales and business positions reported that written descriptions of target applicants resulted in significantly more negative judgements for obese women than for non-obese women (Rothblum, Miller & Gorbutt, 1988). One study used videotaped mock interviews with the same professional actors acting as job applicants for computer and sales positions, in which weight was manipulated with theatrical prostheses (Pingitoire, Dugoni, Tindale & Spring, 1994). Participants indicated that employment bias was much greater for obese candidates than for average-weight applicants, and that the bias was more apparent for women than for men. An earlier study using videotapes of job applicants in simulated hiring settings showed that overweight applicants were significantly less likely to be recommended for hiring than average-weight applicants, and were also judged as significantly less neat, productive, ambitious, disciplined and determined (Larkin & Pines, 1979).

Where overweight individuals have been hired, negative perceptions of them persist throughout their career (Paul & Townsend, 1995). Roehling (1999) summarised numerous work-related stereptypes reported over a dozen laboratory studies. Overweight employees were assumed to lack self-discipline and be lazy, less conscientious, less competent, sloppy, disagreeable and emotionally unstable. Further, these attitudes have a negative impact on wages, promotions and decisions about employment status (Register & Williams, 1990; Rothblum, Brand, Miller & Oetken, 1990).

1.4   Assessing physiognomy

Can physiognomy provide us with reliable cues to a person's underlying character or personality? Are physiognometric measures systematically related to intelligence and ability? Furthermore, can one explain that relationship? Lavater certainly believed this was possible and many psychologists believe that physiognomy is an integral part of social cognition (Hassin & Trope, 2000). However, others have not been so quick to proclaim the universal reliability of physiognomy. The main problem is that in attempting to abstract a static physiognomy from facial features, researchers take an erroneously atemporal view of the face (Magli, 1989). The body and face are continually in flux (Twine, 2002), and can change both in the short and long term: the former being the subtle changes in a face informed by motion and light, and the latter the changes to the body over the life course.

In addition, sociologists point out that the belief that we can assess the morality of a person from their appearance discounts the fact that appearance is *socially constructed*. A person may come to be understood as 'looking intelligent' or 'looking good' but this is merely down to the socially constructed association of one signifier with one signified (Finkelstein, 1991). Sociologically, physiognomic knowledge is problematic because appearance is *unpredictably* located within an array of changeable meanings and also because what we understand as a 'good' or 'bad' character varies across time and space (Twine, 2002).

This is not to say that, in our everyday social practices, we do not use judgements based on physiognomic inferences (Swami & Furnham, 2008). The point, however, is that perception based on such physiognomical inference prevents meaningful interaction with others. While physiognomy can be said to provide for social relations, these are of poor quality. More seriously, they encourage a perceptual filter that objectifies others in ways that are often erroneous and discriminatory. In this sense, though it clearly occurs implicitly, it is extremely unwise to consider using physiogometric data for job selection.

There is a large literature on body build dating from Hippocrates but made most famous by Kretschmer (1925) and later by Sheldon (1940). Kretschmer believed that people could be divided into four distinct categories according to body type: (1) *asthenic* (slight, long-boned, slender persons with a predisposition towards a schizophrenic personality type); (2) *pyknic* (round, stocky, heavy individuals with a predisposition towards manic-depressive reactions; (3) *athletic* (strong, muscular, broad-shouldered people with a tendency more towards schizophrenic than manic-depressive responses); and (4) *dysplastic* (individuals exhibiting disproportionate physical development or features of several body types with personality predispositions similar to the athletic type). The argument was that body shape was systematically related to personality, specifically mental illness.

Sheldon argued for the existence of three distinct body types; *endomorph*, *mesomorph* and *ectomorph*. It represented a long-standing interest in anthropometrics. First a great deal of the research concentrated on the delineation of clear physiological types based on a variety of skeletal measures. This remains far less in contention than the second claim, namely that these types are related to personality and ability. Research in the area produced weak and equivocal correlations between anthropomorphic measures and personality.

Phares (1984) observed that interest in these ideas emerges from time to time but that it is not supported by the data. Furthermore, the ideas never take into consideration the possibility of social behaviours being learnt as a function of interaction.

> For instance, the strongly built individual may learn early that assertiveness and dominance are easily employed to gain his or her ends. The obese person may discover that humour and sociability are ready defenses against a fear of rejection. Or the ectomorph may soon realise that solitary pursuits are more likely to become a source of enjoyment than unsuccessful physical encounters with athletic peers. In any case, however, it would seem that human social behaviour is so complex that mere assignment of people to simple typological categories will never be an adequate basis for prediction or explanation.   (pp. 28–9)

Whilst there is now considerable interest in the psychology of body shapes (Body Mass Index; Waist-to-Hip Ratio), this is concerned with evolutionary psychological explanations of attractiveness. There remains very little evidence that body shape is a robust marker of temperament or ability and should therefore be used for personnel selection. That said, it is to be expected that people's (for example, interviewers') perceptions of others' (e.g., interviewees' or job applicants') psychological traits will be influenced by physical traits, but this will inevitably represent a distorted and erroneous source of information and should therefore be avoided.

That said, there is currently a good deal of interest in related topics like fluctuating asymmetry and digit ratio. Fluctuating asymmetry consists of within-individual differences in left- vs right-side body features (length of ears, fingers, volume of wrists, etc.). Asymmetry is associated with both ill health and lower IQ. In a recent study, Luxen and Buunk (2006) found 20 per cent of the variance in intelligence was explained by a combined measure of fluctuating asymmetry. However, unless these factors are very noticeable in an individual they are unlikely to affect hiring decisions.

The 2D:4D digit ratio has been known for some 100 years and has recently attracted a great deal of attention. The idea is that a person's hand shape – particularly the length of these two digits – is determined by physiological processes in the womb which influence the sex-linked factors (Brosnan, 2006). In line with this view, a seminal study by Lippa (2003) showed that 2D:4D determined sexual orientation (though only for men). Subsequent studies in this area have attempted to link 2D:4D to individual differences in established personality traits, notably those related to aggression or masculine behaviours. Although evidence has been somewhat inconsistent, a number of meaningful connections have indeed been found. In a large-scale study, Lippa (2006) found positive, albeit weak, associations between 2D:4D and Extraversion, as well as a negative, albeit weak, link between 2D:4D and Openness to Experience. Overall, however, associations between finger-length measures and personality were modest and variable.

In a similar, smaller-scale, study, 2D:4D was a significant predictor of different aggression subscales (e.g., sensation-seeking, verbal aggression, etc.) (Hampson, Ellis & Tenk, 2008). The authors concluded that 'the 2D:4D digit ratio may be a valid, though weak, predictor of selective sex-dependent traits that are sensitive to testosterone' (p. 133). More recently, Lindovà, Hruškovà, Pivonkovà, Kubena and Flegr (2008) reported that more feminine women – those with higher right hand 2D:4D ratio – were more neurotic and less socially bold than their less feminine (those with a lower right-hand 2D:4D ratio) counterparts.

Although 2D:4D measures are still unlikely to be used as a personnel selection device, there is growing research in this area and the above-reviewed findings show some promising potential to provide an alternative approach for assessing individual differences (see Chapter 7 for traditional approaches to personality assessment).

1.5   Phrenology

About a quarter of a century after the resurgence of physiognomy under Lavater, a new 'science' claimed to be able to determine character, personality traits and criminality on the basis of the *shape of the head*. Developed by the German physician Franz-Josef Gall at the end of the eighteenth century, phrenology became very popular in the nineteenth century and is usually credited as a protoscience for having contributed to medical science the ideas that the brain is the organ of the mind and that certain brain areas have localised, specific functions.

Although there are important differences between Lavaterian physiognomy and Gall's phrenology, the latter's thinking was clearly influenced by the former. For example, Gall observed that his fellow students who had good memories all had prominent eyes, and so he assumed that the part of the brain concerned with memory was located behind the eyes (Davies, 1955). However, Gall went on to extend these basic ideas into what was, at the time, the most significant theory of mind yet.

In particular, Gall formalised the view that the mind and brain were one and the same thing. His ideas developed the notion of cerebral localisation, that is, the view that various parts of the brain have relatively distinct functions. In his main work, *The Anatomy and Physiology of the Nervous System in General, and of the Brain in Particular* (1796), Gall argued that every brain function could be localised to a particular part of the brain, which was dedicated to that single function alone. For him, understanding the brain would come through identifying which pieces were responsible for which functions.

Subsequent phrenologists like Johann Spurzheim argued that parts of the brain which correspond to functions that an individual used a great deal would hypertrophy, while those functions which were neglected would atrophy. Their vision of the brain, therefore, was that it had a lumpy and bulbous surface, with a landscape unique to each individual based upon their particular set of intellectual and neurological strengths and weaknesses. They further argued that the skull overlying the lumpy parts of the brain would bulge out to accommodate the hypertrophied brain tissue underneath. Therefore, by measuring those bumps, one can infer which parts of the brain are enlarged and therefore which characteristics are dominant (Novella, 2000).

This idea later acquired some fame with the 'phrenology head', a china head on which the phrenological faculties were indicated. This head, while symbolising much of the work of phrenologists, also entailed that phrenology would continue physiognomy's fascination with outward physical appearance. A typical phreno-logical chart outlines thirty-seven brain functions, each with a corresponding bearing upon the shape of one's head (see Davies, 1955, p. 6).

During the nineteenth century, phrenology gained a rapidly growing interest. By the 1820s, every major British city had its own phrenological society, and many people consulted phrenologists to get advice in matters like hiring personnel or finding a marriage partner (see Cooter, 1984; Davies, 1955). Although the theory of phrenology was eventually rejected by official academia, the phrenological parlours remained popular for some time, but they were considered closer to astrology, chiromancy and the like.

In the early twentieth century, phrenology benefited from a new interest, par-ticularly with its greater entwinement with physiognomy. But like physiognomy, much of this resurgence had to do with questions of racial difference and degen-eration (Cooter, 1984). Frequent pictorial representations of racialised groups (notably black Africans and Australian Aborigines) are found within the phreno-logical journals at this time. For their effectiveness, they depended on the view of the external body as a site that could be used to divide assumed racial superiority from inferiority. Phrenology was part of the climate of that time which used science to naturalise racism, class inequality and patriarchy (Gould, 1981).

1.5.1 Appraising phrenology

Gall and other phrenologists were correct when it came to the central debate of neurology of the time (Miller, 1996): the brain is somewhat compartmentalised, with each section serving a specific function. However, the modern 'map' of the brain does not correlate at all with the classic map used by phrenologists. Theirs was more personality (even morality) based, while the modern map is based on fundamental functions, such as the ability to perform mathematical functions (Butterworth, 1999). Furthermore, all the other assumptions of phrenology are false:

• The brain is not a muscle; it does not hypertrophy or atrophy depending on use.
• The brain is very jelly-like in consistency: the soft brain conforms to the shape of the skull and the skull does not conform itself to the brain.

Modern phrenology is not based on head shape but on brain structure and function. In fact the speed of developments in PET scanning and other related technologies suggests that this may be in time the new selection methodology. Understanding individual difference in brain structure and function is the new sci-ence of the twenty-first century. Furthermore, it is possible that future candidates may be brain scanned as part of their selection process. That raises interesting ethical issues, though it will be a long time before the science is going to be sufficiently specific to be used to inform selection decisions.

1.6   Psychognomy, characterology and chiromancy

Although phrenology suffered an early demise, Paul Bouts began working on phrenology from a pedagogical background, using phrenological analysis to define an individual pedagogy. Combining phrenology with typology (characterising a person by personality types) and graphology, he coined a global approach called Psychognomy. Bouts became the main promoter of the renewed twentieth-century interest in phrenology and psychognomy.

A different strand of character reading developed in the 1920s, combining revised physiognomy, reconstructed phrenology and amplified pathognomy (the study of passions and emotions). Designed by McCormick, characterology was an attempt to produce an objective system to determine the character of an individual. In particular, characterology attempted to fix problems in the phrenological systems of Gall and Spurzheim. McCormick suggested that uses for characterology included guiding parents and educators, guidance in military promotion of officers, estimation of the kind of thinking patterns one has, a guide to hiring and a guide to marriage selection.

A more popular pseudoscience is chiromancy (or palmistry), the art of characterisation and foretelling the future through the study of the palm. It consists of evaluating a person's character or future life by 'reading' the palm of that person's hand. There are twenty-nine features that may be read. Various *lines* ('life line', 'heart line' and so on) and *mounts* (bumps) purportedly suggest interpretations by their relative sizes and intersections. Some palmistry mimics physiognomy in claiming that you can tell what a person is like by the shape of their hands. For example, creative people are said to have fan-shaped hands and sensitive people have narrow, pointy fingers and fleshy palms. However, there is about as much scientific support for such notions as there is for characterology or phrenology. There are traditionally seven hard types, including artistic, idealistic and philosophical, while modern classifications tend to have fewer types. Palm readers are more likely to be found at the 'end of the pier' than in a selection interview.

1.7   Astrology

Astrology is any of several traditions or systems in which knowledge of the apparent positions of celestial bodies is held to be useful in understanding, interpreting and organising knowledge about reality and human existence on earth. Most astrologers consider astrology to be a useful intuitive tool by which

Figure 1.3 *Astrological signs*

people may come to better understand themselves and others, and the relationships between them.

Astrology not only fascinates large parts of the general population, but has also been of interest to scientists. Johannes Kepler, one of the modern founders of astronomy, created a surprisingly valid horoscope for Albrecht Wallerstein, the Habsburg monarchy's general in charge during the Thirty Years War (Mann, 1979). Centuries later, Eysenck and his colleagues examined relationships between astrological and personality factors (Gauquelin, Gauquelin & Eysenck, 1979; Mayo, White & Eysenck, 1978). For example, some astrologers claim that Mars occupies certain positions in the sky slightly more often at the birth of sports champions than at the birth of 'ordinary' people (the so-called 'Mars effect', based on Gauquelin, 1969). Indeed, there have been a couple of studies – notably Gauquelin *et al.* (1979) – reporting associations between established traits and astrological factors. More specifically, extraverts were significantly more frequently born just after the rise or upper culmination of Mars and Jupiter, whereas introverts where more frequently born when Saturn had just risen or passed their upper culmination. Psychoticism, on the other hand, has been found to relate to the position of Mars and Jupiter. More recently, Sachs (1999) attempted

to put astrology on a scientific footing by using statistical methods to explore associations between the zodiac and human behaviour (in particular, criminal behaviour).

Although these and various other studies found significant correlations, many other results failed to support the role of astrology in personality (van Rooij, 1994). Carlson (1985) found that astrologers had no special ability to interpret personality from astrological readings and performed much worse in tests than they predicted they would. Similarly, Clarke, Gabriels and Barnes (1996) explored the effect of positions of the sun, moon and planets in the zodiac at the moment of birth, and found no evidence that tendencies towards extraversion and emotionality are explained by such signs.

Even when whole charts are used in 'matching tests', astrology comes out looking unreliable and therefore invalid. Using the Eysenck Personality Inventory, Dean (1987) selected 60 people with a very high introversion score and 60 people with a very high extraversion score. He then supplied 45 astrologers with the birth charts of these 120 subjects. By analysing the charts, the astrologers tried to identify the extraverts from the introverts. The results were disappointing for astrologers: their average success rate was only about 50 per cent (that is, no better than random guessing). Astrologers also fail comprehensive tests when they themselves provide the required information (Nanninga, 1996). In a comprehensive review, Kelly (1997) concluded that:

- The majority of empirical studies undertaken to test astrological tenets did not confirm astrological claims; and
- The few studies that are positive need additional clarification. (p. 1231)

Various authors have similarly dismantled Sachs' (1999) 'scientific' claims, leading at least one group of authors to claim that (von Eye, Lösel & Mayzer, 2003: 89):

1. If there is a scientific basis to astrology, this basis remains to be shown; and
2. If there exists a link between the signs of the zodiac and human behaviour, this link remains to be shown too.

Despite the lack of association between astrological predictions and personality, many people still believe in astrology (Hamilton, 1995) and accept the personality descriptions it offers (Glick, Gottesman & Jolton, 1989). For example, Hamilton (1995) found that undergraduates, presented with one-paragraph descriptions of the characteristics of their own astrological Sun sign and an alternative Sun sign, chose their own Sun sign paragraph as a better representation of their personality than the alternative Sun sign description. Van Rooij (1999) found that participants presented with individual trait words associated with the personality descriptions of each of the twelve Sun signs chose the traits of their own Sun sign as more personally descriptive than the traits associated with the other eleven signs. These results have implications for personnel selection because they indicate that people (employers) are not unlikely to make inferences on others'

Figure 1.4 *Ambiguous inkblot stimulus*

(job applicants' or employees') personality characteristics simply on the basis of their date of birth or zodiac sign. Even if these inferences are invalid, they may have self-fulfilling effects.

Thus one explanation for these results is that individuals who possess astrological knowledge tend to behave according to their respective sign of the zodiac (van Rooij, 1994, 1999). That is, persons exposed to astrological character analysis are likely to incorporate this information into their long-term self-concept. The alternative explanation – that astrology and its derived personality descriptions are valid – is rendered less likely by the finding that this tendency to endorse astrology-consistent personality descriptions is found only in those people with some knowledge of astrology (Hamilton, 1995; van Rooij, 1994).

1.8   Other projective tests

Projective tests (such as graphology) assert that participants project their innermost thoughts and feelings onto the projective stimulus, be it a Rorschach inkblot (Figure 1.4) or Thematic-Apperception-Test (TAT). The TAT was designed by Murray (1943) to assess clinical constructs but was soon widely employed in the context of work psychology. The original version of TAT had twenty black and white pictures of people and objects that enabled respondents to project their own feelings, needs and motives in their interpretations of these images (McClelland, Atkinson, Clark & Lowell, 1953). Thus the TAT manual explains that test stimuli invite respondents to 'expose the underlying inhibited tendencies which the [respondent is] not willing to admit, or cannot admit because he is unconscious of them'.

In a similar vein, other projective tests tend to include ambiguous characters as stimuli in order to enable participants to identify with the hero or central picture. Stimuli come in various different forms including solid objects, even auditory stimuli, as do responses that may include sentence completion or free drawing. Lilienfeld, Wood and Garb (2000) have classified all projective techniques into five types: associations (i.e., Rorschach), construction (e.g., Draw-a-person), completion (sentence completion), arrangement/selection (i.e., Luscher Colour Test) and expression (handwriting analysis).

Kline (1994) listed both psychometric problems with projective tests but also reasons for their continued use, if not popularity. Psychometrically the evidence suggests they have poor reliability and validity; are over-sensitive to contextual effects (i.e., test conditions); have little rationale for their scoring systems and are rarely theoretically driven. However, they continue to be used because they provide a unique data source; they can be powerful techniques for revealing unusually rich insights; and some scoring methods can be insightful.

Studies continue to evaluate the TAT and the *Journal of Personality Assessment* frequently carries articles on the topic (an excellent example is Ackerman, Clemence, Weatherill & Hilsenroth, 1999). Although the psychometric standards of the TAT have been criticised for their low predictive validity (Klinger, 1966) and reliability (Entwisle, 1972; Fineman, 1977), one may argue that projective tests should not be evaluated with the same criteria as psychometric tests. Some studies have shown that TAT-derived profiles – in relation to anxiety and narcissism – are congruent with those sketched using other projective tests, such as Rorschach (Harder, 1979; Hurvich, Benveniste, Howard & Coonerty, 1993; Mayman, 1968). Other studies, however, found very low correlations between performance on TAT and objective or psychometric measures of need for achievement (Hansemark, 1997; Fineman, 1977). In one of the most rigorous longitudinal tests of the validity of TAT – an eleven-year study – Hansemark (2000) concluded that the TAT has no validity at all in the prediction of entrepeneurial activity.

With regard to the Rorschach inkblot test, a seminal review of the validity of this test memorably noted that it 'has the most reviled of all psychological assessment instruments' (Hunsley & Bailey, 1999, p. 266).

Certain areas of the literature have always been interested in projective techniques, particularly those interested in linguistic (Breedin, Saffran & Schwartz, 1998) or discourse-narrative techniques (Billig, 1997). Further, researchers interested in achievement motivation, health and sexual issues have taken particular interest in getting at 'real motives' where participants are as likely to be 'unable' as unwilling to give truthful and insightful answers (McClelland, 1989; Kitzinger & Powell, 1995).

A recent comprehensive review of the validity of all projective techniques is however damning. Lilienfeld *et al.* (2000) wrote:

> We conclude that there is empirical support for the validity of a small number of indexes derived from the Rorschach and TAT. However, the substantial majority of Rorschach and TAT indexes are not empirically supported. The validity evidence of human figure drawings is even more limited. With a few exceptions, projective indexes have not consistently demonstrated incremental validity above and beyond other psychometric data.   (p. 27)

Naturally a consequence of their review is to recommend that less time is devoted to projective techniques and ethical implications of relying on projective indexes that are not well validated.

1.9   The Barnum effect

The most plausible reason why people believe in graphology and astrology is that the interpretations they provide are 'true'. They are true because
they consist of vague positive generalisations with high base-rate validity, yet
are supposedly derived specifically for a named person (Dean, 1987; Furnham,
2001). For several decades, psychologists have investigated the 'Barnum effect'
(sometimes known as the 'Forer effect'), the phenomenon whereby people accept
personality feedback about themselves because it is supposedly derived from personality assessment procedures. In other words, people believe in astrology and
graphology because they fall victim to the fallacy of personal validation. People
accept the generalisations that are true of nearly everybody to be specifically true
of themselves.

Stagner (1948) gave a group of personnel managers a personality test, but
instead of scoring it and giving them the actual answers, he gave each of them
bogus feedback in the form of statements derived from horoscopes, graphological
analyses and so on. Each manager was then asked to read over the feedback (supposedly derived from the 'scientific' test) and decide how accurate the assessment
was. Over half felt their profile was an accurate description of themselves, and
almost none believed it to be wrong (see Table 1.2).

Similarly, Forer (1949) gave personality tests to his students, ignored their
answers, and gave each student an identical evaluation. They were then asked
to evaluate the description from 0 to 5, with 5 meaning the recipient felt the
description was an 'excellent' evaluation and 4 meaning the assessment was
'good'. The class average evaluation was 4.26.

More recently, Furnham (1994) 'tricked' his students with a 'medical Barnum'. Students were told that a 'physical and chemical analysis' of hair can
give clues to body health, and were asked to provide hair samples. The following week, they were shown advertising from an organisation that purported
to do such an analysis, and were given an envelope that contained their hair
samples and Barnum items that they were asked to rate on a seven-point
scale for accuracy (7 being extremely accurate; 1 being not accurate at all).
A third of the feedback items received a score of 60 per cent or above. Some
of the highest ratings were about normality, while other items rated as accurate referred to variability in behaviour. The item that yielded the lowest score
referred to quite specific physical behaviours (for example, urine colour) (see
Table 1.3).

Research on the Barnum effect has, however, shown that belief in bogus
feedback is influenced by a number of important factors (Furnham, 2001): some
to do with the client and the consultant (for example, their personality, naivety)
and some to do with the nature of the test and feedback situation. One of the
most important variables is perceived specificity of the information required. The
more detailed the questions (for example, a horoscope based on the year, month

Table 1.2 *Evaluations of items by sixty-eight personnel managers when presented as a 'personality' analysis*

	Judgement as to accuracy of item: percentage[a] choosing				
	a[b]	b	c	d	e
A. You have a great need for other people to like and admire you.	39	46	13	1	1
B. You have a tendency to be critical of yourself.	46	36	15	3	0
C. You have a great deal of unused capacity which you have not turned to your advantage.	37	36	18	1	4
D. Whilst you have some personality weaknesses, you are generally able to compensate for them.	34	55	9	0	0
E. Your sexual adjustment has presented problems for you.	15	16	16	33	19
F. Disciplined and self-controlled outside, you tend to be worrisome and insecure inside.	40	21	22	10	4
G. At times you have serious doubts as to whether you have made the right decision or done the right thing.	37	31	19	18	4
H. You prefer a certain amount of change and variety and become dissatisfied when hemmed in by restriction and limitations.	63	28	7	1	1
I. You pride yourself as an independent thinker and do not accept others' statements without satisfactory proof.	49	32	12	4	4
J. You have found it unwise to be frank in revealing yourself to others.	31	37	22	6	4
K. At time you are extraverted, affable, sociable, whilst at other times you are introverted, wary, reserved.	43	25	18	9	5
L. Some of your aspirations tend to be pretty unrealistic.	12	16	22	43	7
M. Security is one of your major goals in life.	40	31	15	9	5

Notes: [a] Not all percentages add to 100% because of omissions by an occasional subject.
[b] Definitions of scale steps as follows: (a) amazingly accurate; (b) rather good; (c) about half and half; (d) more wrong than right; (e) almost entirely.

and day of birth, rather than one based on the year and month of birth alone), the more likely it is a person will think it pertains to just themself (Lillqvist & Lindeman, 1998).

Forer's (1949) own explanation for the Barnum effect was in terms of human gullibility. People tend to accept claims about themselves in proportion to their desire that the claims be true rather than in proportion to the empirical accuracy of the claims as measured by some non-subjective standard. This confirms another principle in personality assessment – the 'Polyanna principle' – which suggests that there is a general tendency to use or accept positive words or feedback more frequently than negative words of feedback.

Table 1.3 *Ratings of the feedback from the 'medical Barnum' (from Furnham, 1994b)*

		Accuracy 0–100	Those giving maximum (100%) accurate scores
1.	Your diet, while adequate, would benefit from an increase in fresh fruit and vegetables.	65.6	19.1
2.	You are probably hairier than most other people of your sex and age.	44.9	4.3
3.	Not all your measurements are symmetrical (e.g., your hands, feet, breasts are not exactly the same size/cup).	55.6	2.1
4.	Your sex drive is very variable.	56.3	4.3
5.	There is evidence of a tendency to arthritis in your family.	47.7	12.8
6.	You are prone to feel the cold more than other people.	58.0	19.1
7.	Your skin texture changes under stress.	54.4	10.6
8.	You are prone to occasional patterns of sleeplessness.	62.6	25.5
9.	Your metabolic rate is at the 40 percentile (just below average for your age and sex).	50.1	4.2
10.	You sometimes feel very tired for no reason.	64.7	23.4
11.	You can get depressed for no apparent reason.	58.7	14.9
12.	You are occasionally aware that your breath smells for no reason.	44.9	2.1
13.	Your nose bleeds occasionally.	34.9	8.5
14.	You are more prone to tooth decay than others.	42.8	10.6
15.	Your appetite varies extensively.	63.5	23.4
16.	You have a tendency to put on weight easily.	44.6	8.5
17.	You sometimes experience symptoms of anxiety (e.g., tension headaches, indigestion).	65.9	23.4
18.	There are no major hereditary defects in your family.	75.6	34.0
19.	Your bowel movements are not always regular.	51.3	8.5
20.	Your cardiovascular efficiency is average for your age and sex.	67.7	14.9
21.	You experience frequent changes in your urine colour.	41.3	4.3
22.	You occasionally get a craving for certain food.	66.5	25.5
23.	Your body fat distribution is not perfectly normal.	56.8	12.8
24.	You frequently get indigestion.	43.7	4.3

For example, Glick and colleagues (1989) found that students initially sceptical about astrology were more likely to both accept the personality description it offered them and to increase their belief in astrology as a whole if that description were favourable. In other words, those for whom astrological theory provides a more attractive self-portrait are more likely to express belief in the validity of astrologers (Hamilton, 2001).

Dickson and Kelly (1985) have examined many 'Barnum effect' studies and concluded that overall there is significant support for the general claim that

Barnum profiles are perceived to be accurate by subjects in the studies. Furthermore, there is an increased acceptance of the profile if it is labelled 'for you'. Favourable assessments are more readily accepted as accurate descriptions of subjects' personalities than unfavourable ones. But unfavourable claims are more readily accepted when delivered by people with high perceived status than low perceived status. There is also some evidence that personality variables such as *neuroticism, need for approval* and *authoritarianism* are positively related to belief in Barnum-like profiles (Glick *et al.*, 1989).

Hence the popularity of astronomy and graphology: feedback is based on specific information and it is nearly always favourable. In addition, it is often the anxious who visit astrologers and the like: they are particularly sensitive to objective information about themselves and the future. Thus, for example, research has shown that increasing uncertainty in the environment increases interest in astrology and other paranormal phenomena (Keinan, 1994), and astrological information also verifies an individual's self-beliefs and possibly reduces negative feelings linked with uncertainty (Lillqvist & Lindeman, 1998).

1.10 Accepting feedback

Several studies which have considered the influence of personality factors on the Barnum effect have attempted to show that the acceptance of feedback is consistent with particular traits. The literature has as much to do with self-verification (Swann, 1987), namely the notion that individuals are highly motivated to verify their self-conceptions even if those are negative.

Snyder and Clair (1977) looked at the effects of insecurity on the acceptance of personality interpretations, both as a trait and as situational manipulation. The major finding of this study was that the greater the insecurity of the participants, the greater was the acceptance of feedback. Ruzzene and Noller (1986) noted that individuals who exhibited high levels of desire for feedback did not discriminate between favourable (positive) and unfavourable (negative) accurate feedback, or between accurate and inaccurate favourable feedback. In other words, desire for feedback *per se* did not affect the acceptability of feedback.

Various studies have related Extraversion and Neuroticism to the acceptance of bogus feedback. Layne and Ally (1980) used the Eysenck Personality Inventory, and found that the more accurate the feedback, the more positively it was accepted. Neurotics endorsed neurotic (and accurate) feedback more than stable (inaccurate) feedback, and stable people endorsed stable (and accurate) feedback more than neurotic (inaccurate) feedback. This suggests that some personality variables were logically and predictably related to feedback acceptance. Yet Kelly, Dickson and Saklofske (1986) found no relationship between extraverts' and neurotics' non-neurotics' acceptance of general vs specific positive and negative feedback. They found that extraverts, compared to introverts, showed a significantly greater acceptance of general positive and specific positive feedback. Compared to non-neurotics, neurotics showed a greater acceptance of general positive, specific positive and general negative feedback, but not specific negative feedback. Neurotic extraverts showed significantly more acceptance of general and specific negative feedback. The impulsiveness and low reflectiveness of extraverts accounts for their readiness to accept positive feedback, or the fact that being more sociable, which is a desirable trait, actually results in receiving more positive feedback in everyday life, which was confirmed in this study. Because both introverts and extraverts perceive extraversion as a more desirable or ideal trait than introversion, it is possible that extraverts accept positive feedback as being more accurate than negative feedback (but not vice versa) precisely because it is true.

Fletcher, Taylor and Glanfield (1996) found that subjects who completed the 16PF were able to identify their test-derived personality more accurately than would be expected by chance. However, they did find that education, sex and personality were related to acceptance of feedback. Three personality factors accounted for 22 per cent of the variance in accuracy ratings – these were mental capacity, conscientiousness and imaginativeness. They noted: 'To define which personality characteristics those giving feedback should be wary of would be difficult: on the other hand, some evidence suggests that individuals with less positive charactersitics are less likely to seek test feedback anyway' (Fletcher *et al.*, 1996, p. 155).

1.11   Summary and conclusion

Ideally those in the business of selection want to use reliable and valid measures to accurately assess a person's abilities, motives, values and traits. There are many techniques available and at least a century of research trying to determine the psychometric properties of these methods. Over the past twenty years there have been excellent meta-analyses of the predictive validity of various techniques.

In this chapter we considered some assessment and selection techniques that have alas 'stood the test of time' despite being consistently shown to be both unreliable and invalid. They are perhaps more a testament to the credulity, naivety and desperation of people who should know better.

However, it is important to explain why these methods are still used. One explanation is the Barnum effect whereby people accept as valid about themselves and others high base-rate, positive information. The use to a client of personal validation of a test by a consultant or test publisher should thus be questioned.

Part of the problem for selectors is their relative ignorance of the issues which are the subject of this book. Even specialists in human resources remain uninformed about research showing the poor validity and reliability of different methods. There is, however, one other issue that in part may account for the use and abuse of ineffective methods. This concerns the issue of applicant reaction to testing and the related issue of litigation. The business of selection is a way an organisation can show it is up-to-date and fair in its procedures. However, some candidates do not like tests and processes that have proven to be highly valid, such as intelligence tests (see Chapter 6). They therefore rely on methods that candidates might like but which are very poor indeed as an aid in selecting the best candidates and weeding out the worst.

2   The interview

2.1   Introduction

It seems almost inconceivable that any form of selection task and decision is not informed by one, indeed many, job interviews. These have been used in selection for over two centuries (for example, the Royal Navy used job interviews as early as 1800). Whether it comes at the beginning or the end of the selection process, whether there are one or many interviewers at a time and whether it lasts a few minutes or several hours, the selection interview is thought as a *crucial and central* part of the process whereby the employer and employee can get a good sense of one another. People use the words 'chemistry', 'fit' and 'feel', all of which speak primarily to the intuitive nature of the process. Candidates expect interviews.

An interview candidate may have to sit before large panels of people eager to have a 'good look' at him or her or else go through a large number of sequential 'one-to-ones' from the often many stakeholders in the job. Interviews differ on many dimensions: how long they last, how many interviewers there are; how much they are pre-planned; what the real purpose of the interview is.

The very popularity and ubiquity of interviews has spawned a huge industry in interview training. It has also spawned a number of books for both interviewers and interviewees. Interviewers are 'taught' how to ask 'killer questions' that get 'to the heart of the interviewee'. Equally, interviewees are taught how to give diplomatic (somewhat evasive) answers to those really 'tough' questions. Interviews are therefore presented as a minefield of dishonesty; a game of intellectual charades, where both parties are essentially out to 'trick' and 'out manoeuvre' one another. This is, of course, far from the truth but has no doubt served to influence how both parties see selection interviews.

As a result, some organisations have argued that the data showing the extremely poor reliability and validity of (mostly unstructured) interviews effectively means that they often hinder rather than help effective decision making. Interview data and ratings have been accused of being invalid, unreliable and biased. Further, considerable time and travel costs are often involved for both parties. Hence, in UK it is still common for universities *not* to interview prospective undergraduate students, believing that the school exam results, letters of recommendation and other application form data provide sufficient information for them to make the 'optimal' decision. Some universities do interview for highly selective courses

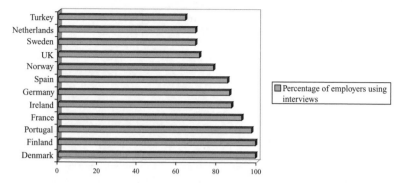

Figure 2.1 *Percentage of employers using interviews (based on Dany & Torchy, 1994)*

because they are interested in *weeding out* unsuitable candidates (as judged by personality, motivation or values) rather than selecting desirable candidates.

Yet interviews are perhaps part of nearly all selection decision, data-gathering methods because they are rated as the most acceptable (fair, reasonable, important) method. They are used to collect information, make inferences about suitability and determine an individual's communication skills. It is estimated that 90 per cent of employment selection decisions involve interviews (Cook, 2004). Figure 2.1 (from a Price Waterhouse Cranfield survey of Western European countries) shows the large percentage of employers in each country using the interview. Although accurate US estimates are harder to come by, US figures can be expected to be at least as high as UK ones and it has been pointed out that the employment interview is the most widely used method of assessment in the US (Judge, Higgins & Cable, 2000). Both parties seem to expect and want them.

This chapter attempts both to review the salient literature on the reliability and validity of information obtained by interview but also to look at the research-based advice to those interested in better interview practice. The literature on this topic is scattered between various academic and applied disciplines from Human Resource Management to Differential Psychology. Some researchers appear to be less disinterested that others in their attempt to demonstrate the validity of particular types of interview techniques or styles. However, there remains considerable consensus on the validity of structured and non-structured interview data. We will start with what is currently considered to be evidence-based good advice for doing interviews.

2.2   Basic guidelines for a good selection interview

The central question for those interested in the selection interview is the old but crucial psychometric issues of reliability and validity. In short, they refer to the question of whether interviewers' ratings of the candidates agree

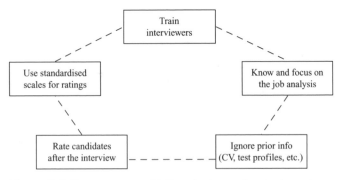

Figure 2.2 *Five common guidelines for improving the interview*

(sufficiently) with one another. Do candidates leave the same impression about their skills, aptitudes, dispositions and attitudes with *all* those that interview them? Second, and always more salient, do the interview ratings predict future job performance? The answer to this simple question is far from simple. The reliability and validity of the interview is dependent on all sorts of things from the skill and training of the interviewers to the types of ratings made and the length of the interview, and rather than asking 'whether' interviews predict performance the question is 'to what extent' they do.

As a consequence of a great deal of research and excellent recent meta-analyses it is possible to list some rules of thumb that have been shown to increase the reliability and validity of the interview: train interviewers; ask standardised questions; do a good job analysis; ignore salient prior information; do the ratings before and after the interviews; make specific ratings (see Figure 2.2).

Interviewers need training in how they present themselves: how to pose questions and how to interpret often subtle non-verbal cues as well as certain answers. This is mainly about social skills and emotional intelligence (see Sections 7.19 to 7.23). More importantly they need to know what salient questions to ask that relate to the very specific nature of the job that they are selecting for. A careful job analysis should reveal the full range of skills, aptitudes and dispositions required. Hence this should drive the interview structure. Interviewers need not only to know *what* questions to ask and *why* but also *how* to interpret the answers. In addition, interviewers need to make judgements on only the salient features of the candidates and to ignore various impression-management techniques (tactics used to portray a desired and planned image to others) that candidates may employ either on the CV or face-to-face.

Next, interviewers need training on how to accurately distinguish between the different criteria assessed. Just as wine and tea tasters have to be taught to make reliable and accurate ratings, so interviewers have to be taught – through both practice and special training – how they and other raters see the same candidate and to ensure that they provide consistent or at lest compatible evaluations. Finally, it is important that the rating scales used by interviewers are clear and comprehensive, allowing a wide range of ratings, including an index of uncertainty.

2.3   Description, types and functions of the interview

Research on the interview addresses a number of quite specific issues. First, it is important to distinguish between different types of interview given both their purpose and methodology. Second, there is a long literature on the cognitive psychology of interviews that looks at how people obtain, evaluate and combine information to derive a final judgement. Third, by far the greatest research effort has gone into looking at the psychometrics (reliability and validity) of the interview, as well a how to improve it. Fourth, there is a growing literature on candidate evaluation of the interview. Fifth, there is a small literature on legal aspects of the interview.

It is difficult to characterise the typical selection interview. Certainly it is probably true to say most are unstructured and semi-structured at best; few interviewers are properly trained; the easiest aspects to assess (i.e., self-confidence, presentation) are frequently relatively unimportant job criteria; the interview is usually done by the person (alone or with others) who will 'manage' the candidate; the only preparation the interviewer has done is a perfunctory reading of the completed application form and the candidate's CV. Despite the wide range of interviews, most tend to ask a relatively invariant number of questions, such as 'What persuaded you to work for us?', 'What are your greatest strengths and weaknesses?' and the cliché finale of 'Have you got any questions for us?' (see Table 2.1, based on www.advancedqanda.com/interview; retrieved 21 Feb 2008).

There are many different types of interview: the appraisal, disciplinary, motivational and selection interviews, though there is probably most research on the selection interview. Certainly people have a clear expectation of interviews, though they vary a great deal in form and content. They usually expect an interview to be thorough, lasting anything from 30 to 120 minutes. They expect the interviewer to be in some sense prepared, to ask most of the questions and to take notes. They expect that they must be smartly dressed (where 'smart' means better dressed than they would normally be in that job!), that they will answer questions honestly and that they will be allowed themselves to ask various questions at some point. Thus there are four phases to the interview: welcome, information gathering, supplying information and the conclusion. The first phase is usually thought of as welcome or courtesy. It lasts a few minutes and is designed to put the candidate at his/her ease. The second phase – gathering data – may constitute as much as 80–90 per cent of the total interview. The third, relatively short phase near the end occurs when the interviewer/s invite/s the candidate to pose any questions he/she might have. Some of these questions are genuine and others often impression-management questions designed to impress the interviewer. The final phase usually involves the interviewers explaining to the candidate the decision-making process and how and when they will be informed as to the outcome.

There are many courses that attempt to teach managers interview skills, especially how to plan and run an interview, as well as how to ask perceptive questions.

Table 2.1 *Typical questions asked in an employment interview*

What information have you got about our company?
What persuaded you to get a job in this company?
Tell us about yourself and your background. How would you/co-workers describe you/yourself?
Why should we hire you? What makes you the right person for this job?
Give us an example of situations in which you displayed attributes that are relevant to this job?
What aspects of your previous experience do you think will be most helpful to you in this role?
What are your greatest strengths and weaknesses?
How do you deal with failure? Please provide an example where you dealt with failure in the past.
How do you feel about working with others/in a team? Please provide examples from the past.
How do you feel about working under pressure/tight deadlines?
How do you react to criticism?
What is your greatest achievement to date?
Why are you thinking of leaving your current job?
Where do you see yourself in five/ten years time?
What other jobs are you applying for?
What kind of salary are you expecting?
When would you be able to start?
Have you any questions for us?

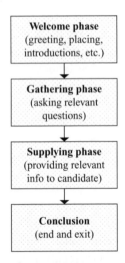

Figure 2.3 *Phases of the interview*

To some extent the issue is how to obtain sufficient valid data upon which to make a good rating.

This, in turn, is different from a target-setting interview, an appraisal and a disciplinary interview. They have various skill requirements in common. Thus one of the major issues for the target-setting interview is agreeing clear,

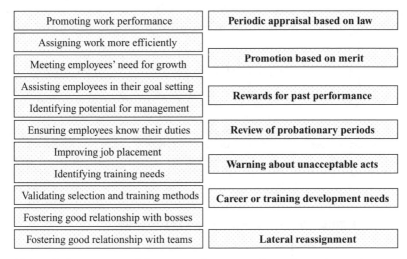

Figure 2.4 *Functions of the appraisal interview (for organisation and employees, and personnel actions)*

measurable targets. These can or should have highly defined criteria measurable usually by one of five factors: time, money, quality, quantity or customer feedback.

All interviews should have an agenda that demonstrates that at least the interviewer has planned the process. Also it should end with a clear summary statement from both parties regarding what they got from the interview.

Appraisal interviews have very specific functions: to improve utilisation of staff resources by promoting work performance, assigning work more efficiently, meeting employee's need for growth, etc. (see Figure 2.4).

Often training programmes concerning interviews spend a great deal of effort on looking at formulating, asking and interpreting the answers to questions. Appraisal interviews, often considered much more problematic, look at how best to give (both positive and negative) feedback. Thus clear recommendations are made such as:

- Begin with a clear brief about the context and purpose of the feedback.
- Start with the positive feedback.
- Be specific in both positive and negative comments.
- Refer always to behaviour that can be changed.
- Offer alternative suggestions to how things can be done differently.
- Always be descriptive rather than evaluative in feedback.
- Attempt to get the person to acknowledge the feedback.
- Check on whether there are any hidden agendas in how, when and why you are giving the feedback.
- Leave the person with choice in how they accept and respond to the feedback.
- Consider what the feedback says about you.

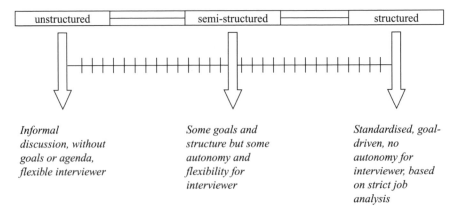

Figure 2.5 *Dimensional structure of interviews*

Equally, it may be advisable to train people in how to receive feedback in interviews. So they are usually advised to listen to, and to consider carefully, precisely what is being said before rejecting it or arguing with the giver. It is important to understand and be clear about what is being said. Receivers of feedback should be encouraged to ask for feedback that they wanted but did not get. They may also be encouraged to check it out with other senior people who know them rather than rely on only one source. Further, they will need to decide on precisely what they intend to do with the feedback.

2.4   Structured vs unstructured interviews

It has long been common practice to differentiate between what have been called structured and unstructured interviews, though strictly speaking they are really on a continuum from completely unstructured (and possibly unplanned) to rigidly and inflexibly structured. The ultimately unstructured interview is a little like an informal discussion where interviewers ask whatever questions come to mind and follow up answers in an intuitive and whimsical way. Crucially, questions are open-minded and attempt to avoid 'leading' the interviewee's answers in any specific direction. The structured interview on the other hand is pre-planned to ensure every candidate receives exactly the same questions in the same order at the same pace. Structured interviews also employ rating scales, checklists for judgement; allow for few or no follow-up questions (to limit interviewees' response time and standardise it); take into account previous job analyses; and leave little autonomy for the interviewer. In that sense, totally structured interviews resemble standardised psychometric tests (see Chapter 7). The question is how much structure vs flexibility should be built in to maximise the point of the whole exercise.

A structured interview is essentially a planned interview. In fact it often requires interviewers to make pre- and post-interview decisions. The idea is that a job

Table 2.2 *Potential qualities assessed by a structured job interview*

Energy and drive	General level of work output, ability to stay with a problem, persistence, enthusiasm, motivation
Work discipline	General efficiency, ability to plan, control and monitor work and time, ability to set objectives and standards
Decision making	Quality of judgement on personnel and technical matters, willingness and ability to make decisions
Intellectual effectiveness	Analytical ability, speed of thinking, creativity
Relationships	Sociability, ability to work individually and in teams, extent of guidance and support needed from boss, ability to delegate
Flexibility	Ability to adapt to new and different people, technology and environments, responsiveness to change
Emotional stability	Ability to work under pressure, response to setback and failures

analysis leads one to decide on a limited number of essential qualities or competencies that one is looking for. These are often a mixture of abilities and personality traits. Consider the potential qualities and areas listed in Tables 2.2 and 2.3.

A structured interview then follows a rigorously planned sequence of question areas in an attempt to get all the salient information upon which to make an accurate rating. This might result in either ratings on each of the dimensions specified in Tables 2.2 and 2.3 or a written report such as the one shown in Box 2.1.

The importance of structured interviews to ensure validity cannot be overrated, as we shall see. As a result, textbook writers often offer hints or tips to those embarking on the process. For example, Figure 2.6 summarises main areas of attention for improving structured interviews (based on Arnold, 2005, p. 182).

2.5 The cognitive basis of interviews

The result of an interview is usually a decision. Ideally this process involves collecting, evaluating and integrating specific salient information into a logical algorithm that has shown to be predictive.

However, there is an academic literature on impression formation that has examined experimentally how precisely people select particular pieces of information. Studies looking at the process in selection interviews have shown all too often how interviewers may make their minds up *before* the interview even occurs (based on the application form or CV of the candidate), or that they make up their minds too quickly based on first impression (superficial data) or their own personal implicit theories of personality. Equally, they overweigh or overemphasise negative information or bias information not in line with the algorithm they use. Earlier research (Harris, 1989) was conducted on whether information was added or weighted, that is, how people combined positive and negative 'pieces

Table 2.3 *Potential areas assessed by a structured job interview*

Upbringing	• Base point against which person makes decisions • Info needed – where born, siblings (ages, academic and work achievements), childhood events *Evaluate: economic and social stability, degree of supportiveness*
Education	• Focus is on intellect • Info needed – schools, university, exam results, other interests and achievements (cultural, social, technical) *Evaluate: choice of subjects, performance, causes and results of failures*
Work history	• Look at most recent experience first • Info needed – job titles, main tasks, relationships, objectives/results, part of job liked/done well and vice versa, reasons for changing *Evaluate: significance of job within the organisation, standing of the firm in the industry, competence of candidate against demands of job*
Aspirations	• Reality check • Info needed – what candidate wants to do in short/long term, what plans for achieving ambitions *Evaluate: how realistic aspirations are when set against academic and work achievements to date plus personal attributes*
Circumstances	• Establish pressures on career • Info needed – willingness to move, marital status, social family constraints, financial liabilities, driving licence *Evaluate: any constraints which may affect work effectiveness by exploring marital and financial stability*
Interests	• Ask what they enjoy about their interests to find out motivations • Info needed – main interests, with what intensity and for how long *Evaluate: to what extent proposed job gives an outlet for these interests, and to what extent it is a barrier*

Box 2.1 Aspects of the candidate assessed in an interview

Energy and drive

The candidate is a very ambitious, focused, task-oriented individual. There is a strong sense of someone who is strongly driven to prove his worth and to achieve specific goals. He has been in HR since the beginning of his career and has a clear vision of where he wants to be. Further, he has the capacity, stamina and drive to achieve those ends.

The candidate is very articulate and honest, and shows particularly high levels of self-insight. He admits to being a driven individual but that of late he is less so, because he has begun to achieve his goals and get recognition for them. This is not to say that his energy has diminished but rather that he is probably more relaxed. He is energetic and enthusiastic – more a socialised extravert than a pure strong extravert. But he is enthusiastic and possibly at times rather too much so.

Work style and values

The candidate is a hard worker. He freely admits that at school and university he had to work hard to 'compensate' for his lack of ability relative to his peer group. He is clearly a 'mover and shaker' preferring to 'get on with it' rather than sit about discussing strategy. His claims he is 'tough on performance' and no doubt drives others as much as he drives himself. Where necessary he says he can be controlling and very directive. He prefers to delegate but only if he believes his people are up to the challenge. Asked what other bosses/appraisers have said about him, he pointed out that they said he always delivered, but there was a hint of 'achievement at what cost?' I do not, however, get the impression that his is ever unfair or unreasonable with his staff, but rather that he wants them, like him, to work at their maximum capacity.

   He seems to like a 'work hard, play hard' culture where you get on with the job but have a lot of fun while doing it. He sees the 'glass half full' and likes to work with people like himself.

Decision making and judgement

Three things characterise his decision-making style. The first is honesty/integrity. He admits that he does not like 'confronting others', but where he feels various ethical, moral and decency barriers are passed he speaks out. Second, he is not risk-averse, which means that he can and does accept failures when they occur. Third, he does not like procrastination and ambiguity. This means that he demands clarity and provides it for those around him. He is clearly a man of both 'heart and head' who can and does balance decisions where necessary. He appears to read situations well.

Flexibility and adaptability

The candidate is fit, curious and ambitious. He has, can and will adapt to situations well. But more than that, he has no problem in trying to adapt and change others and their way of working to achieve certain goals. His self-insight and self-confidence and abilities mean that he can easily rise to challenges requiring adaptation.

Emotional stability and maturity

The candidate comes from a very stable background with an articulate and affectionate mother. He is quite able to cope with stress and very unlikely to buckle under pressure. His coping strategy is primarily cognitive: withdraw, attempt to analyse the situation, get things in proportion...and then get on with it.

Intellectual capacity and effectiveness

The candidate performed well on the tests but not quite as well as one might expect from his academic record. There is no doubt that he is more than capable intellectually of doing the job and learning new things. Further, he has a history of believing that if things are not easily understood and learnt, with effort they can be. He will certainly put effort into doing that. There is no fear of someone whose academic strength and curiosity leads to a situation of 'analysis paralysis'.

Relationships

Asked about relationships, the candidate made some astute and interesting observations. Asked about how he works with others, he made it clear that much depends on the task and the ability of the team. His preference is to be 'first among equals' in a bright and active team. He believes his reports find him energetic, focused, enthusiastic... and, he added, possibly egotistical. He likes to understand the problem, set goals and then delegate.

He claims not to enjoy but to be able, when necessary, to confront poor performance. His agreeableness in that sense should not then prove to be a handicap.

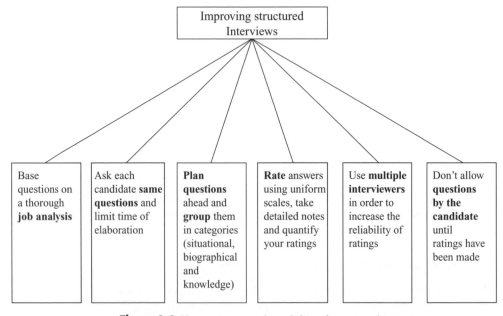

Figure 2.6 *How to improve the validity of structured interviews*

of information' about an individual to come up with some overall rating. Thus researchers in the area of interpersonal perception examined the way interviews looked for 'favourite cues' or facts they believed particularly diagnostic. Some wondered whether people did 'linear regressions' in their head in the sense that they assigned different importance to certain predictors of a given outcome. The question is how interviewers make *configural judgements*: what causes them to have multiple cut-off points (e.g., are candidates qualified enough, young enough, friendly enough, etc.) or, instead, single disqualifying factors, such as evidence of going to a mental hospital or having taken drugs? Clearly, more research is needed to answer these questions.

Social psychologists have also been interested in *implicit personality theories*, which are concerned with how individual, idiosyncratic, lay theories of personality influence a person's judgement in the interview (Cook, 2004). They have also worked for years on *attribution theories*, which are concerned with how people attribute social causation, notably whether they explain success and failure in terms of personal or situational factors. In the interview it is common to ask candidates why certain events occurred, i.e., to try to assess their attribution style, but the interviewer also infers causation. Thus a candidate may be asked why their school results were so different from their university results, or why they seem to change jobs so regularly.

Certainly understanding how people collect and integrate information in the interview must be central to the whole enterprise.

2.6   The psychometrics of interviews

The two strong pillars of psychometrics are *reliability* and *validity*, both of which come in many forms (see Figure 2.7). Further, they are interdependent: interviews cannot be valid if they are not reliable.

For interviews, it is crucial to have inter-interviewer (judge, observer, rater) reliability. This means that two people doing or watching interviews with the same person must have the same ratings. Low reliability, particularly in unstructured interviews, is no doubt mainly due to interviewer variability. Interviewers ask different questions, record and weight answers differently and may have radically different understandings of the whole purpose of the interview. Most reviewers have seen that the single simplest way to improve reliability is to introduce a consistency and structure to the interview. Thus it is almost tautological to suggest that consistency leads to reliability as they are in essence the same thing. Studies also show that it is possible to increase interviewer reliability by different but important steps, including: doing a job analysis; training interviewers; having structured interviews; having behaviourally based and anchored rating scales.

Many studies have examined the issue of reliability with a useful meta-analysis by Conway, Jako and Goodman (1995), who reviewed 160 empirical studies. They

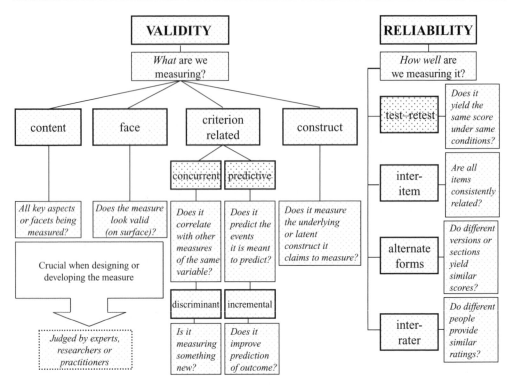

Figure 2.7 *Validity and reliability*

found reliabilities of 0.77 when observers watched the same interview, but that this dropped to 0.53 if they watched different interviews of the same candidate. Given that candidates react to different questions by different interviewees often quite differently, some would argue that 0.53 is surprisingly good.

Research in this area has gone on for fifty years at least. Over the years small, relatively unsophisticated studies have been replaced by ever more useful and important meta-analyses. There are now a sufficient number of meta-analyses that some have done helpful summaries of them. Thus Cook (2004) reviewed Hunter and Hunter (1984) (30 studies); Wiesner and Cronshaw (1988) (160 studies); Huffcutt and Arthur (1994) (114 studies) and McDaniel, Whetzel, Schmidt and Maurer (1994) (245 studies). These meta-analyses covered many different studies done in different countries over different jobs and different time periods, but the results were surprisingly consistent. Results were clear: the validity coefficient for unstructured interviews as predictors of job performance is around r = .15 (range .11 – .18), while that for structured interviews is around r = .28 (range .24 – .34). Cook (2004) calculates the overall validity of all interviews over three recent meta-analyses – taking job performance as the common denominator of all criteria examined – to be around r = .23.

There may be rather different reactions to this validity coefficient. An optimist might point out that given the many differences in interview technique – some are

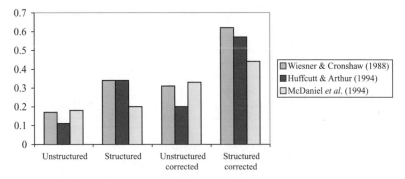

Figure 2.8 *Predictive validity of interviews*

psychological, some situational, some job related – and the fact that they were attempting to assess very different issues from creativity to conscientiousness, the validity is impressively high. Indeed, compared to various other job selection methods, this result is rather impressive (see Figure 2.8).

The pessimist, however, may point out that a value of $r = .25$ means in effect an interview is accounting for a paltry 5 per cent in explaining the variance in later work behaviour. That is, it is not accounting for 95 per cent of the variance. However, given the unreliability of the criterion, the unaccounted variance may be as low as 70 per cent, and even seemingly small percentages of variance explained may have very important utility. If, for instance, 5 per cent of the variance in an outcome is explained, the categorical (yes or no) prediction of that outcome would improve from 50 per cent (the chance rate) to 55 per cent, and probably more (as the 5 per cent figure is 5/70 rather than 5/100). That said, given that interviews are used to infer information about candidates' abilities or personality traits (see Section 2.9 and Chapters 6 and 7), they provide very little unique information about a candidate and show little incremental validity over established psychometric tests (of ability and personality) in the prediction of future job performance (Schmidt & Hunter, 1998).

It is not difficult to list reasons for the relatively low reliability. Essentially, these have to do with three issues: factors associated with the interviewer; factors associated with the interviewee; factors associated with the process.

From an *interviewer's perspective* low validity may be attributable to individual difference in values, intelligence, perceptiveness, etc. of the various interviewers; the motives of interviewers in the selection process; the training they received; their understanding of the job itself. Whatever their training, interviewers differ in terms of their natural ability, perceptiveness and courage to make 'thorough but accurate' ratings. From an *interviewee's perspective* there are two major problems which come under the heading of dissimulation: notably impression management and self-deception. This means in effect not presenting themselves honestly either because of their desire to get the job or not having sufficient self-insight to tell

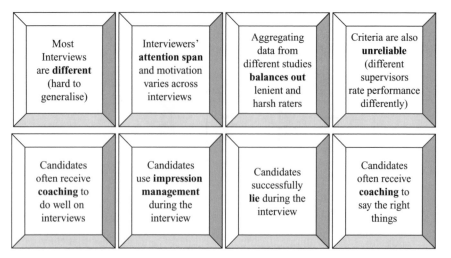

Figure 2.9 *Reasons for low validity of job interview (based on Cook, 2004)*

the truth. Thus the person who is presented at the interviews is not the same as the person at work on the job.

The third factor lies not in the two parties involved but in the *information provided*. What criterion/criteria is the interviewer trying to predict? Is there clear, reliable and valid evidence on the criteria? Is the rating scale such as not to lead to ceiling effects, restriction of range? In short, how easy is it for the interviewer to do a good job even if both parties are well briefed and honest?

Cook (2004) offers evidence-based recommendations for improving interview reliability and validity.

1. *Select interviewers with talent.* As in every aspect of life, some people appear to have the optimal mix of abilities, temperaments and traits to do good interviews. Many studies have demonstrated considerable interviewer variability. Though it can cause organisational problems, it is recommended that interviewers are selected for this task, which inevitably leads to some being rejected. This inevitably leads to the interesting question of how interviewers are selected. Is the best interviewer selected by interview?

2. *Train interviewers in the relevant skills* like asking open-ended questions, doing sufficient preparation, etc. It is possible to improve all skills though training, but only within the limits of the ability of the trainee.

3. *Be consistent using the same interviewers for all interviews.* This simply avoids unwanted variance. Though for practical and political reasons it may not always be possible to have the *same* (well-chosen and well-trained) interviewers for all interviews.

4. *Use dyad, board or panel interviewers* because they are more reliable. This point does not contradict the above point. Rather it suggests that a well-chosen, well-trained, perceptive group of interviewers will be more accurate and reliable.

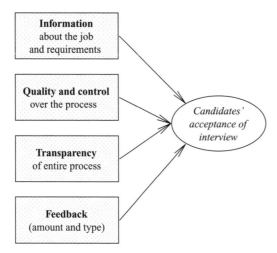

Figure 2.10 *Factors influencing candidates' acceptance of interviews (based on Schuler, 1993)*

5. *Have planned, structured interviews* with clarity about precisely what questions to ask. And when and why. It means taking notes, making systematic ratings and later checking interview reliability and validity.

2.7   The 'acceptability of interviews'

The interview is a two-way process of observation and rating. By and large, candidates approve of interviews and are surprised if they are not asked to them. Thus they have two types of validity: that from the organisational perspective (which has been the focus of academic validity studies on personnel selection techniques) and that from the candidate perspective.

Schuler (1993) described the latter as the social validity of the interview. He argued that people tend to base the social validity of interviews on four factors: how informative they are to the candidate in terms of the total information they get about the job; the quality, quantity and control they have over participation in the process (and its outcome); how transparent the whole approach is; and the amount and type of feedback provided (see Figure 2.10).

Another perspective on the acceptability of interviews is that from social justice theory, which distinguishes between distributive and procedural justice. This allows for the derivation of theory-based, testable hypotheses to predict how fair a candidate finds an interview (Gillibrand, 1993).

Results in this field have led to a number of conclusions. First, when given a list of, or actually exposed to, different selection methods, candidates approve most of the more traditional methods (interview, application form, reference letters) and those clearly job relevant (work samples). By the same token they like lie-detector, graphology or obscure personality tests the least. A recent review of selection methods and how they are perceived around the world reported that interviews are favourably perceived in Europe, the US, Asia and Africa (Lievens, 2007).

Second, although there are broad patterns of agreement in candidates' reactions, there are also cultural differences, not all of which are clearly explicable. Culture dictates what questions may be asked and the sort of answers that are given. Legal, anti-discriminatory changes in legislation mean that in some, predominantly western, countries people are not required to answer questions about their age, previous job history, family structure, etc. The formality of the interview, the probability of group interviews, as well as the length of the interview, are all influenced by corporate and national culture. This means that a person from one culture who is interviewed in another culture may feel unfairly dealt with or simply surprised by the questions that they are asked.

Third, because lay people are not always fully familiar with various methods – they may not be exactly sure what a cognitive ability test or biographical inventory is – their reactions are different depending on whether they rate methods in the abstract or they actually undergo the test (Marcus, 2003).

2.8   Fairness, bias and the law

Most developed countries have legislated against forms of discrimination in terms of age, gender, race and religion. Whilst there are no laws about lookism (discriminating by physical appearance), weightism (discriminating by body mass index), classism (discriminating by dress or accent), there are reasons why individuals and organisations try not to let appearance and social background influence their decision making.

There is plenty of evidence to suggest that interviews in the past have been, and no doubt will continue in the future to be, systematically biased against ethnic minority groups, older people and women (Cook, 2004). This tends to occur where raters are not trained or interviews are not structured. All sorts of extraneous factors like the perfume a person wears at interview have been shown to influence ratings.

The literature is essentially driven by two main areas of research: one well established, namely the social-psychological literature on discrimination, favouritism and prejudice; the other, more recent research on sociolegal features of selection. Studies on the legal and illegal aspects of selection have nearly all come out of the US, whose reputation for litigation is well known. Inevitably one has to acknowledge many national differences in legal procedures and the law itself, suggesting that studies are less likely to generalise.

Table 2.4 *Applicant attributes that affect rating bias*

Attributes	Examples of research findings
Gender bias	Influenced by type of job (role-congruent jobs) and competence. Female interviewers gave higher ratings than male interviewers.
First-impression effect	Early impressions were more important than factual information for interviewer judgements. Decisions to hire were related to the interviewer's causal interpretation (attribution) of an applicant's past outcomes.
Contrast effect	Interviewers' evaluations of job candidates were influenced by the quality and characteristics of the previous candidates.
Non-verbal communication	Applicants who looked straight ahead, as opposed to downwards, were rated as being more alert, assertive and dependable; they were also more likely to be hired. Applicants who demonstrated a greater amount of eye contact, head moving and smiling received higher evaluations.
Physical attractiveness	More attractive applicants received higher evaluations.

However, there do seem to be various principles that emerge from legal cases, all concerned with bias and unfairness in selection procedures. The three themes are:

1. It is believed structured interviews are less biased because all candidates are asked the same questions in the same way.
2. It is argued that if a job analysis is done so that rated criteria are exclusively related to the task itself and specified in objective behavioural terms, discrimination is less likely to occur.
3. It is suggested that interviewers do not use application form biographical data because it often leads them to make unwarranted references about the ability of individuals.

There are many sources of interview-rating bias. Bernardin and Russell (1993) drew up a useful list under three headings (see Tables 2.4, 2.5 and 2.6).

2.9   Interviewing skills

There is no shortage of books, chapters and papers on training people in interviewing skills. These range from describing and listing different skills for different types of interviews (i.e., counselling, disciplinary, survey) to describing the typical styles of interviewers.

Another approach has been to divide skills into different bands. Thus Bogels (1999), in examining the diagnostic interview in mental health care, distinguished

Table 2.5 *Interviewer attributes that affect rating bias*

Attributes	Examples of research findings
Similarity effect	Interviewers gave more positive ratings to applicants perceived to be similar to themselves.
	Interviewers resisted using additional information to evaluate applicants once they perceived the applicants to be similar to themselves.
'Likeability'	Interviewers gave more positive ratings to candidates they liked.
	Interpersonal attraction was found to influence interviewers' perceptions of applicant qualifications.
'Ideal stereotype'	Interviewers judged applicants against their own stereotype of an 'ideal' job candidate.
	These stereotypes may be unique to each interviewer, or they may be a common stereotype shared by a group of raters.
Information favourability	Interviewers weighted negative information more heavily than positive information.
	Interviewers spent more time talking when they had already formed a favourable decision.
Information utilisation	Interviewers placed different importance (weights) on the information content of the interview, resulting in idiosyncratic information-weighting strategies.
	Discrepancies often arose between interviewers' intended (nominal) information weights and the actual information weights they used to arrive at a decision.

Table 2.6 *Situational attributes that affect rating bias*

Attributes	Examples of research findings
Job information	Interviewers who received more information about the job used it for evaluation decisions.
	Increased job information reduced the effect of irrelevant attributes and increased reliability between raters.
Applicant information	Interviewers' pre-interview impressions of applicant qualifications had a strong influence on post-interview impressions and recommendations to hire.
	Interviewers with favourable pre-interview impressions of applicants evaluated those applicants as having done a better job of answering the interview questions.
Decision time	Interviewers reached a final decision early in the interview process; some studies have indicated the decision is made after an average of 4 minutes.
	Decisions to hire were made sooner than decisions not to hire.

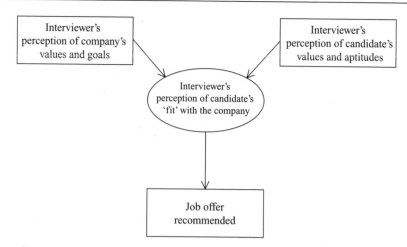

Figure 2.11 *Perceived fit and employment interview (adapted from Judge et al., 2000)*

between *content* skills (getting the required information/data), *process* skills (concerning all the techniques used) and *cognitive* skills (hypothesis formulation and testing and integrating information).

Margie and Tourish (1999) note that skilled interpersonal behaviour, like skilled motor behaviour, has identifiable components. Interpersonal skills manifest in interviewing can be characterised by:

- *Fluency:* smooth, controlled, unflustered progress.
- *Rapidity:* speedy responses to answers and issues.
- *Automaticity:* performing tasks without having to think.
- *Simultaneity:* the ability to mesh and coordinate multiple, verbal and non-verbal tasks at the same time.
- *Knowledge:* Knowing the what, how, when and why of the whole interview process.

Skills also involve understanding the real goal of the interview, being perceptive, understanding what is and what is not being said, and empathy.

Recent research in the past decade has argued that the key issue assessed by the employment interview is the person–organisational *fit* (see also Section 7.26). Thus Judge, Higgins and Cable (2000) argued that when interviewers perceive that the candidate's profile is congruent with (the interviewer's perception of) organisational values and goals, job offers are recommended (see Figure 2.11). Indeed, previous evidence suggested that different interviewers show acceptable levels of agreement in their ratings of 'fit' (Rynes & Gerhart, 1990), though interviewers are not very accurate at assessing the candidate's aptitudes and dispositions (Cable & Judge, 1997). That said, recent evidence suggests that interviewers rarely assess person–organisation fit, preferring to focus on the characteristics of the candidate (even though they are unable to assess these accurately!). In a

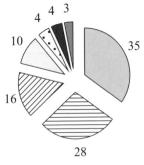

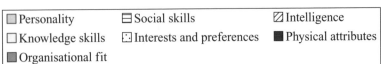

Figure 2.12 *What do interviewers assess?*

meta-analysis, Huffcutt Conway, Roth and Stone (2001) reported that most interviewers try to assess candidate's personality traits, followed closely by social or interpersonal skills, and not that closely by intelligence and knowledge. On a few occasions, interviewers focus on assessing interviewees' preferences or interests and physical attributes, and the variable of least interest appears to be fit (Huffcutt *et al.*, 2001; see Figure 2.12). It is noteworthy that all these variables can be assessed via reliable and valid psychometric tests (see notably Chapters 6 and 7), which begs the question of what if any unique information (that is reliable and valid) can be extracted from employment interviews.

2.10 Summary and conclusion

The interview is a central feature of business life. It seems inconceivable that one would make a selection decision without one or more interviews. Equally, managers are called upon to appraise their staff via interviews as well as occasionally discipline them. Interviews are nearly always face-to-face, though technology allows video conferencing and interviewing these days. Some organisations believe that the time and money cost of interviews, combined with their low validity, means they can and should be dispensed with and replaced by such things as assessment centres. However, candidates like and expect them precisely because they are an inter-view: both parties are able to make a judgement of the other.

Interviews can be designed to ensure they are seen to be fairer and to yield ratings, assessments and evaluations which are reliable and valid: the efforts necessary to do this are clearly worthwhile because of the very poor-quality data which are usually obtained in unstructured, unplanned and unprofessional interviews (appraisal, selection, etc.), which are, alas, all too common.

Quite clearly, validity studies indicate that unstructured interviews are associated with a number of problems and drawbacks that do not affect structured interviews. Thus employers should have a natural tendency to opt for the latter rather than the former. At the same time, structured interviews still do not remove the bias caused by subjective and unstandardised evaluations of the candidates. Moreover, given that interviewers tend to assess factors that can be assessed equally well (or even better) via other means, such as purpose-built and well-established and validated psychometric tests (see Chapters 6 and 7), interviews can be hard to justify at times, especially as they are less cost-effective than remote testing. That said, good interviews still provide important information, even when other methods are taken into account. Astute and perceptive interviewers, attentive to vocal and visual clues, can often assess the truthfulness of a specific answer. Furthermore, the way certain questions are answered means that specific issues can be further probed to reveal opinions and facts that otherwise may not be revealed. Indeed, it is often in conjunction with other methods that interviews work best, though employers tend to overrate the usefulness of interviews compared to other selection methods, like personality and ability tests.

3   Letters of recommendation

3.1   Introduction

Another widely used method in personnel selection is the reference report or letter of recommendation, simply know as *the reference*, whereby a referee (e.g., former employer, teacher or colleague) provides a description and usually, but not always, a statement in support of a candidate or job applicant (see Figure 3.1 for an example). Thus referees are expected to have sufficient knowledge of the applicant's previous work experience and his or her suitability for the job applied for.

References are almost as widely used in personnel selection as the interview (see Chapter 2). The Price Waterhouse Cranfield (Dany & Torchy, 1994) review of assessment methods (see Figure 3.2) found that the vast majority of employers in Europe use references to inform their hiring decisions (especially in Scandinavia and the UK) (Lévy-LeBoyer, 1994), with US estimates (Burean of National Affairs, 1988; Judge & Higgins, 1998; Muchinsky, 1979a, 1979b) similar to UK ones. Yet there has been a surprising dearth of research on the reliability and validity of the reference letter; and, as shown in this chapter, an assessment of the existing evidence suggests that the reference is a poor indicator of candidates' potential. Thus Judge and Higgins (1998) concluded that 'despite widespread use, reference reports also appear to rank among the least valid selection measures' (p. 207).

References are essentially observational data, that is, statements or ratings by bosses or peers, and therefore subjective. There is an extensive literature on multi-source or 360-degree feedback – the process whereby your peers, subordinates and supra-ordinates all provide ratings on you – aimed at assessing the reliability of self- and other-ratings.

3.2   Structured vs unstructured references

Like the employment interview (see Chapter 2), references can be classi-fied on the basis of how structured/standardised they are, ranging from completely unstructured ('What do you think of X?') to totally structured (e.g., standardised multiple choice questions, checklists and ratings). The latter require referees to

Genco Olive Oil

Date: 24 February 2008

Dear Dr Chamorro-Premuzic,

RE: Joey Tattaglia

The above mentioned has applied for a temporary position with our organisation and has given your name to provide a reference on their behalf. We would be most grateful if you would kindly comment on the individual by answering the questions below and then return the completed form by fax/email ASAP.

Dates course started/ended?	2006 -7
Do you consider them to be honest & trustworthy?	YES
No. of sick days taken (if known)	2

PLEASE COMMENT ON THE APPLICANT'S PERFORMANCE

	Excellent	Good	Fair	Poor
Quality of work		X		
Productivity	X			
Commitment to course	X			
Attitude	X			
Attendance/punctuality	X			
Teamwork		X		
Initiative		X		
Communication skills	X			
Leadership skills		X		

Figure 3.1 *Sample reference letter*

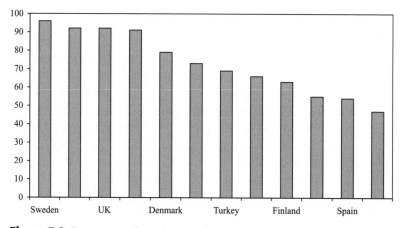

Figure 3.2 *Percentage of employers using references*

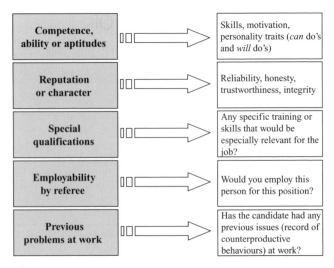

Figure 3.3 *Employment Recommendation Questionnaire (ERQ)*

address predefined areas and often merely tick boxes (see Figure 3.1). One of the most well-known structured references is the US Employment Recommendation Questionnaire (ERQ), developed for the US civil service and investigated in many psychological studies. The ERQ covers five core areas referring to the candidate's (a) competence or ability, (b) reputation or character, (c) special qualifications (relevant to the job offered), (d) employability by the referee and (e) previous record of problems at work (see Figure 3.3).

3.3   Reliability of references

Early research on the reliability of the employment reference produced pessimistic results (Muchinsky, 1979b). For example, a study examining letters of recommendation in the US civil service found that different ratings from different referees correlated only at .40 (Mosel & Goheen, 1959). This value is somewhat lower than – but still comparable to – that obtained in multisource or '360-degree' feedback settings, where the inter-rater reliability can approach .60 (Murphy & Cleveland, 1995). This is to be expected as people may show 'different aspects of themselves' to different people – and, as Murphy and Cleveland argue, there would be little point in using multiple sources if we expected all of them to provide the same information. This is a well-known contradiction in academic grading, where exams are frequently double-marked by faculty only to agree similar marks in the end (Baird, Greatorex & Bell, 2004; Dracup, 1997). However, inter-rater agreements of .60 are low and mean that only 36 per cent of the variance in candidates' attributes is accounted for, leaving a substantial percentage of variance unexplained.

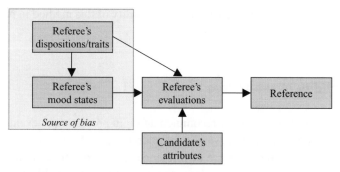

Figure 3.4 *Referees' characteristics bias their evaluations of candidates (based on Feldman, 1981, and Judge & Higgins, 1998)*

The low reliability of references has been explained in terms of evaluative biases (Feldman, 1981) attributable to personality characteristics of the referee (see Figure 3.4). Most notably, the referee's mood when writing a reference will influence whether it is more or less positive (Judge & Higgins, 1998). This is in line with Fiske's well-known finding that emotional labels, notably extreme ones, are used to categorise factual information about others (Fiske, 1980). Thus when referees retrieve information about candidates their judgement is already clouded by emotional information (often as simple and general as 'good' or 'bad'). Some of the sources of such mood states are arguably dispositional (e.g., emotionally stable and extraverted individuals more frequently experience positive affective states, whereas the opposite applies to neurotic introverted people), and personality characteristics can have other (non-affective) effects on evaluations, too. For example, agreeable referees (see Section 7.9) can be expected to provide more positive evaluations, and conscientious/responsible referees (see Section 7.6) may do more rigorous checks on the information they are providing. In that sense references really are in the 'eye of the beholder' because they say more about the referee than the candidate. Thus the ability, personality and values of the referee shape the unstructured reference so much that they have more to do with compatibility between referee and candidate than with the candidate's suitability for the job. It is, however, noteworthy that little research has been conducted in this area so most of these hypotheses are speculative.

More reliable information from reference letters can be obtained if different raters base their ratings and conclusions on the same information. For instance, as early as in the 1940s the UK Civil Service Selection Board (CSSB) examined multiple references for the same candidates (e.g., from school, university, army and previous employment), written by different referees. Results showed that inter-reliabilities for a panel of five or six people can be as high as .73 (Wilson, 1948). However, few employers can afford to examine such detailed information. Furthermore, even if internal consistencies such as inter-rater reliabilities are adequate, that does not mean that employment references will be valid predictors of job-related outcomes. Indeed, the validity of references has been an equally important topic of concern when assessing the utility of this method in personnel selection.

3.4   Validity of references

How valid are letters of recommendation in predicting relevant job outcomes? Again, research into the validity of references has been scarce, especially in comparison to the frequent use of references in personnel selection. This is no doubt partly because it is unclear what the criterion variable is. Most of this research has focused on structured references, not least because it is easier to quantify the validity of these references (particularly compared to the highly variable and, by definition, hard to standardise, unstructured letters of recommendation). For example, studies on the ERQ (see Figure 3.3) showed that reference checks correlated in the range of .00 and .30 with subsequent performance. In a meta-analysis, Reilly and Chao (1982) reported a mean correlation of .18 with supervisory ratings, .08 with turnover and .14 with a global criterion. A more generous (corrected for unreliability and restriction of range) estimate was provided by Hunter and Hunter's (1984) meta-analysis, namely .26, and one of the largest validities was (again, corrected) .36 for head teachers' references and training success in the Navy (Jones & Harrison, 1982). It has been pointed out by Jones and Harrison that teachers' (or, for that matter, professors') references tend to be more accurate because they are more motivated (than past employers) to maintain credibility as they are likely to write more references in the future.

On the one hand, it would be incongruent to expect higher validities from the reference letter if it is not reliable in the first place. On the other hand, there are several other converging factors that threaten the validity of this assessment and selection method, namely:

1. Referees tend to be very *lenient*, which produces highly skewed data (see Figure 3.4 for a hypothetical example). This effect, often referred to as the *Pollyanna effect*, reduces the real variance between candidates (producing more heterogeneous outcomes than predictors) and means that 'most applicants are characterised as somewhat desirable' (Paunonen, Jackson & Oberman, 1987, p. 97). This is hardly surprising since referees are nominated by the candidates themselves and referees' 'primary interests are not with the organisation but with the applicant' (Colarelli, Hechanova-Alampay & Canali, 2002, p. 316). Recent research shows that even in academic settings (grant proposals) applicant-nominated assessors provide biased and inflated reviews of the candidates (Marsh, Bond & Jayasinghe, 2007). Clearly, referees who are asked to provide a reference have no incentives to be harsh and may indeed be afraid of being too harsh as they may be sued by the candidates. Moreover, given that harsh comments are so rare and seen as a 'kiss of death' (typically, negative points are given more weight than positive ones), referees

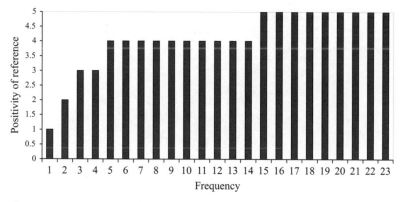

Figure 3.5 *Distribution of negative and positive references*

are even more sensitive about making them, though research suggests that *mixing up* negative and positive comments makes references be perceived as more genuine and even results in positive hiring decisions (Knouse, 1983). It is also likely that referees abstain from providing a reference if they cannot be too positive about the applicant, which would explain the poor response rates found (Schneider & Schmitt, 1986).

2. Referees tend to write *similar references* for all candidates. In fact it has been pointed out that references – particularly unstructured ones – provide more information about the referee than the candidate (Baxter, Brock, Hill & Rozelle, 1981). Moreover, and as mentioned above (Section 3.3), dispositional traits (personality factors) and affective states (mood) distort references significantly (Judge & Higgins, 1998). This leads not only to low reliability but also lower criterion-related validities.

3. Referees (often acting in benefit of the organisation) may wish to *retain good employees* and know that a positive reference may have just the opposite effect. Moreover, for the same reasons they may choose to write overly positive references for staff they are eager to see off. These 'hidden agendas' are hard to verify but indicate that employers' motivations can have a huge effect on the type of reference provided.

There are now many serious legal issues associated with references, so much so that some organisations refuse to give them. People are directed only to say that the candidate was employed for the specified time they worked there and nothing else. Litigation has followed where a person has been hired partly on the basis of a reference only to discover the person was extremely poor at the job. In this instance it appears references have been over-positive to 'get rid' of the employee (see above). However, what has more recently occurred is that people and organisations have been sued if they refused to give a reference knowing the candidate is in some sense problematic (e.g., has criminal or anti-social tendencies). In this sense some employers claim with respect to references you are 'damned if you do, and damned if you don't'.

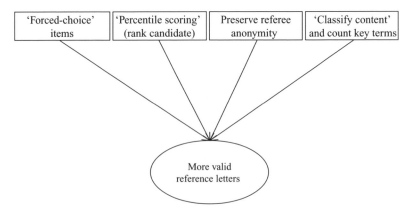

Figure 3.6 *Improving recommendation letters (adapted from Buss, 1955, and Colarelli* et al.*, 2002)*

3.5   How to improve the validity of references

In the light of the above-reviewed literature, it is clear that the extent to which employers use and rely on references is unjustified and not backed up by research evidence. However, research in this area provides some useful guidelines to improve on the validity of recommendations letters (see Figure 3.6).

First, it has long been suggested that 'forced-choice' items, for example does X like 'working in a team *or* working alone', reduce the effects of overall leniency and can increase accuracy (Carroll & Nash, 1972). Yet forced items must be carefully selected and even then it is likely that candidates could be equally described by either extreme (as items are rarely truly mutually exclusive) (see also Section 7.3).

Second, employers should count 'key-words' (e.g., able, creative, reliable, etc.), which are to be previously determined on the basis of job analysis. This technique provides some order to unstructured references, though it is certainly not immune to the referee style. Peres and Garcia (1962) scrutinised over 600 references and identified five key areas that could be used to organise the key-word count: cooperation, intelligence, Extraversion ('urbanity'), vigour, and Conscientiousness ('dependability'). Three decades later Aamodt, Bryan and Whitcomb (1993) analysed students' references and found support for these categories. Although it is questionable whether these categories truly represent the best way to organise and classify the content of references – notably because established personality taxonomies, such as the Big Five, and cognitive ability models (see Chapters 7 and 6, respectively) have a stronger and more generalisable theoretical basis – it is clear that having a taxonomy or framework to assess unstructured references does help.

Third, the predictive validity of references tends to increase when referees are asked to use 'relative percentiles', i.e., comparative rankings of how well the

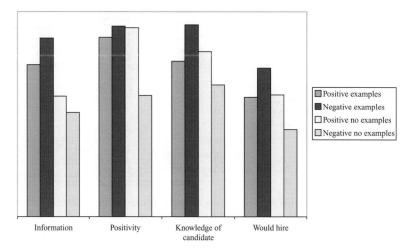

Figure 3.7 *Positivity of information and use of examples in reference letters*

candidate does in any given area relative to the group the referee uses as frame of reference. Although percentiles are not normally distributed and inflated (80th percentiles being the average; McCarthy & Goffin, 2001), they still force referees to distinguish between candidates.

Last, but not least, it has been argued that if the anonymity of the referees were preserved, references would be less lenient, more heterogeneous and more accurate/valid (Ceci & Peters, 1984).

Research also indicates that using concrete examples to back up statements about the candidate's attributes and including both positive *and* negative information about the candidate lead to improved references. This was the conclusion of a study by Knouse (1983). As shown in Figure 3.7, including examples (e.g., 'X's leadership skills are evidenced in his/her roles as president of the management club, rowing society and wine-tasting club') and some negative information ('George tends to be arrogant at times') resulted in references that were rated richer in information, reflected the fact that the referee knew the candidate better and led to more hiring decisions. The worst-case scenario on the other hand was for references that had no examples and included some negative information.

3.6   Popularity of references: an evolutionary perspective

Given the unreliability and poor validity of letters of recommendation, it seems hard to understand why this method of assessment is used so widely. One reason may be that employers are unaware of the problems associated with these data (Terpstra & Rozell, 1997), though given that references are used even in business and psychology schools (where employers have access to this literature and tend to be aware of the low validity and reliability of recommendation letters)

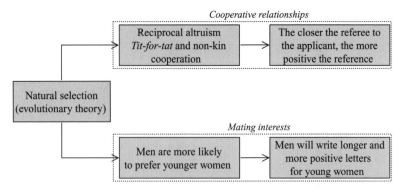

Figure 3.8 *Evolutionary-based hypotheses regarding reference letters*

there may be other reasons. Colarelli *et al.* (2002) explained the widespread use of references in terms of what evolutionary theory calls 'reciprocal altruism' (*tit for tat*), which is the basis of cooperation among non-kin (Buss, 1995). As is usually the case with evolutionary explanations of behaviours, this hypothesis seems untestable and somewhat far-fetched. However, it does offer some interesting insights into the core determinants of the pervasiveness of the reference and, in the absence of any alternative theoretical explanation, it shoud be considered. As shown in Figure 3.8, Colarelli *et al.* applied the principle of reciprocal altruism to the relationship between the applicant and the candidate, specifically how closeness between them determines the favourability of the references. Thus Colarelli *et al.* argued that 'a recommender will be inclined to write favourably if the applicant is perceived as a valuable resource or if there has been a history of mutually beneficial social exchange. An evolutionary psychological perspective suggests that cooperation, status competition and mating interests should affect the tone of letters of recommendation' (2002, p. 325).

A second hypotheses derived from evolutionary theory is that men's preference for younger females should be reflected in more favourable references. Specifically, the authors explained that 'males typically desire attractive, younger females as mating partners because youth and beauty are cues of health and fertility. As such, males are likely to be most solicitous towards younger females and regard them in a positive way. This positive regard, in turn, is likely to be reflected in letters of recommendation' (2002, p. 328). In an analysis of 532 letters referring to 169 candidates, the authors found support for the idea that closeness (strong cooperativeness) of relationship was reflected in more favourable references, even after controlling for competence indicators (publications and years since obtaining a PhD). The second hypotheses – that men would write more positive references for younger women – was not supported, though references for women were more positive than those for men. The authors also note that there was a range restriction in women's age (with over 90 per cent of them aged between 25 and 38).

3.7   Conclusion

The present chapter reviewed the evidence in support of the validity of letters of reference or recommendation as a tool for personnel selection. As seen, the high frequency with which employers use references is unmatched by the predictive power of references, which only have modest validity – especially if they are not structured. Indeed, this has led many employers to ask for references *only after* candidates have been offered the job (and simply as a standard legal requirement but without actually taken into account any evaluative judgements made on the candidates).

Why are references not more valid? Because referees have no interest in helping the potential prospective employers of the candidate by providing accurate information about the candidate (in fact, if the candidate is worth retaining they may be less motivated to speak highly of him/her and if the candidate is not worth retaining they may have an extra incentive to persuade prospective employers to hire him/her!); because referees are biased; because candidates seek referees who can only comment positively on them; and because all to often the same things are said about all candidates (e.g., bright, hard-working, reliable and talented).

All that said, there is the potential of improving the validity of references by using standardised forms, multiple referees and comparative ranking scales, and even by preserving the anonymity of the referee. Still, the question remains as to whether in that case referees can provide any additional information to, say, psychometric tests (see Chapters 5, 6 and 7), interviews (discussed in Chapter 1) and biodata.

4   Biodata

4.1   Introduction

Consider the past and you shall know the future.   Chinese proverb

Biographical data – simply known as *biodata* – have informed selection decisions for many decades and are still widely used in certain areas of employment, such as sales and insurance. In broad terms, biodata include information about a person's background and life history (e.g., civil status, previous education and employment), ranging from objectively determined dates – date of first job, time in last job, years of higher education – to subjective preferences, such as those encompassed by personality traits (see Chapter 7). The diversity of constructs assessed (explicitly or implicitly) by biodata is such that there is no common definition for biodata. Indeed, 'biodata scales have been shown to measure numerous constructs, such as temperament, assessment of work conditions, values, skills, aptitudes, and abilities' (Mount, Witt & Barrick, 2000, p. 300). Some have argued that biodata represent a more valid predictor of occupational success than traditional personality scales (Mumford, Costanza, Connelly & Johnson, 1996), as well as reducing aversive impact in comparison to cognitive ability tests (Stokes, Mumford & Owens, 1994).

The main assumption underlying the use of biodata is that the 'best predictor of future performance is past performance' (Wernimont & Campbell, 1968, p. 372), though biodata focus as much on the *predictors* of past performance as on past performance itself. Indeed, it has been argued that one of the greatest potential routes for understanding and improving the prediction of work performance is the link between individuals' life history and their performance at work (Fleishman, 1988), a question directly related to biodata.

Biodata are typically obtained through *application forms*, which are used extensively in most western countries (see Figure 4.1, based on Dany & Torchy, 1994). It is, however, noteworthy that application forms are generally not treated or scored as biodata. Rather, they represent the collection method for obtaining biographical information and employers or recruiters often assess this information in non-structured, informal, intuitive ways. However, the technical use of biodata adds two important elements to the standard application form, namely:

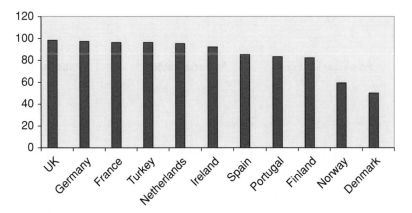

Figure 4.1 *Percentage of employers using application forms*

(a) It collects biographical information that has previously been correlated with desirable work criteria (notably job performance).
(b) It incorporates 'weighted scoring' by which questions are coded and treated as individual predictors of relevant work criteria.

In that sense, biodata represent an approach to treating biographical information (collected through application forms or different means, such as CVs, personal essays or statements, and letters of reference) in a statistically sound way and building up biographical profiles that classify job applicants according to their potential for future work performance.

4.2   Scoring of biodata

A crucial issue with biodata is how to score them. In some cases, it is the very scoring of biodata that sets it apart from the more informal use of application forms, references or CVs (where employers may simply eliminate candidates on basis of eye-balling these documents). A rigorous and effective approach for scoring biodata is the so-called *empirical keying* method (Devlin, Abrahams & Edwards, 1992), which codes each item or question into yes = 1 or no = 0 and weights them according to their correlations with the criterion (as derived from previous samples or a subset of the current sample). Finally, item scores are all added up for each candidate. It has been reported that empirical keying shows incremental validity in the prediction of occupational success over and above personality scales and cognitive ability measures (Mount *et al.*, 2000) (see also Section 4.4).

Empirical keying makes biodata markedly different from standard personality inventories, which are scored in terms of reliability or internal consistencies (e.g., grouping questions that assess the same underlying dimension together) but not on the basis of their association with the criteria they are used to predict. In that

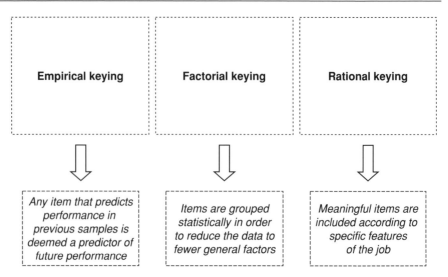

Empirical keying	Factorial keying	Rational keying
⇩	⇩	⇩
Any item that predicts performance in previous samples is deemed a predictor of future performance	Items are grouped statistically in order to reduce the data to fewer general factors	Meaningful items are included according to specific features of the job

Figure 4.2 *Scoring biodata*

sense, personality measures are internally constructed whereas biodata items are externally constructed (Goldberg, 1972). However, biodata can also be scored via *factorial keying*, which identifies higher-order domains or common themes underlying groups of items, just like personality scales group questions on the basis of specific traits. For instance, Mumford and Owens (1987) identified the factors of adjustment, academic performance, extraversion and leadership in over twenty studies. Others have scored biodata items in terms of family and social orientation (Carlson, Scullen, Schmidt, Rothstein & Erwin, 1999) and money management (Stokes & Searcy, 1999) (see also Section 4.5). When this approach is taken, the only difference between biodata and personality inventories is that the latter – but not the former – are designed specifically to assess established individual differences or traits (see Chapter 7). Other than that, factorial-keyed biodata are 'indistinguishable from personality items in content, response format, and scoring. Personality tests typically contain items regarding values and attitudes and biodata items generally focus on past achievements of behaviours, but even this distinction is not obvious in many biodata applications today' (Schmitt & Kunce, 2002, p. 570).

Finally, *rational keying* is used to design biodata inventories that are based on the specific job requirements or characteristics. Fine and Cronshaw (1994) proposed that a thorough job analysis informs the selection of biodata items (see also Stokes & Cooper, 2001). In that sense, rational keying refers to the construction phase rather than the analysis or scoring phase of biodata and there is no reason why it cannot be combined with factorial keying. Drakeley, Herriot and Jones (1988) found rational keying to be more valid than empirical keying, though more recent and robust investigations estimated both methods to have comparable validities (Stokes & Searcy, 1999).

Figure 4.2 summarises the three approaches discussed. Each method has its advantages and disadvantages. The somewhat dated approach of empirical keying is advantageous in that it makes biodata 'invisible' and hard to fake for the respondents, as many predictors of occupational success are bound to be counterintuitive and identified purely on an empirical basis. At the same time, however, this makes the inclusion of certain items hard to justify. As noted by Ree:

> During one typically heated debate [with the US Navy] over the inclusion/exclusion of items, I complained that I found an item that asked about attendance at dance in high school unacceptable [to predict performance in the Navy]. On the surface, this item seemed to measure 'sociability'. I was concerned that it was potentially a surrogate for religious denomination, as certain religions frown upon dancing. This leads to the problem of forbidden questions. In the US, you cannot ask about religion, marital status, and numerous others characteristics, even though they might be empirically predictive.   (Ree, 2003, pp. 506–7)

Two additional problems with empirical keying are that it does not generalise well to other samples and it does not advance our theoretical understanding of the reasons for which items predict occupational success (Mount *et al.*, 2000).

On the other hand, rational keying may be easy to justify from a theoretical point of view and provides an opportunity for excluding items with adverse impact. No wonder, then, that rational keying has been used extensively in recent years (Hough & Paullin, 1994; Schmitt, Jennings & Toney, 1999). However, the advantages of rational keying may come at the expense of making 'correct responses' too obvious for respondents and increasing the likelihood of faking (Lautenschlager, 1994) (see Section 4.3 below).

Finally, factorial keying, whether applied in conjunction with rational keying methods or not, makes biodata identical to personality inventories, especially if attitudinal or subjective items are also included. It has been argued that even experts would fail to distinguish between personality scales and factorial-keyed biodata (Robertson & Smith, 2001). Moreover, personality scales have some advantages over biodata, such as being more 'theory-driven', assessing higher-order and more stable dispositions, and generalising quite easily across settings and criteria (see Chapter 7).

4.3   Verifiability of biodata and faking

The main difference between personality and biodata inventories is that biodata inventories include a larger number of verifiable or 'harder' items, such as basic demographic or background information. These items are uncontrollable (what can one do about one's place of birth or ethnicity?) and intrusive compared to the 'softer', more controllable unverifiable items assessing attitudes and behaviours: e.g., 'What are your views on recycling?', 'How often do you go to the gym?', 'Do you think people should drink less?', 'Do you like country music?' It has, however, been suggested that unverifiable items increase the probability of faking (Becker & Colquitt, 1992). Indeed, although some degree of inflation does

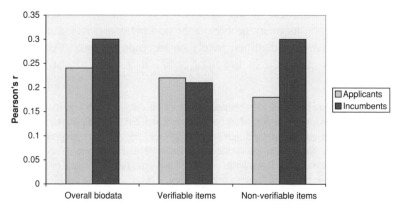

Figure 4.3 *Biodata correlates of job performance in applicants and incumbents*

exit for verifiable items, early studies reported intercorrelations in the region of .95 between responses given to different employers (Keating, Paterson & Stone, 1950; Mosel & Cozan, 1952), showing that verifiable items yield very consistent responses even across different jobs. Yet a thorough review of the literature concluded that faking affects both verifiable and non-verifiable items and that attempts to control it have been largely unsuccessful, though empirical-keying prevents faking more than other keying types (Lautenschlager, 1994).

A recent study compared the validity of verifiable and non-verifiable biodata items in call centre employees and applicants (Harold, McFarland & Weekley, 2006). Results, depicted in Figure 4.3, showed that although applicants did not score significantly higher on overall biodata items than their incumbent counterparts, non-verifiable items had lower validities in the applicant sample. This led Harold *et al.* to conclude that 'the good news is that a biodata inventory comprised of all verifiable items was equally valid across incumbent and applicant samples regardless of the criterion examined', but '[T]he bad news, however, is that the validity of non-verifiable items shrank in the applicant sample' (2006, p. 343).

Regardless of these results, modern jobs, such as services and team work (Hough, 1998a), call for attitudinal and interpersonal constructs to be assessed in order to predict occupational success. Thus non-verifiable, soft, subjective items will inevitably be incorporated in contemporary biodata scales. Schmitt and Kunce (2002) proposed that in order to reduce faking and social desirability respondents should *elaborate* on their answers – a method previously used in 'accomplishment records', e.g., 'Give three examples of situations where you showed to work well under pressure' or 'Can you recall past experiences where you showed strength and leadership?' (Hough, 1984). Examples used by Schmitt and Kunce are reported in Table 4.1.

Results indicated that respondents tended to score lower (be more modest) on items that required elaboration (Schmitt & Kunce, 2002); indeed, scores on elaborative items were .6 SD lower, which is roughly the difference found between

Table 4.1 *Biodata items with elaboration request (based on Schmitt and Kunce, 2002)*

1. How many groups have you led in the past 5 years?	(a) 0, (b) 1, (c) 2, (d) 3, (e) 4 or more. If you answered options (b) to (e), briefly describe the work you did.
2. How often do you rearrange computer files?	(a) Very frequently, (b) often, (c) sometimes, (d) rarely, (e) never. If you answered (a) to (c), provide dates and how much time you spent doing it.
3. In how many previous jobs have you had to interact with clients for more than 1 hour per day?	(a) 0, (b) 1, (c) 2, (d) 3, (e) 4 or more. If you answered (c), (d) or (e), please describe the nature of each job.
4. How many software packages have you used to analyse data?	(a) 0, (b) 1, (c) 2, (d) 3, (e) 4 or more. If you answered (b), (c), (d) or (e), please describe the software packages and nature of the data analyses.

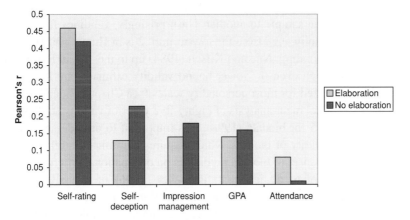

Figure 4.4 *Validity of elaborative vs non-elaborative biodata items*

participants instructed to respond honestly and those asked to 'fake good', in laboratory studies (Ellingson, Sackett & Hough, 1999; Ones, Visvesvarian & Reiss, 1996). Furthermore, a subsequent study showed that the validities of elaborative items were in line with standard biodata items and in some cases even higher (Schmitt *et al.*, 2003). As shown in Figure 4.4, validities (predicting self-ratings, self-deception, impression management, grade point average (GPA) and attendance) were unaffected by elaboration instructions even though lower means were found for the elaborative items.

Other methods for reducing the likelihood of faking in respondents have included *warnings* (Schrader & Osburn, 1977), such as 'Any inaccuracies or fake information provided will be checked and result in your no longer being considered for this job', to the more creative use of 'bogus' (fake) items that may trick respondents into faking good (Paunonen, 1984), for example 'How many years have you been using the HYU-P2 software for?' However, including bogus items is widely deemed unethical.

4.4   Validity of biodata

Just how valid are biodata? Early empirical evidence on the validity of biodata was provided by England (1961), who reported an average correlation of .40 between weighted application blanks and turnover. Another investigation by Wernimont (1962) identified three main variables that predicted length of service in female officers from 1954 to 1959 with similar accuracy, namely high proficiency at shorthand, whether they left their previous jobs because of pregnancy, marriage, sickness or domestic problems, and whether they were willing to start with their news job within the next week.

Since the late 1970s large-scale and robust validity studies on biodata have been reported thanks to the adoption of meta-analytic techniques. Meta-analyses are particularly important in biodata research because of the heterogeneity of different biodata studies and the importance of testing whether validities generalise from one sample to another. Unsurprisingly, validities for biodata have varied significantly, e.g., from the low-to-mid .20s in Hunter and Hunter (1984) and Schmitt, Gooding, Noe and Kirsch (1984) up to the .50s in Reilly and Chao (1982). Although even the lower-bound validity estimates are higher than the validities reported for most personality scales (see Chapter 7), and Schmidt and Hunter's seminal meta-analysis of eighty-five years of validity studies estimated a validity of .35 for biodata (1998), it is important to provide an accurate estimate of the validity of biodata, which requires identification of the factors that moderate the impact of biodata predictors on occupational criteria.

In an attempt to do just that, Bliesener (1996) meta-analysed previously reported meta-analysis paying careful attention to methodological differences among different validity studies. Over one hundred samples including 106,302 participants were examined, yielding an estimated (uncorrected) validity of .38 (SD = .19). However, when correcting for methodological artefacts and statistical errors, the overall validity for biodata inventories dropped to .22 (usually, corrected estimates tend to yield higher rather than lower validities), which still meets the criteria for utility and incremental validity (Barthel & Schuler, 1989). Interestingly, Bliesener's results showed that biodata were a more valid predictor of occupational success for women (.51) than for men (.27). Larger-than-average validities were found for studies that concurrently administered all measures (.35). Figure 4.5 summarises the validities for each criterion (i.e., tenure, training success, performance ratings, objective performance and creativity). Thus Bliesener concluded that 'Biographical data are a valid predictor of an applicant's suitability. This, combined with their high economy, their universal applicability and the ease of combining them with other predictive procedures, makes them a valuable instrument in personnel selection' (1996, p. 118).

With regard to the generalisability of biodata, Carlson et al. (1999) constructed a five-factor biodata inventory, which they found to correlate at .52 with occupational success in one organisation. They then administered the same inventory

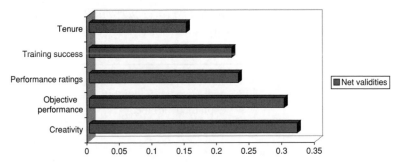

Figure 4.5 *Meta-meta-analytic validities for biodata inventories*

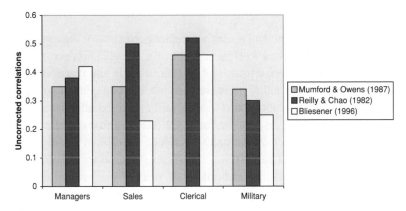

Figure 4.6 *Meta-analytic validities of biodata across job types*

to 24 organisations (including 7,334 employees) and found an overall validity of .48, indicating that biodata scales do indeed generalise to different organisations. That said, validities for biodata scales have been found to vary depending on job type. As shown in Figure 4.6 (based on three meta-analytic sources), biodata have been found to be consistently more valid for clerical jobs, followed by managerial jobs. Sales jobs have yielded more heterogeneous results, and military jobs have produced consistently lower validities.

Studies have also provided evidence for the *incremental validity* of biodata over established personality and cognitive ability measures. These studies are important because of the known overlap between these measures and biodata; they show that even if personality and intelligence are measured and taken into account, biodata scales provide additional useful information about the predicted outcome. Incremental validity of biodata over cognitive ability tests has been demonstrated in samples of army recruits (Mael & Ashforth, 1995) and air traffic controllers (Dean, Russell & Muchinsky, 1999); see also Karas and West (1999). Another study found that people's capacity to cope with change, self-efficacy for change and past experiences, as assessed via biodata items, predicted occupational success over and above cognitive ability (though cognitive ability was a more powerful predictor) (Allworth & Hesketh, 2000). With regard to personality,

Table 4.2 *Incremental validity of biodata (over personality and cognitive ability) in the prediction of four work outcomes (adapted from Mount* et al.*, 2000)*

Criterion	Tenure, cognitive ability and personality (combined explained variance)	Biodata (additional variance explained)
Quantity/quality of work	14%	5%
Problem-solving performance	17%	2%
Interpersonal relationships	5%	7%
Retention probability	8%	17%

studies have shown biodata scales to predict performance outcomes incrementally in US cadets (Mael & Hirsch, 1993); for a replication see McManus and Kelly (1999). Moreover, Mount *et al.*'s (2000) study simultaneously controlled for the Big Five personality traits (see Section 7.3) and general cognitive ability (see Section 6.2), and found that biodata still explained unique variance in four occupational criteria. As seen in Table 4.2 (adapted from Mount *et al.*, 2000), biodata explained 2 per cent of unique variance in problem-solving performance (even this incremental validity was significant, albeit marginally), 5 per cent of unique variance in quantity and quality of work, 7 per cent of additional variance in interpersonal relationships and 17 per cent of extra variance in retention probability.

4.5   Structure of biodata

Until recently, little research had been conducted on the structure underlying biodata (Schmidt, Ones & Hunter, 1992), that is, addressing the question of how large sets of personal data can be organised into and reduced to wider, latent factors or meaningful categories. Mumford *et al.*'s *ecology model* (Mumford, Stokes & Owens, 1990) postulated that biodata can be organised in terms of core knowledge, skill, ability, value and expectancy variables that explain how people develop their characteristic patterns of adaptation at work and beyond. These constructs 'facilitate the attainment of desired outcomes while conditioning future situational choice by increasing the likelihood of reward in certain kinds of situation' (Mumford & Stokes, 1992, p. 81). Nickels (1990) posited that these constructs can be organised as shown in Figure 4.7, namely personality – often inferred by employers when they assess biodata (Cole, Feild, Giles & Harris, 2004) – social and intellectual resources in one block, followed by choice and filter processes as mediators, and performance as well as rewards as criteria.

In a recent study (Dean & Russell, 2005), these constructs were replicated using 142 biodata items and over 6,000 newly hired air traffic controllers. Part

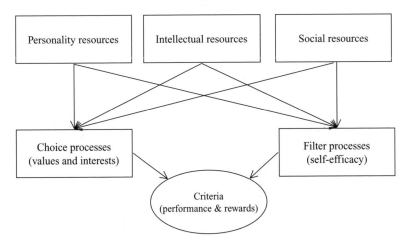

Figure 4.7 *Structure of biodata (adapted from Nickels, 1990)*

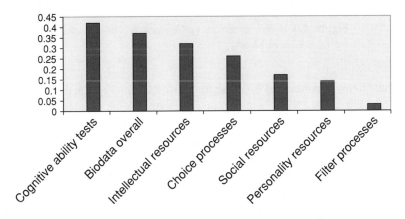

Figure 4.8 *Biodata and cognitive ability correlates of job performance*

of the success of this study can surely be attributed to the fact that the authors combined rationally designed items – based on Mumford and Owens' (1987) approach – with traditional empirical keying (see Section 4.2). Figure 4.8 reports the correlations between the various biodata scales, cognitive ability scores and a composite performance criterion found in this study. As seen, overall bio-data correlated with job performance almost as highly as did cognitive ability. Furthermore, the authors corrected restriction of range in cognitive ability (the uncorrected correlation between cognitive ability and the criterion was only .16, and the corrected correlation for biodata and the criterion was .43).

Although the wider literature has provided compelling evidence for the fact that cognitive ability tests, particularly general mental ability scores, are the best single predictor of work performance (see Chapter 6), Dean and Russell's (2005) results provide a robust source of evidence in support of the validity of coherently constructed and scored biodata scales, not least because they organised

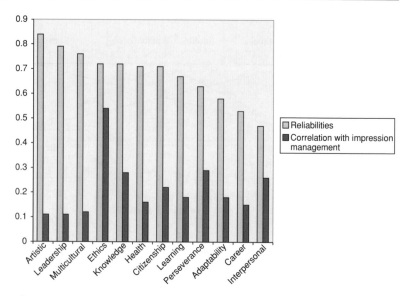

Figure 4.9 *Twelve dimensions of biodata: reliabilities and correlations with impression management*

their items according to established constructs (interpersonal skills, personality and values). Among the different scales or aspects of biodata (as shown in Figure 4.8) intellectual resources predicted job performance best, followed by choice processes, social and personality resources; filter processes were only weakly related to job performance.

Dean and Russell's results also illustrate the validity of biodata as measures of personality. Indeed, recent investigations underline the usefulness of purpose-built biodata inventories as an alternative to traditional self-reports of personality, such as the Big Five (Sisco & Reilly, 2007). As biodata scales place greater emphasis on verifiable and objective items than traditional personality scales do, they are less likely to be affected by respondents' faking and misinterpretations.

Studies have also shown that using purpose-built biodata that include a defined structure (different scales) can be used successfully to predict performance in college, even when entry exam scores (SAT) and personality factors are taken into account (Oswald, Schmitt, Kim, Ramsay & Gillespie, 2004). Oswald and colleagues looked at biodata (115 items) in a sample of 654 college students and identified twelve major dimensions, such as *knowledge* ('Think about the last several times you have had to learn new facts or concepts about something. How much did you tend to learn?'), *citizenship* ('How often have you signed a petition for something you believe in?'), *leadership* ('How many times in the past year have you tried to get someone to join an activity in which you were involved or leading?') and *ethics* ('If you were leaving a concert and noticed that someone left their purse behind with no identification, what would you do?'), which they used to predict final academic grades. Internal consistencies (Cronbach's α) and correlations with an impression management scale are shown in Figure 4.9. As

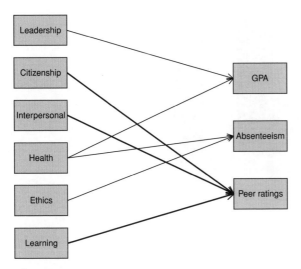

Figure 4.10 *Incremental validity of biodata dimensions (based on Oswald et al., 2004)*

seen, most α's were higher than .6, with the exception of adaptability, career and interpersonal (which had lower internal consistencies). On the other hand, all factors except ethics correlated only modestly with impression management.

Oswald *et al.* also tested the extent to which their twelve biodata factors predicted GPA, absenteeism and peer ratings while controlling for SAT and personality scores. Their results (shown in Figure 4.10) showed that six facets were still significantly linked to these outcomes even when previous academic performance and psychometrically derived trait scores were included in the regression model. As seen, leadership and health were linked to GPA, citizenship, interpersonal and learning-predicted peer ratings, and absenteeism was predicted by health and ethics.

In a recent validity study, Manley and colleagues compared the predictive power of two self-reported measures of personality (locus of control and conscientiousness) with biodata measures of the same constructs (Manley, Benavidez & Dunn, 2007). Results – shown in Figure 4.11 – revealed that the biodata versions of these two constructs predicted ethical decision making better than the self-reported (personality-style) measures did.

4.6   Summary and conclusions

The present chapter examined the usefulness of biographical information – biodata – in personnel selection, which is based on the premise that the best predictor of future performance is past performance. As seen, biodata have been used in personnel selection research and practice for many decades and continue to be used extensively in the developed world. Although biodata vary widely in

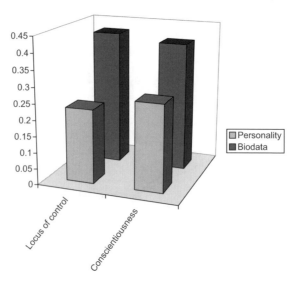

Figure 4.11 *Personality vs biodata as predictors of ethical behaviour (based on Manley* et al., *2007)*

their structure and form, and in how they are collected and scored, they include both objective (hard and verifiable) and subjective (soft and unverifiable) items. The latter are more easily faked – and influenced by socially desirable responding and impression management – than the former, though faking can potentially affect any form of biodata. One way of reducing faking appears to be to request respondents to elaborate further on their answers to biodata items.

Biodata scales can be designed and scored in different ways. Traditionally, the inclusion of biodata items has been guided by a purely empirical approach (empirical keying) based on any variable that has been found to correlate significantly with the desired outcome. Yet this approach is completely a-theoretical, uninformative, hard to justify and quite job-specific. Thus rational keying has been proposed in order to build biodata scales that target relevant constructs in a conceptually valid way. As for the scoring of biodata items, the best approach seems to be to identify higher-order factors (measured by a group of single variables) in the manner of personality inventories.

The most important conclusion with regard to biodata is no doubt that they represent a valid approach for predicting occupational success (in its various forms). Indeed, meta-analytic estimates provided validities for biodata in the region of .25, and this is probably a conservative estimate. In any case, this means that biodata are as valid predictors as the best personality scales, though the fact that biodata scales overlap with both personality and cognitive ability measures limits the appeal of biodata. That said, incremental validity studies have shown that even when established personality and intelligence measures are taken into account, biodata still predict job performance.

5 Situational judgement tests and GPA

5.1 Situational judgement tests

Situational judgement tests (SJTs) – of one form or another – have been used in personnel selection and examined in applied psychological research for many decades. However, the term 'SJT' is relatively more recent and the boundaries of what should constitute a SJT have only been defined relatively recently. In a seminal review of the topic a few years back SJTs were defined as 'any paper-and-pencil test designed to measure judgment in work settings' (McDaniel, Morgeson, Finnegan, Campion & Braverman, 2001, p. 730). Although this definition is too broad in a sense (cognitive ability tests, for instance, are not considered SJTs even though they may be designed to measure judgement at work) and too specific in others (SJTs are not only available in paper-and-pencil forms and can also be used to assess things other than judgement at work), it represents a useful operationalisation of SJTs. Indeed, McDaniel *et al.* organised many decades of research on the SJT on the basis of this operationalisation, as well as providing a widely cited meta-analytic estimate of the correlation between SJT and work criteria on the one hand, and cognitive ability on the other. Needless to say, the SJT is a measurement method rather than a construct (hence it is included in the first half of the current book rather than the second one, which deals with constructs; see, for instance, Chapters 6, 7 and 8).

Although there are many different SJTs, they tend to be similar in the sense that they present test-takers with work-related problems or scenarios that require judgement. Box 5.1 presents a sample scenario from a SJT used during World War II to assess soldiers' judgement (Northrop, 1989, p. 190). Other SJTs assess 'agreement' or 'disagreement' level rather than the ability to identify the correct response. Indeed, even in SJTs containing items such as that in Box 5.1 the 'correctness' of answers may be hard to determine objectively, a key difference from tests of cognitive ability (see Chapter 6). Thus different scoring methods have been used to score SJTs (see Box 5.3).

Based on their initial qualitative review of the literature on eight decades of research on SJTs, McDaniel *et al.* concluded that SJTs were an assessment measurement method rather than construct and that they assessed a variety of constructs depending on the measure. They also noted that most SJTs were standard paper-and-pencil inventories that were administered in written form, and that they comprised similar types of items – hypothetical work scenarios

Box 5.1 SJT sample item or 'Scenario' (based on Northrop, 1989, p. 190)

A man on a very urgent mission during a battle finds he must cross a stream about 40 feet wide.	*Walk to the bridge and cross it.*
A blizzard has been blowing and the stream has frozen over. However, because of the snow, he does not know how thick the ice is.	*Run rapidly across the ice.*
He sees two planks about 10 feet long near the point where he wishes to cross.	*Break a hole in the ice to see how deep the stream is.*
He also knows where there is a bridge about 2 miles downstream.	*Cross with the aid of the planks, pushing one ahead of the other and walking on them.*
Under the circumstances, which of the five options on the right should he consider.	*Creep slowly across the ice.*

Box 5.2 Summary of 1920s–2000s research on SJTs (based on McDaniel et al.'s (2001) review of the literature)

(1) SJTs are a measurement method that can be used to assess various constructs

(2) Most SJTs have similar features: paper-and-pencil (at least until 2000), include hypothetical scenarios that occur at work, require knowledge and judgement

(3) SJTs have demonstrated adequate validity in regards to work-related criteria

(4) Correlations between SJTs and cognitive ability measures have been variable

(as those shown in Box 5.1) being the most obvious. Their initial inspection of the studies also led to suggestions that the SJTs were adequate predictors of work-related criteria, though they tended to be generally correlated with cognitive ability or intelligence tests (although there is no objective statistical cut-off point for determining how high correlations can be before the two measures are deemed conceptually 'too similar', correlation coefficients $>.6$ are generally considered problematic).

Most of McDaniel *et al.*'s conclusions have been supported by subsequent evidence and are still valid, except the remark that 'paper-and-pencil' was the typical way to administer SJTs. In fact a recent study found that with the popularity of the World Wide Web SJTs are increasingly administered online and that this

---

Box 5.3 SJT scoring methods

Empirical: on the basis of previously identified correlations with desired
    outcomes
Theoretical: on the basis of rational relationships established between
    answers and performance differences, as well as desirable traits linked to
    them
Hybridised: combining different methods (for example empirical and
    theoretical)
Expert: asking subject-matter experts (bosses or high-performers) what
    the best and worst response to each scenario would be
Factorial: grouping of items via statistical methods (such as
    factor-analysis); can be used in combination with other scoring methods,
    especially *theoretical*
Subgrouping: grouping respondents – rather than items – who have
    similar patterns of answers

---

form of administration yields better distributional properties, lower means, higher internal consistencies/reliabilities and more variance (Ployhart, Weekley, Holtz & Kemp, 2003), which seems to justify the trend to move from paper-and-pencil to web-based tests (it is noteworthy that these conclusions do not apply only to SJTs but also extend to biodata and personality inventories) (see also McHenry & Schmitt, 1994, and Weekley & Jones, 1997, for video-based situational testing, and McHenry & Schmitt, 1994, for multimedia versions of SJTs and other methods).

To some extent, the constructs measured by SJTs will vary according to the method of scoring employed. For example, cognitive ability will be more important when items have responses that can be objectively rather than subjectively determined, whereas the opposite is true for personality traits (which tap into stylistic dispositions and behaviours rather than maximal performance). Yet it should be noted that SJTs are rarely scored objectively. Rather, a variety of methods – not dissimilar to those discussed in the context of biodata (see Section 4.1) – are available, from theoretical to empirical, and expert to factorial scoring (see Box 5.3). In a recent examination of these scoring methods Bergman and colleagues noted that the validity (construct and predictive) of SJTs is largely moderated by the scoring method (Bergman, Drasgow, Donovan, Henning & Juraska, 2006) (but see next section).

5.2   Validity of SJTs

How valid are SJTs? McDaniel *et al.* (2001) conducted a meta-analysis of 102 coefficients and 10,640 participants, which represents the best available

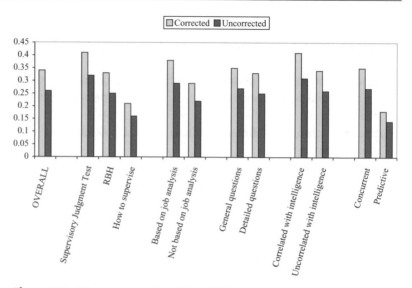

Figure 5.1 *Criterion-related validity of SJTs (McDaniel et al.'s 2001 meta-analysis)*

source to date on the validity of this measurement method. As shown in Figure 5.1, the corrected overall validity of the SJT (adjusted for unreliability in the criterion but not for restriction of range) was almost .35, which is a very healthy figure (see, for instance, Chapter 6 for the criterion-validity of cognitive ability tests, which are the most powerful single predictor of job performance, and Chapter 7 for personality inventories, which tend to yield lower validities than the SJT). A more specific inspection of the results also reveals interesting differences in the validity estimates of the SJT according to the tests examined. As shown, the Supervisory Judgment test was more valid than the Richardson, Bellows & Henry (RBH) and, especially, the How to Supervise test (see Table 5.1); SJTs that took into account the specific characteristics of the job ('based on job analysis') were more valid than those that did not; SJTs that included general questions were slightly more valid than those comprising detailed questions; SJTs that were highly 'g-loaded' (see Sections 6.1 and 6.2), that is, correlated substantially with tests of cognitive ability or intelligence, were more valid than those with low 'g-loadings' ('uncorrelated with intelligence'). Finally (as is often the case in validity studies), concurrent studies – which assessed SJT and the criterion at the same time – showed higher validities than predictive studies (which assessed SJT at time 1 and the relevant work outcomes at time 2, for example three years later).

McDaniel *et al.* also examined the empirical link between SJTs and tests of cognitive ability (described in Sections 6.2, 6.3 and 6.4). Conceptually, it is important to examine the correlation between STJ and standardised cognitive ability tests in order to clarify whether SJT measures or assesses a construct that is different, and potentially unrelated, to intellectual ability. From an applied/personnel selection perspective this question is important as the validity of any new or different

Table 5.1 *SJTs across the decades*

Test	Description	Problems
George Washington Social Intelligence test (subtest: Judgment of Social Situations) (Moss & Hunt, 1926)	Multiple choice test measuring 'keen judgment, and a deep appreciation of human motives, to answer correctly' (p. 26).	Low correlations with social outcomes and high correlations with standard intelligence (Thorndike & Stein, 1937).
Judgment test for soldiers (see Box 5.1)	Multiple choice test measuring 'common sense, experience, general knowledge, rather than logical reasoning' (McDaniel *et al.*, 2001, p. 731).	Too highly correlated with intelligence (Northrop, 1989).
Practical Judgment test (Cardall, 1942); How Supervise? test (File & Remmers, 1946)	Multiple-choice scenarios on everyday social and business situations (no items on factual knowledge or specific information); the test was believed to measure a construct independent of intelligence and academic background.	Correlated highly with intelligence (Carrington, 1949); Millard (1952) reported substantial correlations (.70) between scores on the How Supervise? and cognitive ability tests.
Supervisory Practices test (Bruce & Learner, 1958); Business Judgment test (Bruce, 1953)	Designed to measure supervisory potential (ability to deal with people); scenarios refer to problem that supervisors may face in everyday working life.	Although scores differentiated between supervisors and non-supervisors (Bruce & Learner, 1958), it correlated up to .35 with intelligence (not necessarily a problem).
Supervisory Judgment test (Greenberg, 1963); (Richardson, 1963) (RBH)	Designed to measure knowledge of the human resources industry (similar to the Supervisory Practices test).	See McDaniel *et al.*, below (Section 5.2).

measure should be independent of that of established or previously validated tests. Thus, if SJTs are uncorrelated with existing measures (other assessment methods), their predictive power to explain work-related criteria would be more relevant than if that variance could also be explained by other measures – see again Figure 2.7 for *incremental validity* and the different types of validity.

As shown in Figure 5.2, the overall corrected correlation between SJT and intelligence approaches .50 (at .46 to be precise). The authors also found that this correlation generalised across a number of studies, though they identified some interesting moderators – which are consistent with those reported in Figure 5.1. Again, SJTs where job analysis had been taken into account were more 'g-loaded' than those which did not consider job specificities, and, again, SJTs with general

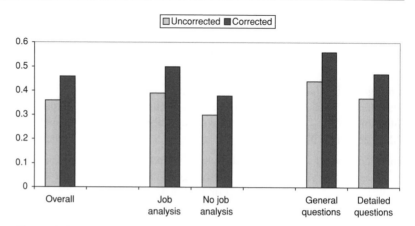

Figure 5.2 *Meta-analytic correlations between SJT and intelligence tests (McDaniel* et al.*'s 2001 meta-analysis)*

rather than detailed questions were more highly related to the intelligence. The authors noted that their estimates are likely to be conservative and underestimate the population-based correlation between SJTs and intelligence tests as they did not correct for restriction of range. Morever, they argued that SJTs have *incremental* validity over and above cognitive ability tests when it comes to explaining work-related outcomes. In fact, they estimated that a composite of SJT and cognitive ability would explain an additional 5–6 per cent of the variance in work-related outcomes than either measure alone (though they based their estimate on a rather low validity of .25 for cognitive ability – see Chapter 6).

Thus McDaniel *et al.*'s conclusion was that:

> It is clear that [SJTs] are good predictors of job performance. Our data suggest that general cognitive ability is a construct partly reflected in such measures, although general cognitive ability does not typically account for all the variance... Future research should repeat our moderator analyses on larger data sets and attempt to identify other possible moderators to allow a more complete understanding of the nomological network within which test situational judgment measures reside.   (2001, p. 738)

Subsequent studies provided additional support for both the predictive *and* incremental validity of SJTs over and above personality and intelligence when it comes to explaining work outcomes. Chan and Schmitt assessed data from 160 Singaporean civil service employees and found that overall job performance, as well as three specific performance dimensions (task, motivational or contextual and interpersonal performance), was linked to SJT scores beyond personality and intelligence measures (Chan & Schmitt, 2002). As shown in Figure 5.3, even when intelligence and major personality dimensions – see Section 7.3 – are taken into account, SJT scores are linked to interpersonal performance (.17), task performance (.24), and especially contextual performance or job dedication (.30). It is noteworthy that Chan and Schmitt also controlled for previous job experience,

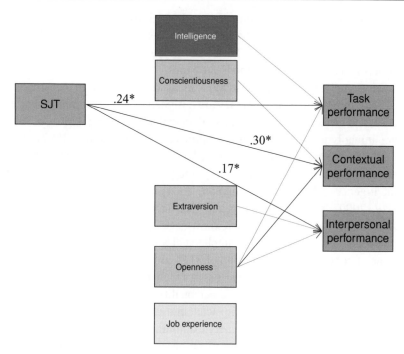

Figure 5.3 *Incremental validity of SJT over personality and intelligence (based on Chan & Schmitt, 2002)*

though this predictor was not significantly related to any of the criteria when other measures were considered.

5.3   What do SJTs actually measure?

Although SJTs are a method rather than a construct, they measure individual differences and therefore latent psychological constructs. Theoretically – and this is a question that is addressed throughout Part 2 (Chapters 6–10 of this book) – it is important to identify the psychological attributes that underlie performance differences in SJTs in order to better understand the determinants of individual differences at work and identify the best ways to assess these differences.

Early SJTs were believed to measure 'keen judgment, and a deep appreciation of human motives' (Moss & Hunt, 1926, p. 26) and fell within the 'social intelligence' or interpersonal competence domain. Since then, a key issue in SJT research has been the distinction between academic and non-academic competencies, where the former fall within the realm of IQ or cognitive ability and the latter are hypothesised as independent and largely unrelated. However, research has repeatedly found that SJTs are *g*-saturated (Northrop, 1989; see Section 5.2

and above), especially in their paper-and-pencil form (Lievens & Sackett, 2006). Despite clear evidence on the associations between traditional ability tests and SJTs, recurrent assumptions have been made on the independence of the constructs assessed by both methods/measures.

McDaniel *et al.* stated that SJTs measure 'a variety of constructs' (2001, p. 732), though in most cases they are designed to assess 'common sense, experience, and general knowledge, rather than logical reasoning' (2001, p. 731), which are arguably job-related skills or abilities (Weekley & Jones, 1997). As obvious as this assertion may sound, there is a long academic dispute in psychology about the extent to which 'common sense' and practical skills – often labelled 'social intelligence' (Peterson & Seligman, 2004), 'practical intelligence' (Sternberg *et al.*, 2000), 'emotional intelligence' (see Section 7.19), 'interpersonal' or 'social skills' (Furnham, 1986) or 'tacit knowledge' (Sternberg & Horvath, 1999) – are independent of 'academic' or intellectual abilities. As seen above, this was an issue of concern in the validation of SJTs, as their usefulness in personnel selection will largely depend on the extent to which they predict work-related outcomes independently of intelligence and personality measures. In a way, the second part of this chapter – which deals with academic achievement – tackles the same problem from the reverse angle, namely examining whether a measure of 'academic' knowledge rather than common sense or street-wisdom can be used to predict performance differences in the rather non-academic world of work (see Sections 5.4 to 5.8).

5.4   Academic performance and general grade-point average (GPA)

Another important, yet often overlooked, factor in the prediction of future work performance is school and/or university academic performance or general grade-point average (GPA). Although GPA is almost as old as education itself, and despite the well-known occupational consequences of educational attainment, GPA-based selection has been the target of recurrent criticisms over the years and there are still many employers and recruiters who are reluctant to select on the basis of GPA. In fact recent evidence suggests that recruiters often ignore GPA when recommending selection and in some circumstances even recommend selecting candidates with lower GPA (McKinney, Carlson, Mecham, D'Angelo & Connerley, 2003), though in general GPA is positively regarded in personnel selection, especially at entry-level (Rynes, Orlitzky & Bretz, 1997).

The validity of GPA is an important issue in personnel selection research, not only because there are large interindividual differences in GPA – such that grades are a robust marker of longitudinal performance differences between people in academic settings – but also because of the added practical value of GPA: information on grades is easily obtainable – for example, via biodata

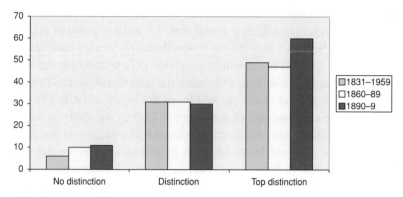

Figure 5.4 *Achievement in life as a function of earlier academic performance (Nicholson, 1915)*

(see Chapter 4) or academic records – and does not require further testing or interviewing, which is why many selection strategies use GPA to 'sift' or select out candidates during the early stages of the selection process. Moreover, there is a bulk of educational and occupational research on academic performance that provides robust evidence on its consequences and causes. Thus in the forthcoming sections we assess the validity of GPA in the prediction of future job performance and occupational success.

5.5   GPA: a poor predictor of success in the real world?

Validity studies examining the predicting power of GPA date back many decades, and even before that psychologists have speculated on the meaning and value of educational outcomes, such as grades. Thus in *The Influence of Selection*, Thorndike noted that 'educational agencies are a great system of means not only of making men good and intelligent and efficient, but also of picking out and labeling those who for any reason are good and intelligent and efficient' (Thorndike, 1903).

In line with Thorndike's assertion, Nicholson (1915) found that outstanding college students were much more likely to succeed in later life than their less outstanding and average counterparts (see Figure 5.4). These results were seen as important because they highlighted the fact that, even among high-achievers (and without correcting for range restriction), differences in academic performance translate into differences in real-world success – and they were the first important longitudinal evidence of this sort.

A few years later one of the first large studies on the validity of academic grades was published in the *Journal of Applied Psychology*. Toops and Pintner hypothesised that 'amount of education' (when they left school) would predict intra-occupation occupational status (trading success), and they classified

924 tradesmen from 30 different trades into three educational and occupational groups. As hypothesised, they found that '(1) median grade of employed men was found to be higher than the unemployed men (2) average trade rank increased in relation to increase in amount of education (3) a relationship existed between intelligence and trade status and (4) industrial selection of men and trade guidance was related to amount of education' (Toops & Pintner, 1919, p. 33).

During the early decades of the twentieth century the study of individual differences received widespread attention from both educational and occupational psychologists, not least due to advances in statistics and measurement methods. In France, Theodore Binet was establishing the foundations of modern IQ testing (Binet & Simon, 1905/1973) (see Section 6.3), whilst in England, Charles Spearman (see Section 6.2 and Figure 6.2) correlated people's grades on different subjects to identify a general factor of intelligence (Spearman, 1904). Accordingly, if academic grades were used to validate psychometric measures as indicators of people's learning potential, it made sense to validate academic grades as predictors of success following formal education, that is, in the real world. Whereas Binet was more interested in the developmental aspects of human abilities and how these can be shaped by education, Spearman – following Francis Galton's premise of hereditary genius – was after a general measure of mental ability that could explain performance differences in any domain because of its capacity to assess individual differences in learning potential.

Despite the large number of validity studies on academic performance conducted in the following decades, evidence for a strong link between GPA and success in the workplace was far from clear (and certainly less compelling than the evidence for the validity of psychometric tests in both educational and occupational settings) (see Chamorro-Premuzic & Furnham, 2005). One of the reasons for the inconclusive evidence for the utility of academic grades was that there is high variability among different educational institutions (Barrett & Alexander, 1989; Humphreys, 1988) as well as careers (Elliott & Strenta, 1988; Schoenfeldt & Brush, 1975).

Bretz identified 50 studies and a total of 62 samples conducted until the late 1970s to explore the validity of grades as predictors of salary and supervisory ratings in various occupational domains (i.e., business, teaching, engineering, medicine). As shown in Figure 5.5, which plots the effect sizes of these studies in chronological order along the x axis (from 1917 at the left to 1977 at the right), the reported results for the validity of GPA were most inconsistent, producing erratic effect size values. The range of correlations between GPA and job success went from $-.25$ ($d = .50$) to r $= .43$ ($d = .95$) (Bretz, 1989).

Bretz meta-analysed the results from these studies. The overall effect sizes are graphically depicted in Figure 5.6. As shown, postgraduate GPA – using as predictor only academic grades obtained after the degree – was a strong predictor of overall job success ($d = .73$). However, when undergraduate GPA is considered, the only significant effect sizes were found for job success in business ($d = .60$) and teaching ($d = .36$). Indeed, using overall job domains, the effect size

Figure 5.5 *Erratic effect sizes for GPA as predictor of job performance between 1922 and 1973*

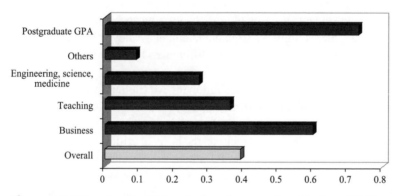

Figure 5.6 *Effect sizes for GPA and job performance found in Bretz (1989)*

for GPA as predictor was ($d = .39$), which narrowly missed significance level. Similar results were found when GPA was tested as predictor of starting salary – though the sample sizes dropped significantly. Thus GPA barely predicted starting salary and no form of GPA predicted salary growth or current salary. These results led the author to the pessimistic conclusion that 'no significant relationship exists between college GPA and job success' (Bretz, 1989, p. 14).

Despite some methodological limitations – mostly regarding the inclusion of studies with very small sample sizes (under fifty participants), Bretz *et al.*'s meta-analysis seem to justify subsequent dismissals of academic performance and GPA as 'just grades'. In fact, these results only confirmed what many already believed about the validity of grades, as evidenced by a widely cited article by McClelland (1973) on the importance of assessing non-academic *competencies* in order to predict occupational success. Although the main target of McClelland's criticisms was IQ (see Chapter 6), he was also sceptical of academic grades, not least because they are used to validated IQ tests. Thus McClelland claimed that 'the games people are required to play on aptitude tests are similar to the games teachers require in the classroom' (1973, p. 1), implying that these *games* finish when people leave school or college to enter the 'real world' of work. Moreover, McClelland argued that grades and intelligence scores were only a substitute for social class and that relying on these predictors was a sort of strategy to handicap minorities and individuals of lower socioeconomic status.

Whilst few people today would question the fact that both academic grades and cognitive ability scores have adverse impact as they are associated with socio-economic, cultural and ethnic group differences (see Section 6.9 for a discussion of group differences in IQ and Roth & Bobko, 2000), McClelland's claims that IQ scores do not predict occupational outcomes – job and training success – were unfounded and seem ludicrous today (see Section 6.4 for a compilation of robust evidence in support of the validity of cognitive ability tests). Fur-thermore, McClelland's conclusion that grades did not predict subsequent job performance – consistent with, but also prior to, Bretz meta-analysis – was based on anecdotal evidence, such as his personal teaching experiences suggesting that top-grade students do as well or as badly after they finish college as low-grade students (interestingly, McClelland taught at Wesleyan University, the same col-lege where Nicholson found clear differences between more and less competent students).

Although in the two decades following McClelland's paper a number of text-books, psychological magazines (notably *Psychology Today*) and newspapers like the *New York Times* (articles by Daniel Goleman, who popularised the concept of emotional intelligence largely on the basis of criticising IQ) (see Sections 7.19 to 7.23) repeatedly stated that IQ grades are unrelated to occupational success and life outcomes (for a review see Barrett & Depinet, 1991), during the same period psychological and educational journals published a growing number of validity studies suggesting that a variety of occupational outcomes – from salary to promotion and supervisory ratings – could be predicted by grades, albeit mod-estly (Samson, Graue, Weinstein & Walberg, 1984). Thus a thorough review of McCelland's claims and the evidence for the validity of GPA and cognitive ability concluded that:

> Despite the wide acceptance of McClelland's (1973) views, the evidence he used to support his arguments leads to conclusions that actually oppose the ones he has proposed. His assertions are contradicted by other evidence. Grades did predict occupational success. Intellectual ability and aptitude tests predicted occupational success even when the aptitude test was . . . not designed for general use. Test results were not an artefact of social status, nor were they unfair to minorities.   (Barrett & Depinet, 1991, p. 1021)

Although this statement provides an accurate reflection of the validity of both cognitive ability tests (see Chapter 6) and GPA in the prediction of relevant work-outcomes (see below for the validity of GPA), it seems to undermine the adverse impact of GPA, which does seem to disadvantage some groups in comparison to others. Roth and Bobko assessed black–white ethnic differences in a sample

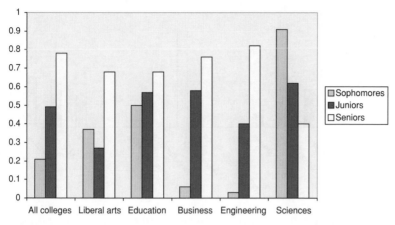

Figure 5.7 *White–black difference in GPA (effect sizes from Roth & Bobko, 2000)*

of 7,498 US university students (Roth & Bobko, 2000). The results, summarised in Figure 5.7, reflect group differences in favour of white students across all colleges and in particular at more advanced levels of the undergraduate degree (sophomores being the lowest, juniors the intermediate and seniors the highest). All effect sizes shown in Figure 5.7 favour whites students. The pattern of results also indicates that for sciences group differences are especially pronounced in sophomores and decrease thereafter. The findings of Roth and Bobko are consistent with the adverse effect reported for intelligence tests (see Section 6.9), which are known to be consistently and often substantially correlated with GPA (Jensen, 1980). It seems that there is a certain level of adverse impact in any test requiring cognitive performance, which is why self-reports – such as personality inventories – have often been proposed as an alternative or complementary method to reduce adverse impact (Hogan, Hogan & Roberts, 1996).

In the past ten years meta-analysis has provided compelling evidence for the validity of GPA in occupational settings. Most notably, Roth and colleagues reported corrected validities above .30 for job performance (Roth, BeVier, Switzer & Schippmann, 1996) and .20 for initial level of earnings (Roth & Clarke, 1998). Figure 5.8 summarises these findings. As shown, the highest validity was found for job performance one year after graduating, with validities decreasing thereafter (see light-grey bars). When salary is taken as the criterion, the highest validity was found for current salary, followed by starting salary, and last for salary growth (dark-grey bars). Finally, when job performance is assessed independently for each job domain, the highest validity is found for educational jobs, followed by military and business, with lower validities for scientific and medical professions (see mid-grey bars). It is noteworthy that the overall corrected validity above .30 for performance and around .20 for salary is at least comparable to and often higher than that of personality traits (see Chapter 7).

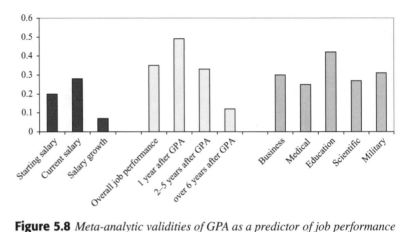

Figure 5.8 *Meta-analytic validities of GPA as a predictor of job performance and salary*

5.6   Why does GPA predict occupational outcomes?

From an applied perspective, it is sufficient to know that GPA predicts the desired occupational outcomes; however, from a theoretical point of view it is important to understand *why*. Moreover, if the relationship between GPA and work outcomes can be explained in terms of other constructs for which alternative and possibly better measures exist, the advantages of GPA over such measures need to be specified.

In order to understand why GPA predicts job performance and salary, one needs to identify the determinants of GPA and test whether these are conceptually and empirically related to the job-related criteria used to validate academic grades. Whereas recruiters tend to interpret GPA in terms of verbal and mathematical abilities as well as motivation or drive (Brown & Campion, 1994), there is a wealth of psychometric evidence for the idea that interindividual differences in academic performance (whether in school, undergraduate or postgraduate education) reflect broader and earlier individual differences in personality and, especially, intellectual ability; for reviews see Chamorro-Premuzic & Furnham (2005, 2006).

Kuncel, Hezlett and Ones (2001) meta-analysed 163 independent samples from 127 studies (totalling 229 correlations and 20,352 participants) on the Miller Analogies Test (MAT) (Miller, 1960), a measure designed to predict academic achievement and used widely in the US for admission to graduate schools and moderate or high-complexity jobs. The test was devised in 1926 and contains 100 analogies (administered in 50 minutes) that assess candidates' capacity to reason and solve problems using their knowledge of sciences, literature, arts, etc. (domain-specific knowledge). Kuncel and colleagues set out to explore the extent to which MAT scores differentially predict academic and occupational outcomes, as well as creativity (see Chapter 8) and career potential (see

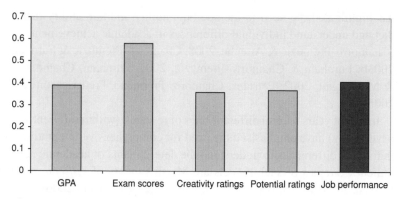

Figure 5.9 *Validity of the MAT predicting academic and occupation success (from Kuncel et al., 2001)*

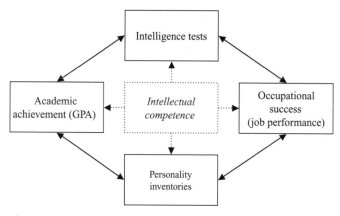

Figure 5.10 *Intellectual competence as the common source of variability in academic and occupational success*

Chapter 10). As shown in Figure 5.9, the estimated true validities (fully corrected correlations) were moderate and similar for GPA, ratings of creativity, potential and measures of job performance (with exam scores yielding even higher validities for the MAT). This indicates quite clearly that the same underlying construct – whatever is measured by the MAT – can explain individual differences in various domains and underlies different academic and occupational criteria. In simple terms, this suggests that the causes of individual differences in GPA are at least in part similar to the causes of individual differences in job outcomes.

In line with Kuncel *et al.*'s findings, GPA could be simply interpreted as a marker of future potential or *intellectual competence* (Chamorro-Premuzic & Furnham, 2004, 2005), which is also the source of interindividual differences in occupational success. Moreover, psychometric measures, such as those designed to assess individual differences in personality and intelligence, are also aimed at assessing people's intellectual competence, whether it is for the job or for college (Figure 5.10 illustrates this point). Our own programme of research has highlighted the need to include both ability and non-ability factors to predict and understand individual differences in academic achievement and beyond (Chamorro-Premuzic & Arteche, 2008; Chamorro-Premuzic & Furnham, 2003a, 2003b; Furnham & Chamorro-Premuzic, 2004; Furnham, Chamorro-Premuzic & McDougall, 2002; Petrides, Chamorro-Premuzic, Frederickson & Furnham, 2005).

In recent years several different lines of research (within different sub-areas of psychology) have emphasised the need for comprehensive integrative models of individual differences to understand the determinants of academic achievement. Salient examples of such models are Marsh's theory of *self-concept* (Marsh & Craven, 2006; Marsh, Trautwein, Lüdtke, Köller & Baumert, 2006) in educational psychology; Eccles' *expectancy-value* theory of motivation (Denissen, Zarrett & Eccles, 2007) in social and development psychology; Ackerman's theory of *adult intellect* and *intelligence as process, personality, interests and knowledge* (Ackerman, 2008; Ackerman & Rolfhus, 1999; Kanfer & Ackerman, 2004) in differential, industrial/organisational and educational psychology; Duckworth's concept of *grit* (Duckworth, 2006; Duckworth, Peterson, Matthews & Kelly, 2007; Duckworth & Seligman, 2005) in social and positive psychology; and our model of *intellectual competence* (Chamorro-Premuzic & Arteche, 2008; Chamorro-Premuzic & Furnham, 2005, 2006).

What these theories have in common is that they explain academic achievement, and often achievement beyond educational life, by including various measures and constructs as predictors of scholastic outcomes, as well as exploring the added predictive value of reciprocal, interactive and mediated effects, in order to identify *synergies* among different individual-difference constructs (e.g., self-confidence and self-perceptions, actual abilities, motivational factors and dispositions). Thus GPA can be conceptually linked to occupational performance in that it carries variance from both ability and non-ability factors that are determinants of individual differences in real-world success (first in school, then in college and finally at work).

Recent studies provide important new evidence for the idea that different achievement criteria (academic and occupational performance) can be explained and are likely to be caused by the same factors. For example, Spinks and colleagues showed that elementary school achievement (grades 3–8) predicted IQ scores in the mid 40s ($r = .64$; Spinks, Arndt, Caspers *et al.*, 2007). Strenze (2007) found that early measures of people's intelligence, socioeconomic status and GPA are all powerful predictors of subsequent success and have comparable validities. Another recent study tested the degree to which cognitive ability and conscientiousness (see Section 7.6) can be used to explain interindividual variability in GPA over the course of students' careers. Although cognitive ability and conscientiousness explained initial differences in GPA, only conscientiousness affected performance change thereafter. However, as initial performance had a negative effect on performance change, cognitive ability and conscientiousness had indirect negative effects on performance. Findings also showed that whereas cognitive ability was more useful to explain initial differences in GPA, conscientiousness explained performance change and GPA beyond the third semester better than did cognitive ability (Zyphur, Bradley, Landis & Thoresen, 2008). Fenollar and colleagues found that study strategies explain the effect of motivation and self-efficacy on GPA (Fenollar, Román & Cuestas, 2007), whereas Farsides and Woodfield found that sex differences in GPA (in favour of women) are partly explained in terms of women's higher Openness to experience (Farsides & Woodfield, 2007). In order to better understand the meaning of these predictors not only of GPA but also of success in the workplace, Part 2 of this book discusses the salient relevant constructs that determine personnel selection-relevant differences and how they can be assessed psychometrically.

5.7   Summary and conclusions

The present chapter discussed the validity of two methods of selection, namely SJTs and GPA. Both methods are similar in that they have a long history in psychology and personnel selection, though significantly more research has been conducted on GPA than on SJTs, not least because of its relevance in educational psychology (something that does not apply to SJTs). These two methods are also quite different in that SJTs require employers or recruiters to design, choose, administer, score and interpret scores on purpose-built tests that need to be taken by the candidate especially for the purpose of getting the job, whereas GPA is merely a number that is available from candidates who have completed higher education (and can provide this via the university, CVs, references of recommendation, etc.).

There are also conceptual similarities between SJTs and GPA as both assess a variety of constructs that are relevant to performance in the workplace. Moreover, the boundaries of what is assessed through both SJTs and GPA vary according to the type of test, in the case of the former, and the type of institution, course and markers, in the case of GPA. Thus both SJTs and GPAs are clearly heterogeneous and markers of a wide range of *traits* or individual attributes that are conceptually and empirically linked to workplace behaviours.

How valid are SJTs and GPA? Although the answer depends on the specific measure in question, meta-analytic evidence provided compelling evidence for the validity and generalisability of both methods and suggests quite clearly that both SJTs and GPA should be used to inform personnel selection, even if the factors determining differences in SJTs and GPA can also be assessed via other methods (such as intelligence or personality tests). Meta-analyses also suggest that there is an overlap between these two measures and established psychometric tests, but that, in the case of SJTs, incremental validity over personality and intelligence factors justifies the use of these measures in selection, whereas in the case of GPA the combination of factors that cause differences in academic performance are also likely to contribute, and in a similar vein, to interindividual differences in occupational performance. The question of what constructs these are is discussed in more depth in the second part of this book, namely Chapters 6–10.

PART 2

Constructs for personnel selection

6 General mental ability

6.1 Introduction: what is intelligence?

Intelligence is arguably the most important construct in personnel selection, but what is its precise meaning, and that of *IQ*, *g*, *general intelligence* and *cognitive abilities*? The following conceptual differences should be noted:

> IQ (a measure) versus *g* (a construct, the primary latent trait that IQ tests actually measure) versus general intelligence (often used as a synonym for *g*) versus intelligence (a lay word with multiple meanings; an umbrella term in science for a wide range of cognitive abilities).   (Gottfredson, 2007, p. 219)

Unfortunately, the above terms are often used interchangeably, producing frequent misunderstandings and unnecessary discussions (that is, discussions based on semantic confusion rather than valid theoretical assertions or empirical evidence). In order to avoid falling into this category we will use each of these terms in the context of Gottfredson's (2007, p. 219) conceptual distinctions. Thus, we will define IQ as intellectual quotient, or the score on a comprehensive battery of tests or global intellectual ability scale (omnibus test) that has a standardised scale with a mean score of 100 and a standard deviation of 15 points (see Section 6.3). On the other hand, the terms '*g*', 'general intelligence' and 'general mental ability' (GMA) will be defined simply in terms of 'the ability to learn' or 'general learning ability' (Hunter, 1986) and used more or less interchangeably. A more detailed definition of GMA would read as follows:

> a very general mental capability that, among other things, involves the ability to reason, plan, solve problems, think abstractly, comprehend complex ideas, learn quickly and learn from experience. It is not merely book learning, a narrow academic skill, or test-taking smarts. Rather, it reflects a broader and deeper capability for comprehending our surroundings – 'catching on,' 'making sense' of things, or 'figuring out' what to do.   (Gottfredson, 1997a, p. 13)

This definition was provided by a panel of fifty-two experts in the field and first appeared on the *Wall Street Journal* in 1994 in response to media and sociological criticisms of the psychological notion of intellectual ability after the publication of *The Bell Curve*. Most experts still agree that it captures the essence of the meaning of *intelligence*, but we will try to avoid using this term from here onwards in order to minimise confusion (with, for example, 'emotional intelligence' or

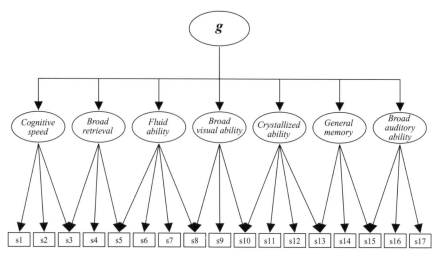

Note: s1…s17 = specific abilities at the lowest hierarchical level

Figure 6.1 *Graphical representation of the hierarchical structure of cognitive abilities identified by John Carroll (based on Carroll, 1993)*

'social intelligence'[1]), preferring to use *g* or GMA instead. Crucially, *g* and GMA emphasise the generality of human intelligence, setting it apart from the more specific *cognitive abilities* (e.g., spatial, numerical and visual). Whereas there is some debate as to how best to conceptualise specific cognitive abilities (Johnson & Bouchard, 2005), there is robust evidence for the existence of a general *g* factor at the broadest level. This factor accounts for 50–80% of the variance in multiple tests of specific abilities (Deary, 2001), leaving some variance unaccounted for. The unaccounted variance is explained first in terms of broad abilities (e.g., cognitive speed, broad retrieval, general memory, etc.), which, in turn, can be broken down into lower-level factors or aspects of cognitive ability, such as induction, language development and word fluency. This *hierarchical structure* of cognitive abilities (graphically depicted in Figure 6.1) represents the state-of-the-art approach to classifying human aptitudes and places *g* or GMA at the highest hierarchical level; it has been found to explain hundreds of robust datasets (Carretta & Ree, 1996; Carroll, 1993; Jensen, 1998; Spearman, 1904).

In purely statistical terms, the *g* factor simply indicates that people's scores on various cognitive ability tests are highly intercorrelated, making differences *within* individuals quite negligible in comparison to differences *between* individuals (which is the same as saying that your scores on different tests are much more similar to each other than your overall score is to the overall score of other people). To illustrate this with another example: suppose you know someone who is not just good at football, but also good at tennis, basketball, rugby, sailing and marathon running. You would probably refer to that person as a good sportsman or *sporty* person. Conversely, imagine you know someone who is bad at all possible sports (not just at one); you would probably think of that person as a bad sportsman or *un-sporty* person. While we can probably all think of people who are good at some sports but not all, when it comes to cognitive ability tests, people who do very well at one or two tests but very badly at others are a notable exception to the norm, though it has been shown that specific abilities are more weakly intercorrelated at higher levels of GMA (Legree, Pifer & Grafton, 1996).

The vast amount of accumulated evidence in support of the *g* factor undermines the validity of alternative ability models that de-emphasise the importance of *g* (Sternberg & Wagner, 1993) or question its usefulness (Guilford, 1988). This applies especially to Gardner's theory of 'multiple intelligences' (Gardner, 1983/2003, 1993b), which assumes the independence of cognitive abilities, as well as the inclusion of non-traditional competencies, such as 'spiritual intelligence' and 'body-kinaesthetic intelligence', in the realm of cognitive abilities (for emotional intelligence, see Sections 7.19 to 7.23). Regardless of the popular appeal of this theory and of any progress – so far there has been little (Chamorro-Premuzic, 2007) – that may come in relation to the measurement of novel abilities herewith defined, few psychological findings are as robust as *g*, that is, the idea that different abilities are highly intercorrelated (Carroll, 1993; Jensen, 1998). It is also noteworthy that even though laypeople are seemingly reticent to accept the idea of *g*, ratings of their own cognitive abilities tend to be strongly intercorrelated, even when novel abilities, such as spiritual and existential abilities, are estimated in relation to mathematical and spatial abilities (Chamorro-Premuzic, Ahmetoglu & Furnham, 2008; Chamorro-Premuzic, 2007; Chamorro-Premuzic & Furnham, 2006a; Furnham & Chamorro-Premuzic, 2007).

The theoretical meaning of *g* is not to be debated in detail here, but we examine why it comes to predict job performance and other occupational outcomes in Section 6.4. It should be noted that, for the purposes of this book, what matters most is how good *g* is at predicting (positively) desirable or (negatively) undesirable occupational outcomes. In that sense, whether we agree or not with the idea that *g* is the best marker of human intelligence really is quite irrelevant.

6.2   A brief history of GMA and Raven's Progressive Matrices

The construct of GMA is widely attributed to Spearman's (1904) finding that performance on different mental tests, as well as grades on different academic subjects, are largely intercorrelated, such that performance on these tests can be explained quite accurately in terms of a general psychometric factor, which he called *g*. Theoretical interpretations of this statistical factor have varied quite markedly, though a majority of intelligence researchers endorse the conceptualisation of *g* as a mainly, if not purely, biological, largely unchangeable, culture-free, measure of individual differences in learning and reasoning capacity, best measured through non-verbal tests, such as Raven's Progressive Matrices (see Figure 6.3). However, Spearman's (1904, p. 276) original data showed that

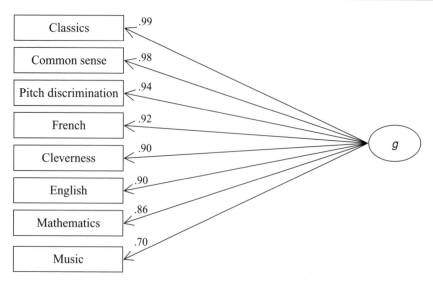

Note: Correlations corrected for measurement error

Figure 6.2 *Some correlates of Spearman's* g *factor (after Spearman, 1904)*

g correlated almost perfectly with knowledge of Greek and Latin (the 'Classics'), which are obviously dependent on previous knowledge and education. Moreover, pitch discrimination, French and 'common sense' correlated more highly with *g* than mathematics did (see Figure 6.2). Nonetheless, Spearman later shifted his interpretation of *g* from a more verbal, knowledge and content-based to a more abstract, non-verbal and process-based conceptualisation of *g*, regarding Raven's Progressive Matrices as the ultimate measure of GMA (Spearman, 1930, 1938). Clearly, Spearman was more interested in the biological aspects of GMA than in the development of adult intellectual abilities (Ackerman, 2008).

The Raven's Progressive Matrices (Raven, Court & Raven, 1998) is a non-verbal, multiple-choice test of abstract reasoning developed in the UK by John C. Raven in 1938 (Raven, 1938). It is widely regarded as a – if not the best single – measure of GMA (Jensen, 1998), though see Carpenter, Just and Schell (1990) and Mackintosh and Bennett (2005) for different views. The test presents test-takers with several series of figures linked by specific implicit rules (see Figure 6.3). Test-takers are required to complete the sequence by identifying the missing figure from a number of possible alternatives given, which requires understanding of the implicit rule by which the given figures are connected. The test has sixty items and is administered in twenty minutes, though different versions exist. The sixty items fall into sets of twelve items and increase in difficulty. Abundant evidence of the test's reliability and validity for a wide range of ages and cultural groups, including clinical and non-clinical groups, has been reported in the manual. The test is used extensively in personnel selection, particularly in the US and the UK (Bertua, Anderson & Salgado, 2005; Jensen, 1998; Raven *et al.*, 1998). Given

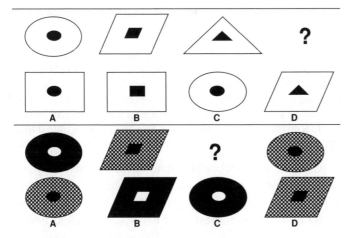

Figure 6.3 *Two examples of Raven-like items*

that this is a non-verbal measure, the Raven's Matrices can be administered in every nation without the need to translate anything more than the instructions. This culture-free element of the test makes it particularly attractive when one wishes to compare the reasoning ability and learning potential of culturally heterogeneous groups of candidates (e.g., applicants from rural China, urban Chile and suburban Germany applying for a postgraduate programme of studies in London or a banking job in New York), which is a common need in globalised job markets and has become increasingly feasible with the growth of the World Wide Web beyond the industrialised world.

6.3   A brief history of IQ and the Wonderlic Personnel Test

At the same time as Spearman's investigations on the *g* factor in the UK, a different approach to the measurement of cognitive abilities was being pioneered in France by Binet and Simon (Binet & Simon, 1905/1973). Unlike Spearman, Binet and Simon were interested in the development of intellectual abilities and 'sum of acquired knowledge' (p. 40), so that their battery of mental tests was directly designed to address *change* in cognitive abilities as a function of chronological age. Binet and Simon's original battery of tests comprised thirty tasks of increasing complexity, ranging from simple items, such as assessing whether children managed to shake hands with the test administrator, to more complex, intellectual problems, such as testing children's ability to memorise drawings and random sequences of digits, to come up with rhymes and to answer questions such as 'My neighbour has been receiving strange visitors. He has received in turn a doctor, a lawyer, and then a priest. What is taking place?' Thus Binet and Simon's approach very much highlighted the practical or common-sense aspects of cognitive ability (as noted in Section 6.2, this interpretation was congruent with Spearman's early findings). Indeed, their definition of cognitive ability stated that:

> It seems to us that in intelligence there is a fundamental faculty, the alteration or the lack of which is of the utmost importance for practical life. This faculty is judgment, otherwise called good sense, practical sense, initiative, the faculty of adapting one's self to circumstances. A person may be a moron or an imbecile if he is lacking in judgment; but with good judgment he can never be either. Indeed the rest of the intellectual faculties seem of little importance in comparison with judgment.   (Binet & Simon, 1916/1973, pp. 42–3)

Children's IQ scores are calculated by dividing their mental age (i.e., the average chronological age of the children who solve problems of similar complexity or level of difficulty) by their chronological age, and then multiplying that by 100. Thus an IQ of 120 may indicate that a 10-year-old child has the mental ability of a typical 12-year-old, i.e., $12/10* 100 = 120$, which would make that child more than 1 standard deviation smarter than most children. This distribution means that 68 per cent of individuals score between 85 and 115 points, and this distribution applies to adults as well as children.

However, as the effects of age on most cognitive abilities vanish by the age of 15, the IQ formula cannot be directly applied to adults. Early attempts to do so, when IQ tests were first implemented in the context of personnel selection, created interpretational problems. Most notably, when an American adult adaptation of Binet and Simon's scale (the Army Alpha test) was administered to 1.7 million conscripts, the reported average age for the sample was 13 years (Ackerman, 2008). However, adult IQ norms were implemented for several scales soon thereafter.

The most widely used adult IQ test (for 16 to 89-year-olds) is the Wechsler Adult Intelligence Scale (WAIS), currently in its third edition (Wechsler, 2002).[2] The first version of the test was designed for the US army seventy years ago by David Wechsler (a student of Spearman's) to measure 'the global capacity of a person to act purposefully, to think rationally, and to deal effectively with his/her environment' (Wechsler, 1939, p. 229). However, the WAIS (which includes fourteen scales and measures the four broad components of verbal comprehension, perceptual organisation, working memory and processing speed) is used primarily in clinical settings, not least because of its lengthy administration time, 75 minutes on average. In research and even in most clinical settings, subscales of this test are employed more often than the full battery. In occupational settings, particularly for personnel selection, shorter IQ tests or omnibus GMA tests are always preferred.

The most widely used IQ test in personnel selection is probably the Wonderlic Personnel Test (Wonderlic, 1992) (Murphy, 1984; Schmidt & Hunter, 2004), an omnibus GMA test developed by Eldon F. Wonderlic in 1937 and used by the US Navy for the selection and training of pilots during World War II. The main advantage of this test is that it is administered in only twelve minutes, meaning it is less intimidating for job applicants and more efficient for employers than long

Table 6.1 *Wonderlic Personnel Test: sample items (adapted from Wonderlic, 1992)*

1. When rope is selling at 20 cents a foot, how many feet can you buy for 60 cents?
2. Assume the first two statements are true. Is the final one: True, False, Uncertain?
   1. The girl is a hockey player.
   2. All hockey players wear hats.
   3. The girl wears a hat.
3. Paper sells for 14 cents per pad. What will four pads cost?
4. How many of the five pairs of items listed below are exact duplicates?
   Ackerman, P. L., Ackerman, P. L., Gottfredson, L. S., Gottfredson, M. R., Thorndike, E. L., Thorndike, P. L., Vernon, P. E., Vernon, P. A., Bach, J. S., Bach, J. A.
5. PREVENT PRESENT – Do these words
   a. Have similar meanings
   b. Have contradictory meanings
   c. Mean neither the same nor opposite?

- **Answers: 1** = *3* / **2** = *True* / **3** = *56 cents* / **4** = *1 (Ackerman, P. L.)* / **5** = c

IQ tests. Despite its short administration time, the Wonderlic produces overall IQ scores that correlate at r = .93 with the WAIS and in 80–90 per cent of cases are within 10 points difference from scores derived from the WAIS (Dodrill, 1981). Moreover, the test–retest reliability of the Wonderlic (r = .94 in five years) approaches that of the WAIS (r = .96) (Dodrill, 1983).

Modified sample items of the Wonderlic are shown in Table 6.1. Even a quick glance at these items suggests a marked difference from the Raven-like items shown in Figure 6.3, namely that Wonderlic (but not Raven) items are mostly verbal. Indeed, the distinction between verbal and non-verbal ability tests is at the heart of a fundamental theoretical distinction frequently applied to the realm of cognitive abilities, that is, the difference between *fluid* and *crystallised* abilities (Cattell, 1943). Fluid intelligence, usually notated as *gf*, refers to individual differences in abstract reasoning and is therefore equivalent to Spearman's late interpretation of *g* and measured by tests such as Raven's Progressive Matrices (see Section 6.2). Crystallised intelligence, usually notated as *gc*, refers to individual differences in acquired knowledge and is therefore measured by tests that require information retrieval (e.g., vocabulary, general knowledge and learned rules).

Although it has been recently questioned whether *gf* and *gc* provide an accurate grouping of cognitive abilities (Johnson & Bouchard, 2005), and whether one can truly measure *gc* without eliminating or 'decanting' variance caused by *gf* (Reeve, Meyer & Bonaccio, 2006), this distinction has important implications for personnel selection because it acknowledges that certain tests are more useful for measuring what people have already learned and already know, whereas other tests are more useful for providing an indicator of what people will be able to learn. For instance, being a physicist or a mathematician will probably require high levels of *gf*, whilst being a historian or a lawyer will probably require high levels of *gc* (McGrew & Flanagan, 1998).

The Wonderlic Personnel Test has been reported to be correlated equally with both *gf* and *gc*, thus measuring both abstract reasoning capability and knowledge possessed (Bell, Matthews, Lassiter & Leveret, 2002). In that sense, the two conceptual differences between IQ and GMA are that IQ tests have standardized scores and also measure *gc*.

6.4   Like no other: the predictive power of GMA

To say that GMA predicts occupational outcomes, such as job or training performance, is as much a truism as an understatement, and is really beyond debate (Murphy, 2002; Schmidt, 2002). Indeed, there is so much evidence for the validity of GMA in the prediction of job and training performance that an entire book could be written simply describing these findings. There are several great and relatively compact sources of reference, the most robust and widely cited (Hunter & Hunter, 1984; Judge, Higgins, Thoresen & Barrick, 1999; Schmidt, 2002; Schmidt & Hunter, 1998, 2004) are discussed in this and the forthcoming sections.[3]

The predictive power of GMA at work is rivalled by no other psychological trait (Ree & Earles, 1992). That said, GMA should not be used as single predictor of job performance as some traits, notably Conscientiousness and Integrity (discussed in Section 7.4), have incremental validity over and above GMA, explaining additional variance in occupational outcomes of interest (Bobko, Roth & Potosky, 1999; Schmidt & Hunter, 1998). The validity of GMA at work has been documented quite systematically since the end of World War I (Harrell & Harrell, 1945; Yerkes, 1921), first in military and then in civil occupations. Yet – as shown in Figure 6.4, based on Dany & Torchy (1994) – most employers do not test for aptitude when selecting their workforce.

The first seminal reviews on the subject (Ghiselli, 1966, 1973) concluded that GMA, as well as spatial, mechanical and perceptual abilities, were the best aptitude predictors of training and job performance, and that for every family of professions (e.g., managerial, clerical, sales and drivers) there is a cognitive ability test that is at least moderately related to these outcomes.

As shown in Table 6.2, average GMA levels tend to increase with occupational level, that is, with the prestige of the job (Jensen, 1980). Furthermore, higher-level jobs tend to have substantially higher levels of inbound GMA, indicating that it is far more unlikely to find low-IQ scorers in high-level professions than it is to find high-IQ scorers in low-level professions. This is probably because laziness can drive bright people to simple jobs, but hard work can hardly push dim people to

Table 6.2 *GMA across civilian jobs in US Army; simplified adaptation of original source (Harrell & Harrell, 1945)*

Jobs	N	M	SD	Range
Accountants	172	128.1	11.7	94–157
Lawyers	94	127.6	10.9	96–157
Repairman	96	115.8	13.1	76–149
Cashier	111	115.8	11.9	80–145
Tractor driver	354	99.5	19.1	42–147
General painter	440	98.3	18.7	38–147
Farmer	700	92.7	21.8	24–147
Farmhand	817	91.4	20.7	24–141

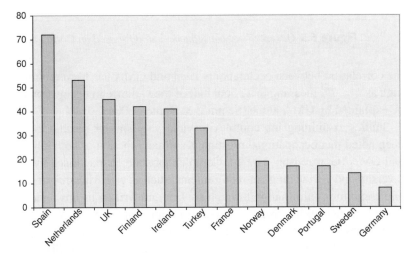

Figure 6.4 *Percentage of employers using aptitude tests in Western Europe (Price Waterhouse Cranfield survey, 1994)*

complex jobs (note, of course, that most but not all complex jobs pay higher wages than simple ones). In addition, the standard deviations tend to decrease as people move up to higher-level professions, showing that these jobs tend to have not only people with higher but also more homogeneous GMA (see also Figure 6.5, taken from Chamorro-Premuzic, 2007, and based on Gottfredson, 2004).

Although the notion that better jobs attract brighter people is not really counterintuitive (think of how many times you surprised yourself when people who did not seem very bright told you they have very well-paid jobs), the strength of the association between GMA and job success is robust. Ratings of occupational level, which are extremely reliable (even when only two or three individuals are asked to independently rank different occupations, they provide very homogeneous rankings), correlate as highly as r = .95 with average IQ scores of people in those jobs (Jensen, 1998). Even at the individual (rather than aggregate) level,

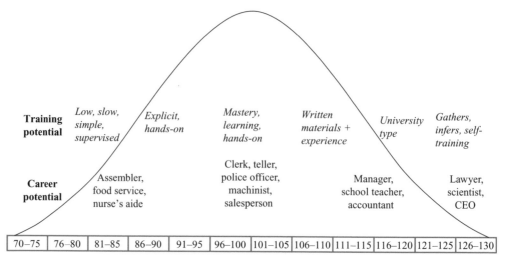

70–75	76–80	81–85	86–90	91–95	96–100	101–105	106–110	111–115	116–120	121–125	126–130

Figure 6.5 *Occupational consequences of IQ (based on Gottfredson, 2004)*

the correlation between occupational level and GMA has been reported to be as high as r = .72, meaning that about half of the variance in occupational level can be explained by GMA alone (Schmidt & Hunter, 2004).

Studies examining job complexity yield very similar results. Indeed, it has been noted that occupational prestige is a direct function of both job complexity and GMA (Gottfredson, 1997b). Complex jobs are characterised by a cognitive diversity and a wide range of requirements, such as gathering, relating, analysing and combining information through spoken and written means under situations of high responsibility and low supervision and substantial psychological pressure. Conversely, low prestige and low-complexity situations – where GMA plays a much more limited role – are characterised by repetitive, systematic, monotonous and physical rather than intellectual tasks; they are also more highly supervised and demand less responsibility from the employee (see Gottfredson, 1997a, pp. 100–5) (see also Figure 6.5, taken from Chamorro-Premuzic, 2007, and based on Gottfredson, 2004).

In a colossal quantitative review and meta-analysis of 425 studies on GMA and job performance across different levels of complexity (Hunter, 1980; Hunter & Hunter, 1984), typically referred to as 'validity studies', GMA was found to correlate significantly with performance at *all* levels of job complexity, though it is clear that the more complex the job, the more important GMA is; hence the common assertion that the relationship between GMA and job performance is *moderated by job complexity*. Indeed, it has been noted that job complexity is one of the few moderators of the effects of GMA on job performance (Murphy, 2002, p. 175).

Table 6.3 summarises the main results from Hunter and Hunter's (1984) meta-analysis. The authors operationalised job performance in terms of supervisory ratings, which are known to be less reliable than objective measures of performance,

Table 6.3 *GMA correlates of job and training performance across various job complexity levels (adapted from Hunter, 1980; Hunter & Hunter, 1984)*

Job complexity	% workforce	Job performance 425 studies	Training performance 90 studies
1 *most complex*	14.7	.58	.59
2	2.5	.56	.65
3	62.7	.51	.57
4	17.7	.40	.54
5 *least complex*	2.4	.23	not reported
Overall *N*		32,124	6,496

and training performance in terms of the degree of learning during training. Correlations corrected for error in the outcome measures but not in the predictor. Thus at the construct level the authors estimated that correlations would be approximately 8.5 per cent higher.

Hunter and Hunter coded different occupations and their complexity level according to the Dictionary of Occupational Titles.[4] Examples of complex jobs (level 1) were professional, scientific and management jobs, where GMA correlated $r = .58$ with job performance and $r = .59$ with training performance. Examples of low-complexity jobs (level 5) were feeding/off-bearing (that is, placing or removing materials from machines that are automatic or operated by others), where GMA correlated $r = .23$ with job performance. On the other hand, Hunter (1986) tested the predictive power of GMA against objective performance measures and found a predictive validity of $r = .75$.

Subsequent meta-analyses in the US were by and large congruent with Hunter's findings (see Table 6.4 for a summary) and highlight the strength of the effects of both GMA and specific abilities on both job and training performance across different occupations. A special issue of the journal *Personnel Psychology* (edited by J. P. Campbell, 1990) was devoted entirely to the discussion of the 'Project A', a huge US-based personnel selection project that cost $25 million and was 'probably the largest and most expensive selection research project in history' (Schmidt *et al.*, 1992, p. 632). Findings showed that military job performance, as operationalised via both technical and general soldiering proficiency, was strongly related to GMA, and that GMA predicted these outcomes better than any other psychological trait. Athough non-ability traits, such as personality, were better predictors of supervisory ratings of effort, leadership and discipline (McHenry, Hough, Toquam, Hanson & Ashworth, 1990), they provided only limited incremental validity over GMA in predicting job performance. Thus project A largely replicated previous findings on the validity of GMA (Schmidt *et al.*, 1992).

More recently, meta-analyses were also conducted in the UK and Europe (see Sections 6.5 and 6.6).

Table 6.4 *Other meta-analyses on the validity of GMA since 1980*

Reference	Outcomes	Validities
(Pearlman, Schmidt & Hunter, 1980)	Clerical occupations (job and training)	Moderate to large (generalise across different samples and jobs)
(Schmidt, Gast-Rosenberg & Hunter, 1980)	Computer programmers (job proficiency and training)	Very large (.73 for job proficiency and .91 for training)
(Hirsh, Northrop & Schmidt, 1986)	Law enforcement jobs (job proficiency and training)	For job proficiency modest (but only spatial-mechanical ability generalised), for training large
(Nathan & Alexander, 1988)	Supervisory ratings and rankings, work samples, production quality and quantity	Moderate to high (.44 for supervisory ratings to .60 for work sample criteria); lower validities for objective job performance but they were not corrected for unreliability
(Hartigan & Wigdor, 1989)	Reanalysed Hunter and Hunter's (1984) data plus new datasets	Substantial (.80 for job performance, .81[5] for training) Job complexity moderates validity of GMA and abilities
(Levine, Spector, Menon, Narayanan & Cannon-Bowers, 1996)	Crafts jobs in utility industry (e.g., mechanical utility, telephone technical and electrical assembly) (job performance)	Moderate for job performance
(Vinchur, Schippman, Switzer & Roth, 1998)	Sales jobs (job performance)	Moderate (.40 for GMA)

6.5   GMA in the UK

Although measures of GMA are used more widely for personnel selection in the UK than the US (Salgado & Anderson, 2002), until recently there was only scattered evidence for the validity of GMA in the prediction of job-related outcomes in UK studies, with most studies traditionally focusing on US data (Anderson, Born & Cunningham-Snell, 2001). However, a comprehensive meta-analysis of UK validity studies (283 independent samples and 75,311 people) has recently provided robust evidence for the power of GMA and specific abilities in the prediction of job performance and training across a wide range of occupations (Bertua, Anderson & Salgado, 2005). Table 6.5 reports the key findings. As shown, the validity of GMA in UK samples is comparable to that reported

Table 6.5 *Ability validities for job and training performance in the UK (based on Bertua et al., 2005)*

Measure	Job performance		Training performance	
	N (60 studies)	Corrected r	N (223 studies)	Corrected r
GMA	2,469	.48	17,982	.50
Verbal	3,464	.39	12,679	.49
Numerical	3,410	.42	15,925	.54
Perceptual	1,968	.50	13,134	.50
Spatial	1,951	.35	15,591	.42
Total	13,262	.42	75,311	.49

in US studies (see again Table 6.4). In addition, the UK results highlight the importance of specific cognitive abilities, particularly perceptual and numerical abilities in relation to both job and training performance, and verbal abilities in relation to training performance. Although the relevance of these specific abilities in UK studies overshadows the validity of specific abilities reported in the US by Hunter (1983b) (see also Section 6.8 below), three important issues should be noted. First, Bertua *et al.* did not test for incremental validity, which means it is uncertain whether the validities reported for specific abilities would have held if GMA had been controlled for. Second (a related issue), each of the specific abilities tested in the UK meta-analysis, especially those that showed the highest validities for both job and training performance, is *g*-saturated, meaning their correlations with job and training performance are at least in part a function of GMA. Third, the UK meta-analysis included many more recent studies than those reported in the above US studies.

Despite these minor methodological differences, one can only conclude that the UK studies on GMA and job performance and training mirror the findings from the US. This is in line with the reported overlap in choices of test for measuring GMA. Indeed, several US-designed tests are commonly used in the UK (e.g., the Differential Aptitude Test and the Minnesota Clerical Test) and vice versa (see Section 6.2 on the Raven's Progressive Matrices).

The UK data also replicated the positive association between the predictive power of GMA and the complexity levels of the job. Figure 6.6 depicts the corrected validities for GMA across various occupations in predicting job (white bars) and training (black bars) performance. As can be seen, professions that are more intellectually demanding, such as professional, engineering and managerial, require more GMA than those less cognitively complex professions (e.g., operator and driver). Interestingly, for complex jobs, GMA is a better predictor of job performance than of job training, whereas for simpler jobs, training seems to require more GMA than performance. This pattern of results is

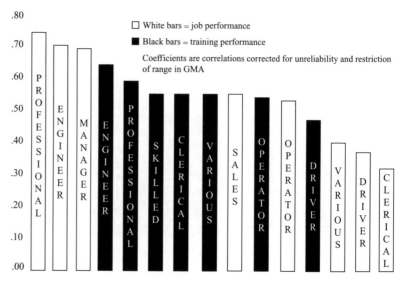

Figure 6.6 *Validity of GMA across occupations in the UK (based on Bertua et al., 2005)*

consistent with the idea that GMA is especially important for explaining individual differences in learning, which, in low-complexity professions, may not be that important after training, but, in high-complexity professions, may be needed especially in the job. However, it is clear (as much in the UK as in the US data) that GMA matters in every job and for both training and performance. Thus the authors concluded that:

> Selection practitioners and HR professionals in UK organisations should be encouraged to use psychometrically developed cognitive ability tests regardless if job type, hierarchical seniority, potential future changes in job role composition, or whether the tests are principally for general or specific abilities. Moreover, these findings highlight the importance of research-based practice in selection psychology and provide unequivocal evidence for the continued and expanded use of GMA tests for employee selection in UK organisations.   (Bertua *et al.*, 2005, p. 403)

6.6   GMA in Europe

Studies in the European Community (EC) echo the pattern of results from US and UK studies. A relatively recent examination of sixteen EC-member nations revealed that GMA tests are used in personnel selection more frequently in European than in US organisations, even though there is a larger percentage of small- and medium-size organisations in the EC than in the US (Salgado & Anderson, 2002). Another difference between the EC and the US is that EC nations are very homogeneous (i.e., there is little variability within countries in the EC) with regard to their testing policies and practices, which vary hugely across the US (Viswesvaran & Ones, 2002). But how comparable are the US validity studies of GMA to those of the EC?

A major meta-analysis (Salgado, Anderson, Moscoso, Bertua & De Fruyt, 2003) examined the results from ten EC nations (*N* range from 946 to 16,065). Salgado *et al.* reported operational validities (corrected correlation coefficients) for GMA of .54 for training and .62 for job performance. Specific cognitive abilities were also found to account for a substantial amount of variance of job and training performance. For training performance, corrected correlations ranged from .25 for perceptual ability to .48 for numerical ability. For job performance, corrected correlations ranging from .35 in the case of verbal ability to .56 in the case of memory ability. Although some of these validities approached the validity of GMA, as in the UK meta-analysis (see Section 6.5), the authors did not examine the incremental validity of specific abilities over and above GMA. However, verbal, spatial, numerical, perceptual and memory abilities had lower validities than GMA. Thus, based on the clear similarity between their own and US findings, Salgado *et al.* concluded that '[T]here is international validity generalisation for GMA and specific cognitive abilities for predicting job performance and training success. In order words, the criterion validity of cognitive measures generalises across different conceptualisations of job performance and training, differences in unemployment rates, differences in tests used, and differences in cultural values, demographics, and languages' (p. 592).

Salgado *et al.* also noted a few differences between their own and US results. At the level of specific abilities, perceptual ability had lower validities predicting training performance in the EC than in the US. At the GMA level, validities were larger in the EC for job performance, but larger in the US for training performance. The authors explained the former in terms of the higher-complexity jobs of the EC jobs examined (compared to the US studies, which included more lower-complexity jobs), and the latter in terms of the fact that US studies tended to measure training performance objectively, whereas EC studies tended to assess it subjectively (i.e., supervisory ratings) (for additional explanations see p. 593 of their article). In all, though, there are clearly more similarities than differences among EC, US and UK studies, and other international studies can be expected to yield very similar validities for GMA and specific abilities. It should, however, be noted that the US, UK and EC studies all looked at GMA in the context of industrialised and globalised economies. Given that the validity of GMA is moderated by job complexity, and since industrialised economies are characterised by a higher proportion of intellectually demanding jobs, one would expect somewhat lower predictive validities for GMA in undeveloped and developing nations, but meta-analytic evidence for these nations is yet to be provided (Lievens, 2007).

In another meta-analysis the same group of researchers examined the validity of GMA across different occupations in the EC (Salgado, Anderson, Moscoso,

Table 6.6 *Ability validities for job and training performance in the EC (Salgado et al., 2003a)*

Measure	Job performance		Training performance	
	N (93 studies)	Corrected r	N (97 studies)	Corrected r
GMA	9,554	.62	16,065	.54
Verbal	4,781	.35	11,123	.44
Numerical	5,241	.52	10,860	.48
Spatial-mechanical	3,750	.51	15,834	.40
Perceptual	3,798	.52	3,935	.25
Memory	946	.56	3,323	.34

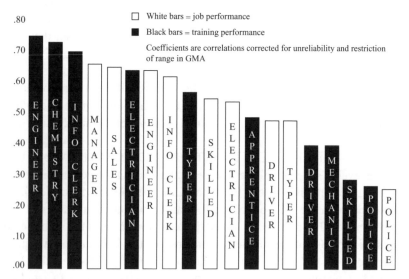

Figure 6.7 *Validity of GMA across occupations in the EC (based on Salgado et al., 2003)*

Bertua, De Fruyt & Rolland, 2003b). Results are graphically depicted in Figure 6.7. As shown, and similarly to Figure 6.6, validities for GMA ranged across occupations for both job and training performance, with GMA having moderate to substantial validities for job performance on all occupations except the police, where it had only modest validity. As regards training, validities showed an even wider range, with the weakest being police force jobs. These results replicate the findings of US meta-analysis (Hirsh, Northrop & Schmidt, 1986; Pearlman, Schmidt & Hunter, 1980), even with regard to the lower validity of police jobs. Thus the authors concluded that '[P]revious meta-analytic findings for the North American continent and now our findings for the European continent unequivocally support the use of tests of GMA for personnel selection regardless of job complexity or job occupation being selected for' (Salgado *et al.*, 2003b, p. 1077).

6.7   Longitudinal evidence

Whilst powerful, the above reviewed studies provide no longitudinal evidence for the predictive power of GMA, making interpretation of causational paths largely speculative. However, there is equally impressive evidence for the longitudinal validity of GMA in the prediction of job performance.

One of the first compelling demonstrations of the longitudinal predictive power of GMA in the context of job outcomes was published by Austin and Hanisch (1990). The authors analysed data from a large sample of the Project Talent dataset and found that GMA measures obtained during high school years predicted occupational attainment eleven years later. Two subsequent studies by Wilk and Sackett provided additional support for the longitudinal importance of GMA, showing that, over a period of five years, people with higher GMA tend to move upwards in the job level scale, whereas lower GMA people tend to move downwards (Wilk, Desmarais & Sackett, 1995). Moreover, congruency between GMA levels and typical GMA levels found for each job also predict people's likelihood of moving upwards or downwards (Wilk & Sackett, 1996).

Quite astonishingly, the longitudinal associations tend to hold even when socioeconomic status (SES) is taken into account. Thus, within the same family (where SES levels are the same for every member) family members with higher GMA tend to have significantly better jobs, and earn more, than their lower GMA relatives (Murray, 1998). In fact, at 1993 figures, and controlling for SES, people with average levels of GMA (IQ = 100) earned almost $20,000 less than siblings who were 20 IQ points brighter, and almost $10,000 more than siblings who scored 20 IQ points lower. These findings are consistent with earlier longitudinal data showing that, when GMA levels go up from one generation to the next, SES levels go up accordingly (Mascie-Taylor & Gibson, 1978). In a similar vein, Jencks *et al.* (1972) reported that sons' occupation and income levels correlated more significantly with their own IQ than with the occupation or educational level of their fathers. Recent studies have replicated these findings. For example, Deary and colleagues found that childhood GMA accounted for 23.2 per cent and parental social class for 17.6 per cent of the total variance in social status attainment in mid life (Deary *et al.*, 2005).

The most compelling evidence for the longitudinal validity of GMA in the prediction of occupational level and income was provided by a study spanning back almost four decades (Judge *et al.*, 1999). The authors reported correlations between GMA at age 12 and occupational level (r = .51) and income (r = .53) almost forty years later. Moreover, a reanalysis of these data (which also included the Big Five personality traits) estimated that the predictive power of GMA was almost 60 per cent higher than that of Conscientiousness (the trait that came second) (Schmidt & Hunter, 2004). Thus even very early measures of GMA – which can be expected to change quite a bit after the age of 12 (Ackerman, 2008, pp. 461–8) – seem to account for over 25 per cent of the variance in occupational status and income over almost two generations later, in a way that no other psychological traits can match.

6.8   Why, then, is IQ so unpopular?

Given the vast amount of compelling evidence for the predictive validity of GMA in the workplace, one has to wonder why IQ has remained such an unpopular and politically contested concept for many decades (Cronbach, 1975; Murphy, 2002). Although the reasons are multiple, let us at least examine some of the most probable causes for the 'bad image' of IQ inside and outside academic and occupational settings. Let us start with the academic counterclaims to the validity and importance of GMA.

A common academic counterclaim (though, given the above-reviewed evidence, the extent to which such claims may be considered academic is rightfully questionable) is that the predictive power of GMA is largely dependent on the specificity of the outcome measure or context. In simple terms, this argument refers to the idea (admittedly intuitive) that no two jobs are the same, and that IQ scores will inevitably be associated with some jobs more than others (just as, say, biodata items may be predictive of certain jobs but not others, as seen in Chapter 3). The alert reader will have already noted that the data reported above is in stark conflict with this assumption (for instance, Tables 6.3 and 6.4 refer to a wide range of studies looking at various types of jobs). Thus the 'situational specificity' argument – as this idea is called – is hard to accept unless one is unaware of the wealth of data mentioned above (see also Hunter & Hirsh, 1987). A more viable way of putting this argument forward, however, may be to argue that *specific* cognitive abilities rather than GMA are necessary to predict job outcomes accurately, or, at least, that specific abilities would be more appropriate predictors of specific job types (if, say, one were to rely on measures of spatial ability measures to predict how quickly an employee would learn a spatial task, e.g., driving, arranging furniture or reading maps). This point is still very intuitive, and respects even the original conceptualisation of GMA (Spearman, 1904), which left some room for specific abilities; but what do the data tell us?

When both specific and general abilities are taken into account, any variance in specific abilities unaccounted for by the general factor g (GMA) seems to be unrelated to job outcomes (Hunter, 1986; Jensen, 1986; Thorndike, 1986). This was the finding of another large-scale study by Hunter, looking at 20,256 US marines' training performance (Hunter, 1983b). As shown in Figure 6.8, when the latent factor of GMA is considered, training performance is not predicted

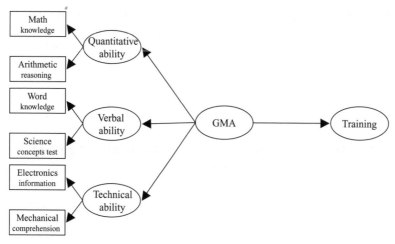

Figure 6.8 *Training performance is predicted by GMA rather than specific abilities (adapted from Hunter, 1983)*

by any specific abilities, i.e., there are no paths from quantitative, verbal or technical aptitudes to training performance. These results were also replicated by later investigations by Ree and colleagues, who reported minimal incremental validity for specific abilities over and above GMA (Ree & Earles, 1991a, 1991b, 1992; Ree, Earles & Teachout, 1994).

With regard to non-academic counterclaims or reasons why laypeople question the validity of IQ tests, perhaps the biggest reason is that laypeople (including the average employee) underestimate the real impact of individual differences underlying performance, masked by everyday behaviours at work. Thus people are quick to judge fellow workers on the basis of how sociable, well or badly behaved, they are at work. The fact of the matter is, though, that social behaviours have little to do with individuals' performance or actual productivity. As noted by Hunter and Schmidt:

> Many people who do not study work scientifically fail to distinguish between poor citizenship behaviour and poor performance. These are not highly correlated. There are people who are poor citizens but who can perform the work well. These poor citizens who can perform well when they perform are the workers that laypeople think of when they say 'Intelligence just doesn't matter that much at work'. However, there are many workers who are excellent citizens but who cannot do the job very well. These poor performers are usually tolerated by supervisors because they obviously try hard. These individuals also tend to be ignored by lay theories.   (1996, p. 449)

Thus laypeople have a natural tendency to judge their co-workers in terms of their social rather than performance-related behaviour. Even supervisory ratings of employees' performance are 'contaminated' by social behaviours (Orr, Sackett & Mercer, 1996), despite the fact that such behaviours bear little relationship to productivity. This is true not only for desirable but also undesirable social behaviours, such that unreliable, disorganised and argumentative employees are likely to be punished by both co-workers and supervisors even though they may be more productive than their reliable, organised and agreeable counterparts, though it has been recently shown that GMA is also associated with a number of counterproductive behaviours at work (see Section 6.11).

6.9   The inconvenient effects of the 'triple g': general, genetic and group differences

It is only when we jointly examine some of the causes and consequences of GMA that we can fully understand the reasons for the low popularity and political delicacy of the notion of IQ. Although a book on the psychology of personnel selection, one may argue, should not devote much time to discussing these issues, it is quite clear that people's conceptions – right or wrong – of GMA and IQ tests threaten the use of these tests in personnel selection. In fact, given the direct economic implications of selecting or not on the basis of GMA, we feel compelled to discuss not only the major controversies surrounding IQ but also some of the claims associated with the idea of using or banning such tests altogether.

As noted above, the first hard-to-digest issue is that GMA is very general and has equally general effects in the workplace, such that it predicts virtually every relevant occupational outcome, and in most cases better than specific abilities do. Thus GMA refers to very *general* differences in aptitudes that are reflected in multiple indicators of job performance in a generic fashion.

The second inconvenient issue is even harder to digest, namely, the well-established fact that there are strong genetic influences on GMA. Correlations between genetic similarity and IQ scores approach $r = .90$ in mid to late adulthood, leaving little room for environmental influences (Bouchard, 1998; Plomin, 2001). Furthermore, most of the environmental effects on GMA are *non-shared* – in broad terms, non-shared environment is what exposes children in the same family to different environmental influences (e.g., differential treatment from parents, school mates and teachers) – and probably 'respond' to genetic influences (Chamorro-Premuzic, 2007, pp. 90–101). For example, if one of two siblings is musically talented, his/her teachers may insist that he/she takes up extra piano lessons, which, in turn, will enhance the differences in musical competence with the other sibling. Although even the most radical geneticists would acknowledge, and often emphasise, that the genetic basis of GMA is far from behavioural determinism, it is hard (and not just for the layman) to see how this could be the case. Occupational success – or failure – is obviously not encoded in the genes, but the psychological traits that facilitate or hinder it most certainly are. It is estimated that about 20–25 per cent of the observed variability in occupational level and income is due to genetic differences in GMA (Gottfredson, 2004), and there are even fewer doubts about the stability of GMA across the lifespan. Studies have shown that, even over a period of sixty-five years, there is little variability in people's IQ scores (Deary, Whalley, Lemmon, Crawford & Starr, 2000), unless crystallised abilities, which increase until the age of 60 (Ackerman, 2008), are considered.

Although the stability of GMA has clear benefits for personnel selection (it would indeed be quite problematic to select someone on the basis of their IQ scores if their GMA levels changed drastically over time), it poses an important political question as to the limited lifelong job prospects of lower-GMA individuals even at an early age, particularly in industrialised nations. If, as we have seen is the case, IQ scores at age 12 are such strong predictors of occupational level and income later (Judge *et al.*, 1999) (see also Section 6.7), and GMA varies little over the lifespan, are lower-GMA individuals already 'condemned' or handicapped by the time they reach adolescence?

As if these two issues were not enough, there is the issue of *group differences* in GMA, which, in the context of personnel selection, tends to fall under the broader discussion of *adverse impact*. Thus '[C]ognitive ability tests represent the best single predictor of job performance, but also represent the predictor most likely to have substantial adverse impact on employment opportunities for members of several racial and ethnic minority groups' (Murphy, 2002, p. 173). For example, several robust studies, particularly in the US, report that whites tend to score higher than Hispanics, who tend to score higher than blacks on IQ tests. Estimates of white–black differences in IQ tend to give whites an average advantage of .85 to 1.00 standard deviation (that is, almost 15 IQ points), which is certainly 'not trivial' (Hough & Oswald, 2000, p. 636). Although group differences in job performance are somewhat less pronounced (Hattrup, Rock & Scalia, 1997; Waldman & Avolio, 1991), the mainstream view in intelligence research is that these differences are not caused by any test biases (Gottfredson, 1986, 1988, 2005; Jensen, 1980, 1998).

When the implications of the three inconvenient *g-facts*, or 'triple *g*' facts (general, genetic and group differences), are combined, they produce a chain of events that has clear social implications. First, it is evident that in globalised times industrialised societies are characterised by increasingly complex and less stable jobs that require more and more GMA. Newer jobs are more 'g-loaded' because they require rapid adaptation and highly effective performers (think, for instance, of the downsizing levels caused by mergers and acquisitions) (Sackett & Lievens, 2008). Second, these jobs also tend to pay more, and have higher occupational status attached, than low-complexity jobs. As a consequence of these two points, it is harder and harder for lower-IQ individuals to be in the higher-earning spectrum of society and to aspire to higher-status jobs. In fact, individuals with lower GMA are also at greater risk of being unemployed as technological advances make it possible to replace repetitive (and unintellectual) manual tasks with machine operations.

Despite this divisive picture of intellectual potential and job opportunities, there is little evidence for the benefits of ignoring GMA when it comes to selecting employees. In fact, most studies report just the opposite, namely detrimental effects of banning IQ-based personnel selection (Hunter & Schmidt, 1996), and its macro-economical consequences have been discussed elsewhere (Hunter & Schmidt, 1996). Given that higher-complexity jobs require higher GMA, and that even in lower-complexity jobs brighter employees are more productive – meaning the higher the GMA of the workforce the smaller the workforce can be – it is easy to imagine what these effects may be. On the other hand, GMA-based selection is not necessarily a disadvantage for any group of society, as individuals would be rated on the basis of their own capability rather than their group membership. Furthermore, social policy can easily address the issue of group inequalities in GMA by providing additional support for individuals with lower GMA, and this can be done at the *individual* rather than group level. Thus, just as people are not selected for their membership of any age, gender or ethnic group, their learning would not be supported on the basis of group membership but individual competence. For example, people with an IQ < 80 (about 10 per cent of whites and 30 per cent of blacks in the US) are currently considered unsuitable for the US army by federal law and there are few civilian employers who would hire under this GMA threshold (Gottfredson, 2005). If these people were equipped with additional training that enabled them to develop extra skills and acquire knowledge in key areas, the performance or training potential gap that separates them from their higher-IQ counterparts (e.g., white *or* black, male *or* female, young *or* old) would probably decrease. Thus social policy can address these issues without causing IQ-based stagnation. It may also be possible to redesign specific jobs in a way that removes unnecessary complexity from them, such that lower-IQ individuals can attain the same level of performance (in training and at work) without scarifying productivity levels, though tailoring the instructions of ability tests to make them more user-friendly for disadvantaged groups does not seem to eliminate group differences (DeShon, Smith, Chan & Schmitt, 1998).

Recent reviews also suggest that GMA differences between blacks and whites may be smaller than previously thought (Sackett & Lievens, 2008), and certainly less marked for specific cognitive abilities. For instance, short-term memory ability (measured via digit span or symbol substitution) yields average differences of less than $\frac{1}{2}$ SD despite having high validities – correlating with job performance at $r = .45$ (Verive & McDaniel, 1996). In addition, it has been noted that selecting on the basis of specific cognitive abilities may also be beneficial for *higher* GMA candidates as specific abilities are more weakly intercorrelated at higher levels of GMA (Lubinski & Benbow, 2000).

More importantly, it is important to emphasise that the effects of GMA are especially consequential ceteris paribus (i.e., all other things being equal) (Ackerman, 2008; Murphy, 2002), but this is rarely the case. In fact, even if group differences in GMA are negligible, applicants' own assessments of what they can and indeed are likely to produce may push them toward, or away from, potential jobs (Wilk & Sackett, 1996), and it is questionable whether taking up jobs that are seen as too demanding has more beneficial than detrimental consequences. In that sense, self-selection occurs regardless of personnel selection, and usually precedes it. This makes recent findings on individual differences in self-assessed intelligence very relevant in regards to career choices and personnel selection (Ackerman & Wolman, 2007; Chamorro-Premuzic, Harlaar & Plomin, 2008; Chamorro-Premuzic & Furnham, 2006b; Furnham & Chamorro-Premuzic, 2007).

6.10 Searching for mediators: GMA predicts job performance and training, but why?

> For practical purposes of prediction in personnel selection, it does not matter why GMA predicts job performance. However, scientific understanding requires theoretical explanation. Theoretical explanation is also required to gain acceptance of findings from those who question the plausibility of a central role for GMA in the determination of job performance. It is easier to accept an empirical finding when there is a theoretical explanation for that finding.   (Schmidt & Hunter, 2004, p. 170)

The main reason why GMA predicts job performance, and related outcomes, is that it causes faster, better, more effective and enduring knowledge acquisition. This is evident in the strong associations between GMA and training success reviewed in Sections 6.4, 6.5 and 6.6. In simple terms, having a higher IQ means being able to learn faster. One of the first psychological figures to formalise this was Edward Lee Thorndike, whose *classic theory* of job performance posited that individual differences in learning are the main driving force of individual differences in job performance (Brolyer, Thorndike & Woodyard, 1927). In occupational settings, formal learning – through training and instruction – as well as learning on the job, is influenced by GMA. As noted, 'because the rate and amount of learning is determined by cognitive ability, the classic theory predicts a high correlation between cognitive ability and learning' (Hunter & Schmidt, 1996, p. 461).

Hunter (1983a) set out to empirically validate this hypothesis by examining fourteen studies that included measures of GMA, job knowledge (a proxy of learning) and job performance as assessed both objectively and subjectively through supervisory ratings. Figure 6.9, adapted from Hunter and Schmidt (1996), summarises the path models for both military and civil samples. As shown, most of the effects of GMA on job performance are explained by job knowledge. Thus, GMA was positively correlated with supervisory ratings because of its positive effects on job knowledge, which means that, once individual differences in job knowledge are taken into account, differences in GMA are not associated with differences in supervisory ratings, though they still translate into higher job performance. It is also clear that job knowledge has a greater impact on supervisory ratings of performance than on actual job performance (Ree, Carretta & Teachout, 1995).

Although the job knowledge mediation suggests that the effects of GMA on job performance, at least as rated by supervisors, could be attenuated by offering more

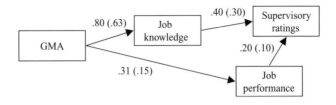

Note: Numbers in brackets show coefficients for military jobs; numbers outside brackets show coefficients for civilian jobs.

Figure 6.9 *Job knowledge mediates the effects of GMA on job performance and ratings (adapted from Hunter & Schmidt, 1996, based on fourteen studies analysed by Hunter, 1983a)*

training to lower-IQ individuals (a clear example of how the above-discussed psychological data could be used to *minimise* rather than maximise the effects of GMA on performance), this is probably not in the current agenda of many organisations, and not just in the western, industrialised world. Clearly, it is cheaper to hire fast learners or people who know their stuff already than to train slow learners or people who have yet to learn their stuff. Nonetheless, if the organisation's priority is to boost group parity, equity, non-discrimination and social diversity, a trade-off between validity and integration can surely be made. As recently noted:

> Reliance on cognitive ability measures in selection is likely to lead to more efficiency (i.e., higher average performance) and less equity (e.g., disparities in selection rates across racial and ethnic groups), whereas avoiding the use of cognitive ability measures is likely to lead to less efficiency and more equity. There is no scientific principle that can tell us which criteria *should* receive more evidence, but scientific research can clearly inform us of the consequences of emphasising one criterion or the other.   (Murphy, 2002, p. 183, italics in the original)

Clearly, criteria are influenced by market demands and in the past decades technological advances in the workplace have certainly increased the importance of individuals' learning potential in comparison to the knowledge and experience they may have already gained.

It appears that even hiring on the basis of previous experience does not diminish the impact of GMA on subsequent training and job performance. In Hunter's (1980) seminal meta-analysis, mean job experience was over five years and GMA still correlated with job performance at r = .51 (see also Hunter, 1986). Indeed, Schmidt and colleagues (Schmidt, Hunter, Outerbridge & Goff, 1988) found that ability differences in job knowledge where as marked after five years as after a single year. On the other hand, research evidence shows that the experience–performance correlation decreases with time in the job (from r = .49 during the first three years to merely r = .15 after twelve years in the job) (McDaniel, Schmidt & Hunter, 1988), whereas the opposite occurs with the

GMA-performance correlation (from r = .35 during the first three years to .r = .59 after 12 years of age) (McDaniel, 1985). That said, knowledge acquisition is not only determined by GMA.

Much of the theoretical and empirical work of Phillip Ackerman and Ruth Kanfer focuses on the 'non-ability' determinants of skills acquisition and adult knowledge. The underlying threat to this programme of research is the idea that GMA is mainly helpful at initial stages of skills acquisition and particularly in so-called 'inconsistent-tasks' (which require ongoing intellectual application). For 'consistent-tasks', however (e.g., typing, driving and answering phone-calls), *typical* levels of performance – what a person is motivated to do and normally does – are more important than *maximal* levels of performance – what a person *can* do (Ackerman, 1987; Cronbach, 1960; Sackett, Zedeck & Fogli, 1988). Performance on short tasks tends to be determined mostly by GMA, whereas performance on longer-term, everyday tasks is strongly influenced by an array of motivational and personality traits, which tend to fluctuate less in short-term performance assignments (Sackett *et al.*, 1988). As discussed in Chapter 7 (see also Hough, Oswald & Ployhart, 2001), these non-ability traits have been less frequent targets of political debate.

Thus, relying on non-ability traits and using multiple methods of assessment should reduce adverse impact without necessarily sacrificing predictive power, though the idea of not resigning predictive power if GMA measures are excluded is close to inconceivable (Gottfredson, 1996; Murphy, 2002).

Another reason why IQ tests predict job performance is that higher GMA is linked to higher *job role breadth*, enabling brighter employees to perform a wider range of tasks and, in turn, be rated more highly by their supervisors (Morgeson, Delaney-Klinger & Hemingway, 2005). These findings are consistent with the idea that higher GMA is associated with higher levels of intellectual curiosity, Openness to Experience and need for cognition (Chamorro-Premuzic & Furnham, 2004, 2005, 2006b), and the importance of problem-solving even beyond tested cognitive ability. For example, recent studies on Openness show that it is a critical determinant of cross-cultural training and coping with organisational change (George & Zhou, 2001), whereas studies on assessment centres show that problem-solving is the most important determinant of candidate's performance (Arthur, Day, McNelly & Edens, 2003).

6.11   GMA and counterproductive work behaviours

Although most applied psychologists employ cognitive ability tests to predict positive outcomes, such as learning, training and job performance (Ones, Viswesvaran & Dilchert, 2005), the importance of GMA at work is not limited to the wide range of desirable outcomes it predicts. Indeed, GMA has been negatively associated with workplace deviance, also referred to as *counterproductive work behaviours* (e.g., employee theft, high absenteeism levels and misuse of resources). These behaviours are commonly encompassed under the heading of workplace deviance, which has been defined in terms of 'voluntary behaviour that violates significant organisational norms and in so doing threatens the well-being of an organisation, its members, or both' (Robinson & Bennett, 1995, p. 556). It has been estimated that these behaviours could cost the US economy as much as $200 billion a year (Greenberg, 1997; Murphy, 1993; Vardi & Weitz, 2004; see also Bennett & Robinson, 2000).

After many decades of little research in this area, a recent US investigation of 1,799 police officers (of similar SES) (Dilchert, Ones, Davis & Rostow, 2007) reported substantial negative associations between IQ – measured during job applications – and several counterproductive behaviours at work – taken from the archive after several months of employment. Examples of counterproductive behaviours assessed in this study were racially offensive conduct, excessive use of force, misused official vehicles and destroying official property. In line with previous theoretical propositions (White, Moffitt & Silva, 1989) the authors interpreted the negative correlation between IQ and workplace deviance in terms of the protective or *inhibitory effects* of higher GMA, which enables brighter individuals to better predict or foresee the negative consequences of deviant behaviours, therefore inhibiting maladaptive behaviours. Particularly lower-GMA individuals would be characterised by 'a deficit in foreseeing temporally remote consequences of actions' (Lubinski, 2000, p. 430). As noted, however, this is a rather new area of research and replication of the negative link between GMA and deviant behaviours at work, particularly from longitudinal studies, is deemed necessary before implementing GMA measures solely for this purpose. Until then, it is more appropriate to associate counterproductive behaviours, and behavioural problems in general, with personality traits rather than cognitive ability, especially the personality trait of Conscientiousness and its primary facet of dependability (Dudley, Orvis, Lebiecki & Cortina, 2006) (see also Section 7.6). Special attention should be devoted to these non-ability traits as they are generally uncorrelated (Bobko *et al.*, 1999; Sackett & Lievens, 2008) – and often even negatively correlated (Ackerman & Heggestad, 1997; Chamorro-Premuzic & Furnham, 2006b) – with cognitive abilities.

6.12   Retesting, practice and coaching effects

Despite their impressive validity as predictors of job outcomes, cognitive ability tests are not perfect measures of GMA because individuals' performance on ability tests is also affected by a number of non-ability factors (e.g., negatively by anxiety and worry, positively by motivation and confidence) (Chamorro-Premuzic & Furnham, 2004). In occupational settings, individuals may wish to retest in order to maximise their chances of employment or promotion, and indeed an estimated 25–50 per cent of people have been reported to retake ability tests in the US (Hausknecht, Halpert, Di Paolo & Di Paulo, 2007). The question therefore arises of whether a one-time measure of GMA can provide the most accurate

Table 6.7 *Explanations for practice effects (test score gains) on IQ*

Source	Explanation
Anastasi, 1981	Development of or improvement in actual abilities (require substantial intellectual investment from the individual)
Messick & Jungeblut, 1981	Decrease in test-anxiety due to previous test experience
Kulik, Kulik & Bangert, 1984	Memory of questions and answers in previous test
Sackett, Burris & Ryan, 1989	Improvement in test-taking strategies
Campbell & Kenny, 1999	Regression to the mean (i.e., the statistical sampling artefact that results from the fact that only people who scored relatively low in the initial test would be expected to request a second testing session, whilst those who did well in the first instance would not return for a second testing session)
Hausknecht *et al.*, 2007	Mere repetition (e.g., enhanced understanding of instructions or items without specific training); may occur even after completing other ability tests; another explanation is formal instruction (coaching) between sessions

indicator of an individual's potential to succeed in the workplace or elsewhere. This led researchers to examine the issue of retesting the same individuals on the same test or slightly modified versions of it, looking at practice effects (i.e., score gains from one test administration to the next) and coaching effects (i.e., assisted practice effects, that is, practice with formal instructions).

On the one hand, the reliability of IQ tests renders substantial intra-individual differences in IQ test performance unlikely, and, indeed, testing agents often invalidate second-attempted scores if they are significantly larger than the original score (Harcourt Assessment, 2005), whereas the US Air Force bans retesting in some of the components of its selection battery for pilots. Yet IQ and other ability tests measure maximal performance at a given time, and a single test administration may not capture the person's GMA accurately if underperformance occurred. Consequently (but in some conflict with the previous point), it has been recommended that 'employers should provide opportunities for reassessment and reconsidering candidates whenever technically and administratively feasible' (SIOP, 2003, p. 57) and that 'every test taker should have a fair chance to demonstrate his or her best performance on an assessment procedure', such that employers should 'consider retesting or using alternative assessment procedures before screening the individual' (US Department of Labor, 1999, Section 4, pp. 8–2).

Although several explanations for practice or unassisted training effects have been proposed (see Table 6.7), the fact is that practice *does* increase ability test performance, albeit marginally. Messick and Jungeblut's (1981) seminal study on the SAT concluded that score increases of approximately 3 per cent would require as much coaching or assisted practice time as full-time school education, and that the effects of coaching tend to decrease after initial coaching time. More recently, a meta-analysis of 107 samples (reported in fifty studies) revealed score gains of about 1/4 of a standard deviation between the first two test sessions and increases of over 1/2 of a standard deviation between the first and the third testing session (Hausknecht *et al.*, 2007). These results imply that candidates scoring in the 50th percentile when initially tested could be expected to score over the 70th percentile on their third attempt, which suggests larger practice effects than those reported by Messick and Jungeblut (1981), though the meta-analysis did confirmed that the effects of coaching diminish over time. In addition, the meta-analysis also highlighted the importance of having at least twelve months' interval between test administrations in order to reduce the risk of score gains due to memory of items.

6.13   Summary and conclusions

The present chapter has examined the validity of GMA – and IQ tests – in the prediction of major job outcomes, such as occupational level, job knowledge and job performance. Regardless of the criterion we choose, it is clear that GMA is a fundamental and very powerful predictor of positive job outcomes. Evidence also indicates that the predictive power of GMA is rivalled by no other psychological construct (see, for instance, Chapters 3 on biodata and 7 on personality to understand how much more valid cognitive ability tests are).

Although GMA is a strong predictor of overall job performance (correlating at about r = .50, and thus explaining 25 per cent of the variance in job performance), it matters most in complex or intellectually demanding jobs (where it correlates at about r = .80 with job performance) and least in unintellectual or cognitively simple jobs (where it correlates with job performance at about r = .20). Objective measures of performance correlate more highly with GMA measures than subjective assessments of performance, such as supervisory ratings, do. This is because the latter – but not the former – are 'intoxicated' by a wide range of job-irrelevant variables, such as sociability, friendliness, looks and compatibility between the worker and the supervisor's personality traits. This is consistent with the finding that personality traits predict supervisory ratings better than objective performance tests (see Section 7.4).

Specific abilities, that is, variance in cognitive abilities unaccounted for by the general GMA factor, are insignificant predictors of job performance and related outcomes once GMA is taken into account. This is counterintuitive to most people because the layperson tends to overestimate the importance of situational and job-specific factors when interpreting the determinants of work performance. Likewise, most people tend to see their abilities as being heterogeneous, though in fact within-individual differences in abilities are marginal compared to interindividual differences.

Why does GMA predict job performance and related outcomes? Primarily because it accounts for individual differences in learning, specifically how quickly and in what depth people can learn a task, and acquire and retrieve information, both through formal training and informally through experience. Thus job knowledge has been found to partly mediate the effects of GMA on job performance, suggesting that the main – but not only – reason why higher-IQ individuals do better is because they are more knowledgeable in the job. The fact that not all the effects of GMA on job performance can be explained by GMA-related knowledge acquisition has been interpreted in terms of the beneficial effects of GMA on those aspects of jobs that are 'less routinised or less closely supervised; more fraught with change, ambiguity, unpredictability, and novelty (and hence are inherently less trainable); or otherwise require greater exercise of independent judgement and innovative adaptation' (Gottfredson, 2004, p. 175).

Despite the overwhelming body of evidence in support of the predictive validity of GMA in the workplace, the use of cognitive ability tests in personnel selection remains somewhat controversial because of the widely replicated *adverse impact* that GMA-based selection has on specific groups. Clearly, a key aim of civilised and industrialised economies is to provide work opportunities for its wide workforce but the fact that top jobs (which tend to be cognitively complex and require fast and efficient learning) seem out-of-reach for lower-GMA individuals, and that these people are found more frequently in some ethnic or gender groups than in others, creates a conflict between economic integration and productivity. That said, GMA is neither morally *wrong* or *right* but simply a useful – and accurate – indicator of people's ability to learn new things, solve complex problems and adapt to the environment. Furthermore, people's differences in GMA are mostly independent of any group differences as within each group individuals differ in cognitive abilities. More importantly, work performance is not only determined by people's cognitive abilities (even in top jobs), which makes it necessary to look at other constructs in other to explain, understand and ultimately predict occupational success.

Notes

1 For many years, however, there has been a tradition in occupational and industrial/organisational psychology to use 'intelligence' to refer to general mental ability after it reached a point of maturity (Hunter & Schmidt, 1996).
2 The fourth edition of the WAIS is in preparation.
3 It has been pointed out (Schmidt, Ones & Hunter, 1992) that some of the most important evidence for the validity of GMA with regard to job performance and similar outcomes is not available in the form of books and journal articles, but only reported in the form of technical reports or manuals, which are often more difficult to access. Anastasi presented a core summary of the main trends in GMA testing until the late 1980s (Anastasi, 1989), and a comprehensive review of the validity studies on GMA conducted on the Armed Services Vocational Aptitude Battery (ASVAB) has also been published (Welsh, Watson & Ree, 1990).
4 Its modern version is O'NET, a computerised delivery system that links jobs to specific attributes; see Hough & Oswald (2000).
5 Corrected only for unreliability in criterion.

7 Personality traits

7.1 Introduction

The previous chapter dealt with the validity of GMA (general mental ability) as a predictor of job and training performance, as well as other work-related outcomes. In the current chapter, we discuss the predictive power of personality traits.

The question then emerges as to what is the difference between GMA and personality traits, and this is a question for which only one simple answer exists: traditionally (in personnel selection as well as in the wider context of psychological assessment), GMA is measured or *tested* via objective performance tests (such as those discussed in Section 6.6 and 6.7), whereas personality traits are *assessed* via subjective inventories, notably self- or other-reports (but especially self-reports). In that sense, one can distinguish between cognitive abilities and personality traits on the basis of assessment methods, whereby the former reflect individual differences in the capacity to identify correct responses to a standardised test (verbal or non-verbal), whereas the latter reflect individual differences in general behavioural tendencies, assessed only subjectively, that is, through people's accounts (one's own or others'). This led to a now well-established distinction in psychology to refer to cognitive abilities in terms of *maximal performance* and personality traits in terms of *typical performance* (Cronbach & Gleser, 1965), though in the case of personality traits 'behaviour' is a more accurate term than 'performance'.

As much as this distinction is straightforward, things get more complex when we try to assess whether measures of ability and inventories of personality may or not be tapping into the same underlying constructs. That is, is the distinction between personality and abilities only relevant at the level of measured constructs, and therefore a purely methodological issue, or are personality inventories and ability tests also assessing similar constructs? Let us chose a simple example to illustrate this question. Let us say that we want to measure individual differences in running, specifically how fast people can run. One option would be to test a number of subjects in a 100 metre race and time how fast they run (using a stopwatch). Another option would be to *ask* people how fast they can run, and we would be willing to bet that at least 90 per cent of our readers would find the first option better than the second. Why? There are two main reasons. First, people may be unaware of how fast they can run. Second, even if they were aware, they may be unwilling to tell us (especially if we were giving out medals or cash to the fastest runners). Thus, they may chose to exaggerate how fast they can run and try to deliberately mislead us. Of course, one may ask other people (their friends or indeed their enemies) how fast our candidates can run, but the same problems apply, i.e., the friends may be as unwilling or unable to provide this information as the runners themselves, and enemies can hardly be expected to be more accurate.

Our readers may have guessed that these two problems also apply to personality inventories, as personality traits are only assessed subjectively. Indeed, this has been the most common objection to using personality scales in personnel selection and, accordingly, a large part of this chapter is devoted to this issue. But let us make clear at the outset that there are some advantages in using subjective[1] reports rather than objective performance tests. In fact, these advantages highlight some of the limitations of objective assessment methods (briefly discussed in Section 6.13) and explain the importance of using personality inventories in personnel selection. The first issue is that subjective reports can take into account aggregate data, that is, how people have been performing or how they perform most of the time (this has already been shown in Chapter 3 on biodata). Thus, in the context of our running example, asking the runners or people who are familiar with them how fast they can run may provide information on how fast these people *usually* run, as well as how fast they have managed to run in the past. If we were only interested in how fast people *can* run, this may or not be a good approach. However, it is clear that if we were interested in how fast they *tend to run*, then objective performance tests would be very poor indicators of this: even Olympic-medal winners don't run as fast as they can most of the time.

There is also a second issue, which is that objective performance tests (i.e., timing people once, or testing their ability once) may not be accurate, especially if factors other than running ability interfere. Examples of such factors can range from fatigue or test-anxiety (including fear of evaluation, which may explain why even professional athletes may record faster times in training than in the actual competition) to a heavy hangover. This phenomenon, simply referred to as *underperformance* (understandably, 'over-performance' is rarely an issue), threatens the validity of objective tests but does not harm subjective reports. In fact, there are two main reasons underlying the fact that psychometric tests do not perfectly predict any outcomes: the first is that they may be failing to measure the construct in a completely accurate manner; the second is that, even if they do, that construct may be only one of the determinants of the outcome we wish to predict. In a sense, these two reasons are the same and merely one: tests that capture not just running ability but also fatigue, test-anxiety and hangover (to stay with the above example) should therefore predict running performance better than tests that capture only one of the predictors. This logic has been applied to personality inventories and ability measures (Chamorro-Premuzic & Furnham, 2006a; Wechsler, 1939). As shown in Figure 7.1, measures of academic performance, such as general point average (GPA), can be used to validate both

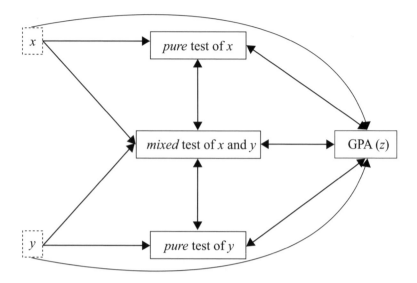

Note: x = 'actual' cognitive ability, y = 'actual' trait anxiety, GPA = grade point average, x and y are predictors, z is the criterion. Since z is influenced by both x and y, tests of x and y will correlate higher with z than *pure* tests of x or y only. ☐ measure ☐ latent ◄───► correlation ───► influence

Figure 7.1 *Ability and non-ability determinants of grade-point average (GPA) (from Chamorro-Premuzic & Furnham, 2006a)*

ability and personality scales. Given that GPA is determined by both ability and personality, tests that capture ability as well as non-ability variance should be stronger predictors of either pure ability or pure personality scales alone.

But we were trying to determine whether personality and ability measures may be assessing similar or at least related constructs, rather than deciding which method is more valid. The truth of the matter is that the only way to determine what any psychological instrument is assessing is to use external validity criteria, and, ironically, that is the very problem with psychological assessment, namely the fact that there is no absolute or ultimate criterion. Thus it is always possible to run faster or slower next time, and in fact very unlikely that anyone runs exactly as fast both times. Moreover, because any variable – whether running ability or personality – correlates with and predicts a wide range of other variables/outcomes, the choice of criterion is rarely unquestionable.

With regard to job and training performance, which have been the criteria *par excellence* in personnel selection for over a century, it is interesting that although GMA is a good predictor of job and training performance, we use maximal performance measures (ability tests) to predict typical performance (aggregate levels of achievement at work, for instance income or occupational level). Further, ability tests rarely account for more than 30 per cent of the real variance in job performance (Schmidt & Hunter, 1998), which is one of the

> *Observation:* Watching what people do most of the time (unfeasible and expensive). Interviews and biodata are largely used to 'observe' (infer) people's personalities.

> *Recommendation letters:* Used extensively. Though not explicit personality tests, they provide information on the personality of the candidate/applicant/etc.

> *Psychometric inventories:* Most common way of assessing personality traits, mainly self-reports but can also be completed on behalf of others (other-reports).

> *Projective tests:* Assume that people's unconscious motives or traits are 'projected' (spontaneously expressed); require interpretation from an expert.

> *Objective tests:* Range from physiological measures (transpiration, heart beat, etc.) to response latency (reaction times in self-report responses); long but failed quest.

> *Situational tests:* Putting people in specific situations to see how they react: e.g., in front of others to see if they can lead; in tempting situations to see if they cheat/steal.

Figure 7.2 *Ways of assessing personality traits*

main reasons why in the past fifteen years a growing number of researchers have examined the predictive validity of subjective inventories. The other main reason is adverse impact, as group differences in personality traits are less pronounced than in GMA (see Section 6.5). But the crucial point is that it would make little sense to assess personality if personality inventories were assessing the same constructs as ability tests (Chamorro-Premuzic & Furnham, 2004). Accordingly, even if personality and ability measures are related, they should be independently related to external criteria.

So, what do personality inventories assess, if not intellectual abilities, and, more importantly, why should personality inventories predict job performance if they do not assess cognitive abilities? This chapter will address these two questions.

It should be noted that personality traits are not only assessed via self-report inventories (though that is indeed the most common way of assessing them). Observation, situational tests, projective techniques and even objective measures can also serve as measures of personality, albeit not explicitly (see Figure 7.2). The most commonly used forms of observation in personnel selection are interviews (see Chapter 2) and biodata (see Chapter 4). Employers may not explicitly state that what they are assessing in an interview or looking for in biodata is indeed traces of personality, but there is longstanding evidence for the fact that candidates'/interviewees' personality traits affect employers' decisions (Wagner, 1949), despite the fact that most interviewees fake (Levashina & Campion, 2007). When employers search biodata records they are looking for markers or consequential outcomes of personality traits. In fact, an individual's background or past would mean very little unless it contributed to predicting what he or she will do in the future (as seen in Chapter 4). Hence consistency underlies the motivation to search for people's biographical records and use that information for organisational decision making. Although biodata measures do overlap with personality inventories (see Section 4.8), they have been shown to have incremental validity over personality (as well as GMA) in the prediction of work performance (Mount, Witt & Barrick, 2000). At the same time, personality inventories have been found to show incremental validity over and above biodata in the prediction of similar outcomes (McManus & Kelly, 1999). Situational tests are a way of 'economising' observations, creating situations that may trigger the behaviours one wishes to observe. Thus they can also be regarded as consequential outcomes of personality traits, though there is longstanding evidence for the fact that personality inventories are only modestly correlated with single behaviours (at a given point in time) (see Box 7.1). On the other hand, the problem with letters of recommendation (and other reports in general) is that they are provided by people who tend to have an interest in the candidate/applicant or at least reasons for being biased in favour of the candidate. Finally, projective tests – which can range from the Rorschach inkblot test (see Section 1.8) to interpretation of dreams – have vanished quite rapidly since the 1970s, although certain techniques, such as graphology (a projective test whereby candidates 'project' aspects of their personality in their writing styles) are still widely employed in certain countries (see Section 1.2), such as France and Argentina, despite evidence that it does not work (Ben-Shakhar, Bar-Hillel, Bilu, Ben-Abba & Flug, 1986; Furnham, Chamorro-Premuzic & Callahan, 2003).

Although it has long been argued that personality traits – or indeed any psychological construct – should not be assessed only with one method, e.g., self-report or interview (Prien, 1977), but with a multi-method approach (Marsh, Martin & Hau, 2006), most researchers and practitioners continue to rely on single methods of assessment and, in the case of personality, that method is self-report inventories. However, it is important to disentangle the variance that is caused by the method of assessment and the actual trait or construct that is being assessed. This is a complex theoretical and methodological issue: for example, self-reports of cognitive ability tend to correlate with performance tests of cognitive ability only at $r = .40$ (Chamorro-Premuzic, Moutafi & Furnham, 2005), meaning they share less than 20 per cent of the variance. This could be indicative of the fact that self-reports and performance-based tests are actually assessing different constructs (and there is wide acceptance that the latter capture the real essence of cognitive ability because they are correlated more highly with performance outcomes). However, with regard to personality traits, objective tests tend to be validated against self-reports, and self-reports are often validated against other-reports (though these are rarely substantially intercorrelated).

Self-report inventories are what people usually call 'personality tests', namely different statements or questions that are answered on a 'yes/no' or 'strongly disagree' to 'strongly agree' response scale. These questions or items are then used to compute overall factors, giving people different scores along different personality dimensions or categorising them in terms of one personality type or another (e.g., 'Extraverted' vs 'Introverted'). What all these variations have

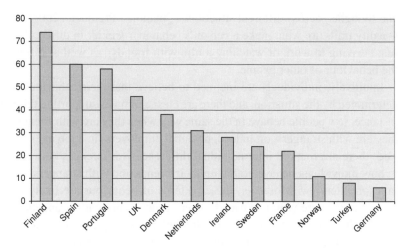

Figure 7.3 *Percentage of companies using psychometric tests in Western Europe (Price Waterhouse Cranfield data, 1994)*

in common is that they assume that respondents are capable of and interested in providing the relevant information about themselves, and that the scores will have cross-temporal reliability (be relatively stable across time) and predictive validity (predict external outcomes, such as job performance). There are four major ways to assess the quality or *construct validity* of personality inventories: (a) *face validity* (in simple terms, how valid do the scales look?); (b) *content validity* (asking questions that genuinely assess the construct we want to assess); (c) *predictive validity* (generating scores that relate to external outcomes); and (d) *factorial validity* (identifying and replicating the same latent dimensions via the same set of items). These four criteria can be applied to the various ways of assessing personality traits specified in Figure 7.2.

The Price Waterhouse Cranfield survey (Dany & Torchy, 1994) found that psychometric testing was used only infrequently in most Western European countries. As shown in Figure 7.3, psychometric tests were used in selection widely only in Finland, and to some extent in Spain and Portugal, but in the remaining Western European countries most companies did not use them and in some countries (Norway, Turkey and Germany) they were barely used at all. US surveys indicate that American organisations (at least in 1997) used personality scales only infrequently. A survey of 251 US employers who were asked to rate how frequently, on a five-point scale (1 = never, 3 = sometimes, 5 = always), they used personality inventories for personnel selection showed the average for both graduate and general jobs to be lower than 2 (closer to 'never' than 'sometimes').

7.2 What are personality traits?

Personality traits are widely defined as stable, inner, personal dispositions that determine relatively consistent patterns of behaviour (including feelings and thoughts) across different situations (Chamorro-Premuzic, 2007). Thus personality traits are what make a person's behaviour similar in different situations (e.g., driving to work or watching a film with friends), as well as different from the behaviour of other people.

Intuitively, individuals are inclined to believe that their behaviour is largely determined by the situation, and there are clear examples supporting this idea. For instance, few people behave in the same way when they are with friends as when they are with strangers, or, indeed, potential employers (in a job interview). That said, there are marked interindividual differences (differences between people) in how individuals behave both with their friends and with strangers – including in a job interview. Moreover, these patterns of behaviour are likely to emerge every time we are with our friends, every time we are with strangers and every time we have a job interview. Thus, although most people are more at ease in the company of friends than in the company of strangers, and although most people are more anxious during a job interview than while watching a film with friends, *some people* are clearly more comfortable interacting with strangers than others, even in a job interview. Likewise, *some people* are characterised by a tendency to worry all the time, even when they are watching a film with friends (in fact, if they are watching a film just before a job interview they may be completely unable to concentrate on the film), whereas *other people* rarely feel worried or anxious about things (in fact, if they are watching a film before a job interview they may be so relaxed that they forget about the interview).

The key to understanding personality traits is understanding both how people differ and how they are similar. In that sense, personality traits are the cause of behavioural differences among individuals in a given situation, and since these differences are maintained across a number of situations, personality traits should predict how people will behave in comparison to other people most of the time. Accordingly, behaviour can be understood as a product of both situational and personal variables (see Figure 7.4).

Situational variables, which have been traditionally studied within social psychology and under laboratory or experimental conditions, make behavioural differences among people less noticeable. An example of a situational variable affecting behaviour in the workplace may be the prospect of a pay rise (reward) or demotion (punishment), both of which should motivate employees to work more. However, not all employees may be equally responsive to this situation; some may be more likely to work more if they are threatened with demotion, whereas others may only be motivated to increase their productivity if they are tempted with a pay rise. Accordingly, the behaviour we are trying to predict, namely *work output* or productivity, is determined by both the situation (the prospect of rewarding or punishing employees) and personality traits (whatever makes one person more responsive to the prospects of reward and punishment than another person). Thus behaviour (b) is determined (=) by situational (S) and personality (P) factors. Moreover, because the effects of one situation will be different for one person than another (see Figure 7.4), the correct formula to

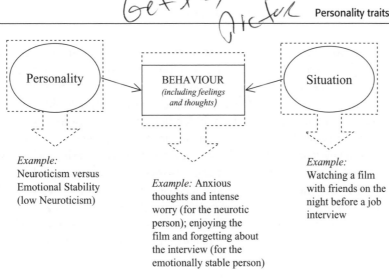

Figure 7.4 *Behaviour as a function of both personality and the situation*

represent the relationship between b, S and P is that of an interaction, namely b = S × P. The multiplication sign illustrates the fact that, if either S or P has a value of 0, the other variable will have no effect on b. For example, an employee may have no ambition of getting a pay rise and may not care about demotion either, which would mean that neither the prospect of a pay rise or a demotion would change his or her work output. Conversely, if an employer is only doing the job for the money and is worried about not earning enough, he or she will be very responsive to the situation.

Box 7.1 Situationalism: undermining personality traits

During the 1960s, the notion of personality traits came under heavy scrutiny when psychologists (especially Walter Mischel) pointed out that personality traits are very weak predictors of behavioural outcomes because behaviour is essentially inconsistent (Mischel, 1968). Thus Mischel concluded that measures of personality (e.g., Extraversion) rarely correlate with behavioural criteria (e.g., being talkative) by more than r = .30. This conclusion had a strong negative impact on the research community and led to stagnation in personality research that was also noticeable in the field of applied psychology and personnel selection. However, Mischel and proponents of *situationalism*, i.e., the idea that behaviour is explained better in terms of contextual factors and weakly in terms of inner dispositions, overlooked the importance of personality traits as predictors of aggregate or long-term behavioural outcomes (Eysenck, 1980). Just as it is hard for weather forecasters to make accurate predictions about the weather until one or two days in advance, personality inventories provide poor information of their behavioural consequences at a specific given time. Like the weather, behaviour does change from one moment to the next. Yet weather forecasts are usually accurate at predicting that the temperature in *x* month will be much warmer than in *y* month, and that, during *x* month, the south will be warmer than the north (Hogan, 1996). Likewise, personality inventories are useful for making predictions of broad behavioural outcomes, especially when situational factors are taken into account (see Section 5.1). In short, personality traits are general constructs and their criteria should be equally general. When this 'bandwith fidelity' is taken into account, trait inventories have shown more than adequate reliability throughout the lifespan, with fifty-year interval test–retest correlations of .25, and usually higher for shorter time periods (Hogan, 1996). Moreover, a meta-analysis reported average test–retest reliabilities for personality in the region of .75 (Viswesvaran, 2000).

7.3   The Big Five: emergence of the five-factor model

The central issue in personality research is not what personality traits are or whether personality traits exist or are useful, but, rather, *which* personality traits should be assessed. In the past twenty years, psychologists have provided compelling evidence for the fact that individual differences in personality can be classified on the basis of five major traits, namely Neuroticism/Emotional Stability, Extraversion/Introversion, Agreeableness, Conscientiousness and Openness to Experience (sometimes referred to as Intellect, Autonomy, or simply 'Factor V'). Indeed, many psychologist believe that these traits capture the essence of interindividual variability by providing a general level of description of the person (P rather than S), which, if valid, should help us predict how people will behave in the future. Although it is questionable whether the Big Five offer the best classification of individual differences (Block, 1995), they are the common currency and universal language in personality research and can be converted or translated into many different taxonomies. Figure 7.5 shows how several different taxonomies and labels can be organised neatly along the five major personality factors. As can be seen, different systems (each row represents a different taxonomy[2]) can be organised quite coherently on the basis of the five personality dimensions lined up at the top (Extraversion, Agreeableness, Conscientiousness, Openness and Neuroticism). Traditionally, this description has not included individual differences in cognitive ability, though in the past ten years a number of researchers have argued that an integration of ability and non-ability traits is needed to provide a more comprehensive picture of the determinants of academic and occupational performance and related outcomes (Ackerman & Heggestad, 1997; Armstrong, Day, McVay & Rounds, 2008; Chamorro-Premuzic & Furnham, 2005; Matthews, 1999).

It is noteworthy that although personality traits were neither identified to predict behaviour at work nor for the purpose of personnel selection, and even though

Extraversion	Agreeableness	Conscientiousness	Openness	Neuroticism
Dominance Initiative	Social orientation	Task orientation		Emotional orientation
Low ego control		High ego control	Ego resiliency	
Activity–Sociability		Impulsivity	Emotionality	
Exvia vs Invia	Pathemia vs Cortertia	Super Ego Strength	Independence Subduedness	Adjusted vs Anxiety
Positive Emotionality		Constraint	Absorption	Negative Emotionality
Extraversion	Psychoticism			Neuroticism
Outgoing, Social, Leadership	Self-protected Orientation	Work Orientation	Aesthetic Intellectual	Dependence
Ambition and Sociability	Likeability	Prudence	Intellect	Adjustment
Extraversion vs Introversion	Feeling vs Perceiving	Judging vs Perceiving	Intuition vs Sensing	Agreeableness

Figure 7.5 *Big Five as universal language of personality. Different rows indicate different researchers' systems*

personality is supposedly unrelated to cognitive ability, the fact that personality traits describe general and consistent differences between individuals means they are useful also in the context of personnel selection, as predictors of work-related behaviours. Moreover, and as mentioned in Section 7.1, if personality traits assess individual differences that are largely independent from cognitive abilities, any information they provide may actually help us improve on the prediction of work-related behaviours beyond cognitive abilities. This is hardly surprising given that people's performance at work is not a 'one off' event but a long-term succession of events where typical behaviour matters more than maximal performance.

Box 7.2 No aversive impact

Hogan (1996) argued that personality inventories generally do not systematically discriminate against any ethnic or national group, and thus may offer more equitable bases for selection (see also John, 1991). There are some sex differences in major personality traits, but these are unlikely to have powerful effects on real-world outcomes and likely to cancel each other out: for instance, women are more neurotic but also more conscientious than men (Feingold, 1994). In addition, there are no personality differences between disabled and non-disabled people, and at least in some personality inventories older individuals (over 40) tend to obtain more favourable or adjusted profiles, probably because they are indeed more mature and balanced. This has no doubt contributed to the growing use of personality inventories in selection. However, evidence suggests that adding personality inventories alongside GMA measures in personnel selection does not seem to compensate for the adverse impact of GMA tests (Ryan, Ployhart & Friedel, 1998).

7.4   Validity of personality traits as predictors of job and training performance

The question of whether personality inventories should be used or not in the context of personnel selection has divided practitioners and researchers for decades. Practitioners tend to assign much more weight to personality than to abilities, but are reluctant to accept the validity of self-reports because common sense indicates that people can and will fake. On the other hand, researchers are still debating whether faking is really a problem and whether the validities of personality inventories are acceptable, meaningless or high. Moreover, unlike with GMA (where higher scores are always better), the same personality traits may be advantageous for some situations but disadvantageous for others, which means that the effects of personality on work-related outcomes are a lot more context-specific and moderated by situational factors than in the case of GMA.

Thus the answer to the question of whether personality tests should be used in personnel selection will depend mostly on who you ask, even if answers are based on exactly the same data. Even if we agree on the fact that personality matters in the workplace, one has to identify exactly what aspects of personality matter in every job, whether we can assess them accurately, and how significant an effect they have on work and training performance; all of these issues have been debated extensively. What is beyond debate is that personality inventories are weaker predictors of job and training performance than are cognitive ability tests (Ghiselli, 1966; Schmidt & Hunter, 1998). In fact, arguments against personality inventories are rarely based on social policy (which, as seen in Section 6.8, is the basis of the common objection to using cognitive ability tests) and mostly based on methodology, namely how personality traits are assessed. Another common criticism of personality traits is based on the magnitude of their associations with job and training performance outcomes. But how valid are personality traits?

Prior to the consolidation of the five-factor model (especially after the first reviews were published in the 1950s and 1960s), researchers and practitioners were generally inclined to believe that personality inventories had very weak validities in personnel selection. Early meta-analytic evidence in support of the validity of personality traits in predicting job performance suggested that, if the right traits are assessed in the right context, personality inventories are significantly, albeit modestly, correlated with work-related outcomes. For instance, one of the first quantitative reviews of different inventories across different jobs

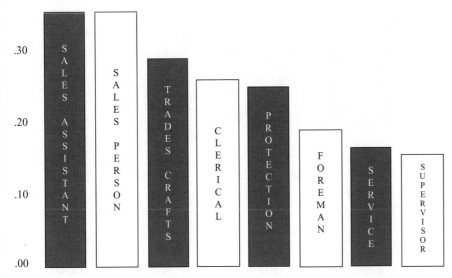

.40

.30

.20

.10

.00

Figure 7.6 *Validity of personality traits across occupations (early meta-analytic evidence) (based on Ghiselli & Berthol, 1953)*

reported uncorrected correlations ranging from .14 to .36 (Ghiselli & Barthol, 1953). As shown in Figure 7.6, the lowest validities were found for supervisory jobs whereas the highest validities were found for sales jobs. However, subsequent reviews during the 1950s and 1960s found that in most studies (80–90 per cent) personality traits did not significantly predict work-related criteria. Until the 1990s, however, there had been little consensus as to the structure of personality, which meant that almost every other researcher had his or her own 'language' for describing major dispositions. This, plus the general lack of quantitative reviews (most reviews were descriptive rather than meta-analytical), contributed to the little support for the idea that self-report inventories assessing stable and general dispositions could be predictive of important work outcomes.

The emergence of the Big Five model provided occupational and I/O researchers with a universal language to compare the results from different validity studies. To be clear, personality experts have and will continue to disagree as to which traits best describe individual differences (Block, 2001), but by the 1990s sufficient evidence had accumulated for the existence of five distinct factors across a wide range of cultures, languages and instruments (Digman, 1990). The first meta-analytic review of findings on the validity of the 'Big Five' (the authors did not refer to these traits as such and also looked at three additional constructs) was provided by Hough and colleagues (Hough, Eaton, Dunnette, Kamp & McCloy, 1990). Results are summarised in Figure 7.7. As shown, personality scales were quite consistently related to individual differences in physical fitness and military bearing (the coefficients shown did not correct for restriction of range,

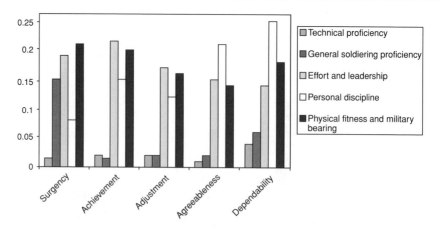

Figure 7.7 *Validities for ABLE personality traits (based on Hough et al., 1990)*

unreliability in the predictor or criterion). There were also several significant associations between personality traits and indicators of effort and leadership, and personal discipline, but the validity of traits in predicting technical proficiency and general soldiering proficiency was considerably lower. Looking at individual traits (Surgency represents Extraversion, Achievement and Dependability represent Conscientiousness, and Adjustment represents Emotional Stability/low Neuroticism), we can see that all traits, especially Extraversion and Conscientiousness, were related to occupational outcomes. Although the authors did not estimate the 'true validities' for these traits (at the level of actual constructs), it is safe to assume that the values would have been much higher.

Although the results of Hough *et al.* added support to the idea that personality traits are valid predictors of job performance, the authors reported data from a single instrument (the ABLE inventory) and military occupations only. Two years later, however, Barrick and Mount's (1991) now widely cited quantitative review meta-analysed the results from 117 investigations (162 samples and 23,994 participants) published between 1952 and 1988, organising their findings according to the five personality traits. The authors looked at five job families, namely professionals, police, managers, sales and skilled/semi-skilled jobs. Results provided compelling evidence for the predictive power of Conscientiousness scales across different settings (predicting job and training performance) and the validity of other traits in specific contexts (for instance, Extraversion was a predictor of managerial and sales jobs, and Openness was a good predictor of training success).

Figure 7.8 depicts Barrick and Mount's validities for the Big Five across different occupational criteria (combining all different job types). As shown, productivity, turnover/tenure, status change, salary and especially subjective ratings where best predicted by Conscientiousness. Indeed, other Big Five traits were inconsistently linked to these five criteria. For example, Openness was related to status change and turnover/tenure but not to salary, subjective ratings and

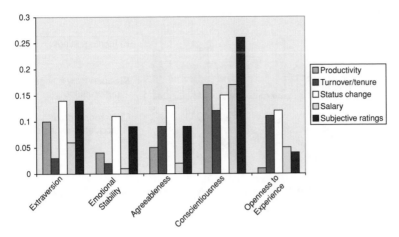

Figure 7.8 *Meta-analysis of Big Five predicting objective and subjective work criteria (based on Barrick & Mount, 1991)*

productivity, whilst Extraversion was linked to status change and subjective ratings but not to turnover/tenure or salary. It is also fair to say that the validities were all modest, even in the case of Conscientiousness, which was by far the best personality predictor of job performance. This led I/O psychologists (both researchers and practitioners) to continue, perhaps even increase, the debate on whether personality inventories should be used in personnel selection, though Barrick and Mount's own conclusion was that the use of personality scales in personnel selection was warranted.

The same year as Barrick and Mount's meta-analysis, Tett and colleagues (Tett, Jackson & Rothstein, 1991) meta-analysed data from 494 studies (97 samples and 13,521 participants), including not only the Big Five but also Type A personality (which combines individual differences in status-consciousness, impatience, restlessness and pro-activity) (Friedman, Hall & Harris, 1985) and locus of control (the tendency to attribute events to personality or situational factors) (Ryckman & Rodda, 1971). Their results replicated several of the findings from Barrick and Mount. Furthermore, Tett *et al.* found that confirmatory studies yielded even higher validities for personality traits as predictors of job performance than thought. However, there were also some 'befuddling' inconsistencies (Goldberg, 1993) between these two meta-analyses. For example, Tett *et al.* reported a validity of .27 for Openness and job proficiency, whereas Barrick and Mount's was −.03. Moreover, the latter found that Conscientiousness was the most solid and powerful predictor of job outcomes but the former found that three other traits (Emotional Stability, Openness and especially Agreeableness) worked better. There were also some discrepancies between these two studies and other meta-analyses. However, Mount *et al.* (2000) and Tett *et al.* justified these discrepancies in terms of differences in statistical methods of analysis and goals between the studies (Ones, Mount, Barrick & Hunter, 1994; Tett, Jackson, Rothstein & Reddon, 1994).

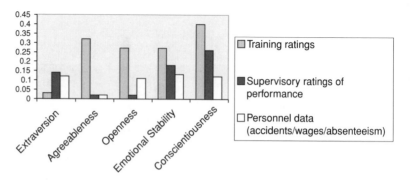

Figure 7.9 *Personality and job performance in the EC (validities from Salgado's meta-analysis)*

7.5   Personality in the European Community

Mount *et al.*'s and Tett *et al.*'s meta-analyses were based on US data. A few years later, a meta-analysis of European validity studies of personality traits by Salgado showed that not only Conscientiousness, but also Emotional Stability (low Neuroticism) had generalisable validities predicting job outcomes (Salgado, 1997). Uncorrected correlations for personality ranged from .00 to .15. The highest observed validities were found for Conscientiousness (.15), Agreeableness (.12), Emotional Stability and training (.11), and Openness (.11) as predictors of training success. Although these coefficients are very modest, the 'true validities' (correlations at the construct level) were at least twice as high (e.g., .39 for Conscientiousness and training, .31 for Agreeableness and training, and .27 for Emotional Stability and training). Moreover, true validities for several traits and supervisory ratings approached these coefficients. Figure 7.9 illustrates the comparative validity of the Big Five (according to Salgado's EC meta-analysis) as predictors of training ratings, supervisory ratings of performance, and 'personnel data' (e.g., absenteeism, salary and accidents at work). As seen, Conscientiousness showed the highest predicted validities across the three criteria – with moderate predictive validity. The figure also highlights the fact that Extraversion was a very poor predictor of training ratings, that Agreeableness was unrelated to both supervisory ratings of performance and personnel data, and that Openness was unrelated to supervisory ratings. Moreover – with exception of Extraversion – the Big Five had higher validities for training than for other criteria.

Whether the results from the US and European meta-analyses should encourage the use of personality inventories in personnel selection or not has been a matter of extensive debate. What is clear, however, is that there has been an exponential increase in research into the validity of personality traits in I/O psychology since these meta-analytic studies and the five-factor model appeared.

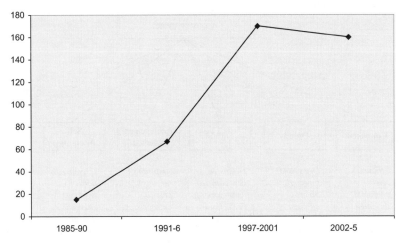

Figure 7.10 *Publications related to personality and selection between 1985 and 2005 (based on Morgeson* et al.*, 2007)*

Figure 7.10 (based on Morgeson, Campion, Dipboye *et al.*, 2007) illustrates the increase in the number of validity studies on personality reported in the main journals of applied psychology and the Society of Industrial and Organisational Psychology. As seen, there were fewer than twenty studies until 1991 (when Barrick and Mount's meta-analysis was published), and three times that amount between 1991 and 1996, and another near-threefold increase between 1997 (the date of Salgado's meta-analysis) and 2001, with a similar number of studies between then and 2005 (the absolute number has dropped slightly but the relative number has gone up as there are two less years in this period).

7.6 Conscientiousness: the most important personality predictor of work outcomes

Regardless of where one stands in relation to the use of personality inventories (criticisms are discussed in Section 7.18), it is clear that Conscientiousness is the most important personality predictor of job performance (Schmidt & Hunter, 1998), and thus the most important non-ability factor in personnel selection, at least among the Big Five personality traits. It has therefore been argued that Conscientiousness is equivalent to GMA in the realm of personality and self-reports. This is hardly surprising given that Conscientiousness assesses individual differences in responsibility, dutifulness, achievement-striving, organised planning and self-control (see Figure 7.11). Thus conscientious people are more likely to both set themselves ambitious goals and work hard to accomplish them (Barrick, Mount & Strauss, 1993; Gellatly, 1996).

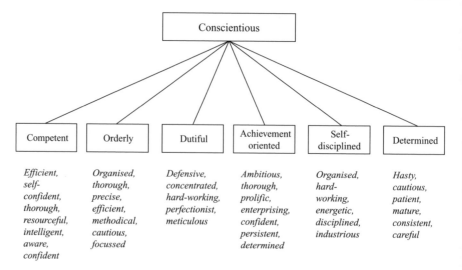

Figure 7.11 *Structure and facets of Conscientiousness (based on Costa & McCrae, 1992)*

That said, measures of Conscientiousness vary quite significantly, with some focusing more on the 'motivational' component (e.g., being ambitious, driven and proactive) and others emphasising the 'tidiness' component (e.g., being organised, clean and somewhat of a perfectionist). Moreover, high correlations between measures of Conscientiousness and Integrity inventories (see Section 7.17) suggest that another important aspect of Conscientiousness is dutifulness or moral responsibility (what Sigmund Freud called the Super-Ego). It has even been suggested that Conscientiousness is one of the main facets of integrity, though given that different integrity scales are often uncorrelated there is some uncertainty as to what integrity scales are assessing in the first place.

The first compelling evidence for the validity of Conscientiousness in the context of personnel settings was provided by Barrick and Mount (1991) (see Section 7.4). Indeed, the consistent validity of Conscientiousness was the major finding in that study. Thus the authors concluded that:

> The major finding [of their meta-analysis] was that one of the Big Five dimensions, Conscientiousness, correlated positively with job performance in all five occupational groups. Individuals who are dependable, persistent, goal directed and organised tend to be higher performers on virtually any job; viewed negatively, those who are careless, irresponsible, low achievement striving and impulsive tend to be lower performers on virtually any job.   (Mount & Barrick, 1998, p. 851)

Unlike GMA, which provides a measure of people's 'can do' or maximal performance, Conscientiousness is especially important as marker of typical performance or people's 'will do'. This is especially noticeable under low extrinsic reward conditions because conscientious individuals will differ from their non-conscientious counterparts in their tendency to strive for excellence and set themselves high targets, which they work hard to achieve. In that sense, Conscientiousness is the ideal 'partner' of GMA and provides the motivational information that GMA tests do not. This is in line with a longstanding tradition in individual differences and I/O psychology to conceptualise aptitudes and conative or motivational traits as essentially independent.

Research evidence from organisational studies suggests that Conscientiousness is negatively related to GMA (Moutafi, Furnham & Paltiel, 2004; Moutafi, Furnham & Tsaousis, 2006) and we have interpreted this association in terms of the compensational function of Conscientiousness in competitive settings. Thus, if employees are not 'equipped' with the necessary cognitive ability levels to perform well at work, they will compensate for this by becoming more conscientious and relying more on their dutifulness, self-discipline and organisational skills (Chamorro-Premuzic & Furnham, 2005). That said, most of the variance in Conscientiousness is unaccounted for by cognitive ability measures, and the effects of Conscientiousness on work-related outcomes – or indeed academic performance (Chamorro-Premuzic & Arteche, in press) – are largely independent of GMA. Thus, it is not difficult to echo Mount and Barrick's conclusion that 'no matter what job you are selecting for, if you want employees who will turn out to be good performers, you should hire those who work smarter and work harder' (Mount & Barrick, 1998, p. 856).

It is also likely that the correlation between Conscientiousness and job performance underestimates the real impact of Conscientiousness at work. First, there is a self-selective bias in any competitive setting that narrows the range in Conscientiousness. Conscientious people are not only more likely to apply for better jobs in the first place, they also have higher levels of organisational switching (the tendency to look for better jobs within and outside one's organisation) (Vinson, Connelly & Ones, 2007). Second, Conscientiousness is negatively related to almost any indicator of counterproductive behaviour, not just at work but in life in general. Indeed, a comprehensive meta-analysis reported that Conscientiousness is negatively correlated with virtually every form of unhealthy and dangerous behaviour (Bogg & Roberts, 2004).

Table 7.1 reproduced from this study summarises the findings. In particular, conscientious people are less likely to drink in excess, use drugs, drive in a risky way and use violence. Although there are ethical boundaries to recruiting on the basis of such behaviours and even asking people to report them, it is hard to conceive of many employers who, on this basis, would prefer to hire individuals who are low in Conscientiousness. The associations reported by Bogg and Roberts highlight the prophylactic nature of this personality trait in relation to counterproductive behaviours (at work and in general). In Section 6.11, we have seen how research evidence has suggested that higher GMA may provide individuals with the necessary cognitive tools to predict the negative consequences of a wide range of counterproductive behaviours (enabling them to foresee potential punishments). In a similar vein, higher Conscientiousness

Table 7.1 *Conscientiousness and health-related behaviours (from Bogg & Roberts, 2004; with permission from Roberts, APA copyright)*

Health behavior	r	No. of studies	N	95% Cl Lower	95% Cl Upper	Q
Activity	.05	17	24.259	.04	.07	136.80
Excessive alcohol use	−.25	65	32.137	−.25	−.24	1,109.89
Drug use	−.28	44	36.573	−.29	−.27	662.21
Unhealthy eating	−.13	14	6.356	−.16	−.11	126.78
Risky driving	−.25	21	10.171	−.27	−.24	422.63
Risky sex	−.13	25	12.410	−.15	−.11	76.75
Suicide	−.12	19	6.087	−.14	−.09	123.47
Tobacco use	−.14	46	46.725	−.15	−.13	352.83
Violence	.25	25	10.277	10.26	−.24	119.22

may strengthen individuals' motivation to avoid these behaviours and is probably a bigger determinant of such behaviours than is GMA: one can easily think of individuals who are bright enough to foresee prospective punishments but lack the necessary ego-strength to inhibit their behaviours. Long before the Big Five taxonomy was established, Hans Eysenck referred to such non-ability predictors of risky and anti-social behaviours in terms of Psychoticism (Eysenck & Eysenck, 1977), which, in the Big Five, is represented in terms of low Agreeableness, high Openness and low Conscientiousness (Costa & McCrae, 1995).

Further evidence for the importance of Conscientiousness in personnel selection derives from the wide range of recent studies that reported consistent positive associations between this personality trait and academic performance, a key antecedent of personnel selection and occupational performance. Several studies reported moderated (uncorrected) validities for Conscientiousness and its primary facets as predictors of various academic performance outcomes (Chamorro-Premuzic & Furnham, 2003a, 2003b, 2004), and recent meta-analytic studies have confirmed that the association of Conscientiousness and post-secondary educational achievement is robust (Noftle & Robins, 2007; O'Connor & Paunonen, 2007). Moreover, newer constructs within the Conscientiousness spectrum have been developed and validated in the context of academic performance, notably the construct of Grit (Duckworth, Peterson, Matthews & Kelly, 2007), highlighting the importance of self-control in achievement-related outcomes.

7.7   Neuroticism: it helps if you are calm

Big Five traits other than Conscientiousness have also been associated with important occupational outcomes, albeit less consistently. Such is the case

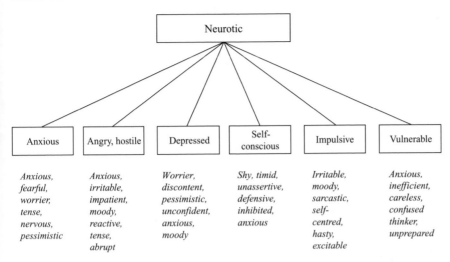

Figure 7.12 *Structure and facets of Neuroticism (based on Costa & McCrae, 1992)*

with Neuroticism (Emotional Stability), which has been linked to job and training performance particularly under stressful conditions. This is consistent with the interpretation of the Neuroticism trait (also known as trait anxiety) as a marker of individual differences in stress-reactivity, the tendency to experience low confidence and heightened negative affect, and a predisposition to anxiety in general (Chamorro-Premuzic, 2007). In the Big Five of Costa and McCrae (1995), Neuroticism comprises the subscales or primary facets of anxiety, angry hostility, depression, self-consciousness, impulsivity and vulnerability (see Figure 7.12). However, it should be noted that Neuroticism inventories assess individual differences in normal rather than clinical samples/subjects, hence they are suitable for personnel selection.

The main meta-analysis on the Big Five and work-related outcomes (reviewed above) yielded inconsistent findings with regard to the validity of Neuroticism. Thus Hough *et al.* (1990) found significant associations for this trait and different measures of military performance (i.e., effort and leadership, personal discipline and physical fitness bearing), and similar associations were found for civil professions by Tett *et al.* Likewise, Hough (1998b) found that emotionally stable recruits performed more effectively in combat, and similar findings were reported for European military samples by Salgado (1998). However, Salgado's (1997) EC meta-analysis reported only a modest correlation between Neuroticism and training success in civil occupations, and, moreover, Barrick and Mount's meta-analyses reported validities close to zero for Neuroticism.

It has even been pointed out that Neuroticism is not always negatively associated with occupational performance outcomes. Indeed, major theories of personality have long postulated that if coupled with specific ability or personality traits Neuroticism may have positive impacts on various task performances. Most

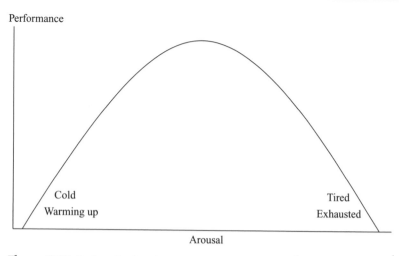

Figure 7.13 *Yerkes–Dodson law*

notably, Gray's (1988) 'reward sensitivity theory' (RST) of personality hypothesises that higher Neuroticism – combined with lower Extraversion – is linked to higher levels of learning in the presence of 'sticks' or punishment, and there is evidence in support of this hypotheses (Corr, Pickering & Gray, 1997). On the other hand, Hans J. Eysenck (1994) argued that Neuroticism and cognitive ability are linked via arousal (baseline levels of cortical arousal or brain reactivity), and Robinson (1997) conducted several EEG studies showing that higher IQ levels are linked to intermediate levels of arousal. Indeed, this idea is consistent with a well-established principle known as the Yerkes–Dodson law, which states that performance is best at an intermediate level of arousal (Yerkes & Dodson, 1908; see Figure 7.13). This explains why, under some circumstances, notably low situational pressure or tasks that are under-arousing, Neurotic individuals have an advantage over their stable counterparts because they are naturally more alert to potential environmental threats. In line with this, studies on air traffic controllers tend to report superior performance by Neurotic individuals (Matthews, 1999).

The fact that meta-analytic studies rarely explored curvilinear effects of Neuroticism on job or training performance may explain the inconsistencies of their results. Moreover, in order to understand the relationship between Neuroticism and job-related outcomes it is fundamental to take into account situational factors such as pressure, whether individuals are motivated by rewards or punishment, and even how hard the task is (for which cognitive abilities should be taken into account).

That said, the bulk of evidence suggests that if any occupational consequences of Neuroticism generalise, these refer to the negative effects of Neuroticism on work-related outcomes and, conversely, the fact that Emotional Stability enables individuals to perform as well as they could in most settings, including under elevated pressure. This idea is in line with recent studies on the

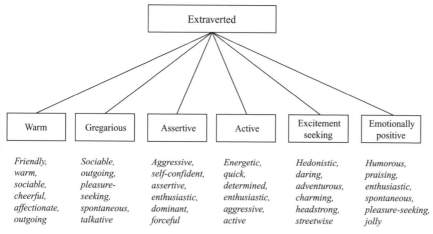

Figure 7.14 *Structure and facets of Extraversion (based on Costa & McCrae, 1992)*

personality–intelligence interface. For example, Moutafi *et al.* (2006) showed that the relationship between Neuroticism and (lower) IQ test performance was explained by test-anxiety; Chamorro-Premuzic, Ahmetoglu and Furnham (2008) showed that Neuroticism was strongly and positively linked to test-anxiety (even when controlling for other individual differences). Perhaps more importantly, Neuroticism has been recently reported to be a consistent negative predictor of post-secondary academic performance (Chamorro-Premuzic & Furnham, 2002, 2003a, 2003b; O'Connor & Paunonen, 2007). Thus even though Neurotic individuals do not differ in cognitive ability levels from their emotionally stable counterparts, they are more likely to underperform in ability tests and real-life tasks, especially in the presence of pressure (Chamorro-Premuzic & Furnham, 2004) (see again Figure 7.1). Recent work on emotional intelligence (see Sections 7.21, 7.22, 7.23), a strong negative correlate of Neuroticism, adds support to the idea that being emotionally stable or in control of one's emotions is beneficial in the workplace.

7.8   Extraversion: positive, sociable people-people

Another trait that has been associated with job-related outcomes, albeit inconsistently, is Extraversion. In the Big Five model of Costa and McCrae (1995) (but see Hogan, 1986, and Hogan & Holland, 2003, for a different view) Extraversion includes the subfacets or primary traits of warmth, gregariousness, assertiveness, activity, excitement seeking and positive affect/emotionality (see Figure 7.14). Thus positive associations between Extraversion measures and performance in managerial and sales jobs have been found and interpreted in terms

Table 7.2 *Task-dependent correlates of Extraversion (based on Matthews, 1999)*

Extraversion level	High	Low
Divided attention	+	−
Long-term memory	−	+
Reflective problem solving	−	+
Resistance to distraction	+	−
Retrieval from memory	+	−
Short-term memory	+	−
Vigilance	−	+

of the higher interpersonal competence of extraverts, something that also applies to more agreeable employees (Mount, Barrick & Stewart, 1998).

Extraversion seems particularly important when 'coupled' with Emotional Stability (low Neuroticism), what some people refer to as the *happy personality* (Chamorro-Premuzic, Bennett & Furnham, 2007). This idea is congruent with two major (pre-Big Five) approaches to personality, namely Hans Eysenck's and Jeffrey Gray's personality models. Eysenck was instrumental in showing that stable Extraverts are better adapted and happier than their introverted counterparts, whereas Gray argued that impulsivity is characterised by a combination of high Extraversion and high Neuroticism. Along these lines, a recent study by Judge and colleagues found that 'happier' employees (those high in Extraversion *and* low in Neuroticism) performed significantly better than extraverted or stable employees alone (Judge & Erez, 2007). Likewise, previous studies found that Neuroticism and Introversion combine to have deleterious effects on performance. For example, a study on fighter jet pilots found that a quick (ten-minute) measure of Extraversion and Neuroticism predicted training success and failure (again, being Extraverted and Stable was linked to success) (Bartram & Dale, 1982). These finding are important because they highlight interactive effects underscored by regression-based studies focussed on the individual contribution of each predictor. Moreover, the common assumption that the Big Five are truly orthogonal (unrelated) underscores potential synergistic effects that may result from the overlap between them, notably Extraversion and Neuroticism (which tend to be negatively correlated) (Chamorro-Premuzic, 2007). Indeed, Judge and colleagues also found that the intersection between Extraversion and Neuroticism predicted job performance better than the unique aspects of these traits.

Unlike Costa and McCrae (1995), Hogan (1986) interpreted the dimensions of Extraversion in terms of sociability, ambition, adjustment, likeability, prudence (lack of) and intellect. The main difference between this model and the one proposed by Costa and McCrae is that Hogan splits Extraversion into the two major subcategories of Sociability and Ambition. Thus some Extraverts may be characterised more by their tendency to experience positive affect, be sociable and enjoy the company of others (as well as dread being alone), whilst in other Extraverts the main trait would be dominance, self-confidence and leadership. As seen, some of these various facets of Extraversion have been conceptualised by Costa and McCrae (1995). However, the issue is whether they really load onto one single higher-order factor or represent two distinct traits (as proposed by Hogan). This is an important question because some aspects of Extraversion may be more beneficial at work than others. Indeed, one may think of jobs that suit 'Sociable' extraverts more than 'Ambitious' extraverts and vice versa.

Last, but not least, the inconsistent associations between Extraversion and job-related outcomes have also been explained in terms of the cognitive characteristics of the Extraversion trait. Specifically, the cognitive nature of the task will determine whether extraverts or introverts are more likely to perform better (Matthews, 1999). Thus extraverts would have an advantage over introverts in tasks that require divided attention (e.g., writing while listening to music, or reading while watching TV) because of their lower levels of distractibility. This is consistent with Eysenck's arousal theory of Extraversion/Introversion. Moreover, Extraverts would also have an advantage in tasks requiring retrieval from short-term memory (and better memory retrieval in general). However, if tasks require vigilance introverts have the advantage over extraverts as the latter would try to compensate for their lower levels of cortical arousals by attending to task-irrelevant stimuli. Tasks that require long-term memory retrieval or problem solving (where accuracy matters more than speed) also benefit Introverts more than Extraverts.

7.9   Agreeableness: getting along, caring and sharing

Agreeableness seems to be advantageous in jobs requiring interpersonal interactions or where *getting along* is paramount (Hogan, Rybicki, Motowildo & Borman, 1998; Mount *et al.*, 1998). A typical case is customer service jobs, and indeed Agreeableness has been found to predict performance on these jobs quite well (Hurtz & Donovan, 2000), especially if based on teamwork rather than individualistic tasks (Barrick, Stewart, Neubert & Mount, 1998). Agreeableness also seems to moderate the effects of Conscientiousness – the strongest personality trait correlate of job performance – or work-related outcomes (Witt & Ferris, 2003). Thus people who are Conscientious but Disagreeable will tend to have conflicts with others, whereas people who are Conscientious and Agreeable will benefit from the synergistic effects of discipline and cooperation.

That said, cooperation is not always a driver of productivity and in some cases may hinder personal success. Thus Hogan and colleagues have argued that individuals higher in Agreeableness are less likely to be driven by social status, particularly if they have to attain it at the expense of others. In situations where collaboration and competition are mutually exclusive, Agreeableness may be

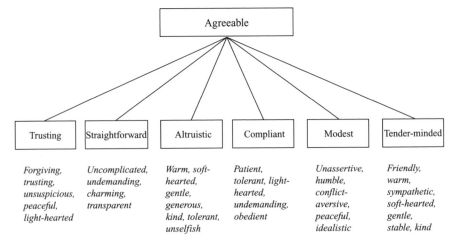

Figure 7.15 *Structure and facets of Agreeableness (based on Costa & McCrae, 1992)*

negatively linked to job performance as disagreeable employees may prioritise *getting ahead* over getting along. Interestingly, and in line with Hogan's idea, most of the empirical evidence suggests that Agreeableness is *negatively* rather than positively linked to career success (operationalized in terms of income). Most notably, two large meta-analytic studies reported associations of $-.24$ (US) and $-.11$ (Europe) for Agreeableness and income (Boudreau, Boswell & Judge, 2001), and a smaller but longitudinal study reported a coefficient of $-.32$ for these variables (Judge, Higgins, Thoresen & Barrick, 1999). This is consistent with the idea that high achievers, and especially leaders, may be characterised by higher levels of Machiavellianism, a trait that assesses individuals' willingness to take advantage of others in order to accomplish their own goals (Austin, Farrelly, Black & Moore, 2007; Drory, 1980).

7.10   Openness: intellectual, imaginative, artistic jobs

The last of the Big Five personality traits is Openness to New Experiences, often simply referred to as 'Factor V', not least because it is unclear what this trait really encompasses. In Costa and McCrae's (1995) model, high Openness scorers are characterised as being driven by fantasy, artistic, feeling-oriented, action-oriented, ideational and having liberal values (see Figure 7.16). Other Big Five taxonomies emphasise the higher levels of need for cognition in open individuals. Openness is correlated with knowledge-based or 'crystallised' aspects of intellectual ability (Ackerman & Heggestad, 1997; Chamorro-Premuzic & Furnham, 2005); artistic professions require higher levels of Openness, an association that has been interpreted in terms of the higher likelihood of Open individuals to 'invest' in intellectual activities and acquire more knowledge

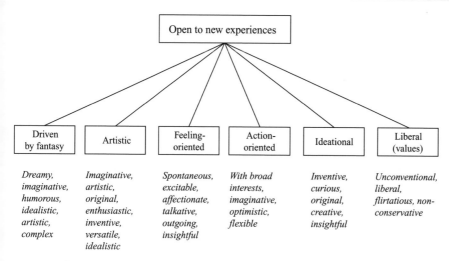

Figure 7.16 *Structure and facets of Openness (based on Costa & McCrae, 1992)*

(Cattell, 1950; Chamorro-Premuzic & Furnham, 2006a). However, Openness has been inconsistently related to work performance and seems relevant only in artistic or creative jobs, though it does affect training success.

7.11   It's not all about performance: validity of the Big Five as predictors of job satisfaction

Although this chapter is primarily concerned with the question of whether personality traits and inventories are useful predictors of work and training performance, performance is not the only thing that matters. Indeed, an important work-related criterion (which may actually drive performance levels itself) is job satisfaction, and psychologists have long argued that individual differences in job satisfaction or the extent to which employees are happy at work are largely influenced by dispositional or personality factors. Moreover, industrialised economies have come to realise in recent times that 'getting richer' does not mean 'getting happier', and in the quest for the right work–life balance an important component is the degree of gratification that people get from their work, and this seems to vary largely independently of performance or financial success.

What personality characteristics determine individual differences in job satisfaction? It seems that emotional adjustment plays the most important role. Almost seventy-five years ago, Hoppock assessed the level of job satisfaction of psychologists and found that those higher in emotional adjustment were more satisfied at work (Hoppock, 1937). Since then a large body of studies has reported consistent associations between affective dispositions (e.g., Neuroticism, emotional intelligence and Extraversion) and various indicators of job satisfaction. However,

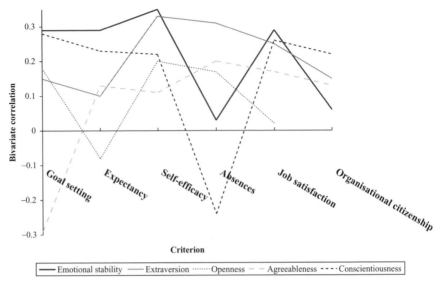

Figure 7.17 *Importance of the Big Five as predictors of motivational outcomes*

until recent meta-analyses made sense of the literature it was difficult to identify overall trends in the data and quantify the impact of major personality dimensions on job satisfaction and related outcomes.

Figure 7.17 (based on Judge & Ilies, 2002; Judge, Heller & Mount, 2002; Judge, 1997; Organ & Ryan, 1995) summarises the meta-analytic evidence for the validity of the Big Five personality traits as predictors of these various motivational outcomes, namely *goal setting*, *expectancy*, *self-efficacy*, *absences* (an indicator of dissatisfaction), *job satisfaction* and *organisational citizenship*. Each trait is represented by a different shade and correlations for different criteria are plotted along the *x* axis. For instance, the correlation between Openness and goal setting was .18, whilst the correlation between Conscientiousness and absences was −.24 (negative correlations are plotted below the *x* axis and vice versa).

As shown, all five factors contributed significantly to the prediction of individual differences in these outcomes, though validities varied according to the outcome and predictor (from −.08 to .35). For example, Openness made a negligible contribution to the prediction of job satisfaction and a very modest contribution to explaining expectancy motivation. Thus whether you are Open or not, your levels of job satisfaction and expectancy motivation remain pretty much the same. On the other hand, Emotional Stability contributed to the prediction of most outcomes but was only weakly related to absences and organisational citizenship. Extraversion and Agreeableness were linked to all outcomes, though sometimes inconsistently: for example, both traits were linked to higher absenteeism rates and disagreeable people had higher levels of goal-setting motivation than their agreeable counterparts did. Thus the only consistent personality predictor of the

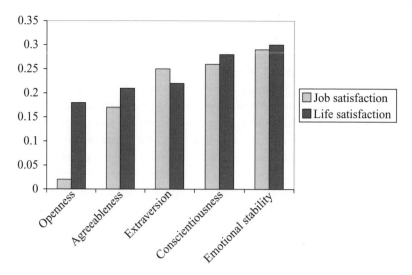

Figure 7.18 *Big Five as predictors of job and life satisfaction*

outcomes examined was Conscientiousness. In fact the validities for Conscientiousness were pretty much equal across all criteria examined.

Research evidence also indicates that satisfaction and dissatisfaction are not two opposite extremes of the same dimension (though see Yik, Russell & Barrett, 1999), but, rather, two distinctive factors. Thus employees may not be satisfied without, however, being dissatisfied, and, likewise, someone may not dissatisfied without, nonetheless, being satisfied (Herzberg, 1965). This is consistent with a well-established tradition in psychology to distinguish between 'positive' and 'negative' affect as two separate dimensions of emotionality. Individuals high in positive affect (who tend to be stable and extraverted) are naturally predisposed to experience joy, excitement and enthusiasm, whereas those high in negative affects have a tendency to experience guilt, anger, fear and concerns (Watson, Clark & Tellegen, 1988). Likewise, Jeffrey Gray's neuropsychological theory of personality postulates the independence of two neural circuits responsible for learning and motivation, namely the behavioural inhibition system (BIS) and behavioural approach system (BAS), which are linked to negative and positive affect, respectively (Gray, 1982). However, for the purposes of predicting job satisfaction, the distinction between positive and negative affect as different dimensions seems overrated, as both factors are linked to job satisfaction measures. For example, a meta-analysis (Connolly & Viswesvaran, 2000) reported that job satisfaction correlated positively with positive affect measures (.49) and negatively with negative affect measures (−.33).

The best meta-analytic estimate of the dispositional basis of job satisfaction was provided by Judge *et al.* (2002) (see Figure 7.18). As shown, Conscientiousness, Emotional Stability and Extraversion had validities larger than .20 in the prediction of job satisfaction, whereas Agreeableness was more weakly but still significantly associated with this outcome (and Openness was unrelated). Interestingly, looking at the correlations between personality and *life satisfaction* – estimates are taken from DeNeve and Cooper (1998) – reveals a very similar pattern of results (the only exception is for open individuals, who seem to be much happier than their less open counterparts in life, but not at work!). Thus dispositional sources underlying individual differences in the extent to which people are happy at work operate in a similar way *beyond the workplace*. This is important because it shows that the scope of personality is not limited to people's jobs, and that selecting employees with a higher dispositional basis for satisfaction (i.e., those emotionally stable, extroverted and conscientious, and to a lesser extent agreeable) will result in employees who are happier in both the job and in general. The authors reported an overall correlation of .41 for all Big Five combined and job satisfaction, which shows that the five factors are good indicators of a person's likelihood to be happy at work.

7.12   Criticisms to the Big Five (and personality inventories in general)

Even since personality inventories were developed there have been objections to the use of such tests in personnel selection (and, in the wider sense, for any decision-making process). In the context of work psychology the two main criticisms are that it is easy to fake responses to a personality inventory and that personality traits are only weak predictors of occupational outcomes. In the forthcoming sections we discuss these two criticisms.

7.13   Faking

Several arguments have been put forward in defence of personality inventories attempting to persuade researchers and practitioners that faking is *not* really problematic in the context of personality assessment. These go as follows:

1. Since applicants are likely to fake good but not to fake bad, the validity of personality inventories is only threatened by faking at the high-end of the distribution (Mueller-Hanson, Heggestad & Thorton, 2003). This means that whereas some candidates will inevitably manage to 'crack the test' and obtain desirable scores simply because they lied and were able to identify the better responses, it is unlikely that candidates with unfavourable profiles would have faked the results. Accordingly, it has been suggested that self-report inventories are used for filtering-out rather than selecting-in candidates.
2. Studies in which faking was detected showed that personality traits still predicted job-relevant outcomes (Hough *et al.*, 1990; Ones, Viswesvaran & Reiss, 1996).

3. Personality inventories administered during high-stake situations still predict job performance and other work-related outcomes (Ones & Viswesvaran, 2003).

4. Laboratory studies, where participants (especially students) are instructed to 'fake good', yield findings that do not necessarily generalise to 'high-stake' settings (see point 1 below) (Viswesvaran & Ones, 1999).

5. The importance of social desirability (as measured by meta-scales that detect extremely positive responses) appears to have been over-rated. First, social desirability scales fail to predict desirable work-outcomes (Viswesvaran, Ones & Hough, 2001). Second, controlling for social desirability has no impact on the validity of personality traits, suggesting that the effects of personality traits on job-related outcomes cannot be accounted for by social desirability scales (Ones *et al.*, 1996). Third, social desirability does not affect the structure of personality inventories (Ellingson, Smith & Sackett, 2001).

6. Being able to fake is a sign of social adjustment in itself (Hogan, 2005). As Hogan pointed out, people's responses to personality items can be interpreted merely as an 'automatic and often non-conscious effort to negotiate an identity with the interviewer/test developer' (Hogan, 1992, p. 902). This is an important point which even critics of personality inventories endorse. Clearly, if you can pretend to be good in a test you can probably do the same in the workplace (and life in general). As summarised neatly by Murphy, 'if faking is defined in terms of saying what you think you ought to say rather than what you want to say that is called civilization' (in Morgeson *et al.*, 2007, p. 712). Social desirability is especially important when it comes to performance assessed by supervisors rather than objective measures. Moreover, in some jobs (highly interpersonal ones, such as customer service and relations, are the obvious ones) the ability to fake good may be essential. Dipboye points out (in Morgeson *et al.*, 2007) that if you are working in Disney you would probably be expected to fake good – and even happiness – most of the time, and the same may apply to McDonalds, at least if you want to make it to employee of the month. Moreover, individual differences in social desirability have been explained in terms of Conscientiousness, Emotional Stability and Agreeableness, and these traits predict performance in the first place.

On the other hand, the most frequently discussed arguments against the validity of personality inventories in personnel selection have highlighted that fact that faking *is* a problem:

1. Several studies have shown that job applicants tend to score 'higher' (i.e., show more favourable or desirable profiles) than incumbents, which can be attributed to the formers' motivation to fake good on these scales (Barrick & Mount, 1996; Hough, 1995; Rosse, Stecher, Miller & Levin, 1998).

2. Laboratory studies, such as those instructing participants to 'fake good', show that it is very easy to identify the desirable or correct responses to a personality inventory (Viswesvaran & Ones, 1999) (though see point 4 above).

Can people fake? → almost 100% of the studies (39) suggest YES
Do they fake? → at least 50% of the studies (14) suggest YES
Do some fake more than others? → 100% of studies (3) suggest YES
Does faking depend on the situation? → at least 70% of studies (7) suggest YES
Are self-deception and impression management different factors? → 80% (4) YES
Does faking harm the validity of personality scales? → 50% (18) YES*
Does faking affect the structure of personality? → 50% (4 studies) YES
Can faking be mitigated? → 30-40% of studies (10) suggest YES
Can faking be detected? → 40% of studies (33) suggest YES

*This point is rejected by one of the authors of the same article, Hollenbeck, who correctly points out that the decrease in validity attributed to faking in those 50% of studies is at most marginal.

Figure 7.19 *Review of faking (by Michael Campion, in Morgeson* et al.*, 2007)*

3. Even if the structure and overall validity of personality inventories may not be affected by faking, faking produces changes in the rank order of candidates – meaning faking will influence hiring decisions – because some may fake more than others, i.e., there are both personality and situational determinants of faking not captured by personality scores (Mueller-Hanson, Heggestad & Thornton, 2006).
4. Even if social desirability scales do not correlate with work-related outcomes, and even if they do not explain the validity of personality traits predicting those outcomes, faking may still be an issue simply because social desirability scales may fail to successfully measure faking in the first place (Ellingson, Sackett & Hough, 1999).

Some of the discrepancies noted above can be attributed to the lack of compelling evidence either against or in support of the idea that faking poses a problem. In an attempt to provide a comprehensive review of the literature, Michael Campion (in Morgeson *et al.*, 2007) examined the salient studies on faking (see Figure 7.19), concluding that:

> Four overall conclusions can be drawn from this review of the research literature on faking in personality tests. First, the total number of studies on the topic is large, suggesting that faking has been viewed as an important problem. Second, people can and apparently do fake their responses on personality tests. Third, almost half the studies where criterion-related validity was studied found some effect of faking on criterion-related validity. Fourth, there has been substantial research devoted to techniques for detecting and mitigating faking, but no techniques appear to solve the problem adequately.   (p. 691)

7.14   How to overcome the problem of faking

Several suggestions have been put forward to overcome the problem of faking (by those who see faking as a problem). These range from simply warning the test-takers (Vasilopoulos, Cucina & McElreath, 2005) to comparing the structure of personality inventories in candidates and low-stake samples (Kuncel & Borneman, 2007). The latter requires test-interpreters to examine whether items that are normally uncorrelated are positively correlated in the applicant/employee/candidate. Others have argued that forced-choice scales, such as asking people whether they are X *or* Y (rather than how representative X is), reduce the problem of faking (Villanova, Bernardin, Johnson & Dahmus, 1994). On the other hand, there is the option of *other-* rather than self-reports, which have been shown to explain additional variance over and above self-reports in the context of occupational (Barrick, Mount & Strauss, 1994), and even secondary school performance (Bratko, Chamorro-Premuzic & Saks, 2006; see also Murphy's comments in Morgeson *et al.*, 2007).

Yet there are issues with all of the recommendations proposed. First, warnings would probably not have the same impact on every test-taker, meaning there are surely individual differences in responses to faking-related warning, which will deter only some of the potential fakers. Second, contrasting the structure of individual responses with previously collected data (from low-stake contexts) may be generally effective but harm honest respondents with an individual or different-from-average-respondents profile. Third, it is not necessarily the case that forced-choice items will prevent 'street-wise' fakers from spotting the most desirable response. For example, a forced-choice item on Conscientiousness may ask candidates to choose between 'Hard-working, reliable and committed' on one hand, and 'Lazy, unreliable and uncommitted' on the other (this is no doubt a somewhat crude example but it does show how forced-choice items are not useful *per se*). In fact, the less obvious forced items are, the more they may compel participants to choose between two options that may both apply to them, e.g., 'Organised, methodical and tidy' versus 'Creative, spontaneous and intuitive' (which may assume that aspects of Conscientiousness and creativity are negatively correlated). Fourth, even if other-ratings have incremental validity over self-reports, it is not easy to collect these data, especially in the context of personnel selection (if recruiting from outside the company). Moreover, it has been pointed out that although the accuracy of other-reports seems to depend on the level of familiarity between the observer and the candidate, familiarity levels may be positively correlated with the observers' motivation to lie and indeed fake good about the candidate (Connolly, Kavanagh & Viswesvaran, 2007). Besides, self- and other-ratings are probably not measuring exactly the same construct.

A somewhat idealistic yet commonsense proposition argued that the way to overcome the problem of faking is to shift from an 'interrogational' or at least inquisitive approach to personality assessment to a more participative, interactive,

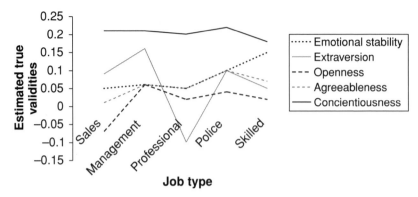

Figure 7.20 *Meta-meta analysis of the Big Five and job performance*

collaborative process where information is not withdrawn from the candidates and where the constructs being assessed are clearly specified to the candidates. Assuming that they will understand the importance of 'fitting' into the right organisation and job (see Section 7.26), they may be expected to respond honestly if this is done (see Dipboye's comments in Morgeson *et al.*, 2007). That said, given that organisations tend to seek the same type of candidates (in personality terms, highly conscientious, stable and perhaps extraverted) it would be impossible for everyone to do well in personnel selection unless they decided to fake good in the expected direction of the employers/recruiters.

7.15   Low validity

Even if faking can be overcome, or in cases where it does not seriously threaten the validity of personality traits as predictors of work-related outcomes, critics of the use of personality inventories in personnel selection have another, often more fundamental, objection, namely the fact that the magnitude of the association between personality traits and the predicted criteria is modest at best, and often non-significant (Morgeson *et al.*, 2007). In fact, meta-analytic estimates that correct for unreliability and range restriction may overestimate the utility of personality traits in the prediction of work and training performance.

The irony is that opposite conclusions are often drawn from exactly the same data. For example, when the first quantitative reviews on the subject appeared in the 1960s researchers' recommendations against the use of personality inventories for work selection was based on an estimated validity of .09 (Guion & Gottier, 1965), whereas Barrick and Mount (1991) recommended using personality inventories based on an overall (corrected) validity of .13 for the Big Five. Although even an optimistic estimate of the validity of personality traits (adjusting and correcting for all possible drawbacks and combining all relevant traits) would hardly account for 15 per cent of the variance in job performance (Murphy,

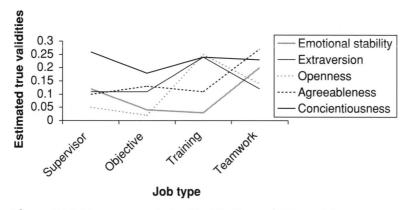

Figure 7.21 *Meta-meta analysis of the Big Five and different job outcomes*

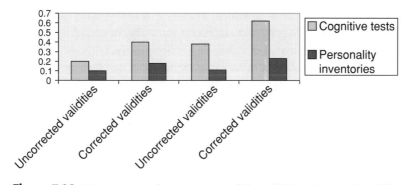

Figure 7.22 *Meta-meta-analytic estimates of the validities of cognitive ability and personality scales*

in Morgeson *et al.*, 2007), utility analyses suggested that this is an acceptable magnitude and supported the inclusion of personality inventories on the basis of the same estimate (Schmidt, Hunter, McKenzie & Muldrow, 1979).

On the other hand, subsequent meta-analyses, particularly in the 1990s (after the consolidation of the Big Five taxonomy), reported validities in the region of .40, that is, 100 per cent larger, though mainly for higher-order or 'compound' traits (Hogan, 2005; Ones, Viswesvaran & Dilchert, 2005) (see Section 7.17).

Figure 7.22 depicts the comparative predictive validity of cognitive ability tests and personality inventories in the prediction of occupational outcomes as estimated by thirteen meta-analyses in the case of cognitive ability tests and twelve meta-analyses in the case of personality inventories. As seen, the comparative validity of personality inventories (in relation to cognitive ability tests) is low, especially in the case of training criteria. However, these figures underestimate the impact of specific personality traits – like Extraversion and Emotional Stability – which may affect performance under certain settings only (unlike Conscientiousness). Thus some traits will work in some situations but not in others (which is hardly true for GMA, as seen in Chapter 6).

7.16   Specific criteria

Regardless of the magnitude of the correlation between personality scores and work-related outcomes, it is clear that the validity of personality inventories is largely dependent on the type of criterion we chose to predict. Thus, unlike with GMA, many factors moderate the effects of personality on job and training performance (though less so for job satisfaction). Of course, it should also be emphasised that the validity of 'personality' depends on what personality trait we are assessing – for example, validities are consistently higher for Conscientiousness than for Agreeableness, though in some cases (jobs low in responsibility but high in interpersonal contact) one may expect Agreeableness to be a better driver of performance than Conscientiousness. Different instruments may also be assessing different constructs, or at least different aspects of the same construct. Most notably, the extent to which 'Factor V' assesses individual differences in Openness to New Experiences, intellect, autonomy or creativity depends largely on the scale used to assess this trait. This reflects the fact that although there is now a large consensus about the explanatory power of the five-factor model, strong preferences for one inventory rather than others remain, and there are debates about how to capture the essence of some of the Big Five, notably Conscientiousness and Openness. Indeed, some of the meta-analytic studies corrected for 'construct invalidity' (Salgado, 1997) on that basis, though this procedure has been shown to overestimate the validity of personality traits (Hurtz & Donovan, 2000).

But some of the moderating factors apply equally to all of the traits. For example, there have been suggestions that the validity of personality traits *increases* with time spent on the job or in the organisation, which is consistent with the idea, albeit contested, that the validity of GMA would decrease over time (Murphy, 1989). Thus maximal performance would be important especially during the transitional phase, at early stages of the job (when motivation is high and more learning is required), but, during the maintenance phase or once employees have acquired the necessary knowledge to perform their job well, the key issue is whether they *want* to perform it or how well they want to do it. For some traits, however, the opposite pattern occurs. For instance, recent evidence suggests that the validity of self-monitoring decreases after the initial 'honeymoon' period has passed (Moser & Galais, 2007).

It is plausible to predict that the validities of personality traits will increase substantially if the correct criteria (or predictors) are chosen. As suggested by Hollenbeck's research, Openness may always be related to performance if performance requires non-conventional methods; Extraversion and Agreeableness may be consistently related to performance if performance is determined by communicational factors and collaboration, respectively, and Neuroticism may be a strong predictor of performance if performance is measured under stressful situations (see Morgeson *et al.*, 2007). To this extent, it has been suggested that practitioners, employers and recruiters design purpose-built inventories and pay particular attention to the behavioural outcomes they wish to predict. Failing that, the best way to detect faking is probably by including 'bogus' items referring to non-existent things (e.g., 'I know how to program with all versions of the Shorkipu software' or 'I have used Mokipu before').

7.17   Integrity inventories

The first thing to say about integrity 'tests' is that they are usually inventories rather than tests (hence the title of this section). The second is that in the past five to ten years they have enjoyed a level of popularity in personnel selection matched only by the Big Five (hence integrity is the first non-Big Five personality trait we review in this chapter). Needless to say, the popularity of integrity inventories is justified by the amount of empirical evidence in support of their validity in the prediction of important job outcomes. Most famously, Schmidt and Hunter's (1998) seminal meta-analysis concluded that the optimal combination of psychological measures in personnel selection consisted of GMA tests plus integrity inventories; but let us examine the concept and measurement of integrity in more detail.

Box 7.3 The polygraph and the quest for an objective personality test

After many decades of intensive use in employment, in 1988, the polygraph or 'lie detector' was banned in the US for the purpose of pre-employment screening under the Employee Polygraph Protection Act (EPPA). Until then, the polygraph was a widely used and trusted tool for spotting dishonest applicants despite the fact that there had been little evidence in support of its validity. Furthermore, a growing number of studies indicated that the number of 'false positives', i.e., honest subjects who are judged dishonest on the basis of the polygraph, was too high (EPPA, 1988). So, how exactly does the polygraph work?

The polygraph provides an objective measure of various physiological markers for anxiety, namely increases in blood pressure, pulse, respiration and skin conductivity. As individuals differ in their levels of arousal (as expressed through each of these markers), the polygraph is based on *within*-subject rather than between-subject comparisons, taking baseline measures of these variables first, and comparing arousal levels at baseline with those measured while the respondent is interrogated. Thus, unlike self-reports of honesty, which ask respondents to report how honest they are in relation to various scenarios or behaviours, participants tested via the polygraph may be asked to answer any question (the content is quite irrelevant) because their honesty is meant to be measured objectively. The problem is that even honest participants are likely to experience heightened levels of arousal when put in these circumstances, and any such changes are likely to be wrongly interpreted as dishonest responding when in fact arousal was triggered by increases in anxiety that are not related to lying.

Although the polygraph has been discredited to the extent of being considered a ludicrous proposition for assessing dishonesty and honesty, it reflects a long psychological quest for the objective assessment of personality traits. Indeed, 'objective personality tests' have been researched for almost a century (Achilles & Achilles, 1917; Ball, 1929; Cattell, 1950), especially by R. B. Cattell. In some cases, such as with the objective measurement of certain primary traits like tolerance for ambiguity or boredom, objective measures of personality (e.g., looking time, response latencies and kinesis) have shown some degree of success (Messick & Hills, 1960). In recent years, there has been a renaissance of objective measures of personality no doubt thanks to the technological improvements in software and computer developments. For example, the Hyperkinetic Syndrome Assessment Method is a software-based test for measuring children's work styles, adaptation to difficulty and adjustment to feedback, and it has shown good reliability and adequate validity in educational, health and clinical settings (Proyer & Häusler, 2007). Moreover, there has also been a recent and relatively successful rediscovery of some of Cattell's objective personality scales, with suggestions that such tests are re-employed in the context of personnel selection (Santacreu, Rubio & Hernández, 2006). However, objective tests that succeed at measuring broad personality dimensions (such as the Big Five traits) or compound traits (such as Integrity) have yet to be discovered (see Sections 7.21, 7.22 and 7.23 for a discussion of objective emotional intelligence measures), and the reliability of objective measures of personality traits is poor compared to that of subjective self-reports.

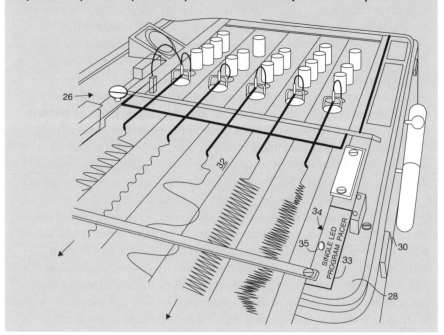

Integrity inventories – based on self-reports – fall into two different categories, namely personality-like and overt (Sackett, Burris & Callahan, 1989). Personality scales for assessing integrity function in the same way as the Big Five or indeed most personality inventories, namely by including various self-report items that tap into an underlying latent dimension of integrity (or indeed several subscales, such as dependability, conformity and risk-taking, which are conceptualised as aspects of integrity). Examples of such items would be 'I am always driven by principles' or 'Even when temptations are strong I manage to exert a great degree of self-control.' The advantage of these scales is that although they rely on self-reported information it is not completely obvious to the respondent what trait or construct is being assessed. Another advantage of these scales is that they assess a broad construct that is likely to be a marker of individual differences across a wide range of contexts.

On the other hand, overt integrity scales include two types of items (Dalton & Metzger, 1993; Dalton, Metzger & Wimbush, 1994). The first type is those items that require the respondent to provide specific information on his or her past wrongdoings. Examples of such items would be 'How many times in your previous employment history have you stolen something from your employer?' or 'Have you ever pretended to be sick in order to miss a day of work?' As can be seen, these items are straight-to-the-point, but it is also easy to identify the direction of the most desirable response. Moreover, honest individuals are probably more likely to 'confess' any behaviours with negative connotations than their less honest counterparts, in which case integrity scales would end up punishing honest rather than dishonest respondents (Karren & Zacharias, 2007).

In some cases so-called 'lie scales' have been introduced to spot unrealistically desirable responses. For example, if the question were 'Have you ever lied to your employer, even on something completely trivial?' and respondents answered 'never', we would probably wonder if we are either in the presence of the most honest person on earth or if the respondent is reporting incorrect information (voluntarily or not). The second type of items for overt integrity scales uses a more impressionistic approach, which is to assess respondents' attitudes towards integrity-related behaviours, though not theirs. For example, respondents may be asked to indicate the extent to which they agree with the following statements: 'Anybody who steels something is a thief and should be punished accordingly' or 'More often than not, lies can be justified and are less damaging than the truth.' Clearly, what is being assessed with such items is people's opinions or attitudes, and the assumption is that there is a link between people's acceptance of others' dishonesty (or, to rephrase, the extent to which people regard various behaviours as morally unacceptable) and their own dishonesty (Murphy, 2000). However, research has shown that more and less honest individuals do not really differ in their attitudes towards morally acceptable or unacceptable behaviours (Nicol & Paunonen, 2002) and, if they do, they may still report similar attitudes.

Box 7.4 Theft estimates in the workplace

The exact amount of theft that goes on in the workplace is hard to estimate given that it varies from one job to the next and, perhaps more fundamentally, that people are unlikely to report theft behaviours candidly. However, a variety of estimates have been made throughout the years. Hollinger and Clark (1983) estimated the non-trivial (i.e., deliberate, substantial and consequential) employee theft to be at least 5 per cent in most settings, though subsequent estimates have been much higher, particularly if they use alternative techniques to assess theft and other sensitive (illegal or counterproductive) behaviours (Dalton, Wimbush & Daily, 1994). Estimates have also varied across job sectors. For instance, Brooks and Arnold (1989) reckoned that for the retail industry theft rates are as high as 35 per cent, and Slora (1989) found that over 4/10 supermarket and over 6/10 fast-food employees confessed to theft (which suggests the real number is even higher). However, these estimates confounded both trivial and non-trivial theft (note that the former may include 'having at least once taken something from your work without paying'). However, studies controlling for methodological artefacts (such as underestimations due to self-reports) and distinguishing between more and less serious forms of theft are far from optimistic. Wimbush and Dalton (1997) estimated overall levels of theft to be as high as 60 per cent. Moreover, even non-trivial theft (e.g., more than $10 in cash or merchandise per a month) was estimated at 35 per cent.

Evidence for the validity of personality-based integrity inventories was reported quite emphatically by the largest meta-analytic study on personality constructs published to date (Ones, Viswesvaran & Schmidt, 1993). In it, Ones and colleagues reported a colossal total of 665 validity coefficients for over half a million subjects. The criteria used to examine the validity of integrity inventories included both self-reported and archival evidence of theft, attendance records and even job performance. The uncorrected average validity for integrity measures as predictors of job performance was .25 (corrected .41), whereas for counterproductive work behaviours (see also Section 6.11) it was .27 (corrected .39). This prompted experts to suggest that if integrity scales are added to GMA tests, the prediction of job performance is practically as good as it gets (Schmidt & Hunter, 1998).

Although critics have argued that most of the studies examined were published by the actual test-publishers (highlighting a potential conflict of interests, unless the publishers have integrity themselves), independent studies reported similar validities (Bernardin & Cooke, 1993). Yet it is true that when it comes to predicting actual theft, which is arguably the obvious criterion for validating any measure of integrity, the validities of integrity scales have been surprisingly low (regardless of where the data came from) (Guastello & Rieke, 1991; Murphy, 2000).

7.18   Criticisms of integrity inventories

Like all psychological assessment tools, integrity inventories have been the target of criticisms, and perhaps even more so than other instruments because of the moral implications of assessing integrity. A recent review (Karren & Zacharias, 2007) has highlighted four major drawbacks of integrity scales, namely:

1. Construct confusion: it is unclear what integrity scales are actually assessing. If the underlying construct is integrity, why are these scales so weakly correlated with theft indicators, and why do they correlate quite systematically with job performance? From an applied perspective, integrity scales are especially needed to reduce or avoid theft (see Box 7.4), yet there are virtually no validity studies providing evidence for the idea that these scales are predictive of theft (Murphy & Dzieweczynski, 2005). Indeed, even in Ones' meta-analysis of integrity scales (see Section 7.17) different integrity scales were weakly intercorrelated, suggesting that different scales are assessing different constructs. Correlations of integrity with Conscientiousness, Agreeableness and Neuroticism (negatively) suggest that integrity is a higher-order or compound trait, but is 'integrity' the accurate name for it? On the basis of its Big Five correlates, one could relabel this trait something like 'Responsible pro-social stability' or 'Pro-active and stable cooperativeness'. It is apparent that the integrity–performance associations cannot be explained by Conscientiousness (Murphy & Lee, 1994), so why are integrity inventories predictive of performance? Finally, what do we know about the temporal and cross-situational stability of integrity, and is it more important in explaining dishonesty than situational factors are (Murphy, 1993)? Evidence suggests that integrity-related behaviours are more affected by situational than personal factors (Mumford, Connelly, Helton, Strange & Osburn, 2001). Indeed, one of the earliest reviews of personality (including integrity or 'character') measures concluded that different measures of honesty are very poorly intercorrelated (May & Hartshorne, 1926), such that people are honest or not depending on the situation and situationally determined motivation (see again Box 7.1).
2. Just like the polygraph (see Box 7.3), integrity scales may underestimate the number of false positive responses, misclassifying honest respondents as dishonest. As said (Section 7.13), 'faking good' about one's past misbehaviours may be picked up by lie scales – especially if one exaggerates. Yet being honest about them is unlikely to result in higher integrity. This problem brings us back all the way to Epimenides' paradox: if someone admits to being a liar, is that person really a liar? Moreover, it would only take a few fakers (who

are capable of not only spotting the correct response but also hiding their past misbehaviours or positive attitudes about immoral behaviours) to make honest respondents seem even more dishonest. It has been estimated that as many as four out of five respondents who end up being classified as dishonest are actually misclassified (Bernardin & Cooke, 1993).

3. In line with point 2, meta-analytic estimates suggest improvements of about 1 standard deviation on integrity 'scores' after test-takers have been instructed to fake good (Alliger & Dwight, 2000). This shows that, regardless of people's motivation to be honest, most individuals are able to identify the correct responses to these inventories. In theory, then, the only thing people would need to fake good is the motivation to do it (though of course some respondents may be particularly worried that they may be found out, especially in high-stake settings). Post hoc enquires to anonymous test-takers after completion of integrity scales indicate that up to 50 per cent of respondents admit having exaggerated or faked good, presenting themselves as more dependable, conscientious and reliable. Additional practice and coaching can cause substantial improvements on overt integrity tests and some improvements on personality-like inventories.

4. Employees and job candidates tend to dislike integrity inventories because of their intrusive nature (Ryan & Sackett, 1987) and the fact that they ask questions that bear little apparent relation to their view of competence. Indeed, many people regret taking such tests and dislike organisations for using them in selection. It has also been argued that integrity scales discriminate against people with certain political attitudes (Faust, 1996). For instance, agreeing with the statement 'It is important to give people a second chance' is seen as a sign of lack of integrity but it also taps into authoritarianism and right-wing personality, both negatively. It is therefore not surprising that people higher in Openness to Experience are more likely to 'fail' or score lower in integrity scales (Guastello & Rieke, 1991).

7.19 Emotional intelligence (EI)

In a broad sense, emotional intelligence (EI) refers to individual differences in the ability to identify and manage one's own and other people's emotions (Goleman, 1995; Salovey & Mayer, 1989). Thus, EI is essentially an ability related to emotional processes, notably the successful manipulation and accurate knowledge of emotional states. That said, just as integrity tests are not actual tests, EI is not really an intelligence; hence 'trait EI' is often used to emphasise the taxonomic position of this construct in the realm of personality rather than intelligence (Brody, 2004; Petrides & Furnham, 2001). But what is EI, and why is it not an actual intelligence? More importantly, how important is EI in personnel selection? Sections 7.20 to 7.23 attempt to answer these questions.

7.20   What is EI?

As said, EI refers to individual differences in emotional identification and management, hence it is generally defined as the ability to identify and manage one's own and others' emotions. However, there has been extensive debate in the past ten years or so as to whether the EI construct fulfils the necessary requirements to be considered an actual intelligence (for a state-of-the-art summary of this debate and a compelling case against the inclusion of EI in the realm of human intelligence the reader is strongly encouraged to consult Brody, 2004). Note that the use of the term 'ability' is neither consistent with how EI tends to be assessed nor sufficient to grant EI a place in the realm of human abilities. Unless, say, we consider any self-report of competence an indicator of intelligence. For example, some people may be better than others at making other people cry, and we may assess these individual differences by asking respondents to agree or disagree with statements such as 'I find it very easy to make others cry' or 'Upsetting others is easy.' But would these questions be measuring an *ability*, let alone intelligence?

Whilst there is no absolute answer to these questions, it is clear that if one conceptualises EI as an intelligence it would be incongruent not to do the same with a wide range of other non-cognitive constructs. In fact, most personality traits would probably have to be rebranded as 'intelligence'. For example, Emotional Stability (low Neuroticism) could be defined as the ability to remain calm under difficult circumstances or the ability to work well under pressure, Extraversion could be defined as the ability to socialise or interact with people even if you don't know them, and Conscientiousness could be defined as the ability to resist one's temptations and trade off instant gratification for relevant long-term goals. Doing this, however, would be incongruent with a well-established tradition in psychology to refer to maximal performance tests as 'ability tests' (see Section 7.1) and typical performance scales as 'personality inventories'. In that sense, there are two radical elements in the concept of EI (though some approaches, such as trait EI, are an exception to this; see Section 7.21), namely (a) it defies the notion of 'intelligence' as being essentially cognitive, and (b) it defies the notion of ability tests as being essentially maximal performance measures. In fact, a third important issue is that ability tests are predictive of individual differences in learning, educational and occupational achievement, where occupational achievement is particularly relevant to this book. Can the same be said about EI scales? Do they predict job and training performance?

7.21   EI: the personality construct

Conceptualisations of EI as a personality construct are congruent with the traditional distinction in psychology of referring to self-reported scales of

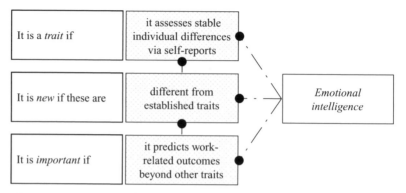

Figure 7.23 *Validating emotional intelligence as a personality construct: three 'ifs'*

typical performance as personality traits and, accordingly, seek to validate scales of EI as personality measures. First, this requires demonstration of the reliability of EI self-reports, that is, showing that these scales have sufficient test–retest reliability to indicate little intra-individual variability and a 'trait-like' disposition. Second, it is also essential to demonstrate that the EI construct is different from established personality traits, otherwise EI would simply be a new name for an already known trait or set of traits (Chamorro-Premuzic & Furnham, 2006a). Third, and perhaps most importantly from an applied point of view, it is important to show that any association between EI measures and relevant outcomes (e.g., job performance, job satisfaction and training success) cannot be explained by established personality traits, such as the Big Five. Thus EI should demonstrate *incremental validity* over and above other traits in the prediction of work-related outcomes.

7.22   Reliability of EI

There is no question that the constellation of behavioural tendencies defined by the EI construct refers to individual differences in stable behavioural patterns, such that one may safely conclude that what EI inventories assess is personality. Moreover, they found that trait EI is significantly correlated with established personality traits. These results provide compelling evidence for the interpretation of EI as a personality trait that is a 'compound' or higher-order factor of individual differences in Emotional Stability, Extraversion, Agreeableness and Conscientiousness (see also Section 7.23). Petrides and Furnham's (2001) original interpretation of 'emotional self-efficacy' emphasises the fact that, from a conceptual point of view, people who are less Neurotic, more Extraverted, Agreeable and Conscientious *rate* their abilities to handle emotionally challenging situations and their abilities to perceive and manage emotions higher than their more neurotic, introverted, disagreeable and less conscientious counterparts. In the tradition of self-expectancy constructs, such as self-efficacy (see

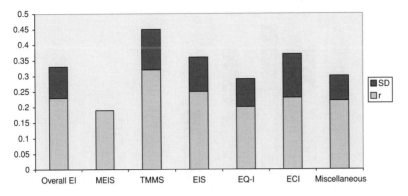

Figure 7.24 *Meta-analytic validities for different EI scales (corrected correlations and their SDs)*

Section 7.24), people's perceptions of their own abilities (emotional or not) are known to have important behavioural consequences regardless of their accuracy. Thus the question for trait EI is whether it can have self-fulfilling effects on performance related to work outcomes; so, just how valid are self-reports of EI in predicting occupational success? (See Section 7.23).

7.23   Validity of EI

The importance of EI in the context of work was demonstrated by a meta-analytic study (Van Rooy & Viswesvaran, 2004). The authors examined data from 59 independent studies (9,522 participants) and reported an operational validity of .23 for measures of EI as predictors of various job outcomes. Associations between EI and the criteria examined depended on what instruments were used (Figure 7.24) and what dimensions or aspects of EI were assessed (Figure 7.25). As seen in Figure 7.24, validities were slightly higher for the trait meta-mood scale (TMMS) (Salovey, Mayer, Goldman, Turvey & Palfai, 1995), followed by the emotional intelligence scale (EIS), emotional competence inventory (ECI) (Sala, 2002), miscellaneous scales, the emotional quotient inventory (EQ-I) (Bar-On, 1997) and finally the multifactor emotional intelligence scale (MEIS) (Mayer & Salovey, 1997).

Figure 7.25 plots the validities of different 'facets' or aspects of EI as estimated by Van Rooy and Viswesvaran's meta-analysis. The four bars on the left represent subscales of the MEIS (based on Salovey and Mayer's framework) and show that assimilation (7 samples and 770 participants) had the highest and perception (21 samples and 3,484 participants) the lowest validities, and that understanding (10 samples and 1,525 participants) and management (18 samples and 2,961 participants) showed the highest variability (as indicated by the SD of the meta-analytic correlations). The five bars on the right of the chart are based on the EQ-i (Bar-On's) subgroupings and indicate that validities were generally lower

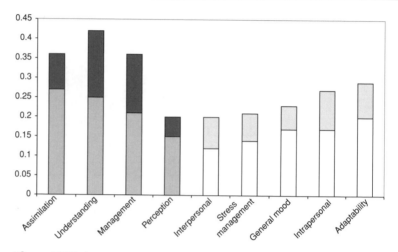

Figure 7.25 *Aspects of EI that predict work outcomes*

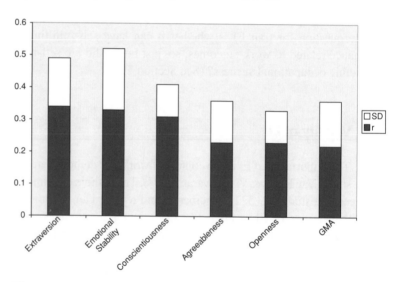

Figure 7.26 *Meta-analytic correlations (and their SDs) of EI with the Big Five and GMA*

and more homogeneous than for the MEIS subscales. The lowest validity was found for the interpersonal facet (22 studies and 4,684 participants), followed by stress management (9 samples and 2,687 participants), followed by general mood (9 samples and 2,687 participants) and intrapersonal (20 studies and 4,548 participants); the highest validity was found for adaptability (20 samples and 4,524 participants).

Van Rooy and Viswesvaran also reported meta-analytic correlations between EI, GMA and the Big Five personality traits. As shown in Figure 7.26, EI correlated at .34 with Extraversion (19 studies and 4,158 participants), 33 with Emotional Stability (23 studies and 4,213 participants), .23 with Openness and Agreeableness (14 studies and 3,306 participants), and .22 with GMA (19 studies and 4,158 subjects). All correlations correct for unreliability in the criterion and observed mean in the predictors.

Moreover, the authors used previous validities for GMA and the Big Five to estimate the incremental validity of EI, and found that EI explained unique and additional variance over and above personality traits, but not GMA. Other studies have also shown that EI inventories are valid predictors of peer nominations of influence (Byrne, Smither, Reilly & Dominick, 2007), though a recent study showed that EI has no incremental validity over GMA and Conscientiousness in predicting educational attainments, social status or income (Amelang & Steinmayr, 2006).

7.24 Self-efficacy

Another personality construct that has long been associated with work performance is self-efficacy, defined broadly as an individual's beliefs about his or her capabilities to affect events and outcomes and produce desired levels of performance (Bandura, 1999). The core idea underlying the notion of self-efficacy is that competency-related self-beliefs have self-fulfilling prophecies and affect performance irrespective of actual abilities. To paraphrase Henry Ford, 'Whether you believe you can do a thing or not, you are right.'

Although self-efficacy has been primarily examined in the context of clinical and social-psychological settings, there is a wealth of published research looking at self-efficacy in work settings too. Judge, Jackson, Shaw, Scott and Rich (2007) note that: 'In industrial–organisational (I-O) psychology, self-efficacy has been remarkably popular as well. In the past 25 years, more than 800 articles on self-efficacy have been published in organisational journals. Virtually every area in organisational research has utilized self-efficacy' (p. 107). Thus Judge *et al.* provided a quantitative estimate of the unique contribution of self-efficacy to work-related outcomes whilst taking into consideration the Big Five traits, GMA and previous job experience. Results showed that overall the contribution of self-efficacy to explaining occupational outcomes was relatively small in comparison to that of other personality traits and GMA. However, there were some exceptions, notably low complexity jobs (this is consistent with Kanfer & Ackerman, 1989) and task rather than job performance, where self-efficacy did provide some important additional information to the prediction of work outcomes (Judge *et al.*, 2007). However, in all the effect of self-efficacy was largely accounted for by personality and GMA.

7.25 Core self-evaluations

The idea that self-beliefs affect performance independently of actual competencies has not only been represented by the notion of self-efficacy but is at the heart of a wide range of self-centred constructs, such as locus of control, self-esteem, self-concept and even Neuroticism. In an attempt to overcome the multiplicity of labels and overlapping constructs referring to individual differences in self-perceptions (e.g., of concept, ability, efficacy, etc.), Judge and colleagues recently conceptualised a higher order construct of 'Core Self-Evaluations' (CSE) (Judge, Erez, Bono & Thoresen, 2003; Judge, Locke, Durham & Kluger, 1998). This work was inspired by the authors' finding (see Section 7.11) of the strong dispositional determinants of job satisfaction. But the key importance of CSE is that it explains the common variance found among a variety of self-centred constructs, such as locus of control, self-efficacy, self-esteem, self-concept and also Neuroticism. Thus high CSE are indicative of positive self-regard in general, and specifically higher self-efficacy, internal rather than external locus of control or attributional style, Emotional Stability rather than Neuroticism, and higher self-concept. Evidence indicated that people with higher CSE are also more likely to hold self-concordant goals and be intrinsically rather than extrinsically motivated, all of which is reflected in higher job satisfaction (Judge, Bono, Erez & Locke, 2005).

7.26 Moving beyond traits: the person–environment fit

Though not new (Pervin & Rubin, 1967), interactive approaches to personality have emphasised the importance of assessing not only traits but also situational factors, specifically the level of congruence between them. Thus such theories posit that occupational outcomes, such as job satisfaction, stress and indeed productivity, will depend not only on the personal characteristics (e.g., Conscientiousness, Integrity or Extraversion) but on whether these *fit* in the context of the organisation (Pervin, 1989). Accordingly, whether specific personality traits affect occupational outcomes and how will depend on whether the environment facilitates or inhibits their effects. For example, Extraversion may be predictive of higher performance in sales jobs only if these environments are sufficiently 'extraverted'. What matters here is the individuals' perception of the environment as well as his or her assessment of how close that environment is to his or her 'ideal' setting. In that sense, three things are needed to assess the level of person–environment fit, namely:

(a) The individual's personality
(b) The environment's 'personality'
(c) The level of congruency between a and b

Recent evidence suggests that the person–environment fit predicts training success in occupational settings. Specifically, a study found that if employees perceived that their training supervisors supported and promoted their creative initiative and respected their preferred workload, they performed better than employees

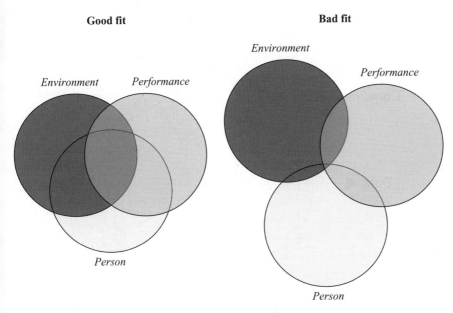

Good fit   **Bad fit**

Figure 7.27 *Performance as a function of the person–environment fit*

who did not feel supported in these areas by their supervisors (Awoniyi, Griego & Morgan, 2002).

Although assessment of environmental factors has been largely overshadowed by the assessment of personality traits, the vocational interests – or simply 'interests' – have embodied a longstanding attempt to bridge the gap between personal and environmental attributes. Within this field, major taxonomies have emerged such as Holland's and Prediger's interests models, which are often conceptualised in terms of personality traits (Holland, 1999). Holland (1959, 1997) classified individuals' vocational preferences and indeed the level of prestige, income and skills associated with these vocations, using a typology that could be simultaneously applied to people and jobs, hence emphasising the importance of 'fitting' the right person to the right job. As seen in Figure 7.28, Holland's typology classifies interests and careers with an hexagon describing Realistic (R), Investigative (I), Artistic (A), Social (S), Entrepreneurial (E) and Conventional (C) jobs/interests, with R-S representing the Things–People dimensions, C-A representing the Conformity (non-Conformity) dimension, and the Data-Ideas and Sociability dimensions at the intersection of C-E/I-A and E-S/R-I, respectively. People's interests have been shown to be at least as reliable as standard personality traits, if not more. For example, Strong reported a twenty-two-year (eighteen years after university) test–retest reliability of .75 for his Interest Inventory (Strong, 1955).

A recent study (Armstrong *et al.*, 2008) reported important data highlighting the interface between personality (e.g., Big Five) and interests (Holland's RIASEC), as well as examining sex differences in these constructs. Results

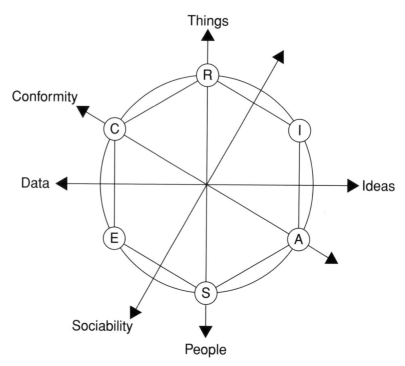

Figure 7.28 *Holland's RIASEC*

indicated that men showed a preference for 'Things' whereas women showed a preference for 'People', which is in line with previous studies (Tracey & Rounds, 1992). Indeed, Lubinski argued that this sex difference is the 'largest of all sex differences on major psychological dimensions' (2000, p. 421). But the most interesting results of Armstrong *et al.*'s investigation concern the associations among different individual difference constructs. As shown in Figure 7.29, different personality dimensions could be organised on the basis of the RIASEC model in a way that is coherent with the meaning of the constructs examined.

7.27   Summary and conclusions

Throughout this chapter we have examined the notion of personality traits and how self-report-based inventories designed to assess them can be used to predict important occupational outcomes. As we have seen, personality traits differ mainly from cognitive ability constructs in that the former are assessed via self-report inventories and refer to individual differences in typical behaviours, whilst the latter (see Chapter 6) measure maximal performance and are measured via timed tests of performance (with objective rather than subjective items). Although the predictive power of personality scales at work is clearly lower and more job-specific than that of ability tests, if the right traits are assessed in the right

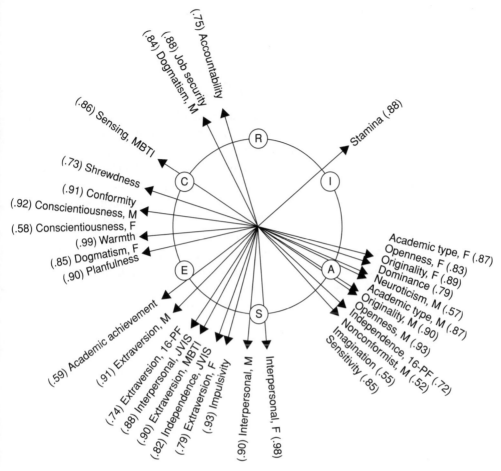

Figure 7.29 *Individual characteristics integrated into a two-dimensional RIASEC interest circumplex (reproduced with permission from Armstrong et al., 2008)*

context, personality inventories add important information to the prediction of future occupational success. Moreover, Conscientiousness, one of the main factors of personality, has general and positive effects on work-related criteria that are independent of GMA as well as preventive and protective health- and real-life-related effects.

Although the face validity of self-reports is threatened by the fact that in high-stake settings people can (and are indeed motivated to) 'fake good' or lie, there is mixed evidence and almost never-ending debate as to the real practical problems that faking poses. What is clear is that we have no 'objective' (ability-like) alternatives for measuring individual differences in personality, and that self-reports still provide incremental validity in the prediction of work outcomes over and above GMA.

Several steps forward have been taken in personality-related personnel selection since the early 1990s. First, meta-analytic estimates have provided reliable and robust quantitative evaluations of the predictive validity and utility of widely used traits. Second, personality researchers have at last agreed on the major personality traits that should be considered to provide a comprehensive picture of individual differences in non-clinical samples, with the Big Five emerging as the dominant taxonomy. Although the emergence of the Big Five should not undermine other models, it is inarguably useful as a universal 'exchange currency' to compare results from different studies (which, for instance, in the case of meta-analytic validations, is of capital importance). Third, 'compound' traits, such as Integrity, EI and self-centred constructs (e.g., self-efficacy or CSE) are also useful explaining non-ability-related variance in occupational outcomes. Last, but not least, recent years have witnessed an exciting attempt to integrate core personality constructs with their 'cousin' constructs of interests and even abilities (Ackerman, 1997; Armstrong *et al.*, 2008; Chamorro-Premuzic & Furnham, 2006). These conceptual efforts are important because of their potential to capitalise on the synergistic (*mediational* and *moderational*) links among the major sources of interindividual differences, in the workplace and beyond.

Notes

1 Throughout this chapter we will use 'subjective' to encompass both self- and other-reports of traits or behaviours, purely in order to distinguish between this form of assessment and 'objective' tests (which have objectively determined correct answers).
2 See www.personality-project.org/perproj/theory/big5.table.html for details.

8 Creativity

8.1 Introduction

Some employees are more creative than others: they are more likely to come up with original thoughts and novel solutions and stand out in organisations for their innovative thinking; they seem to prefer innovation to imitation and even enjoy defying the crowd. In this chapter, we discuss the key psychological factors underlying creativity and what personnel selection can do to select creative people.

Although the topic of creativity has a longstanding history in psychology (dating back to the very beginnings of intelligence testing more than one hundred years ago), creativity researchers have repeatedly complained about the fact that insufficient attention is given to the field (Guilford, 1950; Sternberg & Lubart, 1996). Indeed, despite growing economic interests and being associated with a wide range of concepts, such as intelligence (see Chapter 6), personality (see Chapter 7), leadership (see Chapter 9), imagination, motivation, social influence, intuition and talent (see Chapter 10) (Runco, 2004), creativity continues to be neglected from selection-related research.

In 1950, Guilford highlighted the importance of increasing creativity research after noting that only 186 of the 121,000 psychological studies in databases had dealt with creativity. In line with this finding, Figure 8.1 shows that the number of articles including 'creativity', 'creative' or 'originality' as keywords in the main applied journals (*JAP = Journal of Applied Psychology*; *JCP = Journal of Counselling Psychology*; *JOB = Journal of Organizational Behavior*; *AMR = Academy of Management Review*; *PP = Personnel Psychology*; *JOOP = Journal of Organizational and Occupational Psychology*; and *IJSA = International Journal of Selection and Assessment*) is very low, even for *JAP*, as the total number of articles published by the journal between 1917 and 2008 was 8,932. Needless to say, a great deal of creativity research has been published in other, creativity-specialised journals, such as the *Journal of Creative Behaviour* and *Creativity Research Journal*; however, these publication outlets are rarely concerned with personnel selection and tend to examine student samples.

The generalised lack of applied research on creativity is in stark contrast with the consensus, particularly in industrialised or developed nations, on the importance of investing in creative employees. Thus Porter (1990, p. 73) noted that 'national prosperity is created, not inherited' and Amabile (1990) saw individual

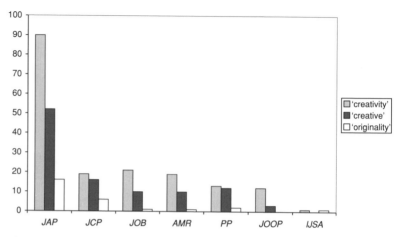

Figure 8.1 *Number of articles with 'creativity', 'creative' or 'originality' as keywords in applied journals until 2008*

creativity as the building block for organisational innovation. Indeed, knowledge-based societies have made creativity a common concept in managerial and macro-economic strategies and a key driver of competitiveness.

Rapid advancements in technology lead to shorter product life cycles and generate intense business competition for innovative ideas (Amabile *et al.*, 1996; Andriopoulos, 2003). Furthermore, cultural, aesthetic and creative aspects of the economies of industrialised nations are growing fast and at unprecedented rates (European Commission, 2001; OECD, 2006; United States Census Reports, 2000). All this means that selecting employees with creative potential is now not only a priority for many sectors of the economy, but also the cause of higher demand for newcomers and the introduction of diverse working teams (Perretti & Negro, 2007), which inevitably impacts on personnel selection.

8.2   Definitions and conceptualisations of creativity

Creativity is part of everyday vocabulary and laypeople have a fairly good idea of how to define it. For example, Sprecher investigated lay conceptions of creativity by asking engineers from a large industrial firm to explain the determinants of creativity in highly ranked co-workers (from research groups, service groups and project groups). Results showed that novelty and worth of ideas were deemed the most relevant factors in creativity, and that independence in problem solving and the achievement of comprehensive answers were also rated highly (Sprecher, 1959). Similar results on lay views of creativity have been reported since (Sternberg & O'Hara, 2000), though laypeople often confound creativity and intelligence, seeing them as the same thing. Indeed, Sternberg (1985a) found a correlation of r = .69 between people's ratings of the creativity and intelligence of imaginary targets.

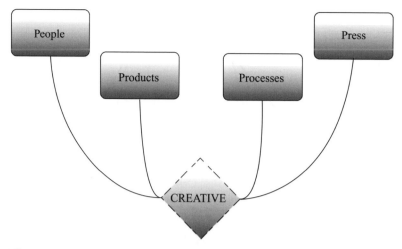

Figure 8.2 *Components of the creative syndrome*

Among experts (both practitioners and researchers), creativity is often defined in terms of *originality*, though this is merely one aspect of creativity. Critics of the conceptualisation of creativity as originality have observed that 'creativity has finished up by being evaluated simply as an oddity or bizarreness of response relative to the population mean . . . [which] comes close to misleading the shadow for the substance' (Cattell, 1971, p. 409). Creative products, then, should not only be original, but also useful. Thus Amabile defined creativity as the 'production of novel and useful ideas' (1988, p. 126), a definition that has since been endorsed by a large number of researchers (e.g., Bailin, 1988; Chamorro-Premuzic, 2007; Mumford & Gustafson, 1988).

Despite consensus in defining creativity, the term is often used in different contexts: there are more and less creative people, ideas, behaviours, works and even jobs (e.g., architect, graphic designer and advertising vs judge, librarian and accountant), though in all jobs some people will be more creative than others. Accordingly, creativity has been conceptualised as a syndrome or complex, rather than a single phenomenon, referring to creative *people*, creative *processes*, creative *products* and environmental influences or *press* on creativity (Rhodes, 1961/1987; Runco, 2004). Figure 8.2 graphically depicts the components of the creativity syndrome, which are discussed in the forthcoming sections.

8.3   Creative people

The *person* or *people* approach to creativity focuses on interindividual differences in creativity and thereby tries to identify and explain the factors that make one person more creative than others. Traditionally, these factors have included cognitive abilities, personality traits and motivation, though in recent years cognitive styles and knowledge have also been emphasised; see,

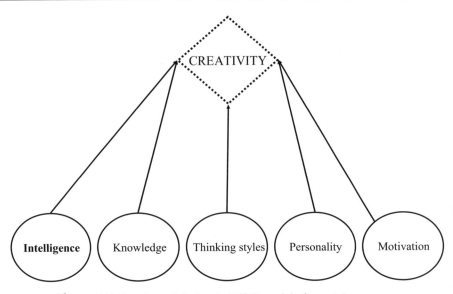

Figure 8.3 *Sternberg & Lubart's (1995) model of creativity*

for instance, Sternberg and Lubart's (1995) conception of creativity, illustrated in Figure 8.3. This multidetermined view of personal creativity has important implications for selection as validated psychometric tests are available for all the individual difference constructs associated with creativity, in particular personality (see again Chapter 7) and intelligence (see again Chapter 6). But is there a specific combination of scores to highlight the creative potential of a person? Over the past century psychologists have tried to address this question, looking at the various dispositional and ability correlates of creativity.

Barron (1963) provided the first comprehensive catalogue of the personality and ability characteristics of more and less creative people. He noted that creative people are 'affected, aggressive, demanding, dependent, dominant, forceful, impatient, initiative, outspoken, sarcastic, strong, and suggestive' if they have lower intellectual abilities, whilst non-cretaive people with higher intelligence are 'mild, optimistic, pleasant, quiet, unselfish' (p. 22). In at least two ways, Barron's description was ahead of its time as it anticipated a subsequent trend in psychological research to examine the psychopathological aspects of creativity (see Section 8.3) as well as the moderating role of cognitive abilities in explaining personality differences in creativity (Peterson & Carson, 2000).

However, most efforts to profile creative people have focused on personality traits. Until the consolidation of the five-factor, or 'Big Five' (see Chapter 7), personality model, psychologists' attempts to identify the key traits that characterise creative people have been somewhat unorganised, such that different labels were often used to refer to the same traits and different levels of generality (from broader trait constructs to primary facets or dimensions of these constructs) were often undermined. Nonetheless researchers by and large identified the 'bulk' of traits that are currently regarded as core personality markers of creativity.

Torrance (1979, p. 360) pointed out that 'creativity is essentially a personality syndrome that includes openness to experience, adventuresomeness, and self-confidence'. In line, creative people have been described as being risk-takers (Sternberg & O'Hara, 2000), self-confident (MacKinnon, 1971; Buel, 1965), nonconformist or autonomous (Buel, 1965; Kabanoff & Bottger, 1991; McDermid, 1965; Keller & Holland, 1978), tolerant of ambiguity – accepting complexity and chaos without becoming anxious (MacKinnon, 1960), and driven to accomplish personal and economic goals (MacKinnon, 1962; Buel, 1965), though studies have also found a negative link between creativity and achievement-drive (Kabanoff & Bottger, 1991).

The most extensive pre-Big Five review of the literature on the personality correlates of creativity was published by Barron and Harrington (1981). The authors concluded that creative individuals had 'high valuation of aesthetic qualities in experience, broad interests, attraction to complexity, high energy, independence of judgment, autonomy, intuition, self-confidence, ability to resolve antinomies or to accommodate apparently opposite or conflicting traits in one's self-concept, and finally, a firm sense of self as "creative"' (p. 453). Further traits used to describe creative persons were 'active, alert, ambitious, argumentative, artistic, assertive, capable, clear thinking, clever, complicated, confident, curious, cynical, demanding, egotistical, energetic, enthusiastic, hurried, idealistic, imaginative, impulsive, independent, individualistic, ingenious, insightful, intelligent, interests wide, inventive, original, practical, quick, rebellious, reflective, resorceful, self-confident, sensitive, sharp-witted, spontaneous, unconventional, versatile, and *not* conventional and *not* inhibited' (p. 454).

The introduction of the Big Five personality traits has made it rather straightforward to identify the core dispositional predictors of creativity. In fact all the personality characteristics mentioned above can be coherently organised on the basis of the Big Five taxonomy, interpreted as 'facets' or lower-order dimensions of the five broad personality factors (see Figure 8.4). In line with this, Chamorro-Premuzic and Furnham (2005) reviewed the Big Five correlates of creativity and concluded that Openness was the most important factor to discriminate between creative and non-creative people, though Extraversion, and to a lesser extent Agreeableness, are also useful to explain individual differences in creativity.

The strong link between Openness and creativity is unsurprising as Openness assesses individual differences in aesthetic preferences, values, fantasy, feeling, actions and ideas related to novelty and intellectual experiences (see Sections 7.3 and 7.10) and is often interpreted as a self-report of creativity (Chamorro-Premuzic & Furnham, 2005; Matthews & Deary, 1998).

Dollinger and Clancy (1993) reported a positive association between participants' Openness and their ability to improvise autobiographical story-essays on the basis of pictures. 'Richness' of essays was mostly correlated with *aesthetic*

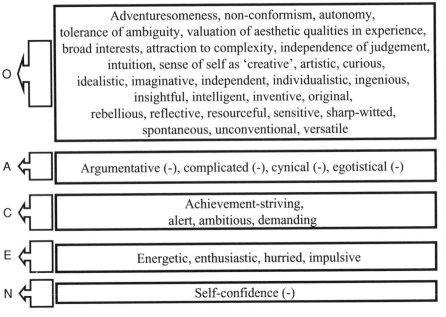

Figure 8.4 *Personality facets associated with creativity (organised by the Big Five)*

openness in men, and *openness to ideas* in women. Multiple regression analysis revealed that Openness was the most significant predictor of creativity (see also Furnham, 1999).

Openness has also been found to be a key determinant of creative performance in work settings (George & Zhou, 2001), particularly when employees are faced with many alternative possibilities for solving a problem or performing a task. In that sense, Openness would have the reverse effect of Conscientiousness, which favours performance on structured, predefined tasks, and is thus detrimental for creativity. In addition, King, Walker and Broyles (1996) found that verbal creativity was positively correlated with Extraversion and Openness to Experience, and negatively with Agreeableness, whereas Chamorro-Premuzic and Reichenbacher (2008) showed that Openness is related to creative task performance (ideational fluency) even when all other factors are taken into account.

Feist (1998) meta-analysed 83 studies reporting associations between creativity and personality, coding personality traits according to the Big Five taxonomy (see Figures 7.4 and 8.4, and Section 7.3) and comparing scientists vs non-scientists, artists vs non-artists, and creative vs less creative scientists. Results showed that Openness, Extraversion and Conscientiousness discriminated between scientists and non-scientists. The traits that most strongly differentiated the creative from less creative scientists were Extraversion and Openness. Artists, on the other hand, were approximately one standard deviation lower on Conscientiousness and half a standard deviation higher on Openness than non-artists.

Feist (1999) concluded that some dispositions, such as higher Openness, unconventionality, self-confidence, drive, dominance and impulsivity could be used to accurately characterise creative individuals in both arts and sciences (consistently with Figure 8.4). On the other hand, artists were found to be more Neurotic, less sociable and less accepting of group norms than their counterpart scientists, who tended to be more conscientious. These findings (like those from Feist, 1998) have important implications for selection and work psychology because they assess the discriminant validity of different traits in explaining the creative behaviours of different vocational types and professions. If creativity is manifested in different personality traits across disciplines or academic domains, the idea of an overarching creative personality may be elusive, especially beyond Openness.

The connections between creativity and personality traits (which are largely stable dispositions) indicate that traits should also predict creative outcomes across time. Accordingly, Feist and Barron (2003) examined the longitudinal predictive validity of personality (over an impressive fifty-five-year period!). Although complete data were only available for 43 subjects, which is understandable given the long time-span, results indicated that personality traits at age 27 predicted originality and creative achievement at age 72, even when early potential indicators and ability scores were taken into account.

Whereas the above findings reveal important personality characteristics of creative individuals – which can be assessed via personality inventories such as those discussed in Chapter 7 – creative people have also been characterised in terms of their higher cognitive abilities, including general mental ability (see Chapter 6).

Sternberg argued that three aspects of intelligence underlie individual differences in creativity, namely, *synthetic*, *analytical* and *practical* intelligences. Synthetic intelligence is used to combine different cognitions and produce novel associations, such as in the case of insight. Analytical intelligence is important because it enables creative individuals to judge the value or appropriateness of an idea. Last but not least, practical intelligence would be advantageous for applying creative ideas in everyday life and 'selling' them to others (see Sternberg & O'Hara, 2000, for a review of Sternberg's creativity theory). This view defines creative people by their social competence as well as their motivation to think differently from the rest. For example, creative people may decide not to sell their houses if a large number of people are selling theirs and their original behaviour may be rewarded by selling at a higher price when there are fewer houses on offer (and more in demand).

However, research into the cognitive abilities that are characteristic of the creative person have tended to focus on 'academic' (IQ, *g* or general mental ability) competence, not least because they can be measured objectively through psychometric tests. Early attempts to document the relationship between intelligence and creativity consisted of biographical studies. Cox (1926) calculated the intelligence and 'creative impact' (opeartionalised in terms of the length of an encyclopaedic entry) of 301 eminencies who lived between 1450 and 1850.

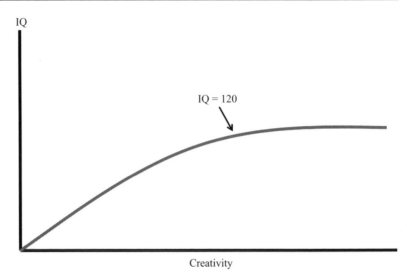

Figure 8.5 *Threshold theory of creativity and intelligence*

The correlation between creative impact and intelligence was significant but modest (at about .16). However, limitations of Cox's study, such as the omission of actual test scores for the examined constructs, underestimated the true association between creativity and intelligence.

In what counts as one of the first methodologically sound studies on creativity and intelligence, Barron (1963) administered divergent thinking (see Section 8.4) and cognitive ability tests to students, army officers, writers, artists and businessmen. Results showed correlations between creativity and intelligence measures in the region of r = .40. However, at higher levels of intelligence, i.e., IQ > 120 (Getzels & Jackson, 1962), the correlation between intelligence and creativity dropped (see Figure 8.5).

For instance, in a sample of army officers with average IQ (100), the correlation between creativity and intelligence was r = .30, but in a sample of architects who scored 2 SD higher in IQ (130) the correlation between intelligence and creativity was very low, and even negative (−.08). This is congruent with the *threshold* theory of creativity and intelligence (Guilford, 1967; Schubert, 1973), which posits that intelligence is necessary but not sufficient to be creative and that after a certain level of intelligence the effects of cognitive ability on creativity are attenuated. Support for this theory was also provided by Guilford and Christensen (1973), who reported that lower-IQ students scored significantly lower in creativity, but that higher-IQ scorers did not differ in creativity.

Non-linear theories of the creativity and intelligence association may explain the variable and inconsistent correlations reported in the literature: in Barron and Harrington's (1981) review correlations ranged from r = −.05 to r = .30, though correlations between intelligence and divergent thinking (see Section 8.7)

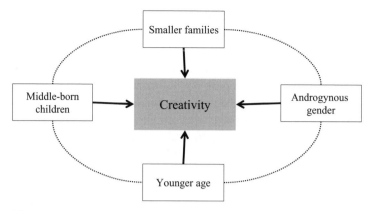

Figure 8.6 *Biodata correlates of creativity*

are typically r =.30 (Chamorro-Premuzic & Reichenbacher, 2008; Horn, 1976; Richards, 1976).

The above-mentioned personality and ability correlates of creativity can all be assessed via validated psychometric tests. However, there are also demographic and biographical factors associated with creativity, which could be assessed using biodata inventories (see Chapter 4). Thus size of family (smaller rather than larger), psychological gender or sexual identity (being androgynous rather than masculine or feminine), age (younger rather than older) and birth order (middle-born children) have all been linked to creativity (Chamorro-Premuzic, 2007; Sulloway, 1996) (see Figure 8.6).

8.4   Creative processes

Attempts to describe the creative *process* have examined the cognitive mechanisms that characterise creative thinking; thus their goal is to explain the general process of creative thinking in all individuals alike rather than profiling more and less creative people. In that sense, the process approach to creativity is within-person and more concerned with actual creativity than creative or non-creative people.

A wide range of studies suggested that creative processes are initiated and fostered by particular attentional patterns that have been describe in terms of reduced filtering of stimuli, lower latent inhibition or over-inclusive thinking. Thus Wallach (1970) argued that defocussed attention is beneficial for creativity as it equips individuals with a wider range of sensory stimuli that serve as raw materials for the production of creative ideas (see also Martindale & Greenough, 1973). In line with this, studies have indicated that broader attention is more likely to occur in the absence of pressure (for example threat of evaluation), which leads individuals to divide attentional resources between task-relevant and task-irrelevant stimuli (Smith, Michael & Hocevar, 1990).

The idea that lower perceptual or attentional censorship is beneficial for creative processes is also consistent with the lack of ideational or cognitive censorship that characterises the technique of *brainstorming*, whereby individuals say everything that comes to their mind about a certain topic (without censoring any ideas) in an attempt to postpone judgement in order to increase fluency of responses and originality (Chamorro-Premuzic, 2007). Other process-centred studies on creativity reported a negative correlation between previous knowledge (which may restrict and eliminate potentially original ideas) and creative performance (Hayes, 1978; Simon & Chase, 1973). In that sense, expertise can have deleterious effects on creative thinking because it reduces flexibility. Indeed, in brainstorming sessions the perceived expertise level of other people in the group/session can inhibit individuals' creativity: Collaros and Anderson (1969) found that subjects felt more inhibited if they were told that the other people in the brainstorming group were experts, and that originality and practicality varied according to the degree of perceived inhibition.

There is an extensive literature showing that the creative process is also fostered by intrinsic rather than extrinsic levels of motivation. Thus creative ideas are more easily generated if one is interested in the task *per se* rather than the potential rewards or punishments (carrots or sticks!) associated with completing or not completing the task, respectively. This is arguably because intrinsic motivation is a marker of a person's orientation or level of enthusiasm for the activity (Amabile (1990). As noted by Csikszentmihalyi (1988, p. 337), 'For no matter how original one might be, if one is bored by the domain, it will be difficult to become interested enough in it to make a creative contribution.' Conversely, if people are performing creative tasks simply for a salary, promotion or social recognition, creative thinking is likely to be constrained by others' evaluations (Amabile, 1990).

The most comprehensive model to date for understanding the creative process is Amabile's (1990, 1997) Componential Model of Organizational Innovation (see Figure 8.7), which identifies three intraindividual variables, namely domain-relevant knowledge, creativity-relevant skills, and motivational orientation, that explain the creative process. Moreover, Amabile's model also conceptualises the environmental characteristics (e.g., of the organisation or company) that facilitate creativity-related processes in an individual, namely organisational motivation to innovate, environmental resources and management practices. Thus creative processes will not only depend on a combination of intraindividual cognitive process (from motivation to knowledge), but also adequate environmental stimuli, as discussed in the forthcoming section.

8.5   Creative work environments: the press approach to creativity

The *press* approach to creativity looks at the relationship between individuals as creators and their environments. It therefore deals with the contextual

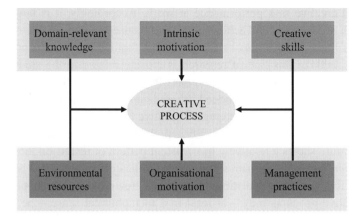

Figure 8.7 *Amabile's componential model of organisational innovation*

or situational determinants of creativity, including the effects of other people or groups on an individual's creativity. Thus creative environments may 'press' individuals to be more creative, accounting for intra- rather than interindividual differences in creativity. For instance, 'freedom, autonomy, good role models and resources (including time), encouragement specifically for originality, [and] freedom from criticism' (Runco, 2004, p. 662) are all contextual factors that can be expected to boost creative production and facilitate creative thinking. Conversely, organisations that frequently downsize increase employees' perceived job insecurity, which in turn hinders creativity (Probst, Stewart, Gruys & Tierney, 2007).

Contextual determinants of creativity include the effects and role of leadership and leadership styles on group and individual performance. Studies have shown that groups with participatory leaders tend to be superior at least in the fluency of ideas or quantity of creative outputs, whereas groups under supervisory leaders tend to produce better-quality creative ideas (Anderson & Fielder, 1964). A more recent study showed that in the presence of creative co-workers, supervision has deleterious effects on group-members' creativity, particularly for employees with less creative personalities (Zhou, 2003). However, leadership styles that contribute to increasing subordinates' self-efficacy tend to raise individual and group creativity (Mumford, Gessner, Connelly, O'Connor *et al.*, 1993). It has also been pointed out that individualistic organisational values promote creativity as they tend to encourage uniqueness and originality, especially if people are instructed to be creative (Goncalo & Staw, 2006).

8.6 Creative products

The *product* approach to creativity studies the characteristics of creative outcomes or products, such as art works (e.g., paintings, designs and sculptures) and scientific publications (e.g., theories, experiments and discoveries), and indeed creative task performance at work. Accordingly, it is largely concerned with productivity and achievement, and focuses on individuals' creations, rather than their personalities or the processes facilitating creative production (Simonton, 2004). This line of research is closely related to the study of creative genius and psychopathology, and has often implied that 'there is a thin line between genius and insanity'. Indeed, 'there is a long "Western" tradition from Plato to Freud that has tended to regard creative products are being "divergent, impulsive and "messy"' (De Bono, 1992, p. 2). However, a closer examination of the literature shows a relatively inconsistent pattern of results on the relationship between creativity measures and diverse indicators of abnormal behaviour. Moreover, it is important to distinguish between creativity and psychopathology: whilst creative products may – at least in a metaphorical sense – be regarded as the symptoms of creativity, the psychopathological conception of symptoms refers to the expression of unbearable, painful and uncontrollable psychological or physical outcomes. Thus creative individuals may have every intention to produce original associations, whilst psychotic individuals may have little alternative and control over their original, unusual or eccentric ideas. Accordingly, Barron referred to creativity in terms of 'controlled weirdness'. Mental patients on the other hand may not even be aware of the creative nature of their ideas (Merten & Fischer, 1999, p. 941).

8.7   Assessing and measuring creativity

Despite the potential conceptual usefulness of the above-reviewed approaches for defining and understanding creativity, psychological research in this area can only have applied or practical implications, particularly for personnel selection, if it provides robust psychometric information on how to assess and measure creativity. Indeed, psychometric research has explored the question of how to capture individual differences in creativity and some of the salient methods and tests are discussed in this section.

Guilford (1967), one of the pioneers in the assessment of creativity, proposed a comprehensive, multidimensional model of intelligence that encompasses more than 120 abilities. One of the core intellectual operations described by Guilford was *divergent thinking production*, which refers to an individual's production of multiple solutions to problems, rather than the identification of a single, correct response (as in traditional cognitive ability tests, such as those discussed in Chapter 6). Unlike convergent thinking, divergent thinking, by definition, cannot be measured by multiple-choice items as objective scoring is not possible unless a predefined correct response is known. However, Guilford (1975) provided four scoring criteria to measure performance differences, namely *flexibility, fluency, originality* and *elaboration,* which would set the foundations for later creativity tests (see Figure 8.8, adapted from Chamorro-Premuzic, 2007). For example, the

- **Originality** – each response is compared with all other responses from all of the people you gave the test to. Reponses that were given by only 5% of the sample are unusual (1 point), responses that were given by only 1% of your group are unique (2 points).

- **Fluency** – quantity regardless of quality (the higher the fluency, the higher the originality; this 'contamination' problem can be corrected by using the formula: originality = originality/fluency).

- **Flexibility** – or use of different categories.

- **Elaboration** – amount of detail (for example, 'a doorstop' = 0 whereas 'a door stop to prevent a door slamming shut in a strong wind' = 2 (one for explanation of door slamming, two for further detail about the wind)).

Figure 8.8 *Guilford's scoring criteria for divergent thinking tasks*

- **Consequences Test** (Guilford, 1954): Imagine what might happen if all laws were suddenly abolished.
- **Unusual Uses Tests** (Guilford, 1954): Find as many uses as you can think of for A. toothpick; B. brick; C. paper clip.
- **Word Association Test** (Getzels & Jackson, 1962): Write as many meanings as you can for the following: A. duck, B. sack, C. pitch.
- **Creative Test Battery** / Torrance Test of Creative Thinking (TTCT): Three picture-based exercises and six word-based exercises (figural and verbal). Does a good job of identifying gifted students.

Figure 8.9 *Creativity measures*

alternative or 'unusual uses' test requires individuals to provide 'as many uses as possible' for different objects (e.g., paper-clip, brick, pen, etc.). Test-takers can be compared on the basis of how many responses they provide, regardless of whether they are original or appropriate (fluency); on how 'different' or flexible their responses are from each other; how detailed they are (elaboration); and finally how 'unique' or original each answer is in comparison to the rest of the sample tested, or population in the case of having normative data.

Tests of *divergent thinking* represent the most widely employed measure of creativity and have been reported to be good predictors of creative achievement across a variety of settings (Barron & Harrington, 1981; Harrington, 1972), and at all levels of education (Anastasi & Schaefer, 1971; Torrance, 1974; Vernon, 1971). The best-known and most widely validated battery of divergent thinking is the Torrance Tests of Creativity and Thinking (TTCT) (Torrance, 1974), which measures divergent production of semantic units, e.g., 'Name all the things you can think of that are red and edible', alternative relations, e.g., 'In what different ways are dogs and cats related' and production of systems, e.g., 'Write as many sentences you can using the words "rain", "station" and "summer".' Torrance spent several decades conducting follow-up studies and reanalysing datasets to validate his test. Longitudinal studies have shown that the aggregated creativity score provided by the different sections of the TTCT correlated in the region of $r = .51$ with creative achievement measures (Torrance, 1975). Torrance also reported that intelligence and creativity were only moderately associated, such that 'no matter what measure of IQ is chosen, we would exclude about 70% of our most creative children if IQ alone were used in identifying giftedness' (Torrance, 1963, p. 182). These findings are important because they highlight the need to include actual creativity measures to test creativity (rather than a battery of personality and convergent thinking tests).

Another widely used measure of creativity is Mednick and Mednick's (1967) Remote Associates Test. Like traditional GMA tests, this thirty-item psychometric test includes items with correct responses rather than open-ended questions. Mednick's idea was that remote or unusual associations would be indicative of an individual's capacity for generating novel ideas, as remote combinations are generally more original. For example, participants may be asked to identify a fourth word that is associated with each of the following triads of words:

(a) rat-blue-cottage-???
(b) railroad-girl-class-???
(c) surprise-line-birthday-???
(d) wheel-electric-high-???
(e) out-dog-call-???

Although the answers[1] are less objective than standard IQ test items, Mednick and Andrews (1967) found correlations of $r = .55$ between IQ and a Remote Associates Test.

The above-reviewed tests of creativity (which mainly measure divergent thinking) represent useful performance-based alternatives to standardised tests of cognitive ability and differ from GMA and IQ tests in that they require divergent rather than convergent responses. However, creativity can also be assessed via self- and other-reports which are more akin to personality inventories. In fact, as seen in Section 8.7, there is a substantial conceptual and methodological overlap between inventories assessing creativity and those assessing the trait of Openness to Experience. For many years (even before the construct of Openness was identified as a core domain of personality), psychologists have used these scales to assess individual differences in creativity. Examples of such inventories are the Vocational Preference Inventory (VPI), Welsh's Figure Preference Test (FPT), Gough's Adjective Check List (ACL), the Concept Mastery Test (CMT) and the Biographical Information (form) for Research and Scientific Talent (BIRST).

Smith and colleagues administered a biographical inventory to a group of petroleum research scientists employed in a research lab of Standard Oil and reported adequate discriminant validity for the measure (Smith, Albright & Glennon, 1961). McDermid (1965) investigated peer- and self-ratings of creativity (of engineers and technicians) and concluded that self-reports and biographical data, especially related to creative interests and achievements, are effective predictors of creative performance in real-life situations. However, Tucker, Cline and Schmitt (1967) found low convergence between self- and other-ratings of creativity in pharmaceutical employees. Jones collected self-report data from managers and industrial scientists and found that performance and self-reports correlated up to .67, corrected for bias (Jones, 1964). Likewise, Datta (1964b) reported a correlation of .31 between Remote Associates Test scores and supervisory ratings of creativity in a sample of US engineers.

In more recent years, there have been some interesting innovations in creativity testing, notably by Sternberg and colleagues. For example, Sternberg's (1982) adaptation of the Goodman (1955) induction riddle requires participants to manipulate imaginary concepts such as 'bleen' (blue until 2004, but green after that year), or 'grue' (green until the year 2004, and blue after that). In a similar fashion, Sternberg and Gastel (1989) designed a test that requires individuals to evaluate logically valid, but factually false, statements, such as 'lions can fly'. Assuming that these items are useful to test individuals' flexibility, Sternberg's tests of induction are measuring an important component of creativity. Indeed, moderate correlations between these measures and fluid ability tests may be indicative of the discriminant validity of Sternberg's tests. Whether these tests measure creativity, flexibility or something else is a matter of interpretation, though.

8.8   Summary and conclusions

Rapid technological advances are creating an increasingly complex world where adaptation to changing environments is crucial. This *cultural*, as opposed to biological, evolution demands more flexibility from individuals than ever before. Given that creativity contributes to greater flexibility (Flach, 1990; Runco, 1986), creative individuals may be more prepared to adapt to the changes in everyday life and remain flexible in their responses to the environment. Thus 'creativity is a useful and effective response to evolutionary changes . . . because older adults tend to rely on routines and, unless intentionally creative, become inflexible' (Runco, 2004, p. 658). This may explain why several studies found creativity indicators to be significantly correlated with late-life adaptation and growth (e.g., Dudek & Hall, 1991; Gott, 1992).

Despite wide agreement that creativity is an important adaptational tool, which is beneficial for both the individual and society, there are many unaddressed psychological questions regarding creativity. Throughout this chapter, we have seen that the creativity *syndrome* is a complex and multidetermined psychological construct that may rarely be measured objectively and accurately. Whereas personality and intelligence are important to explain some of the characteristics of creative and non-creative individuals, individual differences in creativity cannot be explained merely in terms of personality and ability factors, but may also depend on individuals' interests, self-belief and motivation; and even if these variables are considered, it may still be impossible to predict a person's level of creative achievement, because there are few objective criteria to determine such a thing.

Note

1 Correct answers were: (a) cheese, (b) working, (c) party, (d) chair or wire, (e) house. All items taken from Sternberg and O'Hara (2000).

9 Leadership

9.1 Introduction

The current chapter examines some of the salient psychological approaches to leadership. These approaches attempt to explain the emergence and effectiveness of leaders in terms of psychological variables, notably individual differences in the capacity to influence others. Psychology has provided valuable information to explain *why* certain individuals are more likely to become successful leaders than others. Indeed, leadership has been studied in psychology for over a century and the past twenty-five years or so have seen an exponential increase in the number of peer-reviewed research articles on the subject. This pattern (shown in Figure 9.1) is by and large a consequence of the revival of the person or *trait* approach to leadership (discussed in Sections 9.2 and 9.5), which emphasises the personal attributes (e.g., personality, charisma, intelligence and creativity) that explain interindividual differences in leadership. Importantly, the validation of the trait approach to leadership has key implications for assessment and personnel selection as it provides a conceptual and methodological framework for predicting future leadership at work and for hiring applicants with the greatest leadership potential; hence a great deal of this chapter is dedicated to the trait approaches to leadership.

So, what is leadership, what do psychologists understand when they talk about leadership, and is there an overarching psychological definition or meaning of the term 'leadership'? Chamorro-Premuzic argued that regardless of the framework and approaches used to conceptualise leadership, the term always denotes:

(a) Excellence and outstanding *achievement* within one field or professional career. Thus leaders are people who excel at what they do and are recognised as competent by other people in the field.
(b) The capacity to *influence* others. This influence may involve direct leadership when there is personal interaction with the leader, or indirect leadership, if the leader's impact is merely based on his/her ideas or products.   (Chamorro-Premuzic, 2007, p. 143)

At the same time, the literature on leadership can be divided into two broad camps and ways of thinking about leadership. On the one hand, psychologists have regarded leadership as a *process*, namely the 'process of social influence in which one person is able to enlist the aid and support of others in the accomplishment of a common task' (Chemers, 2000, p. 27). On the other hand, leadership has been

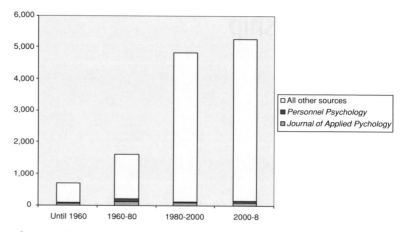

Figure 9.1 *Leadership-related articles published throughout the years*

defined as 'the ability to build, motivate and maintain high performing teams, groups, departments and organisations' (Chamorro-Premuzic, 2007, p. 144). The former has focused on the situational factors that 'make leadership happen' pretty much in every individual alike, whereas the latter has tried to identify why some people are more able to lead than others, focusing on the specific traits that differentiate between leaders and non-leaders.

Thus trait approaches to leadership seek to identify the distinctive psychological characteristics that explain the unequal emergence and effectiveness of leadership among people, whilst situational leadership theories, also known as *contingency* models, assume that leadership is more determined by situational than by personal characteristics, implying that anybody has the potential to become a leader as long as they are 'in the right place at the right time' (think Chance Gardener or Forrest Gump).

In the past decades, a third approach, known as the *behavioural* approach to leadership, has also been adopted to investigate the different behavioural patterns or leadership *styles* that explain both intraindividual and interindividual differences in leadership. Different leadership styles can be expected to have different effects on people and involve different psychological processes and techniques and are therefore worthy of studying. Figure 9.2 summarises the key points of each approach. Because of their relevance with regard to understanding individual differences, in this book we focus on trait and behavioural theories of leadership.

9.2   The trait approach to leadership

Historians, novelists and businessmen have always speculated about the characteristics of great leaders. Psychological theories focusing on leaders' personality or *traits* were influenced by Carlyle's (1907) 'Great Man' theory of leadership, which posited that 'the history of the world [was] the biography of

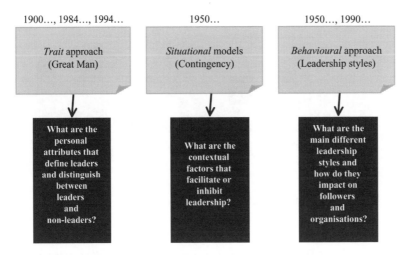

Figure 9.2 *Approaches to leadership*

great men' (Carlyle, 1907, p. 18). Carlyle was certain that leaders possessed certain attributes or personal characteristics that were absent in most individuals or followers, a view that implied that a limited number of core individual attributes could be used to distinguish between leaders and followers. For example, physical features, such as height and energy, demographic background variables (see Chapters 5 and 4), such as education and socioeconomic status, and personality characteristics, such as assertiveness, self-confidence and the capacity to tolerate stress, were crucial to discern between leaders and followers. This intrinsic view of leadership attempted to answer three main questions:

(a) What traits best describe great leaders?
(b) Can one assess leadership potential on the basis of these traits?
(c) Can leadership be learned?

Stogdill (1948) reviewed three decades of research and concluded that a handful of traits, namely dominance, self-confidence, diplomacy, extraversion, ambition, integrity, emotional control, sociability, responsibility, cooperation and especially intelligence (see Chapter 6 and Figure 9.3), set leaders apart from followers and even explained why some leaders are more successful than others. However, he also concluded that none of these attributes were universal predictors of leadership in that their validity was always moderated by situational factors. Indeed, Stogdill stated that 'leadership is a relation that exists between persons in a social situation, and that persons who are leaders in one situation may not necessarily be leaders in other situations' (p. 65), and in the following two decades psychologists echoed these pessimistic remarks, expressing a great deal of scepticism with regard to the trait approach to leadership. For example, Ghiselli and Brown (1955, p. 47) noted that '[U]nder one set of circumstances an individual will be a good leader and under others he will be a poor one' and Baron and Byrne

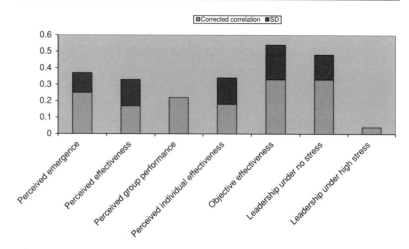

Figure 9.3 *Validity of intelligence as predictor of different leadership criteria*

observed that '[T]he conclusion... that leaders do not differ from followers in clear and easily recognised ways, remains valid' (1987, p. 405).

As pointed out in a recent state-of-the-art review on leadership by Zaccaro (2007, p. 10), the above remarks overlooked the wider conclusions by Stogdill and represented a biased account of his review. In fact the following fragment (from the same page as the above quote) by Stogdill has been widely omitted from the literature, especially by critics of the trait approach to leadership: 'Must it then be assumed that leadership is entirely incidental, haphazard, and unpredictable? Not at all. The very studies which provide the strongest arguments for the situational nature of leadership also supply the strongest evidence that leadership patterns as well as non-leadership patterns of behaviour are persistent and relatively stable' (1948, p. 65).

Although after the 1950s psychologists continued to explore the trait attributes linked to leaders and non-leaders (Atkinson, 1958; McClelland & Winter, 1969), subsequent years were characterised by a growing emphasis on situational or contingent approaches (at least until the late 1980s) (see Section 9.4). Towards the 1970s there was some consensus on the idea that good leaders tended to exhibit higher levels of need for power and lower levels of need for affiliation (McClelland, 1975; McClelland & Burham, 1976). Leaders were also described as being more focused on, or motivated by, influencing others' thoughts, emotions and behaviours (Winter, 1973), and establishing, maintaining and restoring relationships with others (Heyns, Veroff & Atkinson, 1958). But in the absence of a universal personality framework to classify the trait correlates of leadership and the widely endorsed view that situational factors undermine the importance of interindividual differences in leadership, interest in person-centred research on leadership decreased substantially.

Two important publications in the mid 1980s anticipated a revival of the trait approach to leadership. The first was a seminal book on the topic of presidential leadership by Simonton (1986), who combined psychometric and biographical analyses to identify the attributes of successful American presidents. He listed a total of fourteen, namely moderation, friendliness, intellectual brilliance, Machiavelism, poise and polish, achievement drive, forcefulness, wit, physical attractiveness, pettiness, tidiness, conservatism, inflexibility and pacifism. Barber (1992) provided a shorter, albeit largely overlapping, list of presidential attributes, namely 'Machiavellian, forceful, moderate, poised and polished, and flexible' (p. 153). A recent review article by Goethals (2005) concluded that successful American presidents could be characterised by their higher levels of *activity, intelligence, optimism* and *flexibility.*

The second publication was a meta-analysis on cognitive ability and leadership by Lord, De Vader and Alliger (1986), who reported a correlation of $r = .50$ between leadership and intelligence. Although this figure overestimated the importance of intelligence when it comes to explaining individual differences in leadership, it reminded psychologists just how important a single personal attribute can be for predicting leadership. More recently, Judge, Colbert and Illies (2004) re-examined the link between cognitive ability and leadership by meta-analysing data from 40,652 participants and 151 independent samples. They reported a 'true validity' of $r = .27$, which is considerably lower than the one reported by Lord *et al.* (1986). However, Judge *et al.* (2004) identified several moderating factors in the leadership–intelligence link.

As shown in Figure 9.3 (negative correlations have been reversed for the sake of simplicity), correlations between leadership and intelligence varied according to the criteria examined. The highest validity for tested cognitive ability was found when leadership was operationalised in terms of objective effectiveness (corrected $r = .33$, $SD = .21$), followed by perceived emergence ($r = .25$, $SD = .12$) and perceived group performance ($r = .22$, $SD = .00$). Correlations between tested cognitive ability and both perceived effectiveness and perceived individual effectiveness were somewhat lower. Moreover, results revealed a substantial difference between tests of cognitive ability as predictors of leadership under no stress ($r = .33$, $SD = .15$) and higher stress ($r = -.04$, $SD = .00$; in Figure 9.3 this correlation is shown as positive for the sake of clarity). Thus intelligence is only useful for explaining leadership in low-stressful conditions.

Judge *et al.* (2004) also emphasised the distinction between 'objective' and 'perceived' attributes when it comes to understanding the link between leadership and abilities: when 'estimated' rather than objectively tested abilities are considered, the correlation between perceived leadership emergence and intelligence is substantial (corrected $r = .65$, $SD = .28$). The importance of attributions in the study of leadership is discussed in the next section.

9.3   Perceptions of leadership

In the period from 1960 until 1980, research into leadership emphasised the importance of followers' perceptions of leaders and endorsed the idea that leadership is largely determined by followers' choices. Personal attributes, such as charisma, were 'considered to be invested by followers and accorded or withdrawn by them' (Hollander, 1993, p. 41), such that leaders are *legitimated* by the group (an idea already noted by Freud, 1921). Accordingly, there was 'no way of measuring leadership apart from social perceptions, [and] leadership exists primarily as an *attribution* rather than a testable construct' (Chemers, 2000, p. 32, italics added).

Implicit theories of leadership, which study the nature of laypeople's beliefs and perceptions of leaders, suggested that leaders are generally regarded as caring, outgoing, honest, competent, verbally skilled, decisive, educated, dedicated, aggressive and elegant (Lord *et al.*, 1984). In line with this view, Kenney, Balscovich and Shaver (1994) found that four latent factors explained conceptions of leadership:

1. Leaders' ability to know the group's goals
2. Leaders' capacity for being in command
3. Leaders being perceived as a 'nice person'
4. Leaders' emotional calmness (low Neuroticism)

The most important legacy of implicit theories of leadership is the idea that leadership effectiveness should be judged in terms of followers' perceptions rather than the leaders' performance. Thus leaders may rate themselves highly (or even be rated highly by supervisors) and yet fail to have an impact on others. In the words of Hogan, Curphy and Hogan (1994, p. 496): 'there is a kind of manager who routinely over-evaluates his or her performance, and that tendency is associated with poor leadership'. This is why implicit theories of leadership are generally better at explaining leadership *emergence* than leadership effectiveness, as people may often be 'chosen' as leaders when they lack the necessary qualities to perform well.

9.4 Contingency and the situational determinants of leadership

As discussed (Section 9.2), interpretations of Stogdill's (1948) review of the leadership literature led to suggestions that leadership could not be understood merely in terms of personal characteristics, opening the door to contingency or situational approaches to leadership.

This view was received with academic enthusiasm after Fiedler's influential laboratory studies in the 1960s. Fiedler's (1967, 1993) contingency model is based on the distinction between task vs emotional leadership roles (see also Bales, 1958, and Section 9.6 on *behavioural* approaches). Task-oriented leaders are believed to care about the appropriate execution of the task and are negatively predisposed towards low-performing individuals. On the other hand, emotionally oriented leaders emphasise the importance of good interpersonal relations and are therefore more likely to tolerate and accept poor-performing individuals.

There are specific conditions – Fiedler argues – under which task and emotionally oriented leaders may or not be effective, and different individuals make better leaders under different circumstances. The extent to which the situation is favourable to the leader, in the sense of increasing his/her certainty, predictability and control over the group, is reflected in the dimension of *situational favourableness* or situational control.

Thus different situations may require different styles: 'When the task is clear and followers supportive, the leader should use more time-efficient, autocratic styles. If the task or information is unclear, using [the] consultative strategies increases the information yield and likelihood of a higher quality decision. When the leaders lack follower support, the participative strategy helps to ensure follower commitment to the decision and its implementation' (Chemers, 2000, p.30).

Although Fiedler's theory remained more popular within social than differential psychology, today even trait advocates and psychometricians accept that context matters, often more than individual traits (Simonton, 1987).

9.5   Rebirth of the trait approach

There is no doubt about the revival in the past fifteen to twenty years of the trait approach to leadership (Zaccaro, 2007), and one of the reasons for this revival is the emergence of the five-factor model of personality (see Section 7.3). In a widely quoted article, Locke (1997b) identified various leadership traits, which he regarded as *timeless* and *universal*. Locke organised the trait correlates of leadership onto higher-order factors (see Table 9.1). Thus he conceptualised 'cognitive ability and thinking modes' (e.g., active mind, intelligence and vision), 'motivation, values and action' (e.g., action commitment, ambition, and effort and tenacity) and attitudinal variables, namely 'attitudes toward subordinates' (respect for ability and commitment for justice). Though this represented a step forward in the organisation of both ability and non-ability attributes associated with leadership, a bigger 'boost' for trait approaches was to come from the introduction of the five-factor model of personality to leadership research.

Furnham (1994) speculated about the role of the Big Five personality traits at work, arguing that in modern organisations leaders are more likely to be Open, Conscientious, Stable, Agreeable and Extraverts than followers. In line, Hogan *et al.* (1994) organised Stogdill's list of leadership-related personality characteristics on basis of the Big Five and pointed out that leaders tend to show higher levels of emotional balance, adjustment and confidence (all of which are emblematic of low rather than high Neuroticism scorers), higher levels of dominance and sociability (which characterise Extraversion rather than Introversion), higher intelligence and creativity (which are emblematic of higher rather than lower Openness), higher social awareness and friendliness (which are typical of

Table 9.1 *Locke's (1997b) leadership traits (adapted from Locke, 1997b, and Chamorro-Premuzic & Furnham, 2005)*

Cognitive ability and thinking modes	Motivation, values and action	Attitudes toward employees (subordinates)
(1) *Reality focus*: not susceptible to evasions and delusions, but facing reality however grim it may be	(7) *Egoistic passion for work*: intrinsic motivation, workaholic	(11) *Respect for ability*: hiring and developing people with drive, talent and right attitudes
(2) *Honesty*: realistic assessment (accurate insight) of one's and others' abilities and weaknesses	(8) *Action commitment*: doing (not just thinking)	(12) *Commitment to justice*: Rewarding (and punishing) people appropriately
(3) *Independence/self-confidence*: 'thinking outside the box', innovating, breaking new ground	(9) *Ambition*: personal drive and desire to achieve expertise and responsibility	
(4) *Active mind*: constantly searching for new ideas and solutions	(10) *Effort and tenacity*: Hard-working, resilient, not discouraged by failure	
(5) *Intelligence* (*IQ*): ability to reason, learn and acquire knowledge		
(6) *Vision*: Innovative, long-term plan, 'thinking ahead'		

Agreeableness) and high levels of responsibility, achievement striving and ethical conduct (which refer to individual differences in Conscientiousness).

Cross-cultural studies have generally replicated the pattern of Big Five correlates of leadership hypothesised by Furnham (1994) and Hogan *et al.* (1994). For instance, Silversthorne (2001) found that effective leaders tended to score significantly higher on Extraversion, Agreeableness and Conscientiousness, and lower on Neuroticism, than non-effective leaders in US as well as Chinese samples. However, previous studies indicated that, whilst Conscientiousness and Emotional Stability (low Neuroticism) tend to represent sociably desirable traits in almost every culture, Extraversion (with its primary facets of assertiveness and dominance) is less likely to be regarded as a virtue in eastern, than western, cultures (Redding & Wong, 1986).

Judge *et al.* (2002) reviewed the extensive literature on personality and leadership. Ten writers, mainly from the 1990s, listed what they regarded as intrinsic traits of effective or emergent and effective leaders. They observed considerable overlap, such that most writers included self-confidence, adjustment, sociability and integrity, whilst a minority listed persistence and masculinity (see Table 9.2).

Table 9.2 *Traits of effective or emergent leaders as identified by past reviews (adapted from Judge et al., 2002)*

Study	Traits
Stogdill (1948)	Dependability, sociability, initiative, persistence, self-confidence, alertness, cooperativeness, adaptability
Mann (1959)	Adjustment, extraversion, dominance, masculinity, conservatism
Bass (1990)	Adjustment, adaptability, aggressiveness, alertness, ascendance, dominance, emotional balance, control, independence, nonconformity, originality, creativity, integrity, self-confidence
Kirkpatrick & Locke (1991)	Drive (achievement, ambition, energy, tenacity, initiative), honesty/integrity, self-confidence (emotional stability)
Yukl & Van Fleet (1992)	Emotional maturity, integrity, self-confidence, high energy level, stress tolerance
Hogan *et al.* (1994)	Extraversion, Agreeableness, Conscientiousness, Emotional Stability
House & Aditya (1997)	Achievement motivation, pro-social influence motivation, adjustment, self-confidence
Northouse (1997)	Self-confidence, determination, integrity, sociability
Yukl (1998)	Energy level and stress tolerance, self-confidence, internal locus of control, emotional maturity, personal integrity, socialized power motivation, achievement orientation, low need for affiliation
Daft (1999)	Alertness, originality, creativity, personal integrity, self-confidence

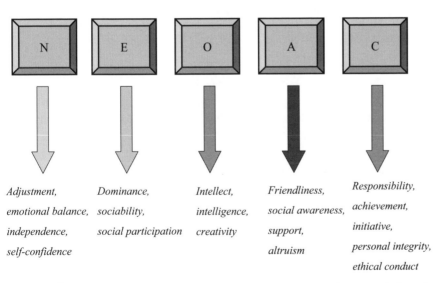

Figure 9.4 *Stogdill's (1974) leadership traits in Big Five language (adapted from Hogan et al., 1994)*

After this qualitative analysis of the literature, Judge *et al.* performed a large-scale quantitative meta-analysis, which included 222 correlations from 73 studies. Results showed that Emotional Stability, Extraversion, Openness and Conscientiousness were all positively correlated with both leadership emergence (perceived leadership) and effectiveness (leadership performance). Judge *et al.* (2002) concluded that Extraversion is the strongest predictor of both leadership and emergence and effectiveness, no doubt because of the assertiveness, dominance and sociability of extraverts.

However, the authors accept that the research does not always explain why these traits related to leadership:

> Is Neuroticism negative because neurotic individuals are less likely to attempt leadership, because they are less inspirational, or because they have lower expectations of themselves or others? Similarly, Extraversion may be related to leadership because extraverts talk more, and talking is strongly related to emergent leadership. Alternatively, it may be that individuals implicitly expect leaders to be extraverted. Implicit views of leaders include aspects of both sociability ('outgoing') and assertiveness ('aggressive', 'forceful'), or extraverts could be better leaders due to their expressive nature or the contagion of their positive emotionality. Open individuals may be better leaders because they are more creative and are divergent thinkers, because they are risk-takers, or because their tendencies for esoteric thinking and fantasy make them more likely to be visionary leaders. Agreeableness may be weakly correlated with leadership because it is both a hindrance (agreeable individuals tend to be passive and compliant) and a help (agreeable individuals are likeable and empathetic) to leaders. Finally, is Conscientiousness related to leadership because conscientious individuals have integrity and engender trust because they excel at process aspects of leadership, such as setting goals, or because they are more likely to have initiative and persist in the face of obstacles? Our study cannot address these process oriented issues, but future research should attempt to explain the linkages between the *Big Five* traits and leadership.   (Judge *et al.*, 2002, p. 774)

Recent trait approaches to leadership have not focussed only on positive personality characteristics, but also on maladaptive traits. Indeed, Hogan *et al.* (1994) highlighted the 'dark side' of leadership when it comes to explaining the well-known case of derailed leadership; they named arrogance, hostility, passive aggressiveness, compulsiveness and abrasiveness as the main traits. Along these lines, a recent article by Judge, LePine and Rich (2006) looked at the relationship between leadership and Narcissism. Results (depicted in Figure 9.6) found Narcissism to be positively related to self-ratings of leadership (r = .22) but negatively linked to other-ratings (−.20). Moreover, when other-ratings are used to assess leadership, Narcissism correlated negatively with contextual performance (r = −.25) and task performance (r = −.11), as well as relating positively to workplace deviance (r = .24). These results provide evidence in support of Hogan's view that there is an underlying 'dark side' to many leaders.

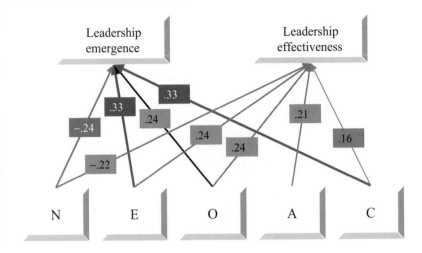

N = Neuroticism, E = Extraversion, O = Openness, A = Agreeableness, C = Conscientiousness

Figure 9.5 *Big Five correlates of leadership emergence and effectiveness: meta-analytic findings by Judge et al. (2002)*

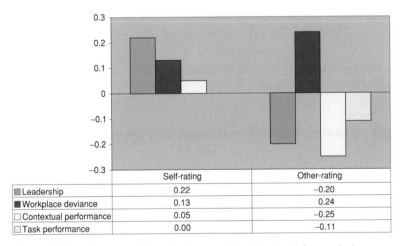

	Self-rating	Other-rating
■ Leadership	0.22	−0.20
■ Workplace deviance	0.13	0.24
□ Contextual performance	0.05	−0.25
□ Task performance	0.00	−0.11

Figure 9.6 *Predicating self- and other-rated work criteria by narcissism scores (based on Judge, Lepine & Rich, 2006)*

Although situationalist models no longer threaten the position of trait approaches in the realm of leadership research, trait approaches are so closely linked to the five-factor model that many of the criticisms of the Big Five also extend to the study of leadership. Thus some have argued that a more causal and theoretically founded personality model is needed to understand leadership (Spangler, House & Palrecha, 2004), particularly if motivational elements are to be considered. Moreover, despite the wide acceptance of the Big Five as a useful

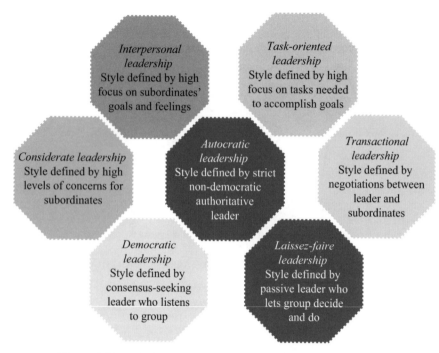

Figure 9.7 *Early descriptions of leadership styles*

model for describing individual differences in non-clinical samples, the model is not without critics (Block, 1995).

9.6   Leadership styles: behavioural approaches to leadership

Behavioural approaches to leadership attempt to conceptualise different leadership styles, as well as their effects on subordinates. In a sense, this approach combines both trait and situational paradigms as it accepts both the idea that different people tend to have different styles (interindividual differences in leadership), but also that in different roles the same individuals may assume different leadership styles. In that sense, behavioural approaches acknowledge the influence of both situational and personal factors on leadership. In this chapter we shall focus on the latter.

Social psychology has long emphasised the distinction between different strategies adopted by leaders and defined their relationship with others/a group (see again Section 9.4, as well as seminal studies by Kurt Lewin, i.e., Lewin, Lippit & White, 1939). However, the behavioural approach soon combined with psychometric techniques, specifically self- and other-reports, in order to identify leadership styles in real-world samples.

One of the first consistent findings from behavioural approaches (see Figure 9.7 for a summary of early descriptions of styles) was that leaders differed in terms of how considerate they were of their subordinates' feelings and needs. Unlike trait approaches, which would interpret this behavioural pattern as a natural consequence of internal dispositions, such as Agreeableness, behavioural approaches simply state that certain leadership styles are more likely than others to take into consideration the behaviour of followers. Accordingly, the emphasis is on the causes as well as consequences of this leadership style.

In the 1950s (e.g., Bales, 1950; Hemphill & Coons, 1957), psychology introduced another distinction that would later be applied to the study of leadership styles, namely between *task-oriented* and *interpersonally oriented* leadership. Task-oriented leadership is characterised by a pragmatic and focused leader who is mainly concerned with the completion of a set of relevant tasks that would enable the accomplishment of specific goals, whereas interpersonally oriented leadership is defined by the leader's concern with maintaining good relationship with the group.

Another classification of leadership style was the distinction between *democratic* and *autocratic* leaders, also referred to as *participative* and *directive* leadership, respectively. Thus leaders differ in the extent to which they seek (democratic/participative) or avoid (autocratic/directive) the participation of their followers/subordinates in key decision making and planning. Psychologists have also conceptualised the *laissez-faire* (literally 'let do') style, which is characterised by a passive leader who tends to avoid decision making and escape responsibilities for group outcomes.

From the late 1970s onwards, leadership research has tended to emphasise the effects of leaders on subordinates with particular focus on leaders' capacity to inspire, motivate and empower their followers, enabling them to perform at their best. Such attempts are best subsumed in the concepts of *charismatic* and *transformational* leadership (Burns, 1978) (see Sections 9.7 and 9.8, respectively).

Another salient leadership style – often opposed to the transformational/charismatic style – is *transactional* leadership (Avolio, 1999; Bass, 1998), which consists of the mere exchange of interests between the leader and subordinates. Thus leaders focus on their followers' needs and establish a relationship with them based on transactions (negotiations) that keep those needs satisfied. Transactional leadership is commonly used to describe the prototypical relationship between work manager and employees, as well as the inherent processes of rewards (carrots) and punishment (sticks) that are used to motivate them. Thus a key difference between transactional and transformational leadership is that the former uses extrinsic factors to motivate subordinates whereas the latter is largely based on intrinsic motives.

9.7   Charismatic leadership

In recent decades, behavioural approaches to leadership have paid increasing attention to the construct of charismatic leadership (Bass, 1997;

Conger & Kanungo, 1987; House & Shamir, 1993), which is characterised by visionary leaders who are able to stimulate subordinates' aspirations and motives. Moreover, charismatic leaders are capable of injecting optimism in others, defy the status quo through innovative thinking and serve as inspirational role models to their followers. It is therefore not surprising that charismatic leadership – more so than other leadership styles – has been found to be linked to superior communicational skills. Thus charismatic leaders 'speak with a captivating voice tone; make direct eye contact; show animated facial expressions; and have a powerful, confident, and dynamic interactional syle' (Kilkpatrick & Locke, 1996, p. 38).

Unlike other leadership styles (notably autocratic or laissez-faire), charismatic leaders are particularly likely to raise followers' feelings of self-efficacy, motivation and self-confidence (Bass, 1997). This *empowerment* is achieved through the leader's ability to provide the vision of 'a better future for followers' (House & Shamir, 1993), which is why followers would be more likely to emulate their leaders by taking risks, challenging given rules and searching for creative solutions to problems (House & Shamir, 1993). Indeed, charismatic leadership has been linked to creativity (see Chapter 8) (Bono & Judge, 2003; Sosik, Kahai & Avolio, 1998), as, rather than giving orders or transmitting a specific set of instructions, charismatic leaders would enable followers/the group to come up with their own solutions and therefore encourage creative behaviours (Dvir *et al.*, 2002). Thus leaders who motivate and inspire their subordinates are more likely to facilitate subordinates' creativity. The link between creativity and leadership has been the topic of much recent debate in both academia and industry because 'managing creative talent' is widely regarded as one of the biggest challenges to management as well as personnel selection (Hogan & Hogan, 2002) (see Chapter 10).

Many psychologists have emphasised that charismatic leadership is mainly a 'perceived' construct or leadership style (see again Section 9.3). In line with this, charismatic leadership is often assessed by using *other-* rather than *self-estimates* of charisma, such as the 'transformational' scale of the Multifactor Leadership Questionnaire (Bass & Avolio, 1985, 1995) (shown in Table 9.3). This inventory has Likert-type items that assess inspirational motivation, attributed charisma and idealised influence, such a 'displays a strong sense of power and purpose' and 'acts in ways to build your trust'. In that sense, one may almost recognise charismatic leadership as the leadership style that is positively rated by others, in the sense of being associated with positive attitudes, perceptions and performance of followers.

Although there is wide consensus on the benefits of charismatic leadership for both the organisation and the individual, identification with the leader and empowerment of subordinates also generate high *dependence* of subordinates on the leader. Conger and Kanungo (1988) argued that dependence is an intense (almost Freudian) identification whereby followers are overly reliant on the leader's approval, i.e., moral and psychological recognition, disregarding potentially important goals for the group and the organisation. Charismatic leaders

Table 9.3 *Leadership styles as defined by the Multifactor Leadership Questionnaire (adapted from Avolio et al., 1999, and Eagly et al., 2003)*

Scales and subscales	Description of leadership style
1. Transformational	
(a) *Idealised influence (attribute)*	Shows qualities that generate respect and pride from others associated with him/her
(b) *Idealised influence (behaviour)*	Communicates values, goals and importance of organisation's aims
(c) *Inspirational motivation*	Is optimistic and excited about goals and future plans
(d) *Intellectual stimulation*	Looks at new ways of solving problems and completing tasks
(e) *Individualised consideration*	Develops and mentors followers and attends to their needs
2. Transactional	
(a) *Contingent reward*	Rewards others for good performances
(b) *Management by exception (active)*	Attends to followers' failures and mistakes to meet standards
(c) *Management by exception (passive)*	Waits for problems to become serious before intervening
3. Laissez-faire	Frequently absent and not involved in critical decision-making processes/stages

strengthen subordinates' level of *social identification* (Ashforth & Mael, 1989), the process by which individuals identify with the group or organisation, to the extent that subordinates are happy to replace their own selfish goals with those of the group. However, due to the strong dependence, the leader's departure can generate withdrawal-like symptoms that 'will result in a crisis, intense feelings of loss and severe orientation problems on the part of the followers' (Shamir, 1991, p. 96).

In all, though, charismatic leadership is rightly regarded as a positive form of leadership. Indeed, recent studies show that leaders who succeed at raising subordinates' level of social identification also increase subordinates' eagerness to engage with, and contribute to, group goals and projects. Moreover, some have argued that the consequences of social identification are more favourable than those of personal identification as the latter (but not the former) lead to increased dependence on the leader.

9.8 Transformational leadership: leaders as mentors

In recent years, the concept of charismatic leadership has been progressively replaced (and absorbed) by that of transformational leadership. In fact, as shown in Table 9.3, the subscale of the Multifactor Leadership Questionnaire is called 'transformational' rather than 'charismatic'. Although there is some debate as to whether charismatic and transformational leadership should be considered synonymous, it is clear that there is a substantial conceptual overlap between both constructs. In fact some have interpreted transformational leadership as the effects of charismatic leadership (House & Shamir, 1993). Others have differentiated between the two constructs in terms of higher- and lower-order levels of leadership style. Most notably, Bass (1997) conceptualised charisma as the overarching factor of transformational leadership, which includes the minor dimensions of motivation, inspiration and consideration. In that sense, transformational leadership is essentially a type of charismatic leadership style.

The notion of transformational leadership owes much credit to Freud's (1921) conceptualisation of leadership, which was based on the idea that, when in a group, 'an individual readily sacrifices his personal interest to the collective interest' (Freud, 1921, p. 75, quoting LeBon). Freud hypothesised this to be a process underlying any form of leadership and group psychology, and did not distinguish between transformational and other forms of leadership, at least not explicitly. Yet transformational leadership, which is largely defined by the effects it exerts on others, seems to represent the essence of the Freudian notion of leadership. In both Freud's notion of leadership and the modern concept of transformational leadership, followers identify strongly with their leader and are very dependent on him/her and ultimately 'transformed' by the leader. This transformation involves a fundamental change in the attitudes, values, expectations and motivations of the followers (Yukl, 1998), and to some extent leaders too. Thus transformational leadership 'occurs when one or more persons *engage* with others in such a way that leaders and followers raise one another to higher levels of morality' (Burns, 1978, p. 20, italics in the original).

The construct of transformational leadership has attracted widespread attention from both academic and business settings because of consistent claims and accumulating evidence that transformational leadership plays a substantial role in the processes that enhance employee motivation and performance (Barling, Weber & Kelloway, 1996; Dvir, Eden, Avolio & Shamir, 2002). Thus several experts have indicated that in most contemporary organisational settings (at least in western/industrialised economies), transformational leadership is highly effective and has benefits for the organisation, the group and the leader, and numerous studies reported that followers' commitment loyalty, attachment and satisfaction are all significantly related to transformational leadership (Becker & Billings, 1993; Conger & Kanungo, 1998).

Psychologists have also pointed out that transformational leaders (like charismatic ones) tend to be creative, innovative and strive for changes and improvements. Accordingly, they 'state future goals and develop plans to achieve them. Sceptical of the status quo, they innovate, even when the organisation that they lead is generally successful. By mentoring and empowering their followers, transformational leaders encourage them to develop their full potential and thereby

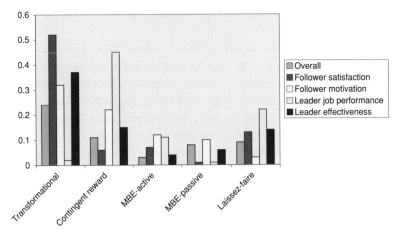

Figure 9.8 *Regression of five leadership styles onto five work criteria (based on Judge and Piccolo's meta-analyses). Note: Negative beta coefficients (for example, for laissez-faire) have been reversed for the sake of simplicity.*

to contribute more capably to their organisation' (Eagly, Johannesen-Schmidt & van Engen, 2003, p. 570).

Judge and Piccolo (2004) reported meta-analytic evidence for the validity of transformational leadership at work, comparing it to different leadership styles (see Section 9.10 on transactional leadership). Results – shown in Figure 9.8 – provide evidence for the predictive validity of transformational leadership style at work, though its predictive power varies according to the criterion examined. For instance, if leadership success is operationalised in terms of followers' satisfaction, transformational leadership is highly predictive. However, if success is measured in terms of job performance, contingent reward (a type of transactional leadership) is more beneficial. In all, though, results showed quite clearly that transformational leadership is the most positive leadership style in the workplace, followed by contingent reward leadership styles.

Besides the benefits for the organisation, transformational leadership may have a positive effect on the psychological aspects of the followers who experience growth, independence and empowerment (Bass, 1995), although dependence on the leader may impose limitations on the subordinates (Howell, 1988). Whilst empowerment increases the subordinates' independence and autonomy, dependence requires constant leader approval to maintain high self-esteem.

Several authors have therefore argued that dependence may be the most common disadvantage (for both individuals and organisations) of transformational leadership. Unlike empowerment, which boosts subordinates' self-efficacy, motivation and performance, dependence creates submissive loyalty, conformity and blind obedience in subordinates (Howell, 1988). However, future research is needed to clarify the extent and direction to which dependence and empowerment interact in both charismatic and transformational leadership (Kark, Shamir & Chen, 2003).

Traditionally, the concepts of empowerment and dependence have been treated as opposite, but in a recent study it was argued that, 'in early stages of the relationship, some dependence on the leader is a necessary condition for the leader's empowering effects, whereas in later stages the empowerment effects would depend on the followers achieving independence from the leader and on their need for affirmation and recognition' (Kark et al., 2003, p. 253). Further, personality traits and specificities of the task may contribute to an interaction between feelings of dependence and empowerment.

9.9   Personality of transformational leaders

If, as has been the case, leadership styles are defined as 'stable patterns of behaviours displayed by leaders' (Eagly et al., 2003, p. 569), there is a clear conceptual overlap between the concept of leadership style and personality traits. Accordingly, the question arises as to what specific personality dimensions are associated with each leadership style.

In the past two decades several studies have aimed at answering this question by articulating or integrating established individual difference constructs with different leadership styles. In particular, recent research has increasingly focussed on the personality characteristics of transformational leaders, looking at empirical or psychometric links between measures of the Big Five and transformational leadership. Hogan and Hogan (2002) argued that charismatic/transformational leaders tend to be more Agreeable, Open and Extraverted, especially compared to transactional leaders (see Section 9.10). Transformational leaders need acceptance and status, which they would achieve by being generous and sensitive (agreeable). Transformational leaders also need to be expressive, dominant and persuasive for which their high Extraversion would be advantageous, whilst their high Openness score may be particularly beneficial to enable them to 'do things differently', that is, innovate and create through an imaginative vision of the future.

Judge and Bono (2000) looked at fourteen samples of leaders in 200 organisations to see which of the Big Five traits predicted transformational leadership. They hypothesised that low Neuroticism, high Extraversion, high Openness to Experience and high Agreeableness would be linked to higher ratings of effective leadership behaviours. Results (illustrated in Figure 9.9) were only partly supportive, as Extraversion ($r = .28$) and Agreeableness ($r = .32$), but not Emotional Stability and Conscientiousness, were related to leadership effectiveness. Correlations between Extraversion and transformational leadership were mainly attributed to the 'dominance' components of Extraversion (see Section 7.8 on Extraversion facets), whilst correlations between transformational leadership and Agreeableness were interpreted in terms of the 'empathy' components

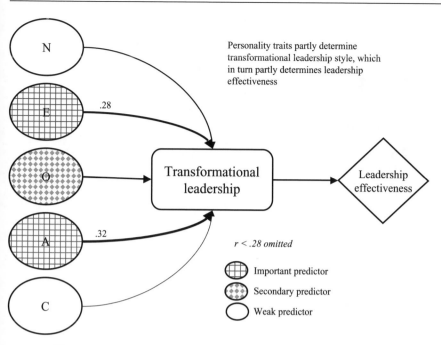

Figure 9.9 *Personality traits, transformational leadership and leadership effectiveness (from Chamorro-Premuzic, 2007)*

of Agreeableness. In addition, there was also a significant correlation between transformational leadership and Openness to Experience, though this correlation dropped to non-significant levels when Extraversion and Agreeableness were taken into account.

9.10   Transactional leadership: controlling rather than inspiring

Burns (1978, 2003) and Bass (1985, 1998) distinguished between *trans-formational* (Sections 9.8 and 9.9) and *transactional* leadership styles, where the latter is characterised by the leaders' tendency to *control* followers' behaviours and apply corrective transactions or negotiations (between leader and follower) that lead to effective problem solving. Transactional leaders achieve influence on their subordinates as an exchange of rewards (securing economic benefits) and compliance. In return, subordinates will grant authority to the leader. Consequently, a recent study found that transactional leaders were perceived as having lower moral standards than transformational leaders (Turner, Barling, Epitropaki, Butcher & Milner, 2002).

Judge and Piccolo's meta-analyses (see again Figure 9.8, but mainly Figure 9.10) showed that different facets of transactional leadership exhibited quite opposite patterns of validity. As shown in Figure 9.10, active management

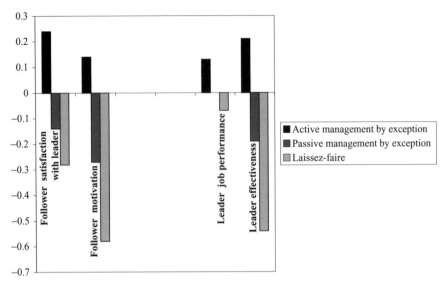

Figure 9.10 *Validity of two management-by-exception and laissez-faire styles at work (Judge & Piccolo's meta-analysis)*

by exception (see Table 9.3) was linked to positive work outcomes (followers' satisfaction with the leader and followers' motivation on the one hand, and leader's job performance and effectiveness on the other), whereas passive management by exception was negatively correlated with the same outcomes. However, the worst effects were identified for laissez-faire leadership style.

The main differences between transformational (as well as charismatic) and transactional leadership is that empowerment of followers only occurs in the former. Thus transformational and charismatic leaders may influence not only subordinates' behaviours, but also their motivation, self-efficacy and self-esteem, whereas transactional leaders will only affect subordinates' behaviours. More crucially, transformational and charismatic leaders manage to influence subordinates to think beyond their personal interests and act according to the interest of the whole group, whereas transactional leaders *base* their influence on the personal interests of the subordinates.

This theoretical distinction is manifested in the practicalities of everyday transactional leadership, which, unlike transformational leadership, does not include a high degree of delegation of responsibilities and decision making on the subordinates (Dvir *et al.*, 2002). Rather, transactional leadership is based on a pragmatic exchange relationship between leader and follower that resembles a commercial/business agreement. For example, employees work in return for the boss's salary/payment, and follow the boss's orders and rules as long as they are satisfied with the rewards they get in exchange. Thus, if the salary is too low, they may choose to 'break' the agreement and finish their transactional relationship with their boss by moving to another company.

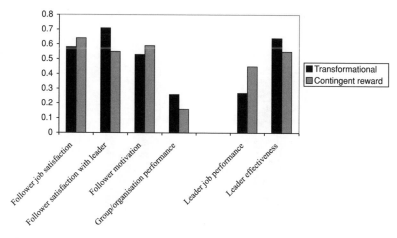

Figure 9.11 *Validity of transformational and contingent reward leadership at work (Judge & Piccolo's meta-analysis)*

Figure 9.11 shows the comparative predictive validity of transformational and contingent reward (a type of transactional leadership) styles as per Judge *et al.*'s meta-analytic review. As seen, both styles exhibited good validities. On the left the criteria are 'perceptions' (or followers' attributions), and similar validities were obtained for both styles, though transformational leadership appears to be more advantageous. However, if the leader's job performance is considered, contingency reward is slightly more positive – though for leader effectiveness the validities are again higher for transformational leadership.

Finally, Figure 9.12 compares the validity of transformational and contingent reward styles (from the same meta-analysis) across different work settings. As seen, contingent reward styles work much better in business than any other setting, whereas for transformational leadership moderational effects of work setting are less salient. Thus transformational leadership is similarly beneficial in military, public sector, business and even college settings, whereas contingent rewards work quite poorly in educational settings, slightly better (but still modestly) in the public sector and the military, and better than transformational leadership in business environments. Thus employers should bear in mind what kind of leadership their organisations are likely to benefit from the most.

9.11 Leadership and gender

There has been a longstanding popular and academic debate on whether salient gender differences in leadership potential and effectiveness exist. This debate is usually motivated by the observable larger proportion of men than women occupying leadership positions in almost every occupational field (Eagly

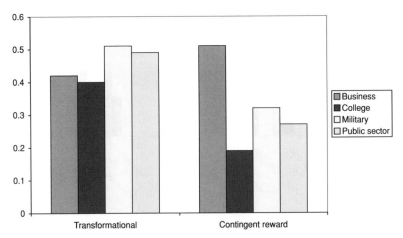

Figure 9.12 *Transformational and contingent reward leadership styles as predictors of occupational criteria across different settings*

et al., 2003; Miller, Taylor & Buck, 1991). For example, only 5 per cent of the top corporate and 1 per cent of chief executive officers amongst America's top 500 companies are women (Catalyst, 2002a, 2002b). To some, this imbalance is indicative of males' superior leadership potential, but to others, it is only a natural heritage of the unequal job opportunities available to women throughout past generations (and in many countries still today).

During the 1970s and 1980s experimental/laboratory evidence suggested that female and male leaders do not differ in their leadership potential, effectiveness (Bartol & Martin, 1986; Nieva & Gutek, 1981) or style (Bass, 1981). However, later correlational studies on larger datasets revealed consistent stylistic differences in the leadership style of men and women.

Theoretically, three main avenues have been pursued when it comes to explaining the basis and causes of observable sex differences in leadership:

(1) Men and women differ biologically and evolutionarily, having different physical traits, adaptational styles and evolutionary goals. Theories of aggression have long highlighted biological sex differences in a number of socially relevant behaviours, which is in line with the notion of biologically based sex differences in leadership styles (Bettencourt, Talley, Benjamin & Valentine, 2006).

(2) Culturally, men and women have different roles. In developed western countries, these differences are less pronounced now than ever, but still cultural differences persist. Given that most societies view women as more friendly, kind and unselfish than men, the very notion of leadership may be constructed upon male-like attributes, such as dominance, masterfulness and assertiveness.

(3) People's perceptions of men and women are associated with implicit theories of sex differences in leadership. As stated (see Section 9.3), attributions and implicit views of leadership have an effect on leadership emergence and effectiveness, acting as self-fulfilling prophecies. Thus, if people perceive

men to be more dominant and better leaders than women, women will find it harder to become leaders than men. Further, perceived (learned) gender roles would cause male leaders to behave in ways that are consistent with the 'male-leader stereotype' and female leaders to act according to established 'female-leader stereotypes' (Cross & Madson, 1997). Accordingly, Schein (2001) concluded that, for most people, the 'think manager, think male' (p. 676) rule is deeply internalised. In fact, we may have all come across situations in which successful female leaders have been more or less deliberately compared with males, or described as more masculine than other women.

It has, however, been argued that feminine traits (whether perceived or real), 'such as warmth, nurturance, and flexibility, made women better leaders and managers than power-oriented male leaders' (Chemers, 2000, p. 33). Eagly and Johnson (1990) meta-analysed 162 studies (during the period 1961–87), looking at gender differences in autocratic vs democratic leadership styles. Results showed that women tended to be more democratic than men, whilst men tended to be more autocratic than women. These findings were replicated in a more recent meta-analysis (van Engen, 2001) and run counter to previous claims on gender differences (and similarities) in leadership.

The most compelling source of evidence for gender differences in leadership was provided by a recent meta-analysis on gender differences in transformational, transactional and laissez-faire leadership styles. Eagly *et al.* (2003) analysed data from 45 different studies (during the period 1985–2000) in order to test whether women and men differed in their *typical* leadership styles.

Results (shown in Figure 9.13, with grey bars on the left representing effect sizes in favour of women and black bars on the right representing effect sizes in favour of men) indicated that women rated higher on several dimensions of transformational leader, namely individualised consideration, idealised influence (trait) and charisma, as well as the contingent reward dimension of transactional leadership. On the other hand, men rated higher on management by exception (passive), which revealed the most prominent gender difference of all styles, as well as laissez-faire and active management by exception. Overall, then, female leaders tended to be more transformational than their male counterparts, whilst male leaders were generally more likely to adopt transactional and laissez-faire leadership styles.

Although effect sizes were generally small, the authors concluded that 'positive' features of leadership are manifested more clearly in female than male leaders, so that, if anything, women would have an *advantage* over men with regard to leadership effectiveness. This is consistent with several claims by other authors that female leaders tend to be less hierarchical, more cooperative and other-oriented than their male counterparts (Helgesen, 1990; Loden, 1985). It has therefore been noted that, in today's organisations, women's typical leadership styles would lead to greater effectiveness than males' (Eagly *et al.*, 2003; Sharpe, 2000), mainly because of their ability to display a transformational repertoire of leadership.

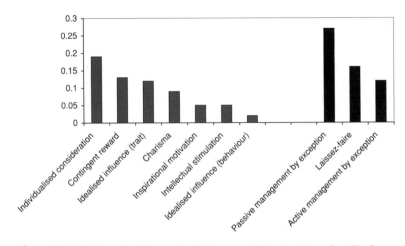

Figure 9.13 *Effect sizes for gender differences in leadership styles (Eagly et al.'s 2003 meta-analysis)*

9.12   Summary and conclusions

This chapter reviewed the most salient literature on the psychology of leadership, with particular focus on the trait approach to leadership. As seen, the concept of leadership has an integral place in the realm of individual differences and has important implications for personnel selection because of its relevance in organisational settings. Thus a key goal of applied psychological research is to enhance our understanding and improve our prediction of leadership by answering questions such as 'Who will lead?' and 'Who will make a successful leader?'

After an initial emphasis on the personal attributes that best distinguish between leaders and non-leaders (a paradigm that was the focus of much psychological research into leadership until the 1950s), situational approaches emerged as the dominant paradigm for understanding leadership, and viewed leadership as a process of influence that is contingent and dependent on contextual rather than interindividual factors. However, the past twenty years or so have witnessed a renaissance of trait approaches to leadership, especially since the consolidation of the five-factor model and application of meta-analytic techniques to provide a robust quantitative estimate of the validity of leadership and its determinants at work.

Recent theoretical efforts have attempted to 'bridge the gap' between situational and trait approaches by integrating interindividual and contextual influences on leadership. Thus Chemers (2000) proposed three major goals that leaders must fulfil in order to be successful:

> [First] a leader must build credibility in the legitimacy of his or her image that arouses feelings of trust in followers (*image management*). [Second] a leader must develop relationships with subordinates that enable those subordinates to

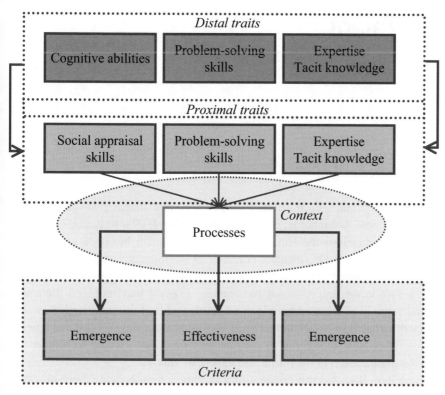

Figure 9.14 *Zaccaro's integrative model of leadership*

move toward individual and collective goal attainment (*relationship development*). Finally, leaders must effectively use the knowledge, skills, and material resources present within their groups to accomplish the group's mission (*resource development*).   (p. 37)

In a similar vein, Zaccaro's (2007) recent review of the leadership literature concluded that leadership frameworks cannot be limited to the identification of broad trait attributes that differentiate between leaders and non-leaders, and that even if robust taxonomies (such as the Big Five) are used to coherently organise the higher- and lower-order attributes that define leaders, non-linear relationships should also be explored. Moreover, Zaccaro argued that some traits – such as emotional or social competence – may highlight leaders' capacity to adopt different leadership styles under different situational demands, blurring the boundaries between intra- and interindividual differences in leadership. Thus 'some attributes will be more stable and cross-situational in their influences, whereas others will be more situationally bound (indicating another important role for the leadership situation' (Zaccaro, 2007, p. 7). An integration of the different approaches *and* attributes underlying leadership is graphically depicted in Figure 9.14 (adapted from Zaccaro, Kemp & Bader, 2004).

10 Talent

10.1 Introduction

Few people can have escaped noticing that 'talent management' has become the new, fashionable, buzzword (Athey, 2004; Gladwell, 2002). Indeed, in some organisations the Human Relations department has been renamed the 'Talent Management Department' (Economist Intelligence Unit, 2006).

Popular magazines, management conference speakers and business journalists over a decade ago talked about the *war for talent*. Many assumed there was an undersupply of talented people at all levels and thus organisations were in a competitive battle to attract and retain as well as develop these special, but crucial, people. They were thought of as the new generation who would be required to lead the organisation in the future and ensure its survival.

Some have disputed this concept of war. Others have become more obsessed by who owns the process of talent management. Far fewer have tried to define the concept of talent from a behavioural or psychological point of view. Hence it remains unclear what talent actually is, whether it needs special nurturing to last and what it predicts. For instance, is talent different from the non-cognitive traits discussed in Chapter 7 (personality) or the cognitive abilities examined in Chapter 6? If talent is not merely a new name for an old construct or set of constructs, what does it comprise?

There are, according to those who write about the topic of talent, various specific questions for those trying to assess and evaluate talent. These include:

- How does one define or operationalise talent?
- How best to select the really talented?
- Are expectations of the talented too high?
- What are the lessons to be learned from the turnover of talented people?
- What is the role of 'experience' in talent search?
- What definable skills, qualities and abilities are required?
- What is potential?
- What about the less talented (average) person?

From a management perspective there seem to be four salient questions:

- *Attracting talent.* This involves the definition of talent, identifying the best methods to assess it and finding ways to persuade talented people to join the organisation. This may mean doing the 'milk round' to attract people from universities as well as various forms of advertising aimed at making these especially (and perhaps unusually) talented people favourably disposed to the organisations such that they apply for advertised positions.

- *Retaining talent.* This involves keeping talented people after they have been selected. It involves understanding their particular and specific 'package' and training needs. They might be quite differently motivated than less talented groups and the task is to find how to keep them both happy and productive. The question is whether they need anything different compared to good management practices and equitable rewards to ensure they stay working for the organisation.
- *Developing talent.* One of the concepts associated with talent is the idea of potential to rise up the organisation to ever more important and challenging jobs. For this it is thought (even) talented people require particular training, coaching or mentoring. This can, and should, be done on an individual basis as well as on a corporate level through leadership development, succession planning to new job integration and assimilation initiative.
- *Transferring talent.* Inevitably, talented people move – they move up the organisation (almost by definition); they move to sister companies; they may head up overseas divisions of the company. Furthermore, they leave the organisation. It is important to ensure that all issues associated with out-placement, relocation and retirement are done well.

Talent management, however, follows talent spotting and selection. It is therefore extremely important to have an operational definition of the concept of talent so as to know what to look for. Yet, despite the increasing number of books written in the area, the concept remains unclear. Talent is, quite simply, not a psychological concept. One approach is to list possible synonyms for talent. These include: blessedness; exceptionality; being experienced; flair; genius; giftedness; high potential; precociousness; prodigy; superstars; wonderkids or wunderkinds.

Of the above it is really only 'giftedness' that has received any serious academic consideration. There is an extensive literature on gifted children which is consistent in what it highlights (Brody & Mills, 2005; Gagne, 2004; Heller, Monks & Passow, 1993; Shavinina, 2004). This, therefore, is a good place to begin to define talent. Research on gifted children tends to highlight the following characteristics. Such children

- Excel at *memory* activities beyond what one would expect at the given age level.
- Demonstrate unusually *mature thinking* on tasks that are complicated, learn very quickly new information or ways of doing things, or perceive hidden meanings.
- Show *advanced understanding* or precocious development of a specific skill area, e.g., early reading or mathematics without having been directly instructed, or rapid development when provided the opportunity in arts.
- Show *self-management* of their own learning.

- Have a high need for a *variety of experiences*, seek new and different opportunities to investigate and seem to delight in novel problems to solve.
- Seek *older children* as playmates and engage in especially creative imaginative play scenarios.
- Have an *advanced vocabulary* and enjoy playing with words or other means of symbolically representing their world.
- Demonstrate notable *variability* between very sophisticated thinking and behaviour in other ways that indicates they are still young children.

There are many such lists but these characteristics appear to identify very specific features or dimensions associated with giftedness. There seem to be three or four distinct clusters of characteristics. The first is both general and specific *ability*. Thus gifted children are described as observant, inquisitive, smart. They learn quickly, have a big vocabulary and enjoy intellectual challenges. At a more specific level (A level II), as defined by Carroll (1993), they have good memory, advanced comprehension skills and wide general knowledge (see Section 6.1). They are also well coordinated; dextrous, athletic and energetic (i.e., have advanced psychomotor skills). They can also show impressive visual, spatial, auditory skills. Perhaps it is their advanced vocabulary which most clearly marks them out as different.

Second, gifted children are known for their *creative thinking*. They are innovators, improvisers, independent and original thinkers. They enjoy coming up with several solutions to standard problems. They also do not mind standing out from a crowd. Unlike adults they are uninhibited about their creative products and express interest and confidence in the process.

Third, highly gifted children appear to have higher levels of *social intelligence*. They are expressive, self-confident, popular and able. They show good social judgement and are able to foresee the consequences and implications of their judgements. They often assume responsibility in social settings, which is accepted by others. In this sense they get elected to positions of leadership by both their peers and their teachers.

Finally, they tend to have higher levels of task commitment. They are able to concentrate easily. Often they also show other characteristics, like assuming task leadership roles in situations as well as advanced psychomotor coordination and visual perception. Not all gifted children grow up to be talented adults, and not all talented adults were gifted children, but it does seem that this is a rich source of hypotheses from which to consider the dimension of talent in adults.

10.2 Business reports

There have been a number of serious business reports on talent, partly because of an increasing interest in intangible assets. They focus on such issues as the relative decline in the number of trained graduates entering the workplace well below projected needs. They mention people feeling unfairly rewarded, as well as new types of jobs. Whilst governments use mechanisms like taxation and immigration to improve the situation, big companies seem worried about to find and attract these young (and not so young) people.

The expectations and lifestyle of people in the west are changing and businesses have to take that into consideration in talent spotting and management. There is the perception of a marketplace of talent: a limited pool of individuals whose talent is portable and transferable across corporate and national boundaries. Further, those talented people are seen to have specific characteristics (creativity, drive, energy, insight) to help companies both thrive and survive.

The Economist Intelligence Unit (2006) produced a case study report which showed that CEOs as well as HR managers are spending more of their time (around 25 per cent) engaged in talent management because it is believed to drive corporate performance, even though its impact is hard to measure. The CEOs see this process as identifying and grooming those at all levels so that they can rise faster up the corporate ladder. Performance evaluations and assessment/developmental centre reports provide the data to decide on programmes, projects and relocations which provide the experience to test and train (and unleash) the talent.

Many believe, quite simply, that talent management is a source, often a major source, of competitive advantage. Talented leaders enhance productivity supposedly through a high-performance culture. It is little more than getting the right people in the top places. It is seen inevitably as both a selector/assessment but also a training/mentoring activity. It is inevitably caught up with all the issues around success management. It is often seen as doing accelerated leadership development on highly selected individuals. In short it is identifying the CEOs of the future.

The Economist report notes that 'a rigorous approach to obtaining reliable performance data is essential' (p. 11), but as ever there is little indication of *what* to measure and *how*. Far too much reliance appears to be put on company appraisal scheme data and not enough on psychometrically proven assessment and developmental centre data.

A Deloitte Research Study on talent by Athey (2004) also covers much of this ground. Thus she argues CEOs are worried about the dwindling supply of talent, the problem of their 'star talent' being poached by the opposition, but also (and paradoxically) that when they poach others they rarely perform as hoped. The demographic time-bomb worries them, as does the education system and evidence of growing employee disengagement.

Athey (2004) presented a fairly standard four-stage model – acquire, deploy, develop and retain talent. Curiously, relatively little is said on acquiring talent, which seems the fundamental process. Much more is said about the developmental process – to give talented people the educational experiences. The 'deploy' part is particularly interesting and important and has three components: (a) identify the 'deep-rooted' skills, interests and knowledge of the individual; (b) find their best fit in the organisation; (c) craft the job design and conditions that help them perform. This is a particularly interesting idea though not fully explored. It is the idea not only of finding the super-adaptive and flexible individual, but also of making sure the organisation is adaptive enough to the profile of the individual.

Part of this plan is ensuring that the corporate culture helps the process. Thus command and control should be replaced by trust and respect. Win–lose must be replaced by a connected and collaborative culture. The idea is that talented people are attracted to companies where employees are aligned, capable, committed and therefore productive. Athey (2004, p. 12) notes the following:

Box 10.1 How do you identify your critical talent?

Critical talent are the people who create the value an organisation needs to succeed. Answering the following four questions can help leaders to isolate these groups and individuals.

1. Which strategies, skills and capabilities are crucial to your current and future success?
2. What emerging workforce trends (e.g., supply and demand of engineers) will impact on your ability to deliver value?
3. Who supports your critical segments of talent within their network? Are these supporting people difficult to replace?
4. Within your critical workforce segments, who possesses the greatest current and future potential?

Alas, like so many other well-researched and interesting reports in the area, the fundamental question (i.e., number 1 in Box 10.1) is never answered. Most writers assume that talent resides within the individual in terms of abilities (see Chapter 6), traits and motives/values (see Chapter 7). They also assume that these are pretty well independent of sector, that is, universally applicable. Yet a comprehensive list is never forthcoming. Nor is there any case study data or theoretical foundation or explanation as to why certain qualities labelled talent have any beneficial effects in the organisation. Further, even if there was an explanation, there is little suggestion about how best these characteristics are (more accurately, reliably, validly) assessed. Finally, one has to turn to organisational psychology to find any empirical evidence that certain characteristics are at all linked to any particular performance outcome.

10.3   The psychology of giftedness

This topic goes back to the 1920s and has been the focus of developmental and educational psychologists. It has been recognised for centuries that some children are quite simply, and very notably, gifted. They are different from their peers of the same age in terms of their cognitive ability, creativity and task commitment and complexity. They perform at many years above their chronological age and appear to sustain remarkably high levels of achievement and creativity. They seem to pick things up quickly, are deeply curious about their environment and proactive.

The question is whether studies on gifted children can inform studies on talented adults. Not all gifted children can and do go on to be talented adults (however defined), but they do so in sufficient numbers for researchers to believe that the concepts and thinking in the area of 'gifted chidren' may act as an excellent proxy for the study of talented adults.

What, therefore, are the distinguishing characteristics of the gifted child? Reviews list characteristics (many related) that parents and teachers of gifted children frequently report (Clark, 1988). Typically, the gifted child

- Shows superior reasoning powers and marked ability to handle ideas; can generalise readily from specific facts and can see subtle relationships; has outstanding problem-solving ability.
- Shows persistent intellectual curiosity; asks searching questions; shows exceptional interest in the nature of man and the universe.
- Has a wide range of interests, often of an intellectual kind; develops one or more interests to considerable depth.
- Is markedly superior in quality and quantity of written and/or spoken vocabulary; is interested in the subtleties of words and their uses.
- Reads avidly and absorbs books well beyond his or her years.
- Learns quickly and easily and retains what is learned; recalls important details, concepts and principles; comprehends readily.
- Shows insight into arithmetical problems that require careful reasoning and grasps mathematical concepts readily.
- Shows creative ability or imaginative expression in such things as music, art, dance, drama; shows sensitivity and finesse in rhythm, movement and bodily control.
- Sustains concentration for lengthy periods and shows outstanding responsibility and independence is classroom work.
- Sets realistically high standards for self; is self-critical in evaluating and correcting his/her own efforts.
- Shows initiative and originality in intellectual work; shows flexibility in thinking and considers problems from a number of viewpoints.
- Observes keenly and is responsive to new ideas.
- Shows social poise and an ability to communicate with adults in a mature way.
- Gets excitement and pleasure from intellectual challenge; shows an alert and subtle sense of humour.

There are many similar lists. To a large extent this seems a helpful way of thinking about how to define talented adults. Certainly those who have thought and written about high-flyers (Cox & Cooper, 1988; Spreitzer, McCall & Maloney,

1997; Locke, 1997) do include the above factors: cognitive ability (see Chapter 7), creativity social intelligence (see Chapter 8). It is important to note that personality, motivation and value-type beliefs tend not to appear on these lists. This may reflect the preference of social psychologists not to use trait-type descriptions when describing organisational success.

Finally, there is in the gifted child literature one other important theme: *the cost of giftedness*. As well as the immense benefits of being gifted, researchers have pointed to disadvantages and drawbacks. Three are often mentioned:

- Raised expectations of others – it is clear why this occurs but it can put pressure on gifted children always, and everywhere, to excel at every task. Lack of achievement can erroneously be seen as laziness. This raises questions as to whether organisations are wise to 'anoint' people as members of a high-flyer group.
- Perfectionism – it has been noticed that some gifted children show signs of perfectionistic obsessionality. This trait can slow down the rate of their performance and leads to both anxiety and depression. Perfectionists set themselves too high a target in all they do; they often fail to achieve these targets and hence feel dejected by failure.
- Self-doubt – it is indeed paradoxical that gifted children can show considerable self-doubt. This may be caused by the implicit and explicit expectations others (especially parents and teachers) have of them and which they feel they cannot easily fulfil. It may also be caused by feeling they have always to excel at everything, which is very demanding.

There is an 'adult version' of these problems in successful (if not gifted, talented) adults, which has been described as the *imposter phenomenon* (Harvey & Katz, 1985). The characteristic of this is that the successful person, often suddenly propelled into the limelight in the arts or business, feels like a fake: an imposter not worthy of the accolade or deserving of success. As a result, they tend to discount their success by attributing it to luck, chance and circumstance. Indeed, they tend to become fearful of success because they see it as causing problems for themselves. The strategy many apply is self-handicapping, which prevents them from failing, maybe through drink, drugs or illegal activities. They feel strongly the need to reduce the pressure not to fail.

This is the dark side of giftedness and talent. It seems, then, that I/O psychologists may have overlooked the gifted child literature which offers considerable empirical and theoretical insight into the concept of talent.

10.4 The psychology of high-flyers

Usually the definition of a high-flyer is a talented individual capable of taking on more and more senior and responsible jobs. Their talent is manifest in

Box 10.2 Performance/promotability matrix

	1	2	3
1	Highly promotable within organisation: significant leadership potential. Exceeds performer – exceeds requirements.	Promotable – one level maximum. Exceptional performer – exceeds requirements.	At level. Exceptional performance – exceeds requirements.
2	Highly promotable within organisation; significant leadership potential. Effective performer – fully meets requirements.	Promotable – one level maximum. Effective performer – fully meets requirements.	At level. Effective performer – meets requirements.
3	Has potential to be highly promotable within organisation. Partially meets requirements. Needs improvement (new in current position).	Has potential to be promoted – one level maximum. Partially meets requirements. Needs improvement.	At level. Partially meets requirements. Needs significant improvement.

their ability to adapt, learn fast and cope with complex tasks, be it in the public or private sector.

When people are asked to evaluate and assess young (or not so young) people at an assessment centre for selection, promotion or succession management reasons, the 'top' category usually refers to a small group of high-flyers who supposedly can 'make it to the top', implying that they can reach board or CEO level. For many assessors the result of an assessment exercise is to classify people by a performance vs potential promotability grid, as set out in Box 10.2. The y axis is performance, the x axis promotability, with 1 being a high score and 3 a low score.

Naturally there has been a great deal of speculation over a long period of time as to what characteristics these very special people manifest. Cox and Cooper (1988) identified 'key personal characteristics' which are related to success. These were:

1. Determination: a characteristic often derived from childhood experiences where they had to take personal responsibility for themselves.

2. Learning from adversity: using adversity and setbacks to learn better coping strategies and learning new skills.

3. Seizing chances: not the same as opportunism but enthusiastically taking on very difficult decisions early in life.

4. Being achievement orientated: being ambitious and positive and after long-term big prizes.

5. Internal locus of control: being a self-confident instrumentalist, not fatalist.

6. Having a well-integrated value system: having a clear, integrated and lived-by value system (valuing integrity, independence, initiative, etc.).

7. Effective risk management: moderate, but calculated, risk takers.

8. Having clear objectives: having both long- and short-term objectives and striving constantly for them.

9. Dedication to the job: feeling the job was the most important aspect of life yet not being a workaholic.

10. Intrinsic motivation: finding energy and enthusiasm in the job, not simply being motivated by extrinsic reward.

11. Well-organised lifestyle, which prevents conflicts between work and home life.

12. A pragmatic rather than intellectual approach: having practical interests and pursuits rather than intellectual ones.

13. Analytic and problem-solving skills: perhaps seeming intuitive rather than rational.

14. Exemplary people skills: being socially skilled, open and consultative; however, also being authoritative.

15. Being innovative: not being constrained by procedures, current systems and assumptions.

16. Having a competitive, hard-driving lifestyle, sometimes called the type A lifestyle.

They noted:

> One quality which does seem to be universal among high-flyers is *resilience* and the ability not only to cope with but also to learn from adversity. This characteristic is a function of their strong *internal locus of control*, aided by a clear *value system* and strong *self-concept*. In other words, people who reach the top are clear about *who they are* and *what they believe in*. This aspect of personality is strongly influenced by early experience and so probably has to be considered as a quality required at the selection stage, rather than as something which can be trained by the organisation. Even so, some development can possibly be offered through the medium of such activities as 'outward bound' programmes, which certainly aid in the development of the capacity to overcome adversity, and do often force individuals to confront their assumptions about themselves and their values. Sensitive and skilled mentoring can also aid this process.   (p. 147)

Locke (1997) also devised a three-category list of what can be called predictors of success:

Cognition: reality focus; honesty; independence and self-confidence; active mind; competence/ability; vision.
Motivation: egotistic passion for the work; commitment to action; ambition; effort and tenacity.
Attitude towards employees: respect for ability; commitment to justice; rewarding merit.

However, he wisely speculated on various related and important questions in this area:

1. What methods could be used to infer quality of a trait possessed by a deceased business leader based on biographical and autobiographical material? Can trait measurements of such people be made reliably?
2. How well can these traits be measured in existing business leaders (e.g., assessment centres, tests, interviews, peer ratings)? Howard and Bray (1988) found that intelligence and ambition, measured by tests and interviews, were the best predictors of advancement of AT&T managers over a 25-year period.
3. Could such traits be measured early in a person's career as a way of identifying 'prime mover' potential? Howard and Bray's results suggest that they could, but their dependent variable was promotion rather than wealth creation.
4. Would qualitative analysis support 12 distinct traits, or could they be grouped into smaller numbers without loss of important information? My prediction is that they can be combined into a smaller number.
5. Do the traits operate independently (i.e., in additive fashion) or are there interactions between them? I have one prediction here: I think dishonesty negates all a person's other virtues in that it divorces a person from reality in principle. An implicating factor, however, is that people are not always consistent in their honesty or dishonesty.
6. Do the same traits produce wealth creation in all cultures? I would say yes, although there may be culture-specific traits as well.
7. Do prime movers and (lower-level) managers differ in their traits only in degree, or are there more fundamental differences? I would predict big difference in degree on some traits (e.g., ability, ambition). In the case of vision, on the other hand, some managers may not have any at all. (Locke, 1997: 92)

Yet another list based on opinion, as opposed to research, is set out in Table 10.1.

While lists are impressively long and fairly commonsensical they have the traditional drawbacks of such an approach. The data are based on self-report (interviews and questionnaires) and it may be that beliefs and behaviour patterns are ignored or 'repackaged' to make them seem more attractive. Certainly many high-flyers have a reputation for being egotistical, ruthless and amoral, though this is not how they present themselves to the world.

The lists are long but not rank ordered. Are some characteristics more important than others? And, if so, which? What is the relationship between these different

Table 10.1 *Most and least important skills and attributes for effective leadership (Corporate Leadership Council, 2001)*

Ten most important characteristics		Ten least important characteristics	
1. Honesty and integrity	61%	31. Committed to continuous	11%
2. Clearly communicates expectations	49%	personal relationships	
		32. Thinks analytically	10%
3. Recognises and rewards achievements	39%	33. Sensitive to others' needs	10%
		34. Has perseverance	8%
4. Adapts to changes	37%	35. Creates clear work plans and timetables	8%
5. Inspires others	34%		
6. Puts the right people in the right holes at the right time	33%	36. Breaks down project into manageable components	7%
7. Has passion to succeed	33%	37. Strong commitment to diversity	5%
8. Identifies and articulates long-term vision for future	31%	38. Properly manages relationships with third parties	5%
9. Persuades and encourages others to move in desired direction	31%	39. Has years of experience in positions of management	2%
10. Accepts responsibility for success or failure	29%	40. Is original	1%

characteristics? How are they related? Can they be reduced to a more parsimonious and clearer list? Indeed, this is why the early trait approach to leadership failed: there was no agreement on, or good empirical evidence in support of, a parsimonious list of identical traits.

Jennings, Cox and Cooper (1994) reported numerous famous 'entrepreneurs' (people who build and control companies) and 'elite entrepreneurs' (people who have worked themselves up to the CEO position in organisations). These individuals may or may not be classified as talented or high-flying. Jennings *et al.* examined early childhood experiences; socio-demographic origins; education; specific support from others; their approach to work and their work ethic; their personality traits and their philanthropic interests. They focussed on three spheres of life–work (education and work history), personality with developmental history, and non-work/family environment. Their results were surprisingly similar to the earlier study (Cox & Cooper, 1988).

Essentially the method was retrospective and biographical. This is often the approach of historians. Borrowing heavily on other explanatory systems, Cox and Cooper (1988) also present a developmental model for managerial success. First, they note the importance both of parental attitudes and values, but also early trauma associated with separation of one kind of another. Next, they did not find schooling at a primary, secondary or tertiary level was particularly influential or important. Indeed, choice of institution may well reflect parental values, which are the really important issue. Early experience at work is seen to be most important,

Box 10.3 Factors contributing to high-flyer performance

DEVELOPMENTAL EXPERIENCES	THE INDIVIDUAL	DETERMINANTS OF PERFORMANCE
EARLY EXPERIENCE	PARENT	MANAGEMENT PHILOSOPHY
Develops reliance on own resources and achievement orientation	Well-integrated value system – integrity – self-reliance – achievement – initiative Control	Balanced task/person orientation Tendency to be authoritarian
EDUCATION	ADULT	MANAGEMENT SKILLS
Including management education, if any Develops rational and social skills	Very effective analysis and problem-solving skills	Helicopter quality People skills
CAREER EXPERIENCE	CHILD	MOTIVATION
Successful response to challenge 'make-or-break' opportunities	Intuition Creativity Enthusiasm Energy	Intrinsic Leadership Motivation pattern

particularly having a helpful early mentor or model and succeeding when early 'make-or-break' opportunities presented themselves. Their model is shown in Box 10.3.

According to Gunter and Furnham (2001), there are three major problems with the high-flyer biographical method. The first is specifying what constitutes a high-flyer. No single criterion suffices. Inevitably luck and chance play a part; hence the particular characteristics high-flyers have may be little more than opportunism-spotting and exploiting entrepreneurial opportunities faster and more successfully than others. The business of defining a high-flyer or a member of a successful business elite is by no means simple. Ideally researchers would specify objectively and explicitly a range of criteria that would explain the principle by which certain people are included and others excluded from the sample.

The second problem is actually getting the nominated high-flyers to take part in the study by agreeing to an interview or completing a survey. High-flyers soon get 'over-researched', receiving little personal benefit from being research participants. Hence many of those carefully selected refuse to take part, forcing the researchers to weaken their criteria and indeed the study as a whole.

Third, these sorts of studies almost never have a control group of those matched on a number of criteria who simply did not 'make it'. Thus one can never really say whether the special characteristics identified by researchers of high-flyers are unique to them or indeed played any part in their success.

McCall and colleagues have attempted to identify executive potential, or executive competences, also known as end-state skills (McCall, 1994, 1998; McCall, Lombardo & Morrison, 1988; Spreitzer et al., 1997). To a large extent this team argue that the ability to learn from experience is the fundamental key to managerial potential.

They argue that a review of the diverse literature on the early identification of executive success through the assessment centre literature indicates five themes or areas of importance.

1. **General intelligence:** simple IQ or cognitive ability is clearly related to business-related issues, such as analytic agility, reasoning, incisiveness, synthetic and visionary thinking.
2. **Business knowledge:** this is an understanding of the company and sector's products, markets and policies as well as a breadth of awareness and interest in trends of the market as a whole.
3. **Interpersonal skills:** social skills are important in handling relationships, team building, the capacity to motivate and inspire as well as align people behind particular strategies.
4. **Commitment:** this can be expressed in various ways, such as a passion for success, personal drive and perseverance. They all refer to extreme interest in, and commitment to, work.
5. **Courage:** to a large extent this means non-risk-averse and willing to take actions to ensure that things happen. It is related to self-confidence but not arrogance.

A theme identified strongly by this team is the ability to learn from experience. Those with potential take a proactive approach to learning, learn from their mistakes, adapt well to difficult circumstances as well as seek and use feedback in order to make sense of their work environment.

In later work McCall identified eleven dimensions he believes relate to being a high-flyer:

1. **Seeks opportunities to learn.**
   Has demonstrated a pattern of learning over time. Seeks out experiences that may change perspective or provide an opportunity to learn new things. Takes advantage of opportunities to do new things when such opportunities come along. Has developed new skills and has changed over time.

2. **Acts with integrity.**
   Tells the truth and is described by others as honest. Is not self-promoting and consistently takes responsibility for his or her actions.

3. **Adapts to cultural differences.**
   Enjoys the challenge of working in, and experiencing cultures different from, his or her own. Is sensitive to cultural differences, works hard to understand them and changes behaviour in response to them.

4. **Is committed to making a difference.**
   Demonstrates a strong commitment to the success of the organisation and is willing to make personal sacrifices to contribute to that success. Seeks to have a positive impact on the business. Shows passion and commitment through a strong drive for results.

5. **Seeks broad business knowledge.**
   Has an understanding of the business that goes beyond his or her own limited area. Seeks to understand both the products or services and the financial aspects of the business. Seeks to understand how the various parts of the business fit together.

6. **Brings out the best in people.**
   Has a special talent with people that is evident in his or her ability to pull people together into highly effective teams. Is able to work with a wide variety of people, drawing the best out of them and achieving consensus in the face of disagreement.

7. **Is insightful: sees things from new angles.**
   Other people admire this person's intelligence, particularly his or her ability to ask insightful questions, identify the most important part of a problem or issue, and see things from a different perspective.

8. **Has the courage to take risks.**
   Will take a stand when others disagree, go against the status quo, persevere in the face of opposition. Has the courage to act when others hesitate and will take both personal and business risks.

9. **Seeks and uses feedback.**
   Pursues, responds to and uses feedback. Actively asks for information on his or her impact and has changed as a result of such feedback.

10. **Learns from mistakes.**
    Is able to learn from mistakes. Changes direction when the current path isn't working, responds to data without getting defensive and starts over after setbacks.

11. **Is open to criticism.**
    Handles criticism effectively: does not act threatened or get overly defensive when others (especially superiors) are critical. (McCall, Spreitzer & Mahoney, 1994).

   The high-flyer approach has fundamental problems, the greatest of which is the identification of these people in the first place. The criteria for being considered a high-flyer are rarely explicit or consensually agreed upon. Worse, it is not unusual for an identified high-flyer to seriously 'fall to earth' not long after a study is complete. Given that the whole approach attempts to find out what is unique to the psyche of the high-flyer, this is a most fundamental issue.

10.5   The Icarus syndrome and talent derailment

Furnham (2003) spelt out a theory as to why talented people derail. He argued that the Greek story of Icarus was a good example to help in understanding the syndrome.

In Greek mythology, Icarus was the son of the inventor Daedalus. Cretan King Minos locked the father and son up in a high tower. The talented Daedalus made two sets of wings of feathers and wax, which they would use to escape; he told his son that the only 'design fault' was that the wax might melt if they flew too close to the sun. Icarus ignored the good advice of his wise father, flew too high, melted his wings and crashed into the sea and drowned.

It is not clear from the myth precisely why Icarus disobeyed his father. Was he a sensation seeker prone to accidents? Did he do it out of boredom? Was he a disobedient, rebellious child? Was he simply beguiled by his own hubris?

We don't know the answers. Indeed, it is the function of myths and case studies that they allow for multiple interpretations. We do know that the modern derailed high-flyer bears an uncanny resemblance to Icarus. But how and why are they chosen? What did the assessors miss? Or was the problem in the way they were managed? Yet there is a growing literature on management derailment and why it occurs particularly in those once labelled as talented.

Later Furnham (2007) argued that three categories or types of personality disorders and traits are most commonly implicated in management derailment: antisocial (psychopath), narcissistic and histrionic. Machiavellianism (which is not strictly a personality disorder) has been considered another dimension. These have been variously described as the dark triad of personality (Paulus & Williams, 2002), though there is some disagreement about all dimensions. In lay terms, psychopaths are selfish, callous, superficially charming, lacking empathy and remorseless; narcissists are attention seeking, vane, self-focussed and exploitative; while Machiavellians are deceptive, manipulative and deeply self-interested.

Furnham (2007) noted that, paradoxically, it is often these disorders that prove to be an asset in acquiring and temporarily holding down senior management positions. The charm of the psychopath, the self-confidence of the narcissist, the clever deceptiveness of the Machiavellian and the emotional openness of the histrionic may be, in many instances, useful business traits. When candidates are physically attractive, well-educated, intelligent and have a dark triad profile, it is not difficult to see why they are selected for senior positions in management. In this sense assessors and selectors must bear part of the blame for not selecting out those who so often so spectacularly derail. They do not recognise in the biography of the individual all the crucial indicators of the disorder.

Alternatively, the biography as portrayed in the CV may easily be a work of fiction.

When thinking of a psychopath, the layperson often conceives of a dangerous mass murderer or perhaps the amazing successful confidence trickster. Similarly, many would admire the self-confidence of the person with narcissistic personality disorder. Further, the emotional lability and showiness of the histrionic-personality-disordered manager in a creative job may result in them being rated as creative rather than disturbed. The clever deviousness of the Machiavellian may also be admired as an indication of toughness. In this sense 'mild' forms of these pathologies could appear generally, or at specific times, which could be very advantageous.

Dysfunctional managers, particularly those with some evidence of antisocial personality disorder, may appear toxic. Furnham (2003) notes that the results from studies on the origin of delinquency and criminality make for depressing reading. When you observe young children in a clearly toxic family, you feel they really have little possibility of growing up as healthy, responsible, adaptable individuals. The person with an antisocial personality has often had a miserable upbringing, which, alas, he or she often perpetuates, producing a cycle of misfortune, neglect, unhappiness and crime.

Reading the list of typical characteristics of the dysfunctional parent in the toxic family, it is not difficult to see why children from these families end up as they do. Moody, egocentric, uneducated, immoral 'caregivers' give little real care.

The same can happen at work. Dysfunctional managers create toxic offices. Often in a brief period of time, they manage to create mayhem, distrust and disaffection. This can have long-term consequences even in stable adults. That perfidious issue of 'stress at work' and its more serious cousin, the nervous breakdown, are often caused by the dysfunctional manager.

He lists nine typical symptoms of toxicity:

- *Inconsistency and unpredictability*. This is often the hallmark of the type. They are unpredictable to staff, clients and customers, even to their family. You can never be sure what they will say or do. They are fickle and capricious. The job of a parent and manager is often to create stability in a world of chaos, a sense of security in an insecure world, not the opposite. Dysfunctional managers are often more than inconsistent in that they give contradictory and mixed messages that are very difficult to interpret.
- *Low tolerance of provocation and emotional sensitivity*. Dysfunctional managers easily fly off the handle. They are known for their moodiness. You quite literally have to read around them very gently. Jokes backfire, unless they themselves make them. They take offence, harbour grudges and can show great mood swings, especially when stressed.
- *Hedonism and self-indulgence*. Dysfunctional managers are not puritans; they like pleasure. The golf round on Friday afternoon, expensive meals and over-priced office furniture are ways dysfunctional managers please themselves.

They are often deeply selfish. There can be real problems if their pleasures are addictive, which so often they can be. The hedonistic, addictive personality is a real nightmare not only from a financial point of view.

- *Now-ness and lack of long-term planning.* Dysfunctional parents and dysfunctional managers live each day as it comes, not for religious reasons, but because they can't or won't plan for the future. They don't understand postponement of gratification. Hence, they experience serious setbacks when unexpected things happen. They can't or won't plan for future eventualities for themselves, their staff, or their product.
- *Restlessness and excitement seeking.* Dysfunctional managers are always on the go. They get easily bored and can't seem to pay attention. They seem to have an adult form of Attention Deficit Hyperactivity Disorder (ADHD). They appear to need thrills and variety to keep them going. Inevitably, they find themselves in situations that are commercially, even physically, dangerous. They change often, can't sit still, and rarely pay attention to others.
- *Learning problems.* Dysfunctional managers don't learn from their mistakes. In fact, they don't like learning at all. The skill-based seminar is not for them. Outdoor, physical training perhaps, but not the conference centre. Many have few educational qualifications. They don't value them in their staff or themselves. Hence, they do not encourage learning of any sort, often pooh-poohing the educated staff member.
- *Poor emotional control.* Dysfunctional managers are the opposite of the stereotypical reserved and controlled Englishman. They shout, weep, sulk and gush with little embarrassment or control. They become well known for their outbursts. This is not the result of therapy: in fact, they have little self-control.
- *Placing little value on skill attainment.* The dysfunctional manager does not have an MBA. They despise attempts of the staff to upgrade their skills. They talk about gut feelings, experience or, worse still, luck. They are loath to invest in training on the job.
- *Perpetual low-grade physical illness.* Dysfunctional bosses always seem to be ill. They get coughs, colds, flu, whatever is going around. They certainly are not health conscious, and they are very liable to absenteeism.

The above list of toxic factors may give one a really good insight into those traits or disorders that one does not want. In this sense these are select-out factors for talent management.

10.6 Practical implications

A great deal has been written on the 'war for talent': mainly about recruiting, developing and retaining talented people. What is perhaps most surprising about this literature is that it appears to flourish without any real clear understanding of what talent is, where it comes from and how it changes over time.

Thus Michaels, Handfield-Jones and Axelrod (2001, p. 165) ask proactively 'Are you prepared to win the war for talent?'

1. Is talent one of your top three priorities?
2. Are you spending 30 per cent or more of your time strengthening your talent pool? Have you made talent your job?
3. Are you and all your key people explicitly held accountable for strengthening their talent pool?
4. Do you have a winning employee value proposition that attracts talented people to your organisation?
5. Do you know the attrition rate of your young, high-performing managers and why they are leaving? Do you have initiatives in place to reduce these regretted losses?
6. Are you aggressively recruiting for new faces in new places at all levels, including senior levels of your organisation?
7. Does your unit have a robust written recruiting strategy, similar in rigour to your marketing strategies?
8. Do you give your top performers accelerated opportunities, significantly differentiated compensation and real mentoring?
9. Does your organisation have a culture of candid feedback and helpful coaching?
10. Does your organisation have a talent review process that has the importance and intensity of the budget process and that cascades throughout your organisation?
11. Is the review session filled with candour and does it result in real consequences for those discussed?
12. Is your annual forced attrition rate in the top 5 or 10 per cent range, and are you continuously dealing with underperformers?

They also challenge readers by rhetorically asking them to check their mindset. Inevitably the 'correct' answer is yes.

- Do you believe having better people is how you will win in your business?
- Do you believe strengthening your talent pool is a crucial part of *your* job?
- Do you convince all your managers to make talent a crucial part of *their* job?
- Have you established a gold standard for talent in your organisation that is widely understood and drives people decisions?
- Are you deeply involved in key people decisions two and three levels below you? Do you probe, help and challenge?
- To instil a talent mindset in others, do you model great talent management and talk to your people about talent frequently?
- Have you demonstrated a willingness to invest real money in talent?
- Are you holding each of your leaders (and yourself) accountable for three to six highly specific and measurable actions to strengthen their talent pool over the coming years?

Like others in the area, they are eager to contrast the 'old' and the new world: new reliable employee expectations, pay philosophies, recruiting strategies, ethics, approaches to development and a new review process. The bottom line is the pool of very talented individuals is small and one has to be aware that finding, managing and retaining them is a seriously challenging and important issue.

Many have written about how to build a talent management system, but they all look very much like one another and similar to older HR systems that never used the concept of talent management (Berger & Berger, 2004).

Others have addressed how to develop talent. Thus Berger (2004) lists twelve approaches, from on-the-job coaching and mentoring, through job rotation and emergency fill-in assignments, to a variety of courses. Ideas about talent management appear to draw heavily upon currently fashionable concepts like emotional intelligence, coaching, levering diversity, to a reinvention of the succession management literature under new guises. Some believe that talented people require special or particular compensation schemes.

However, what remains missing at the heart of the HR-based, rather than differential psychology-based, literature is a theory of, and empirical evidence for, a specific profile of 'talented' people. This would require an explanation for the origin and development of talent, a description of the processes associated with talent, and, most importantly, discriminant and predictive validity showing that talented people are 'special' at work in terms of a number of important output variables like productivity, morale and leadership.

10.7 Summary and conclusions

Despite the popularity of the concept, the definition of talent remains even more problematic than that of creativity. If it essentially means having and wisely applying intelligence in a business context the problem is easily solved. However, just as the 'gurus' of emotional intelligence claim cognitive ability is itself not enough to explain business success, so those writing about talent claim it has other facets. The one issue that underlies a great deal of this work is the concept of motivation, sometimes called drive or determination or ambition, which both researchers and business people recognise as very important but which psychometricians have never had a great success in defining or measuring.

References

Aamodt, M. G., Bryan, D. A. & Whitcomb, A. J. (1993). Predicting performance with letters of recommendation. *Public Personnel Management*, 22(1), 81–90.

Achilles, P. S. & Achilles, E. M. (1917). Estimates of the military value of certain character qualities. *Journal of Applied Psychology*, 1(4), 305–16.

Ackerman, P. L. (1987). Individual differences in skill learning: an integration of psychometric and information processing perspectives. *Psychological Bulletin*, 102, 3–27.

(2008). Knowledge and cognitive aging. In T. A. S. Fergus & I. M. Craik (eds.), *The Handbook of Aging and Cognition*, pp. 445–90. New York: Psychology Press.

Ackerman, P. L. & Heggestad, E. D. (1997). Intelligence, personality, and interests: evidence for overlapping traits. *Psychological Bulletin*, 121, 219–45.

Ackerman, P. L. & Rolfhus, E. L. (1999). The locus of adult intelligence: knowledge, abilities, and nonability traits. *Psychology and Aging*, 14(2), 314–30.

Ackerman, P. L. & Wolman, S. (2007). Determinants and validity of self-estimates of abilities and self-concept measures. *Journal of Experimental Psychology: Applied*, 13, 57–78.

Ackerman, S., Clemence, A., Weatherill, R. & Hilsenroth, M. (1999). Use of TAT in the assessment of DSM-IV Cluster B personality disorder. *Journal of Personality Assessment*, 73, 422–48.

Alley, T. R. (1988). Physiognomy and social perception. In T. R. Alley (ed.), *Social and Applied Aspects of Perceiving Faces*, pp. 167–86. Hillsdale, NJ: Erlbaum.

Alliger, G. M. & Dwight, S. A. (2000). A meta-analytic investigation of the susceptibility of integrity tests to faking and coaching. *Educational and Psychological Measurement*, 60, 59–72.

All-issa, I. (1972). Stimulus generalization and over-inclusion in normal and schizophrenic subjects. *Journal of Clinical Psychology*, 39, 182–6.

Allport, G. W. & Vernon, P. E. (1933). *Studies in Expressive Movement*. New York: Macmillan.

Allworth, E. & Hesketh, B. (2000). Job requirements biodata as a predictor of performance in customer service roles. *International Journal of Selection and Assessment*, 8(3), 137–47.

Amabile, T. M. (1990). Within you, without you: the social psychology of creativity, and beyond. In M. A. Runco & R. S. Alber (eds.), *Theories of Creativity*, pp. 61–91. Newbury Park, CA: Sage.

(1997). Motivating creativity in organizations: on doing what you love and loving what you do. *California Management Review*, 40(1), 39–58.

Amabile, T. M., Conti, R., Coon, H., Lazenby, J. & Herron, M. (1996). Assessing the work environment for creativity. *Academy of Management Journal, 39*(5), 1154–84.

Amelang, M. & Steinmayr, R. (2006). Is there a validity increment for tests of emotional intelligence in explaining the variance of performance criteria? *Intelligence, 34*(5), 459–68.

Anastasi, A. (1981). Coaching, test sophistication, and developed abilities. *American Psychologist, 36*, 1086–93.

(1989). Ability testing in the 1980s and beyond: some major trends. *Public Personnel and Management Journal, 18*, 471–84.

Anastasi, A. & Schaefer, C. (1971). Note on the concepts of creativity and intelligence. *Journal of Creative Behavior, 5*, 113–16.

Anderson, L. R. & Fielder, F. E. (1964). The effect of participatory and supervisory leadership on group creativity. *Journal of Applied Psychology, 48*, 227–36.

Anderson, N., Born, M. & Cunningham-Snell, N. (2001). Recruitment and selection: applicant perspectives and outcomes. In N. Anderson, D. S. Ones, H. K. Sinargil & C. Viswesvaran (eds.), *Handbook of Industrial, Work and Organizational Psychology*, vol. 1. London and New York: Sage.

Anderson, N. & Cunningham-Snell, N. (2000). Personnel selection. In N. Chmiel (ed.), *Introduction to Work and Organisational Psychology*, pp. 69–99. Oxford: Blackwell.

Andriopoulos, C. (2003). Six paradoxes in managing creativity: an embracing act. *Long Range Planning, 36*(4), 375–88.

Armstrong, P. I., Day, S. X., McVay, J. P. & Rounds, J. (2008). Holland's RIASEC model as an integrative framework for individual differences. *Journal of Counseling Psychology, 55*(1), 1–18.

Arnold, J. (2005). *Work Psychology*. New York: Prentice Hall.

Arthur, W., Day, E. A., McNelly, T. L. & Edens, P. S. (2003). A meta-analysis of the criterion-related validity of assessment center dimensions. *Personnel Psychology, 56*, 125–54.

Ashforth, B. E. & Mael, F. (1989). Social identify theory and the organisation. *Academy of Management Review, 14*, 20–39.

Athey, R. (2004). It's 2008: do you know where your talent is? Deloitte Research Study.

Atkinson, J. W. (ed.) (1958). *Motives in Fantasy, Action, and Society*. Princeton, NJ: Van Nostrand.

Austin, E. J., Farrelly, D., Black, C. & Moore, H. (2007). Emotional intelligence, Machiavellianism and emotional manipulation: does EI have a dark side? *Personality and Individual Differences, 43*(1), 179–89.

Austin, J. T. & Hanisch, K. A. (1990). Occupational attainment as a function of abilities and interests: a longitudinal analysis using project TALENT data. *Journal of Applied Psychology, 75*, 77–86.

Avolio, B. J. (1999). *Full Leadership Development: Building the Vital Forces in Organisations*. Thousands Oaks, CA: Sage.

Avolio, B. J., Bass, B. M. & Jung, D. I. (1999). *Manual for the Multifactor Leadership Questionnaire (Form 5X)*. Redwood City, CA: Mind Garden.

Awoniyi, E. A., Griego, O. V. & Morgan, G. A. (2002). Person-environment fit and transfer of training. *International Journal of Training and Development, 6*(1), 25–35.

Bailin, S. (1988). The something more. In *Achieving Extraordinary Ends: An Essay on Creativity*, pp. 109–33. Dordrecht: Kluwer.

Baird, J.-A., Greatorex, J. & Bell, J. F. (2004). What makes marking reliable? Experiments with UK examinations. *Assessment in Education: Principles, Policy & Practice, 11*(3), 331–48.

Bales, R. F. (1950). *Interaction Process Analysis: A Method for the Study of Small Groups*. Cambridge, MA: Addison-Wesley.

Ball, R. J. (1929). An objective measure of emotional instability. *Journal of Applied Psychology, 13*(3), 226–56.

Bandura, A. (1986). *Social Foundations of Thought and Action: A Social Cognitive Theory*. Englewood Cliffs, NJ: Prentice Hall.

(1999). A social–cognitive theory of personality. In L. Pervin & O. John (eds.), *Handbook of Personality*, 2nd edn, pp. 154–96. New York: Guilford Press.

Barber, J. D. (1992). *The Presidential Character: Predicting Performance in the White House*. Englewood Cliffs, NJ: Prentice-Hall.

Barling, J., Weber, T. & Kelloway, E. K. (1996). Effects of transformational leadership training on attitudinal and financial outcomes: a field experiment. *Journal of Applied Psychology, 81*, 827–32.

Bar-On, R. (1997). *Bar-On Emotional Quotient Inventory: Technical Manual*. Toronto: Toronto Multihealth Systems.

Baron, R. A. & Byrne, D. (1987). *Social Psychology: Understanding Human Interaction*, 5th edn. Needham Heights, MA: Allyn & Bacon.

Barrett, G. V. & Alexander, R. A. (1989). Rejoinder to Austin, Humphreys, and Hulin: critical reanalysis of Barrett, Caldwell, and Alexander. *Personnel Psychology, 42*(3), 597–612.

Barrett, G. V. & Depinet, R. L. (1991). A reconsideration of testing for competence rather than for intelligence. *American Psychologist, 46*(10), 1012–24.

Barrick, M. R. & Mount, M. K. (1991). The Big-Five personality dimensions in job performance: a meta-analysis. *Personnel Psychology, 44*, 1–26.

(1996). Effects of impression management and self-deception on the predictive validity of personality constructs. *Journal of Applied Psychology, 81*, 261–72.

Barrick, M. R., Mount, M. K. & Strauss, J. P. (1993). Conscientiousness and performance of sales representatives: test of the mediating effects of goal setting. *Journal of Applied Psychology, 78*(5), 715–22.

(1994). Antecedents of involuntary turnover due to a reduction in force. *Personnel Psychology, 47*(3), 515–35.

Barrick, M. R., Stewart, G. L., Neubert, M. J. & Mount, M. K. (1998). Relating member ability and personality to work-team processes and team effectiveness. *Journal of Applied Psychology, 83*(3), 377–91.

Barron, F. (1963). The needs for order and disorder as motives in creative action. In C. W. Taylor & F. Barron (eds.), *Scientific Creativity: Its Recognition and Development*, pp. 139–52. New York: Wiley.

(1969). *Creative Person and Creative Process*. New York: Holt, Rinehart & Winston.

Barron, F. & Harrington, D. M. (1981). Creativity, intelligence, and personality. *Annual Review of Psychology, 32*, 439–76.

Barthel, E. & Schuler, H. (1989). Nutzenkalkulation eignungsdiagnostischer Verfahren am Beispiel eines biographischen Fragebogens. / Utility calculation of personnel selection methods using the example of a biographical questionnaire. *Zeitschrift für Arbeits- und Organisationspsychologie, 33*(2), 73–83.

Bartol, K. M. & Martin, D. C. (1986). Women and men in task groups. In R. D. Ashmore & F. K. Del Boca (eds.), *The Social Psychology of Female–Male Relations*, pp. 259–310. Orlando, FL: Academic Press.

Bartram, D. & Dale, H. C. (1982). The Eysenck Personality Inventory as a selection test for military pilots. *Journal of Occupational Psychology, 55*(4), 287–96.

Bass, B. M. (1981). From leaderless group discussions to the cross-national assessment of managers. *Journal of Management, 7*, 63–76.

(1985). *Leadership and Performance Beyond Expectations.* New York: Free Press.

(1990). *Bass and Stogdill's Handbook of Leadership: Theory, Research, and Managerial Applications*, 3rd edn. New York: Free Press.

(1995). Theory of transformational leadership redux, *Leadership Quarterly, 6*(4), 463–78.

(1997). Does the transactional-transformational leadership paradigm transcend organisational and national boundaries? *American Psychologist, 52*, 130–9.

(1998). *Transformational Leadership: Industry, Military, and Educational Impact.* Mahwah, NJ: Erlbaum.

Bass, B. M. & Avolio, B. J. (eds.) (1985). *Leadership Performance Beyond Expectations.* New York: Free Press.

(1995). *MLQ Multifactor Leadership Questionnaire for Research: Permission Set.* Palo Alto, CA: Mind Garden.

Baxter, J. C., Brock, B., Hill, P. C. & Rozelle, R. M. (1981). Letters of recommendation: a question of value. *Journal of Applied Psychology, 66*(3), 296–301.

Bayne, R. & O'Neill, F. (1988). Handwriting and personality: a test of some expert graphologists' judgments. *Guidance and Assessment Review, 4*, 1–3.

Becker, G. (1978). *The Mad Genius Controversy.* Newbury Park, CA: Sage.

Becker, T. E. & Billings, R. S. (1993). Profiles of commitment: an empirical test. *Journal of Organisational Behaviour, 14*, 177–90.

Becker, T. E. & Colquitt, A. L. (1992). Potential versus actual faking of a biodata form: an analysis along several dimensions of item type. *Personnel Psychology, 45*(2), 389–406.

Bell, N. L., Matthews, T. D., Lassiter, K. S. & Leveret, J. P. (2002). Validity of the Wonderlic Personnel Test as a measure of fluid or crystallized intelligence: implications for career assessment. *North American Journal of Psychology, 4*, 113–20.

Bennett, R. J. & Robinson, S. L. (2000). Development of a measure of workplace deviance. *Journal of Applied Psychology, 85*, 349–60.

Ben-Shakhar, G. (1989). Non-conventional methods in personnel selection. In P. Herriot (ed.), *Assessment and Selection in Organizations*, pp. 469–85. Chichester: Wiley.

Ben-Shakhar, G., Bar-Hillel, M., Bilu, Y., Ben-Abba, E. & Flug, A. (1986). Can graphology predict occupational success? Two empirical studies and some methodological ruminations. *Journal of Applied Psychology, 71*, 645–53.

Berger, L. (2004). Creating a talent management system for organisation excellence. In L. & D. Berger (eds.), *The Talent Management Handbook*, pp. 3–21. New York: McGraw-Hill.

Berger, L. & Berger, D. (eds.) (2004). *The Talent Management Handbook*. New York: McGraw-Hill.

Bergman, M. E., Drasgow, F., Donovan, M. A., Henning, J. B. & Juraska, S. E. (2006). Scoring situational judgment tests: once you get the data, your troubles begin. *International Journal of Selection and Assessment, 14*(3), 223–35.

Bernadin, H. & Russell, J. (1993). *Human Resource Management*. New York: McGraw-Hill.

Bernardin, J. J. & Cooke, D. K. (1993). Validity of an honesty test in predicting theft among convenience store employees. *Academy of Management Journal, 36*, 1097–1108.

Berry, D. S. (1990). Taking people at face value: evidence for the kernel of truth hypothesis. *Social Cognition, 8*, 343–61.

 (1991). Accuracy in social perception: contributions of facial and vocal information. *Journal of Personality and Social Psychology, 6*, 298–307.

Bertua, C., Anderson, N. & Salgado, J. F. (2005). The predictive validity of cognitive ability tests: a UK meta-analysis. *Journal of Organizational and Occupational Psychology, 78*, 387–409.

Bettencourt, B. A., Talley, A., Benjamin, A. J. & Valentine, J. (2006). Personality and aggressive behavior under provoking and neutral conditions: a meta-analytic review. *Psychological Bulletin, 132*(5), 751–77.

Billig, M. (1997). Discursive, rhetorical and ideological messages. In C. McGarty & S. Haslam (eds.), *The Message of Social Psychology*, 36–42. Oxford: Blackwell.

Binet, A. & Henri, V. (1896). La psychologie individuelle. *Année Psychologique, 2*, 411–65.

Binet, A. & Simon, T. (1905/1973). *The Development of Intelligence in Children*, trans. E. Kite. New York: Arno Press.

Bliesener, T. (1996). Methodological moderators in validating biographical data in personnel selection. *Journal of Occupational and Organizational Psychology, 69*(1), 107–20.

Block, J. (1995a). A contrarian view of the five-factor approach to personality description. *Psychological Bulletin, 117*(2), 187–215.

 (1995b). Going beyond the five factors given: rejoinder to Costa and McCrae (1995) and Goldberg and Saucier (1995). *Psychological Bulletin, 117*(2), 226–9.

 (2001). Millennial contrarianism: the five-factor approach to personality description 5 years later. *Journal of Research in Personality, 35*(1), 98–107.

Bobko, P., Roth, P. L. & Potosky, D. (1999). Derivation and implications of a meta-analytic matrix incorporating cognitive ability, alternative predictors, and job performance. *Personnel Psychology, 52*, 561–89.

Bogels, S. M. (1999). Diagnostic interviewing in mental health care: methods, training and assessment. In A. Memon & R. Bull (eds.), *Handbook of the Psychology of Interviewing*. Chichester: Wiley.

Bogg, T. & Roberts, B. W. (2004). Conscientiousness and health-related behaviours: a meta-analysis of the leading behavioural contributors to mortality. *Psychological Bulletin, 130*(6), 887–919.

Bono, J. E. & Judge, T. A. (2003). Self-concordance at work: understanding the motivational effects of transformational leaders. *Academy of Management Journal, 46*, 554–71.

Bouchard, T. J. Jr (1998). Genetic and environmental influences on adult intelligence and special mental abilities. *Human Biology*, *70*, 257–79.

Boudreau, J. W., Boswell, W. R. & Judge, T. A. (2001). Effects of personality on executive career success in the United States and Europe. *Journal of Vocational Behavior*, *58*(1), 53–81.

Bratko, D., Chamorro-Premuzic, T. & Saks, Z. (2006). Personality and school performance: incremental validity of self- and peer-ratings over intelligence. *Personality and Individual Differences*, *41*(1), 131–42.

Breedin, S. D., Saffran, E. & Schwartz, M. (1998). Semantic factors in verbal retrieval: an effect of complexity. *Brain and Language*, *63*(1), 1–31.

Bretz, R. D. (1989). College grade point average as a predictor of adult success: a meta-analytic review and some additional evidence. *Public Personnel Management*, *18*(1), 11–22.

Brody, N. (2004). What cognitive intelligence is and what emotional intelligence is not. *Psychological Inquiry*, *15*, 234–8.

Brody, L. & Mills, C. (2005). Talent search research. *High Ability Studies*, *16*, 96–111.

Brolyer, C. R., Thorndike, E. L. & Woodyard, E. R. (1927). A second study of mental discipline in high school studies. *Journal of Educational Psychology*, *18*, 377–404.

Brooks, P. & Arnold, D. (1989). *Reid Report Examiners Manual*. Chicago, IL: Reid Psychological Systems.

Brosnan, M. (2006). Digit ratio and faculty membership. *British Journal of Psychology*, *97*, 455–66.

Brown, B. K. & Campion, M. A. (1994). Biodata phenomenology: recruiters' perceptions and use of biographical information in resume screening. *Journal of Applied Psychology*, *79*(6), 897–908.

Brown, R. T. (1989). Creativity: what are we to measure? In J. A. Glover, P. R. Ronning & C. R. Reynolds (eds.), *Handbook of Creativity*. New York. Plenum Press.

Brtek, M. & Motowildo, S. (2002). Effects of procedure and outcome accountability on interview validity. *Journal of Applied Psychology*, *87*, 185–91.

Bruce, M. M. (1953). *Business Judgment Test* [Test booklet with manual]. Oxford: Author.

Bruce, M. M. & Learner, D. B. (1958). A supervisory practices test. *Personnel Psychology*, *11*, 207–16.

Bruchon-Schweitzer, M. & Ferrieux, D. (1991). Une enquête sur le recrutement en France [A study of recruitment in France]. *European Review of Applied Psychology*, *41*, 9–17.

Buel, W. D. (1965). Biographical data and the identification of creative research personnel. *Journal of Applied Psychology*, *49*(5), 318–21.

Bureau of National Affairs (1988). *Recruiting and Selection Procedures*. Washington, DC: Bureau of National Affairs.

Burns, J. M. (1978). *Leadership*. New York: Harper & Row.
  (2003). *Transformational Leadership*. New York: Scribner.

Buss, D. M. (1995). Evolutionary psychology: a new paradigm for psychological science. *Psychological Inquiry*, *6*(1), 1–30.

Butterworth, B. (1999). *The Mathematical Brain*. London: Macmillan.

Byrne, J., Smither, S., Reilly, R. & Dominick, G. J. (2007). An examination of the discrim-
     inant, convergent, and criterion-related validity of self-ratings on the emotional
     competence inventory. *International Journal of Selection and Assessment, 15*,
     343–55.

Cable, D. M. & Judge, T. A. (1997). Interviewers' perceptions of person-organization fit
     and organizational selection decisions. *Journal of Applied Psychology, 82*(4),
     546–61.

Campbell, D. T. & Kenny, D. A. (1999). *A Primer on Regression Artifacts.* New York:
     Guilford Press.

Cardall, A. J. (1942). *Test of Practical Judgment; for 12th Grade Level and Above.* Oxford:
     Science Research Associates.

Carlson, S. (1985). A double-blind test of astrology. *Nature, 318*, 419–25.

Carlson, K. D., Scullen, S. E., Schmidt, F. L., Rothstein, H. & Erwin, F. (1999). General-
     izable biographical data validity can be achieved without multi-organizational
     development and keying. *Personnel Psychology, 52*(3), 731–55.

Carlyle, T. (1907). *On Heroes, Hero-Worship, and the Heroic in History.* Boston:
     Houghton Mifflin.

Carpenter, P. A., Just, M. A. & Schell, P. (1990). What one intelligence test measures: a
     theoretical account of the processing in the Raven's Progressive Matrices Test.
     Psychological Review, 97, 404–31.

Carretta, T. R. & Ree, M. J. (1996). Factor structure of the Air Force officer qualifying
     test: analysis and comparison. *Military Psychology, 8*, 29–42.

Carrington, D. H. (1949). Note on the Cardall Practical Judgment Test. *Journal of Applied
     Psychology, 33*(1), 29–30.

Carroll, J. B. (1993). *Human Cognitive Abilities: A Survey of Factor-Analytic Studies.*
     New York: Cambridge University Press.

Carroll, S. J. & Nash, A. N. (1972). Effectiveness of a forced-choice reference check.
     Personnel Administration, 35(2), 42–6.

Carson, D. K. & Runco, M. A. (1999). Creative problem solving and problem findings in
     young adults: interconnections with stress, hassles, and coping abilities. *Journal
     of Creative Behavior, 33*, 167–90.

Catalyst (2002a). Catalyst census makes gains in number of women corporate officers
     in America's largest 500 companies [Press release, 19 November]. Retrieved
     20 February 2003, from www.catalystwomen.org/press_room/factsheets/fact_
     women_ceos.htm.
     (2002b). Fact sheet: women CEOs. Retrieved 6 October 2002, from www.
     catalystwomen.org/press_room/factsheets/fact_women_ceos.htm.

Cattell, R. B. (1943). The measurement of adult intelligence. *Psychological Bulletin, 40*,
     153–93.
     (1950). *Personality: A Systematic Theoretical and Factual Study.* New York: McGraw-
     Hill.
     (1971). The process of creative thought. In R. Cattell (ed.), *Abilities: Their Structure,
     Growth, and Action*, pp. 407–17. Boston: Houghton Mifflin.

Ceci, S. J. & Peters, D. (1984). Letters of reference: a naturalistic study of the effects of
     confidentiality. *American Psychologist, 39*(1), 29–31.

Chamorro-Premuzic, T. (2007). *Personality and Individual Differences.* Oxford:
     Blackwell.

Chamorro-Premuzic, T., Ahmetoglu, G. & Furnham, A. (2008). Little more than personality: trait determinants of test anxiety. *Learning and Individual Differences*, *18*(2), 258–63.

Chamorro-Premuzic, T. & Arteche, A. (2008). Intellectual competence and academic performance: preliminary validation of a model. *Intelligence*, *18*(6), 564–73.

Chamorro-Premuzic, T., Bennett, E. & Furnham, A. (2007). The happy personality: mediational role of trait emotional intelligence. *Personality and Individual Differences*, *42*(8), 1633–9.

Chamorro-Premuzic, T. & Furnham, A. (2002). Neuroticism and 'special treatment' in university examinations. *Social Behavior and Personality*, *30*(8), 807–11.

   (2003a). Personality predicts academic performance: evidence from two longitudinal university samples. *Journal of Research in Personality*, *37*(4), 319–38.

   (2003b). Personality traits and academic examination performance. *European Journal of Personality*, *17*(3), 237–50.

   (2004). A possible model to understand the personality – intelligence interface. *British Journal of Psychology*, *95*, 249–64.

   (2005). *Personality and Intellectual Competence*. Mahwah, NJ: Erlbaum.

   (2006a). Intellectual competence and the intelligent personality: a third way in differential psychology. *Review of General Psychology*, *10*, 251–67.

   (2006b). Self-assessed intelligence and academic performance. *Educational Psychology*, *26*, 769–79.

Chamorro-Premuzic, T., Harlaar, N. & Plomin, R. (In press). More than just IQ: incremental validity of self-perceived ability in the longitudinal prediction of school performance. *Intelligence*.

Chamorro-Premuzic, T., Moutafi, J. & Furnham, A. (2005). The relationship between personality traits, subjectively-assessed and fluid intelligence. *Personality and Individual Differences*, *38*(7), 1517–28.

Chamorro-Premuzic, T. & Reichenbacher, L. (2008). Effects of personality and threat of evaluation on divergent and convergent thinking. *Journal of Research in Personality*, *42*(2), 1095–1101.

Chan, D. & Schmitt, N. (2002). Situational judgment and job performance. *Human Performance*, *15*(3), 233–54.

Chapman, L. J. & Chapman, J. P. (1967). Genesis of popular but erroneous psychodiagnostic observations. *Journal of Abnormal Psychology*, *72*, 193–204.

Chemers, M. M. (2000). Leadership research and theory: a functional integration. *Group Dynamics: Theory, Research, and Practice*, *4*, 27–43.

Clarke, B. (1988). *Growing up Gifted*. Columbus, OH: Charles E. Merrill.

Clarke, D., Gabriels, T. & Barnes, J. (1996). Astrological signs as determinants of extroversion and emotionality: an empirical study. *Journal of Psychology*, *130*, 131–40.

Cohen, R. (1973). *Patterns of Personality Judgements*. New York: Academic Press.

Colarelli, S. M., Hechanova-Alampay, R. & Canali, K. G. (2002). Letters of recommendation: an evolutionary psychological perspective. *Human Relations*, *55*(3), 315–44.

Cole, M. S., Feild, H. S., Giles, W. F. & Harris, S. G. (2004). Job type and recruiters' inferences of applicant personality drawn from resume biodata: their relationships with hiring recommendations. *International Journal of Selection and Assessment*, *12*(4), 363–7.

Collaros, P. A. & Anderson, L. R. (1969). Effect of perceived expertness upon creativity of members of brainstorming groups. *Journal of Applied Psychology*, *53*(2, part 1), 159–63.

Conger, J. A. & Kanungo, R. N. (1987). Toward a behavioural theory of charismatic leadership in organisational settings. *Academy of Management Review*, *16*, 262–90.

(1988). Toward a behavioural theory of charismatic leadership. In J. A. Conger & R. N. Kanungo (eds.), *Charismatic Leadership: The Elusive Factor in Organisational Effectiveness*, pp. 78–97. San Francisco: Jossey-Bass.

(1998). *Charismatic Leadership in Organisations*. Thousand Oaks, CA: Sage.

Connolly, J. J. & Viswesvaran, C. (2000). The role of affectivity in job satisfaction: a meta-analysis. *Personality and Individual Differences*, *29*(2), 265–81.

Connolly, J. J., Kavanagh, E. J. & Viswesvaran, C. (2007). The convergent validity between self and observer ratings of personality: a meta-analytic review. *International Journal of Selection and Assessment*, *15*, 110–17.

Conway, J., Jako, R. & Goodman, D. (1995). A meta-analysis of inter-rater and internal consistency reliability of selection interviews. *Journal of Applied Psychology*, *80*, 565–79.

Cook, M. (2004). *Personnel Selection*. Chichester: Wiley.

Cooter, R. (1984). *The Cultural Meaning of Popular Science: Phrenology and the Organization of Consent in Nineteenth-Century Britain*. Cambridge: Cambridge University Press.

Corr, P. J., Pickering, A. D. & Gray, J. A. (1997). Personality, punishment, and procedural learning: a test of J. A. Gray's anxiety theory. *Journal of Personality and Social Psychology*, *73*(2), 337–44.

Costa, P. T., Jr & McCrae, R. R. (1985). *NEO Personality Inventory Manual*. Odessa, FL: Psychological Assessment Resources.

(1995). Primary traits of Eysenck's P-E-N system: three- and five-factor solutions. *Journal of Personality and Social Psychology*, *69*(2), 308–17.

Cox, C. M. (1926). The early mental traits of three hundred geniuses. In L. Terman (ed.), *Genetic Studies of Genius*, vol. 2. Stanford, CA: Stanford University Press.

Cox, C. & Cooper, C. (1988). *High Flyers: An Anatomy of Managerial Success*. Oxford: Blackwell.

Crepieux-Jamin, J. (1909). *L'écriture et la caractère*. Paris: Alcan.

Cronbach, L. J. (1960). *Essentials of Psychological Testing*, 2nd edn. Oxford: Harper.

(1975). Five decades of public controversy over psychological testing. *American Psychologist*, *30*, 1–14.

Cronbach, L. J. & Gleser, G. C. (1965). *Psychological Tests and Personnel Decisions*. Urbana, IL: University of Illinois Press.

Cross, S. E. & Madson, L. (1997). Models of the self: self-construals and gender. *Psychological Bulletin*, *122*, 5–37.

Csikszentmihalyi, M. (1988). Society, culture, and person: a systems view of creativity. In R. J. Sternberg (ed.), *The Nature of Creativity: Contemporary Psychological Perspectives*, pp. 325–39. New York: Cambridge University Press.

Daft, R. L. (1999). *Leadership: Theory and Practice*. Orlando, FL: Dryden Press.

Dalton, D. R. & Metzger, M. B. (1993). Integrity testing for personnel selection: an unsparing perspective. *Journal of Business Ethics*, *12*, 147–56.

Dalton, D. R., Metzger, M. B. & Wimbush, J. C. (1994). Integrity testing for personnel selection: a review and research agenda. In G. Ferris (ed.), *Research in Personnel and Human Resources Management*, vol. 12, pp. 125–60. Greenwich, CT: JAI Press.

Dalton, D. R., Wimbush, J. C. & Daily, C. M. (1994). Using the unmatched count technique (UCT) to estimate base rates for sensitive behavior. *Personnel Psychology, 47*(4), 817–28.

Dany, F. & Torchy, V. (1994). Recruitment and selection in Europe: policies, practices and methods. In C. Brewster & A. Hegewisch (eds.), *Policy and Practice in European Human Resource Management: The Price Waterhouse Cranfield Survey*, pp. 68–85. London: Routledge.

Datta, L. E. (1963). Test instructions and identification of creative scientific talent. *Psychological Reports, 13*, 495–500.

(1964a). A note on the remote associates test, United States culture, and creativity. *Journal of Applied Psychology, 48*(3), 184–5.

(1964b). Remote associates test as a predictor of creativity in engineers. *Journal of Applied Psychology, 48*(3), 183.

Davey, D. M. (1989). *How to Be a Good Judge of Character: Methods of Assessing Ability and Personality*. London: Kogan Page.

Davies, J. D. (1955). *Phrenology, Fad and Science: A Nineteenth-Century American Crusade*. New York: Yale University Press.

Dean, G. (1987). Does astrology need to be true? Part 2: The answer is no. *Skeptical Inquirer, 11*, 257–73.

(1992). The bottom line and effect size. In B. L. Beyerstein & D. F. Beyerstein (eds.), *The Write Stuff: Evaluations of Graphology, the Study of Handwriting Analysis*, pp. 269–341. Buffalo, NY: Prometheus Books.

Dean, M. A. & Russell, C. J. (2005). An examination of biodata theory-based constructs in a field context. *International Journal of Selection and Assessment, 13*(2), 139–49.

Dean, M. A., Russell, C. J. & Muchinsky, P. M. (1999). Life experiences and performance prediction: toward a theory of biodata. In G. Ferris (ed.), *Research in Personnel / Human Resources*, pp. 245–81. Westport, CT: JAI Press.

Deary, I. J. (2001). Human intelligence differences: a recent history. *Trends in Cognitive Sciences, 5*, 127–30.

Deary, I. J., Taylor, M. D., Hart, C. L., Wilson, V., Davey Smith, G., Blane, D. & Starr, J. M. (2005). Intergenerational social mobility and mid-life status attainment: influences of childhood intelligence, childhood social factors, and education. *Intelligence, 33*, 455–72.

Deary, I. J., Whalley, L. J., Lemmon, H., Crawford, J. R. & Starr, J. M. (2000). The stability of individual differences in mental ability from childhood to old age: follow-up of the 1932 Scottish mental survey. *Intelligence, 28*, 49–55.

De Bono, E. (1992). *Serious Creativity: Using the Power of Lateral Thinking to Create New Ideas*. London: HarperCollins.

DeNeve, K. M. & Cooper, H. (1998). The happy personality: a meta-analysis of 137 personality traits and subjective well-being. *Psychological Bulletin, 124*(2), 197–229.

Denissen, J. J. A., Zarrett, N. R. & Eccles, J. S. (2007). I like to do it, I'm able, and I know I am: longitudinal couplings between domain-specific achievement, self-concept, and interest. *Child Development, 78*(2), 430–47.

DeShon, R. P., Smith, M. R., Chan, D. & Schmitt, N. (1998). Can racial differences in cognitive test performance be reduced by presenting problems in a social context. *Journal of Applied Psychology, 83*, 438–51.

Devlin, S. E., Abrahams, N. M. & Edwards, J. E. (1992). Empirical keying of biographical data: cross-validity as a function of scaling procedure and sample size. *Military Psychology, 4*(3), 119–36.

Dickson, D. H. & Kelly, I. W. (1985). The 'Barnum effect' in personality assessment: a review of the literature. *Psychological Reports, 57*, 367–82.

Digman, J. M. (1990). Personality structure: emergence of the five-factor model. *Annual Review of Psychology, 41*, 417–40.

Dilchert, S., Ones, D., Davis, R. D. & Rostow, C. D. (2007). Cognitive ability predicts objectively measured counterproductive work behaviors. *Journal of Applied Psychology, 92*, 616–27.

Dodrill, C. B. (1981). An economical method for the evaluation of general intelligence in adults. *Journal of Consulting and Clinical Psychology, 50*, 668–73.

(1983). Long-term reliability of the Wonderlic Personnel Test. *Journal of Consulting and Clinical Psychology, 52*, 316–17.

Dollinger, S. J. & Clancy, S. M. (1993). Identity, self, and personality: II. Glimpses through the autophotographic eye. *Journal of Personality and Social Psychology, 64*, 1064–71.

Domino, S. J. (1974). Assessment of cinematographic creativity. *Journal of Personality and Social Psychology, 30*, 150–4.

Dracup, C. (1997). The reliability of marking on a psychology degree. *British Journal of Psychology, 88*(4), 691–708.

Drakeley, R. J., Herriot, P. & Jones, A. (1988). Biographical data, training success and turnover. *Journal of Occupational Psychology, 61*(2), 145–52.

Driver, R., Buckley, M. & Frink, D. (1996). Should we write off graphology? *International Journal of Selection and Assessment, 4*, 78–86.

Drory, A. & Gluskinos, U. (1980). Machiavellianism and leadership. *Journal of Applied Psychology, 65*(1), 81–6.

Duckworth, A. L. (2006). Intelligence is not enough: non-IQ predictors of achievement. *Dissertation Abstracts International: Section B: The Sciences and Engineering*, vol. 67(3-B).

Duckworth, A. L., Peterson, C., Matthews, M. D. & Kelly, D. R. (2007). Grit: perseverance and passion for long-term goals. *Journal of Personality and Social Psychology, 92*(6), 1087–1101.

Duckworth, A. L. & Seligman, M. E. P. (2005). Self-discipline outdoes IQ in predicting academic performance of adolescents. *Psychological Science, 16*(12), 939–44.

Dudek, S. Z. & Hall, W.B. (1991). Personality consistency: eminent architects 25 years later. *Creativity Research Journal, 4*, 213–31.

Dudley, N. M., Orvis, K. A., Lebiecki, J. E. & Cortina, J. M. (2006). A meta-analytic investigation of conscientiousness in the prediction of job performance: examining the intercorrelations and the incremental validity of narrow traits. *Journal of Applied Psychology, 91*, 40–57.

Dvir, T., Eden, D., Avolio, B. J. & Shamir, B. (2002). Impact of transformational leadership on follower development and performance: a field experiment. *Academy of Management Journal*, *45*, 735–44.

Eagly, A. H. & Johnson, B. T. (1990). Gender and leadership style: a meta-analysis. *Psychological Bulletin*, *108*, 233–56.

Eagly, A. H., Johannesen-Schmidt, M. C. & van Engen, M. (2003). Transformational, transactional, and laissez-faire leadership styles: a meta-analysis comparing women and men. *Psychological Bulletin*, *129*, 569–91.

Economist Intelligence Unit (2006). *The CEOs Role in Talent Management*. London: Economist.

Edwards, A. G. P. & Armitage, P. (1992). An experiment to test the discriminating ability of graphologists. *Personality and Individual Differences*, *13*, 69–74.

Ellingson, J. E., Sackett, P. R. & Hough, L. M. (1999). Social desirability corrections in personality measurement: issues of applicant comparison and construct validity. *Journal of Applied Psychology*, *84*(2), 155–66.

Ellingson, J. E., Smith, D. B. & Sackett, P. R. (2001). Investigating the influence of social desirability on personality factor structure. *Journal of Applied Psychology*, *86*, 122–33.

Elliott, R. & Strenta, A. C. (1988). Effects of improving the reliability of the GPA on prediction generally and on comparative predictions for gender and race particularly. *Journal of Educational Measurement*, *25*(4), 333–47.

Employee Polygraph Protection Act (EPPA) (1988). Legislative history, United States Code Congressional and Administrative News (USCCAN). Paper presented at the 100th Congress, 2nd Session.

England, G. W. (1961). *Development and Use of Weighted Application Banks*. Dubuque, IO: Brown.

Entwisle, D. R. (1972). To dispel fantasies about fantasy-based measures of achievement motivation. *Psychological Bulletin*, *77*, 377–91.

European Commission (2001). Employment trends and sectors of growth in the cultural economy. Final report. European Commission, DG Employment and Social Affairs.

Eysenck, H. (1970). *The Structure of Human Personality*. London: Methuen.

(1994). Personality and intelligence: psychometric and experimental approaches. In R. J. Sternberg & P. Ruzgis (eds.), *Personality and Intelligence*, pp. 3–31. New York: Cambridge University Press.

(1999). Personality and creativity. In M. A. Runco (ed.), *Creativity Research Handbook*. Cresskill, NJ: Hampton Press.

Eysenck, H. J. & Eysenck, S. B. G. (1975). *Manual of the Eysenck Questionnaire*. San Diego, CA: Edits.

(1976). *Psychoticism as a Dimension of Personality*. London: Hodder & Stoughton.

Eysenck, M. W. & Eysenck, H. J. (1980). Mischel and the concept of personality. *British Journal of Psychology*, *71*(2), 191–204.

Eysenck, H. J. & Furnham, A. (1993). Personality and the Barron-Welsh art scale. *Perceptual and Motor Skills*, *76*, 837–8.

Eysenck, H. J. & Gudjonsson, G. (1986). An empirical study of the validity of handwriting analysis. *Personality and Individual Differences*, *7*, 263–4.

Farmer, E. W. (1974). Psychoticism and person-orientation as general personality characteristics. BSc thesis, University of Glasgow.

Farsides, T. & Woodfield, R. (2007). Individual and gender differences in 'good' and 'first-class' undergraduate degree performance. *British Journal of Psychology*, *98*(3), 467–83.

Faust, Q. C. (1996). Integrity tests: do they have any integrity. *Cornell Journal of Law and Public Policy*, *6*, 211–32.

Feingold, A. (1994). Gender differences in personality: a meta-analysis. *Psychological Bulletin*, *116*(3), 429–56.

Feist, G. J. (1998). A meta-analysis of personality in scientific and artistic creativity. *Personality and Social Psychology Bulletin*, *2*, 290–309.

(1999). The influence of personality on artistic and scientific creativity. In R. J. Sternberg (ed.), *Handbook of Human Creativity*, pp. 273–96. New York: Cambridge University Press.

Feist, G. J. & Barron, F. (2003). Predicting creativity from early to late adulthood: intellect, potential, and personality. *Journal of Research in Personality*, *37*, 62–88.

Feldman, J. M. (1981). Beyond attribution theory: cognitive processes in performance appraisal. *Journal of Applied Psychology*, *66*(2), 127–48.

Fenollar, P., Román, S. & Cuestas, P. J. (2007). University students' academic performance: an integrative conceptual framework and empirical analysis. *British Journal of Educational Psychology*, *77*(4), 873–91.

Fiedler, F. E. (1967). *A Theory of Leadership Effectiveness*. New York: McGraw-Hill.

(1993). The leadership situation and the black box in contingency theories. In M. M. Chemers & R. Ayman (eds.), *Leadership Theory and Research*, pp. 1–28. San Diego, CA: Academic.

(2002). The curious role of cognitive resources in leadership. In R. E. Riggio, S. E. Murphy & F. J. Pirozzolo (eds.), *Multiple Intelligences and Leadership*, pp. 91–104. Mahwah, NJ: Erlbaum.

File, Q. W. & Remmers, H. H. (1946). Studies in supervisory evaluation. *Journal of Applied Psychology*, *30*(5), 421–5.

Fine, S. A. & Cronshaw, S. (1994). The role of job analysis in establishing the validity of biodata. In G. S Stokes, M. D. Mumford & W. A. Owens (eds.), *Biodata Handbook*, pp. 39–64. Palo Alto, CA: Consulting Psychologists Press.

Fineman, S. (1977). The achievement motive construct and its measurement: where are we now? *British Journal of Psychology*, *68*, 1–22.

Finkelstein, J. (1991). *The Fashioned Self*. Cambridge: Polity Press.

Fiske, S. T. (1980). Attention and weight in person perception: the impact of negative and extreme behavior. *Journal of Personality and Social Psychology*, *38*(6), 889–906.

Flach, F. (1990). Disorders of the pathways involved in the creative process. *Creativity Research Journal*, *3*, 158–65.

Fleishman, E. A. (1988). Some new frontiers in personnel selection research. *Personnel Psychology*, *41*(4), 679–701.

Fletcher, C., Taylor, P. & Glanfield, K. (1996). Acceptance of personality questionnaire feedback. *Personality and Individual Differences*, *20*, 151–6.

Forer, B. R. (1949). The fallacy of personal validation: a classroom demonstration of gullibility. *Journal of Abnormal Psychology*, *44*, 118–21.

Frensch, P. A. & Sternberg. R. J. (1989). Expertise and intelligent thinking: when is it worse to know better? In R. J. Sternberg (ed.), *Advances in the Psychology of Human Intelligence*, vol. 5. Hillsdale, NJ: Erlbaum.

Freud, S. (1921). Group psychology and the analysis of the ego. In J. Strachey (ed.), *The Standard Edition of the Complete Works of Sigmund Freud*, vol. 28: *Beyond the Pleasure Principle, Group Psychology and Other Works*, pp. 65–143. London: Hogarth Press.

Friedman, H. S., Hall, J. A. & Harris, M. J. (1985). Type A behavior, nonverbal expressive style, and health. *Journal of Personality and Social Psychology*, *48*(5), 1299–1315.

Funder, D. C., Parke, R. D., Tomlinson-Keasey, C. & Widaman, K. (1993). *Studying Lives through Time: Personality and Development* (APA Science Volumes). Washington, DC: American Psychological Association.

Furnham, A. (1986). Social skills training with adolescents and young adults. In C. R. Hollin & P. Trower (eds.), *Handbook of Social Skills Training*, pp. 33–57. Oxford: Pergamon.

  (1988). Write and wrong: the validity of graphological analysis. *Skeptical Inquirer*, *13*, 64–9.

  (1994a). *Personality at Work*. London: Routledge.

  (1994b). The Barnum effect in medicine. *Complementary Therapies in Medicine*, *2*, 1–4.

  (1999). Personality and creativity. *Perceptual and Motor Skills*, *88*, 407–8.

  (2001). *All in the Mind: The Essence of Psychology*, 2nd edn. London: Whurr.

  (2003). The Icarus syndrome: talent management and derailment in the new millennium. In M. Effron, R. Gandossy & M. Goldsmith (eds.), *Human Resources in the 21st Century*, pp. 99–108. New York: Wiley.

  (2004). Personality and organisation: a European perspective on personality assessment in organisations. In B. Schneider & D. Smith (eds.), *Personality and Organisation*, pp. 25–57. Mahwah, NJ: Lea.

  (2007). Personality disorders and derailment at work: the paradoxical positive influence of pathology in the workplace. In J. Langen-Fox, C. Cooper & R. Klimoski (eds.), *Management Challenges and Symptoms of the Dysfunctional Workplace*. Cheltenham: Elgar.

Furnham, A. & Chamorro-Premuzic, T. (2004). Personality and intelligence as predictors of statistics examination grades. *Personality and Individual Differences*, *37*(5), 943–55.

  (2007). Self-assessed intelligence and confidence for the acquisition of skills. *Zeitschrift für Personalpsychologie*, *6*, 28–36.

Furnham, A., Chamorro-Premuzic, T. & Callahan, I. (2003). Does graphology predict personality and intelligence? *Individual Difference Research*, *1*, 78–94.

Furnham, A., Chamorro-Premuzic, T. & McDougall, F. (2002). Personality, cognitive ability, and beliefs about intelligence as predictors of academic performance. *Learning and Individual Differences*, *14*(1), 47–64.

Furnham, A. & Gunter, B. (1987). Graphology and personality: another failure to validate graphological analysis. *Personality and Individual Differences*, *8*, 433–5.

Furnham, A. & Vartan, C. (1988). Predicting and accepting personality test feedback. *Personality and Individual Differences*, *9*, 735–48.

Gagne, F. (2004). Transforming gifts into talents. *High Ability Studies, 15,* 119–47.

Gardner, H. (1983/2003). *Frames of Mind: The Theory of Multiple Intelligences.* New York: Basic Books.

(1993a). *Creative Minds.* New York: Basic Books.

(1993b). *Multiple Intelligences: The Theory in Practice.* New York: Basic Books.

(1995). *Leading Minds: An Anatomy of Leadership.* New York: Basic Books.

Gauquelin, M. (1969). *The Scientific Basis for Astrology.* New York: Stein & Day.

(1975). Spheres of influence. *Psychology Today, 7,* 22–7.

Gauquelin, M., Gauquelin, F. & Eysenck, S. B. G. (1979). Personality and the position of the planets at birth: an empirical study. *British Journal of Social and Clinical Psychology, 18,* 71–5.

George, J. M. & Zhou, J. (2001). When openness to experience and conscientiousness are related to creative behavior: an interactional approach. *Journal of Applied Psychology, 86,* 513–24.

Gellatly, I. R. (1996). Conscientiousness and task performance: test of cognitive process model. *Journal of Applied Psychology, 81,* 474–82.

Getzels, J. M. & Jackson, P. W. (1962). *Creativity and Intelligence.* New York: Wiley.

Ghiselli, E. E. (1966). *The Validity of Occupational Aptitude Tests.* New York: Wiley.

(1973). The validity of aptitude test in personnel selection. *Personnel Psychology, 26,* 461–77.

Ghiselli, E. E. & Barthol, R. P. (1953). The validity of personality inventories in the selection of employees. *Journal of Applied Psychology, 37*(1), 18–20.

Ghiselli, E. E. & Brown, C. W. (1955). *Personnel and Industrial Psychology,* 2nd edn. New York: McGraw Hill.

Gilliland, S. (1993). The perceived fairness of selection systems. *Academy of Management Review, 18,* 694–734.

Gladwell, M. (2002). The talent myth. *The New Yorker,* 28 July, p. 33.

Glick, P., Gottesman, D. & Jolton, J. (1989). The fault is not in the stars: susceptibility of skeptics and believers in astrology to the Barnum effect. *Personality and Social Psychology Bulletin, 15,* 572–83.

Goethals, G. R. (2005). Presidential leadership. *Annual Review of Psychology, 56,* 545–70.

Goldberg, L. R. (1972). *Parameters of Personality Inventory Construction and Utilization: A Comparison of Prediction Strategies and Tactics* (Multivariate Behavioral Research Monographs, no. 59). Fort Worth, TX: Texas Christian University Press.

(1986). Some informal explorations and ruminations about graphology. In B. Nevo (ed.), *Handbook of Scientific Aspects of Graphology,* pp. 281–93. Springfield, IL: Thomas.

(1990). An alternative 'description of personality': the Big-Five factor structure. *Journal of Personality and Social Psychology, 59,* 1216–1229.

(1993). The structure of personality traits: vertical and horizontal aspects. In D. C. Funder, R. D. Parke, C. Tomlinson-Keasey & K. Widaman (eds.), *Studying Lives through Time: Personality and Development* (APA Science Volumes), pp. 169–88. Washington, DC: American Psychological Association.

Goleman, D. (1995). *Emotional Intelligence.* New York: Bantam Books.

Goncalo, J. A. & Staw, B. M. (2006). Individualism-collectivism and group creativity. *Organizational Behavior and Human Decision Processes, 100*(1), 96–109.

Goodman, N. (1955). The new riddle of induction. In *Fact, Fiction and Forecast*, pp. 72–83. Cambridge, MA: Harvard University Press.

Gott, K. (1992). Enhancing creativity in older adults. *Journal of Creative Behavior*, 26, 40–9.

Gottfredson, L. S. (1986). Societal consequences of the *g* factor in employment. *Journal of Vocational Behavior*, 29, 379–410.

(1988). Reconsidering fairness: a matter of social and ethical priorities. *Journal of Vocational Behavior*, 33, 293–319.

(1996). Racially gerrymandering the content of police tests to satisfy the US Justice Department: a case study. *Psychology, Public Policy, and Law*, 2, 418–46.

(1997a). Mainstream science on intelligence: an editorial with 52 signatories, history and bibliography. *Intelligence*, 24, 13–23.

(1997b). Why *g* matters: the complexity of everyday life. *Intelligence*, 24, 79–132.

(2004). Intelligence: is it the epidemiologists' elusive 'fundamental cause' of social class inequalities in health? *Journal of Personality and Social Psychology*, 86, 174–99.

(2005). What if the hereditarian hypothesis is true? *Psychology, Public Policy, and Law*, 11, 311–19.

(2007). Applying double standards to 'divisive' ideas: commentary on Hunt and Carlson (2007). *Perspectives on Psychological Science*, 2, 216–20.

Götz, K. O. & Götz, K. (1979a). Personality characteristics of professional artists. *Perceptual and Motor Skills*, 49, 327–34.

(1979b). Personality characteristics of successful artists. *Perceptual and Motor Skills*, 49, 919–24.

Gough, H. G. (1976). Studying creativity by means of word association tests. *Journal of Applied Psychology*, 61, 348–53.

Gould, S. J. (1981). *The Mismeasures of Man*. Harmondsworth: Penguin.

Graham, J. (1961). Lavater's physiognomy in England. *Journal of the History of Ideas*, 22, 561–72.

Gray, J. A. (1982). Précis of *The Neuropsychology of Anxiety: An Enquiry into the Functions of the Septo-Hippocampal System*. *Behavioral and Brain Sciences*, 5(3), 469–534.

(1988). The neuropsychological basis of anxiety. In M. Hersen (ed.), *Handbook of Anxiety Disorders*, pp. 10–37. New York: Pergamon Press.

Greasley, P. (2000). Handwriting analysis and personality assessment: the creative use of analogy, symbolism and metaphor. *European Psychologist*, 5, 44–51.

Greenberg, J. (1997). *Occupational Crime*, 2nd edn. Chicago: Nelson-Hall.

Greenberg, S. H. (1963). *Supervisory Judgment Test Manual*. Washington, DC: US Civil Service Commission.

Guastello, S. J. & Rieke, M. L. (1991). A review and critique of honesty test research. *Behavioural Sciences and the Law*, 9, 501–23.

Guilford, J. P. (1950). Creativity. *American Psychologist*, 5, 444–54.

(1967). *The Nature of Human Intelligence*. New York: McGraw-Hill.

(1975). Creativity: a quarter century of progress. In I. A. Taylor & J. W. Getzels (eds.), *Perspectives in Creativity*, pp. 37–59. Chicago: Aldine.

(1988). Some changes in the Structure-of-Intellect Model. *Educational & Psychological Measurement*, 48, 1–4.

Guilford, J. P. & Christensen, P. R. (1973). The one-way relation between creative potential and IQ. *Journal of Creative Behavior*, 7, 247–52.

Guion, R. M. & Gottier, R. F. (1965). Validity of personality measures in personnel selection. *Personnel Psychology*, *18*, 135–64.

Gunter, B. & Furnham, A. (2001). *Assessing Business Potential*. London: Whurr.

Haensly, P. A. & Reynolds, C. R. (1989). Creativity and intelligence. In J. A. Glover *et al.* (eds.), *Handbook of Creativity*. New York: Plenum Press.

Hamilton, M. M. (1995). Incorporation of astrology-based personality information into long-term self-concept. *Journal of Social Behavior and Personality*, *10*, 707–18.

(2001). Who believes in astrology? Effect of favorableness of astrologically derived personality descriptions on acceptance of astrology. *Personality and Individual Differences*, *31*, 895–902.

Hampson, E., Ellis, C. L. & Tenk, C. M. (2008). On the relation between 2D:4D and sex-dimorphic personality traits. *Archives of Sexual Behavior*, special issue: *Biological Research on Sex-Dimorphic Behavior and Sexual Orientation*, *37*, 133–44.

Hansemark, O. C. (1997). Objective vs. projective measurement of need for achievement and the relation between TAT and CMPS. *Journal of Managerial Psychology*, *12*, 280–9.

(2000). Predictive validity of TAT and CMPS on the entrepreneurial activity, 'start of a new business': a longitudinal study. *Journal of Managerial Psychology*, *15*, 634–50.

Harcourt Assessment, I. (2005). *Miller Analogies Test: Scoring and Score Reporting*. Retrieved 5 June 2005, from www.milleranalogies.com.

Harder, D. (1979). The assessment of ambitious−narcissistic character style with three projective tests: the early memories, TAT and Rorschach. *Journal of Personality Assessment*, *I*, 23–32.

Harold, C. M., McFarland, L. A. & Weekley, J. A. (2006). The validity of verifiable and non-verifiable biodata items: an examination across applicants and incumbents. *International Journal of Selection and Assessment*, *14*(4), 336–46.

Harrell, T. W. & Harrell, M. S. (1945). Army general classification test scores for civilian occupations. *Educational and Psychological Measurement*, *5*, 229–39.

Harrington, D. M. (1972). Effects of instructions to 'Be creative' on three tests of divergent thinking abilities. PhD thesis, University of California Berkeley.

Harris, M. M. (1989). Reconsidering the employment interview: a review of recent literature and suggestions for future research. *Personnel Psychology*, *42*(4), 691–726.

Hartford, H. (1973). *You Are What You Write*. New York: Macmillan.

Hartigan, J. & Wigdor, A. K. (eds.) (1989). *Fairness in Employment Testing. Validity Generalization, Minority Issues, and the General Aptitude Test Battery*. Washington, DC: National Academy Press.

Harvey, J. & Katz, C. (1985). *If I'm So Successful, Why Do I Feel Like a Fake? The Imposter Phenomenon*. New York: St Martins.

Hassin, R. & Trope, Y. (2000). Facing faces: studies on the cognitive aspects of physiognomy. *Journal of Personality and Social Psychology*, *78*, 837–52.

Hattrup, K., Rock, J. & Scalia, C. (1997). The effects of varying conceptualizations of job performance on adverse impact, minority hiring, and predicted performance. *Journal of Applied Psychology*, *82*, 656–64.

Hausknecht, J. P., Halpert, J. A., Di Paolo, N. T. & Di Paulo, M. M. (2007). Retesting in selection: a meta-analysis of coaching and practice effects for tests of cognitive ability. *Journal of Applied Psychology, 92*, 373–85.

Hayes, J. R. (1978). *Cognitive Psychology*. Homewood, IL: Dorsey.

Helgesen, S. (1990). *The Female Advantage: Women's Ways of Leadership*. New York: Doubleday Currency.

Heller, K., Monks, F. & Passow, A. (eds.) (1993). *International Handbook of Research and Development of Giftedness and Talent*. New York: Pergamon.

Helson, R. (1970). Sex-specific patterns in creative literary fantasy. *Journal of Personality, 38*, 344–63.

  (1971). Women mathematicians and the creative personality. *Journal of Consulting and Clinical Psychology, 36*, 210–20.

Hemphill, J. K. & Coons, A. E. (1957). Development of the leader behaviour description questionnaire. In R. M. Stogdill & A. E. Coons (eds.), *Leader Behaviour: Its Description and Measurement*, pp. 6–38. Columbus, OH: Bureau of Business Research.

Herzberg, F. (1965). The motivation to work among Finnish supervisors. *Personnel Psychology, 18*(4), 393–402.

Heston, J. J. (1966). Psychiatric disorders in foster home reared children of schizophrenic mothers. *British Journal of Psychiatry, 112*, 819–25.

Heyns, R. W., Veroff, J. & Atkinson, J. W. (1958). A scoring manual for the affiliation motive. In J. W. Atkinson (ed.), *Motives in Fantasy, Action, and Society*, pp. 205–18. Princeton, NJ: Van Nostrand.

Hirsh, H. R., Northrop, L. & Schmidt, F. L. (1986). Validity generalization results for law enforcement occupations. *Personnel Psychology, 39*, 399–420.

Hogan, J. & Hogan, R. (2002). Leadership and sociopolitical intelligence. In R. E. Riggio, S. E. Murphy & F. J. Pirozzolo (eds.), *Multiple Intelligences and Leadership*, pp. 75–88. Mahwah, NJ: Erlbaum.

Hogan, J. & Holland, B. (2003). Using theory to evaluate personality and job-performance relations: a socioanalytic perspective. *Journal of Applied Psychology, 88*(1), 100–12.

Hogan, J., Rybicki, S. L., Motowildo, S. J. & Borman, W. C. (1998). Relations between contextual performance, personality, and occupational advancement. *Human Performance, 11*(2–3), 189–207.

Hogan, R. T. (1986). *Hogan Personality Inventory Manual*. Minneapolis, MN: Natonal Computer Systems.

  (1992). Personality and personality measurement. In M. D. Dunnette & L. M. Hough (eds.), *Handbook of Industrial and Organizational Psychology*, 2nd edn, pp. 873–919. Palo Alto, CA: Consulting Psychologists Press.

  (2005). In defense of personality measurement: new wine for old whiners. *Human Performance, 18*, 331–41.

Hogan, R., Curphy, G. J. & Hogan, J. (1994). What we know about leadership: effectiveness and personality. *American Psychologist, 49*, 493–504.

Hogan, R., Hogan, J. & Roberts, B. (1996). Personality measurement and employment decisions: questions and answers. *American Psychologist, 51*(5), 469–77.

Holland, J. L. (1959). A theory of vocational choice. *Journal of Counseling Psychology, 6*(1), 35–45.

(1997). *Making Vocational Choices: A Theory of Vocational Personalities and Work Environments*, 3rd edn. Odessa, FL: Psychological Assessment Resources.

(1999). Why interest inventories are also personality inventories. In M. Savickas & A. R. Spokane (eds.), *Vocational Interests: Meaning, Measurement, and Counseling Use*, pp. 87–101. Palo Alto, CA: Davies-Black.

Hollander, E. P. (1993). Legitimacy, power, and influence: a perspective on relational features of leadership. In M. M. Chemers & R. Ayman (eds.), *Leadership Theory and Research*, pp. 29–48. San Diego, CA: Academic Press.

Hollinger, R. C. & Clark, J. P. (1983). *Theft by Employees*. Lexington, MA: D. C. Heath / Lexington Books.

Hoppock, R. (1937). Job satisfaction of psychologists. *Journal of Applied Psychology*, *21*(3), 300–3.

Horn, J. L. (1976). Human abilities: a review of research and theory in the early 1970's. *Annual Review of Psychology*, *27*, 437–85.

Hough, L. M. (1984). Development and evaluation of the 'accomplishment record' method of selecting and promoting professionals. *Journal of Applied Psychology*, *69*(1), 135–46.

(1995). Applicant self descriptions: evaluating strategies for reducing distortion. Paper presented at the Annual meeting of the Society of Industrial and Organisational Psychology, Orlando, FL.

(1998a). Effects of intentional distortion in personality measurement and evaluation of suggested palliatives. *Human Performance*, *11*(2–3), 209–44.

(1998b). The millennium for personality psychology: new horizons or good ole daze. *Applied Psychology*, *47*(2), 233–61.

Hough, L. M., Eaton, N. K., Dunnette, M. D., Kamp, J. D. & McCloy, R. A. (1990). Criterion-related validities of personality constructs and the effect of response distortion on those validities. *Journal of Applied Psychology*, *75*, 581–95.

Hough, L. M. & Oswald, F. L. (2000). Personnel selection: looking toward the future – remembering the past. *Annual Review of Psychology*, *51*, 631–64.

Hough, L. M., Oswald, F. L. & Ployhart, R. E. (2001). Determinants, detection and amelioration of adverse impact in personnel selection procedures: issues, evidence and lessons learned. *International Journal of Selection and Assessment*, *9*, 152–94.

Hough, L. M. & Paullin, C. (1994). Construct-oriented scale construction: the rational approach. In G. S. Stokes, M. D. Mumford & W. A. Owens (eds.), *Biodata Handbook: The Use of Biographical Information in Selection and Performance Prediction*, pp. 109–46. Palo Alto, CA: Consulting Psychologists Press.

House, R. J. & Aditya, R. N. (1997). The social scientific study of leadership: quo vadis? *Journal of Management*, *23*, 409–73.

House, R. & Shamir, B. (1993). Toward the integration of transformational, charismatic and visionary theories. In M. Chemers & R. Ayman (eds.), *Leadership Theory and Research: Perspectives and Directions*, pp. 81–107. San Diego, CA: Academic Press.

Howard, A. & Bray, D. (1988). *Managerial Lives in Transition: Advancing Age and Changing Times (Adult Development and Aging)*. New York: Guilford Press.

Howell, J. M. (1988). Two facets of charisma: socialized and personalized leadership in organisations. In J. A. Conger & R. N. Kanungo (eds.), *Charismatic Leadership*, pp. 213–36. San Francisco: Jossey-Bass.

Huffcutt, A. & Arthur, W. (1994). Hunter and Hunter (1984) revisited: interview validity for entry level jobs. *Journal of Applied Psychology, 79*, 184–90.

Huffcutt, A. I., Conway, J. M., Roth, P. L. & Stone, N. J. (2001). Identification and meta-analytic assessment of psychological constructs measured in employment interviews. *Journal of Applied Psychology, 86*(5), 897–913.

Huffcutt, A. & Woehr, D. (1999). Further analysis of employment interview validity. *Journal of Organisational Behaviour, 20*, 549–60.

Hull, C. L. & Montgomery, R. B. (1919). An experimental investigation of certain alleged relations between character and handwriting. *Psychological Review, 26*, 63–75.

Humphreys, L. G. (1988). Trends in levels of academic achievement of blacks and other minorities. *Intelligence, 12*(3), 231–60.

Hunsley, J. & Bailey, J. (1999). The clinical utility of the Rorschach: unfulfilled promises and an uncertain future. *Psychological Assessment, 11*, 266–77.

Hunter, J. E. (1980). *Test Validation for 12,000 Jobs: An Application of Synthetic Validity and Validity Generalization to the General Aptitude Test Battery (GATB)*. Washington, DC: US Department of Labor.

   (1983a). A causal analysis of cognitive ability, job knowledge, job performance, and supervisor ratings. In S. Z. F. Landy & J. Cleveland (eds.), *Performance Measurement Theory*, pp. 257–66. Hillsdale, NJ: Erlbaum.

   (1983b). The prediction of job performance in the military using ability composites: the dominance of general cognitive ability over specific aptitudes (no. F41689–83-C-0025).

   (1986). Cognitive ability, cognitive aptitudes, job knowledge, and job performance. *Journal of Vocational Behavior, 29*, 340–62.

Hunter, J. E. & Hirsh, H. R. (1987). Applications of meta-analysis. In C. L. Cooper & I. T. Robertson (eds.), *International Review of Industrial and Organizational Psychology*, pp. 321–57. Chichester: Wiley.

Hunter, J. E. & Hunter, R. F. (1984). Validity and utility of alternative predictors of job performance. *Psychological Bulletin, 96*(1), 72–98.

Hunter, J. E. & Schmidt, F. L. (1996). Intelligence and job performance: economic and social implications. *Psychology, Public Policy, and Law, 2*, 447–72.

Hurtz, G. M. & Donovan, J. J. (2000). Personality and job performance: the big five revisited. *Journal of Applied Psychology, 85*, 869–79.

Hurvich, M., Benveniste, P., Howard, J. & Coonerty, S. (1993). Assessment of annihilation anxiety from projective tests. *Perceptual & Motor Skills, 77*, 387–401.

Jencks, C., Smith, M., Acland, H., Bane, M. J., Cohen, D., Gintis, H. *et al.* (1972). *Inequality: A Reassessment of the Effect of Family and Schooling in America*. New York: Basic Books.

Jennings, R., Cos, C. & Cooper, C. (1994). *Business Elites: The Psychology of Entrepreneurs*. London: Routledge.

Jensen, A. R. (1980). *Bias in Mental Testing*. New York: Free Press.

   (1986). G: artifact or reality? *Journal of Vocational Behavior, 29*, 301–31.

   (1998). *The g Factor: The Science of Mental Ability*. Westport, CT: Praeger.

John, C. A. (1991). Adolescent competence and the life course: or why one social psychologist needed a concept of personality. *Social Psychology Quarterly*, *54*(1), 4–14.

Johnson, W. & Bouchard, T. J. Jr (2005). The structure of human intelligence: it is verbal, perceptual, and image rotation (VPR), not fluid and crystallized. *Intelligence*, *33*, 393–416.

Jones, A. & Harrison, E. (1982). Prediction of performance in initial officer training using reference reports. *Journal of Occupational Psychology*, *55*(1), 35–42.

Jones, F. E. (1964). Predictor variables for creativity in industrial science. *Journal of Applied Psychology*, *48*(2), 134–36.

Judge, T. A. & Bono, J. E. (2000). Five-factor model of personality and transformational leadership. *Journal of Applied Psychology*, *85*, 751–65.

Judge, T. A., Bono, J. E., Erez, A. & Locke, E. A. (2005). Core self-evaluations and job and life satisfaction: the role of self-concordance and goal attainment. *Journal of Applied Psychology*, *90*(2), 257–68.

Judge, T. A., Bono, J. E., Illies, R. & Gerhardt, M. W. (2002). Personality and leadership: a qualitative and quantitative review. *Journal of Applied Psychology*, *87*, 765–80.

Judge, T. A., Colbert, A. E. & Illies, R. (2004). Intelligence and leadership: a quantitative review and test of theoretical propositions. *Journal of Applied Psychology*, *89*, 542–52.

Judge, T. A. & Erez, A. (2007). Interaction and intersection: the constellation of emotional stability and extraversion in predicting performance. *Personnel Psychology*, *60*(3), 573–96.

Judge, T. A., Erez, A., Bono, J. E. & Thoresen, C. J. (2003). The core self-evaluations scale: development of a measure. *Personnel Psychology*, *56*(2), 303–31.

Judge, T. A., Heller, D. & Mount, M. K. (2002). Five-factor model of personality and job satisfaction: a meta-analysis. *Journal of Applied Psychology*, *87*(3), 530–41.

Judge, T. A. & Higgins, C. A. (1998). Affective disposition and the letter of reference. *Organizational Behavior and Human Decision Processes*, *75*(3), 207–21.

Judge, T. A., Higgins, C. A. & Cable, D. M. (2000). The employment interview: a review of recent research and recommendations for future research. *Human Resource Management Review*, *10*(4), 383–406.

Judge, T. A., Higgins, C. A., Thoresen, C. J. & Barrick, M. R. (1999). The big five personality traits, general mental ability, and career success across the life span. *Personnel Psychology*, *52*, 621–52.

Judge, T. A. & Ilies, R. (2002). Relationship of personality to performance motivation: a meta-analytic review. *Journal of Applied Psychology*, *87*(4), 797–807.

Judge, T. A., Jackson, C. L., Shaw, J. C., Scott, B. A. & Rich, B. L. (2007). Self-efficacy and work-related performance: the integral role of individual differences. *Journal of Applied Psychology*, *90*(1), 107–27.

Judge, T. A., LePine, J. A. & Rich, B. L. (2006). Loving yourself abundantly: relationship of the narcissistic personality to self- and other perceptions of workplace deviance, leadership, and task and contextual performance. *Journal of Applied Psychology*, *91*(4), 762–76.

Judge, T. A., Locke, E. A., Durham, C. C. & Kluger, A. N. (1998). Dispositional effects on job and life satisfaction: the role of core evaluations. *Journal of Applied Psychology*, *83*(1), 17–34.

Judge, T. A. & Piccolo, R. F. (2004). Transformational and transactional leadership: a meta-analytic test of their relative validity. *Journal of Applied Psychology*, *89*(5), 755–68.

Kabanoff, B. & Bottger, P. (1991). Effectiveness of creativity training and its relation to selected personality factors. *Journal of Organizational Behavior*, *12*(3), 235–48.

Kanfer, R. & Ackerman, P. L. (1989). Motivation and cognitive abilities: an integrative/ aptitude-treatment interaction approach to skill acquisition. *Journal of Applied Psychology*, *74*(4), 657–90.

   (2004). Aging, adult development, and work motivation. *Academy of Management Review*, *29*(3), 440–58.

Karas, M. & West, J. (1999). Construct-oriented biodata development for selection to a differentiated performance domain. *International Journal of Selection and Assessment*, special issue: *Background Data and Autobiographical Memory*, *7*(2), 86–96.

Kark, R., Shamir, B. & Chen, G. (2003). The two facets of transformational leadership: empowerment and dependency. *Journal of Applied Psychology*, *88*, 246–55.

Karren, R. J. & Zacharias, L. (2007). Integrity tests: critical issues. *Human Resource Management Review*, *17*, 221–34.

Katz, A. (1997). Creativity in the cerebral hemispheres. In M. A. Runco (ed.), *Creativity Research Handbook*, pp. 203–26. Cresskill, NJ: Hampton Press.

Keating, E., Paterson, D. G. & Stone, C. H. (1950). Validity of work histories obtained by interview. *Journal of Applied Psychology*, *34*(1), 6–11.

Keinan, G. (1994). Effects of stress and tolerance of ambiguity on magical thinking. *Journal of Personality and Social Psychology*, *67*, 26–55.

Keller, R. T. & Holland, W. E. (1978). Individual characteristics of innovativeness and communication in research and development organizations. *Journal of Applied Psychology*, *63*(6), 759–62.

Kelly, I. W. (1997). Modern astrology: a critique. *Psychological Reports*, *81*, 1035–66.

Kelly, I. W., Dickson, D. & Saklofske, D. (1986). Personality and the acceptance of Barnum statements under a condition of ambiguous relevance. *Perceptual and Motor Skills*, *63*, 795–800.

Kenney, R. A., Blascovich, J. & Shaver, P. R. (1994). Implicit leadership theories: proto-types for new leaders. *Basic Applied Social Psychology*, *15*, 409–37.

King, L., Walker, L. & Broyles, S. (1996). Creativity and the five-factor model. *Journal of Research in Personality*, *30*, 189–203.

King, R. & Koehler, D. (2002). Illusory correlations in graphological evidence. *Journal of Experimental Psychology*, *6*, 336–48.

Kirkpatrick, S. A. & Locke, E. A. (1991). Leadership: do traits matter? *Academy of Management Executive*, *5*, 48–60.

   (1996). Direct and indirect effects of three core charismatic leadership components on performance and attitudes. *Journal of Applied Psychology*, *81*, 36–51.

Kitzinger, C. & Powell, D. (1995). Engendering infidelity: essentialist and social con-structionist readings of a story completion task. *Feminism and Psychology*, *5*, 345–72.

Klages, L. (1917). *Handschrift und Charakter: Gemeinverständlicher Abriss der graphol-ogischen Technik* [*Handwriting and character*]. Leipzig: Johann Ambrosius Barth.

(1930). *Graphologisches Lesebuch* [*A graphology reader*]. Leipzig: Johann Ambrosius Barth.

Klimoski, R. J. & Rafael, A. (1983). Inferring personal qualities through handwriting analysis. *Journal of Occupational Psychology*, *56*, 191–202.

Kline, P. (1994). *The Handbook of Psychological Testing*. London: Routledge.

Kline, P. & Cooper, C. (1986). Psychoticism and creativity. *Journal of Genetic Psychology*, *147*, 183–8.

Klinger, E. (1966). Fantasy need achievement as a motivational construct. *Psychological Bulletin*, 291–308.

Knouse, S. B. (1983). The letter of recommendation: specificity and favorability of information. *Personnel Psychology*, *36*(2), 331–41.

Kravitz, D., Stinson, S. & Chavez, T. (1996). Evaluation of tests used for making selection and promotion decisions. *International Journal of Selection and Assessment*, *4*, 131–9.

Kretschmer, E. (1925). *Physique and Character*. New York: Harcourt Brace.

Kulik, J. A., Kulik, C. C. & Bangert, R. L. (1984). Effects of practice on aptitude and achievement test scores. *American Educational Research Journal*, *21*, 435–47.

Kuncel, N. R. & Borneman, M. J. (2007). Toward a new method of detecting deliberately faked personality tests: the use of idiosyncratic item responses. *International Journal of Selection and Assessment*, *15*, 220–31.

Kuncel, N. R., Hezlett, S. A. & Ones, D. S. (2001). A comprehensive meta-analysis of the predictive validity of the graduate record examinations: implications for graduate student selection and employment. *Psychological Bulletin*, *27*(1), 162–81.

Lavater, J. C. (1775–8/1840). *Essays on Physiognomy*. London: Thomas Tegg.

Lavell, P. (1994). Taking note of handwriting. *Solicitors Journal*, 3 June, pp. 36–8.

Larkin, J. C. & Pines, H. A. (1979). No fat persons need apply: experimental studies of the overweight stereotype and hiring preferences. *Sociology of Work and Occupations*, *6*, 312–27.

Lautenschlager, G. J. (1994). Accuracy and faking of background data. In G. S. Stokes, M. D. Mumford & W. A. Owens (eds.), *Biodata Handbook*, pp. 391–419. Palo Alto, CA: Consulting Psychologists Press.

Layne, C. & Ally, G. (1980). How and why people accept personality feedback. *Journal of Personality Assessment*, *44*, 541–6.

Legree, P., Pifer, M. E. & Grafton, F. C. (1996). Correlations among cognitive abilities are lower for higher ability groups. *Intelligence*, *23*, 45–57.

Lester, D. (1999). Sylvia Plath. In M. A. Runco & S. R. Plitzker (eds.), *Encyclopedia of Creativity*. San Diego, CA: Academic.

Lester, D., Mclaughlin, S. & Nosal, G. (1977). Graphological signs for extraversion. *Perceptual and Motor Skills*, *44*(1), 137–8.

Levashina, J. & Campion, M. A. (2007). Measuring faking in the employment interview: development and validation of an interview faking behavior scale. *Journal of Applied Psychology*, *92*(6), 1638–56.

Levine, E. L., Spector, P. E., Menon, S., Narayanan, L. & Cannon-Bowers, J. (1996). Validity generalization for cognitive, psychomotor, and perceptual tests for craft jobs in the utility industry. *Human Performance*, *9*, 1–22.

Lévy-LeBoyer, C. (1994). La sélection du personnel en Europe. / Personnel selection in Europe. *Orientation Scolaire et Professionnelle*, *23*(1), 27–34.

Lewin, K., Lippitt, R. & White, R. K. (1939). Patterns of aggressive behaviour in experimentally created social climates. *Journal of Social Psychology*, *10*, 271–301.

Lewinson, T. S. (1986). The classic school of graphology. In B. Nevo (ed.), *Scientific Aspects of Graphology*, pp. 4–46. Springfield, IL: Thomas.

Lievens, F. (2007). Research on selection in an international context: current status and future directions. In M. M. Harris (ed.), *Handbook of Research in International Human Resource Management*, pp. 107–23. Mahwah, NJ: Erlbaum.

Lievens, F. & Sackett, P. R. (2006). Video-based versus written situational judgment tests: a comparison in terms of predictive validity. *Journal of Applied Psychology*, *91*(5), 1181–8.

Lilienfeld, S., Wood, J. & Garb, H. (2000). The scientific status of projective techniques. *Psychological Science in the Public Interest*, *1*, 347–402.

Lillqvist, O. & Lindeman, M. (1998). Belief in astrology as a strategy for self-verification and coping with negative life-events. *European Psychologist*, *3*, 202–8.

Lindovà, J., Hrušková, M., Pivonkovà, V., Kubena, A. & Flegr, J. (2008). Digit ratio (2D:4D) and Cattell's personality traits. *European Journal of Personality*, *22*, 347–56.

Linton, H., Epstein, L. & Hartford, H. (1962). Personality and perceptual correlates of primary beginning strokes in handwriting. *Perceptual and Motor Skills*, *15*, 159–70.

Lippa, R. A. (2003). Are 2D:4D finger-length ratios related to sexual orientation? Yes for men, no for women. *Journal of Personality and Social Psychology*, *85*, 179–88.

  (2006). Finger lengths, 2D:4D ratios, and their relation to gender-related personality traits and the Big Five. *Biological Psychology*, *71*, 116–21.

Locke, E. A. (1997a). Primemovers: the traits of great business leaders. In C. Cooper & S. Jackson (eds.), *Creating Tomorrow's Organisations*, pp. 75–96. Chichester: Wiley.

  (1997b). The motivation to work: what we know. *Advances in Motivation and Achievement*, *10*, 375–412.

Loden, M. (1985). *Feminine Leadership or How to Succeed in Business without Being One of the Boys*. New York: Times Books.

Lombroso, C. (1895). Criminal anthropology. *The Forum*, *20*, 33–49.

Lord, R. G., De Vader, C. L. & Alliger, G. M. (1986). A meta-analysis of the relation between personality traits and leadership perceptions: an application of validity generalization procedures. *Journal of Applied Psychology*, *71*, 402–10.

Lord, R. G., Foti, R. J. & De Vader, C. L. (1984). A test of leadership categorization theory: internal structure, information processing, and leadership perceptions. *Organisational Behaviour and Human Performance*, *34*, 343–78.

Lubinski, D. (2000). Scientific and social significance of assessing individual differences: 'sinking shafts at a few critical points'. *Annual Review of Psychology*, *51*, 405–44.

Lubinski, D. & Benbow, C. (2000). States of excellence: a psychological interpretation of their emergence. *American Psychologist*, *55*, 137–50.

Luxen, M. & Buunk, B. (2006). Human intelligence, fluctuating asymmetry and the peacok's tail. *Personality and Individual Differences*, *41*, 897–901.

MacKinnon, D. W. (1960). The highly effective individual. *Teachers College Record*, *61*, 367–78.

(1962). The nature and nurture of creative talent. *American Psychologist*, *17*, 484–95.

(1971). Creativity and transliminal experience. *Journal of Creative Behavior*, *5*(4), 227–41.

Mackintosh, N. J. & Bennett, E. S. (2005). What do Raven's Matrices measure? An analysis in terms of sex differences. *Intelligence*, *33*, 663–74.

Mael, F. A. & Ashforth, B. E. (1995). Loyal from day one: biodata, organizational identification, and turnover among newcomers. *Personnel Psychology*, *48*(2), 309–33.

Mael, F. A. & Hirsch, A. C. (1993). Rainforest empiricism and quasi-rationality: two approaches to objective biodata. *Personnel Psychology*, *46*(4), 719–38.

Magli, P. (1989). The face and the soul. In M. Feher (ed.), *Fragments for a History of the Human Body*, part 2, pp. 86–127. New York: Zone Books.

Manley, G. G., Benavidez, J. & Dunn, K. (2007). Development of a personality biodata measure to predict ethical decision making. *Journal of Managerial Psychology*, *22*(7), 664–82.

Mann, G. (1979). *Wallenstein*, 7th edn. Frankfurt: S. Fischer.

Mann, R. D. (1959). A review of the relationships between personality and performance in small groups. *Psychological Bulletin*, *56*, 241–70.

Marcus, B. (2003). Attitudes towards personnel selection methods. *Applied Psychology*, *52*, 515–32.

Margie, P. & Tourish, D. (1999). The psychology of interpersonal skill. In A. Memon & R. Bull (eds.), *Handbook of the Psychology of Interviewing*. Chichester: Wiley.

Marsh, H. W., Bond, N. W. & Jayasinghe, U. W. (2007). Peer review process: assessments by applicant-nominated referees are biased, inflated, unreliable and invalid. *Australian Psychologist*, *42*(1), 33–8.

Marsh, H. W. & Craven, R. G. (2006). Reciprocal effects of self-concept and performance from a multidimensional perspective: beyond seductive pleasure and unidimensional perspectives. *Perspectives on Psychological Science*, *1*(2), 133–63.

Marsh, H. W., Martin, A. J. & Hau, K.-T. (2006). A multimethod perspective on self-concept research in educational psychology: a construct validity approach. In M. Eid & E. Diener (eds.), *Handbook of Multimethod Measurement in Psychology*, pp. 441–56. Washington, DC: American Psychological Association.

Marsh, H. W., Trautwein, U., Lüdtke, O., Köller, O. & Baumert, J. (2006). Integration of multidimensional self-concept and core personality constructs: construct validation and relations to well-being and achievement. *Journal of Personality*, *74*(2), 403–56.

Martindale, C. & Dailey, A. (1996). Creativity, primary process cognition, and personality. *Personality and Individual Differences*, *20*, 409–14.

Martindale, C. & Greenough, J. (1973). The differential effect of increased arousal on creative and intellectual performance. *Journal of Genetic Psychology*, *123*, 329–35.

Martindale, C. & Hasenfus, N. (1978). EEG differences as a function of creativity, stage of the creative process, and effort to be original. *Biological Psychology*, *6*, 157–67.

Mascie-Taylor, C. G. & Gibson, J. B. (1978). Social mobility and IQ components. *Journal of Biosocial Science*, *10*, 263–76.

Maslow, A. H. (1971). *The Farther Reaches of Human Nature*. New York: Viking Press.

Matthews, G. (1999). Personality and skill: a cognitive–adaptive framework. In P. L. Ackerman, P. C. Kyllonen & R. D. Roberts (eds.), *Learning and Individual Differences: Process, Trait, and Content Determinants*, pp. 437–62. Atlanta: Georgia Institute of Technology.

Matthews, G. & Deary, I. J. (1998). *Personality Traits*. Cambridge: Cambridge University Press.

Maurer, T. & Salomon, J. (2006). The science and practice of a structured employment interview coaching program. *Personnel Psychology*, *59*, 533–6.

May, M. A. & Hartshorne, H. (1926). Personality and character tests. *Psychological Bulletin*, *23*(7), 395–411.

Mayer, J. D. & Salovey, P. (1997). What is emotional intelligence? In P. Salovey, M. A. Brackett & J. D. Mayer (eds.), *Emotional Intelligence: Key Readings on the Mayer and Salovey Model*, pp. 29–59. Port Chester, NY: Dude.

Mayman, M. (1968). Early memories and character structure. *Journal of Projective Technique and Personality Assessment*, *32*, 303–16.

Mayo, J., White, O. & Eysenck, H. J. (1978). An empirical study of the relation between astrological factors and personality. *Journal of Social Psychology*, *105*, 229–36.

McCall, M. (1994). Identifying leadership potential in future international executives. *Consulting Psychology Journal*, *46*, 49–63.

   (1998). *High Flyers: Development the Next Generation of leaders*. Cambridge, MA: Harvard University Press.

McCall, M., Lombardo, M. & Morrison, A. (1990). *The Lessons of Experience: How Successful Executives Develop on the Job*. Lexington, MA: Lexington Books.

McCall, M., Spreitzer, G. & Mahoney, J. (1994). *Identifying Leadership Potential in Future International Executives: A Learning Resource Guide*. Lexington, MA: International Consortium for Executive Development, 1994.

McCarthy, J. M. & Goffin, R. D. (2001). Improving the validity of letters of recommendation: an investigation of three standardized reference forms. *Military Psychology*, *13*(4), 199–222.

McClelland, D. C. (1973). Testing for competence rather than for 'intelligence'. *American Psychologist*, *28*(1), 1–14.

   (1975). *Power: The Inner Experience*. New York: Irvington.

   (1989). Motivational factors in health and illness. *American Psychologist*, *44*, 219–33.

McClelland, D., Atkinson, J. W., Clark, R. A. & Lowell, E. L. (1953). *The Achievement Motive*. New York: Free Press.

McClelland, D. C. & Burham, D. (1976). Power is the great motivator. *Harvard Business Review*, *25*, 159–66.

McClelland, D. C. & Winter, D. G. (1969). *Motivating Economic Achievement*. New York: Free Press.

McDaniel, M. A. (1985). The evaluation of a causal model of job performance: the interrelationships of general mental ability, job experience, and job performance. MS, George Washington University.

McDaniel, M. A., Morgeson, F. P., Finnegan, E. B., Campion, M. A. & Braverman, E. P. (2001). Use of situational judgment tests to predict job performance: a clarification of the literature. *Journal of Applied Psychology*, *86*(4), 730–40.

McDaniel, M. A., Schmidt, F. L. & Hunter, J. E. (1988). Job experience correlates of job performance. *Journal of Applied Psychology*, *73*, 327–30.

McDaniel, E., Whetzel, D., Schmidt, F. & Maurer, S. (1994). The validity of employment interviews: a comprehensive review and meta-analysis. *Journal of Applied Psychology*, *79*(4), 599–616.

McDermid, C. D. (1965). Some correlates of creativity in engineering personnel. *Journal of Applied Psychology*, *49*(1), 14–19.

McGrew, K. S. & Flanagan, D. P. (1998). *The Intelligence Test Desk Reference (ITDR): Gf-Gc Cross-Battery Assessment*. Needham Heights, MA: Allyn & Bacon.

McHenry, J. J., Hough, L. M., Toquam, J. L., Hanson, M. L. & Ashworth, S. (1990). Project A validity results: the relationship between predictor and criterion domains. *Personnel Psychology*, *43*, 335–54.

McHenry, J. J. & Schmitt, N. (1994). Multimedia testing. In M. G. Rumsey & C. B. Walker (eds.), *Personnel Selection and Classification*. Hillsdale, NJ: Erlbaum.

McKinney, A. P., Carlson, K. D., Mecham, R. L., III, D'Angelo, N. C. & Connerley, M. L. (2003). Recruiters' use of GPA in initial screening decisions: higher GPAs don't always make the cut. *Personnel Psychology*, *56*(4), 823–45.

McManus, M. A. & Kelly, M. L. (1999). Personality measures and biodata: evidence regarding their incremental predictive value in the life insurance industry. *Personnel Psychology*, *52*(1), 137–48.

Mednick, M. T. & Andrews, F. M. (1967). Creative thinking and level of intelligence. *Journal of Creative Behavior*, *1*, 428–31.

Mednick, S. A. & Mednick, M. T. (1967). *Examiner's Manual, Remote Associates Test*. Boston: Houghton Mifflin.

Memon, A. & Bull, R. (eds.) (1999). *Handbook of the Psychology of Interviewing*. Chichester: Wiley.

Merten, T. (1995). Factors influencing word-association responses: a reanalysis. *Creativity Research Journal*, *8*, 249–63.

Merten, T. & Fischer, I. (1999). Creativity, personality and word association responses: associative behavior in 40 supposedly creative persons. *Personality and Individual Differences*, *27*, 933–42.

Messick, S. & Hills, J. R. (1960). Objective measurement of personality: cautiousness and intolerance of ambiguity. *Educational and Psychological Measurement*, *20*, 685–98.

Messick, S. & Jungeblut, A. (1981). Time and method in coaching for the SAT. *Psychological Bulletin*, *89*, 191–216.

Michaels, E., Handfield-Jones, H. & Axelrod, B. (2001). *The War for Talent*. Boston, MA: Harvard Business School.

Michon, J. H. (1872). *Système de la graphologie [A system for graphology]*. Paris: Garnier Frees.

Millard, K. A. (1952). Is 'How Supervise?' an intelligence test? *Journal of Applied Psychology*, *36*(4), 221–4.

Miller, D. T., Taylor, B. & Buck, M. L. (1991). Gender gaps: who needs to be explained? *Journal of Personality and Social Psychology*, *61*, 5–12.

Miller, E. (1996). Phrenology, neuropsychology and rehabilitation. *Neuropsyhological Rehabilitation*, *6*, 245–55.

Miller, W. S. (1960). *Technical Manual for the Miller Analogies Test*. New York: The Psychological Corporation.

Mischel, W. (1973). Toward a cognitive social learning reconceptualisation of personality. *Psychological Review, 80,* 252–83.

(1981). Current issues and challenges in personality. In L. T. Benjamin, Jr (ed.), *The G. Stanley Hall Lecture Series,* vol. 1, pp. 85–99. Washington, DC: American Psychological Association.

Morgeson, F. P., Delaney-Klinger, K. & Hemingway, M. A. (2005). The importance of job autonomy, cognitive ability, and job-related skill for predicting role breadth and job performance. *Journal of Applied Psychology, 90,* 399–406.

Morgeson, F. P., Campion, M. A., Dipboye, R. L., Hollenbeck, J. R., Murphy, K. & Schmitt, N. (2007). Recosidering the use of personality tests in personnel selection contxts. *Personnel Psychology, 60*(3), 683–729.

Mosel, J. N. & Cozan, L. W. (1952). The accuracy of application blank work histories. *Journal of Applied Psychology, 36*(6), 365–9.

Mosel, J. N. & Goheen, H. W. (1959). The employment recommendation questionnaire: III. Validity of different types of references. *Personnel Psychology, 12,* 469–77.

Moser, K. & Galais, N. (2007). Self-monitoring and job performance: the moderating role of tenure. *International Journal of Selection and Assessment, 15,* 83–93.

Moss, F. A. & Hunt, T. (1926). Ability to get along with others. *Industrial Psychology, 1,* 170–8.

Mount, M. K. & Barrick, M. R. (1998). Five reasons why the 'Big Five' article has been frequently cited. *Personnel Psychology, 51*(4), 849–57.

Mount, M. K., Barrick, M. R. & Stewart, G. L. (1998). Five-factor model of personality and performance in jobs involving interpersonal interactions. *Human Performance, 11,* 145–65.

Mount, M. K., Witt, L. A. & Barrick, M. R. (2000). Incremental validity of empirically keyed biodata scales over GMA and the five-factor personality constructs. *Personnel Psychology, 53*(2), 299–323.

Moutafi, J., Furnham, A. & Paltiel, L. (2004). Why is conscientiousness negatively correlated with intelligence? *Personality and Individual Differences, 37*(5), 1013–22.

Moutafi, J., Furnham, A. & Tsaousis, I. (2006). Is the relationship between intelligence and trait Neuroticism mediated by test anxiety? *Personality and Individual Differences, 40*(3), 587–97.

Muchinsky, P. M. (1979a). Some changes in the characteristics of articles published in the *Journal of Applied Psychology* over the past 20 years. *Journal of Applied Psychology, 64*(4), 455–9.

(1979b). The use of reference reports in personnel selection: a review and evaluation. *Journal of Occupational Psychology, 52*(4), 287–97.

Mueller-Hanson, R., Heggestad, E. D. & Thorton, G. C., III. (2003). Faking and selection: the use of personality from select-in and select-out perspectives. *Journal of Applied Psychology, 88,* 348–55.

(2006). Individual differences in impression management: an exploration of the psychological processes underlying faking. *Psychology Science,* special issue: *Considering Response Distortion in Personality Measurement for Industrial, Work and Organisational Psychology Research and Practice, 48*(3), 288–312.

Mumford, M. D., Connelly, M. S., Helton, W. B., Strange, J. M. & Osburn, H. K. (2001). On the construct validity of integrity tests: individual and situational factors as predictors of test performance. *International Journal of Selection and Assessment*, *9*, 240–57.

Mumford, M. D., Costanza, D. P., Connelly, M. S. & Johnson, J. F. (1996). Item generation procedures and background data scales: implications for construct and criterion-related validity. *Personnel Psychology*, *49*(2), 361–98.

Mumford, M. D., Gessner, T. L., Connelly, M. S., O'Connor, J. A. *et al.* (1993). Leadership and destructive acts: individual and situational influences. *Leadership Quarterly*, *4*(2), 115–47.

Mumford, M. D. & Gustafson, S. B. (1988). Creativity syndrome: integration, application, and innovation. *Psychological Bulletin*, *103*, 27–43.

Mumford, M. D. & Owens, W. A. (1987). Methodology review: principles, procedures, and findings in the application of background data measures. *Applied Psychological Measurement*, *11*(1), 1–31.

Mumford, M. D. & Stokes, G. S. (1992). Developmental determinants of individual action: theory and practice in applying background measures. In M. D. Dunnette & L. M. Hough (eds.), *Handbook of Industrial and Organizational Psychology*, 2nd edn, pp. 61–138. Palo Alto, CA: Consulting Psychologists Press.

Mumford, M. D., Stokes, G. S. & Owens, W. A. (1990). *Patterns of Life History: The Ecology of Human Individuality* (Series in Applied Psychology). Hillsdale, NJ: Erlbaum.

Murphy, K. R. (1984). The Wonderlic Personnel Test. In D. J. K. R. D. Sweetland (ed.), *Test Critiques*, vol. 1, pp. 769–75. Kansas City, MO: Test Corporation America.

 (1989). Is the relationship between cognitive ability and job performance stable over time? *Human Performance*, *2*, 183–200.

 (1993). *Honesty in the Workplace* (Cypress Series in Work and Science). Belmont, CA: Brooks/Cole.

 (2000). What constructs underlie measures of honesty or integrity? In R. Goffin & E. Helmes (eds.), *Problems and Solutions in Human Assessment: A Festschrift to Douglas N. Jackson at Seventy*, pp. 265–84. London: Kluwer.

 (2002). Can conflicting perspectives on the role of g in personnel selection be resolved? *Human Performance*, *15*, 173–86.

Murphy, K. R. & Cleveland, J. N. (1995). *Understanding Performance Appraisal: Social, Organizational, and Goal-Based Perspectives*. Thousand Oaks, CA: Sage.

Murphy, K. R. & Dzieweczynski, J. L. (2005). Why don't measures of broad dimensions of personality perform better as predictor of job performance? *Human Performance*, *18*, 343–57.

Murphy, K. R. & Lee, S. L. (1994). Does conscientiousness explain the relationship between integrity and job performance? *International Journal of Selection and Assessment*, *2*, 226–33.

Murray, C. (1998). *Income and inequality*. Washington, DC: AEI Press.

Murray, H. A. (1938). *Explorations in Personality*. New York: Oxford University Press.

 (1943). *Thematic Apperception Test, Manual*. Cambridge, MA: Harvard Psychological Clinic.

Nanninga, R. (1996). The astrotest. *Correlation*, *15*, 14–20.

Nathan, B. R. & Alexander, R. A. (1988). A comparison of criteria for test validation: a meta-analytic investigation. *Personnel Psychology*, *41*, 517–35.

Neter, E. & Ben-Shakhar, G. (1989). The predictive validity of graphological inferences: a meta-analytic approach. *Personality and Individual Differences, 10*(7), 737–45.

Nevo, B. (1988). Yes, graphology can predict occupational success: rejoinder to Ben-Shakhar *et al. Perceptual and Motor Skills, 69*, 92–94.

Nicholson, F. W. (1915). Success in college and in after life. *School and Society, 12*, 229–32.

Nickels, B. J. (1990). The construction of background data measures: developing procedures which optimized construct, content, and criterion-related validities. *Dissertation Abstracts International*, vol. 51(4-B), 2099–2100.

Nickerson, R. S. (1998). Confirmation bias: a ubiquitous phenomenon in many guises. *Review of General Psychology, 2*, 175–220.

Nieva, V. F. & Gutek, B. A. (1981). *Women and Work: A Psychological Perspective*. New York: Praeger.

Nicol, A. M. & Paunonen, S. V. (2002). Overt honesty measures predicting admissions: an index of validity or reliability. *Psychological Reports, 90*, 105–15.

Nobel, E. P., Runco, M. A. & Ozkaragoz, T. Z. (1993). Creativity in alcoholic and nonalcoholic families. *Alcohol, 10*, 317–22.

Noftle, E. E. & Robins, R. W. (2007). Personality predictors of academic outcomes: big five correlates of GPA and SAT scores. *Journal of Personality and Social Psychology, 93*(1), 116–30.

Northouse, P. G. (1997). *Leadership: Theory and Practice*. Thousand Oaks, CA: Sage.

Northrop, L. C. (1989). *The Psychometric History of Selected Ability Constructs*. Washington, DC: US Office of Personnel Management.

Novella, S. (2000). Phrenology: history of a pseudoscience. *New England Journal of Skepticism, 3*, 1–7.

Ochse, R. (1990). *Before the Gates of Excellence: The Determinants of Creative Genius*. Cambridge: Cambridge University Press.

O'Connor, M. C. & Paunonen, S. V. (2007). Big Five personality predictors of post-secondary academic performance. *Personality and Individual Differences, 43*(5), 971–90.

Ones, D. S., Mount, M. K., Barrick, M. R. & Hunter, J. E. (1994). Personality and job performance: a critique of the Tett, Jackson, and Rothstein (1991) meta-analysis. *Personnel Psychology, 47*(1), 147–56.

Ones, D. S. & Viswesvaran, C. (2003). Job-specific applicant pools and national norms for personality scales: implications for range-restriction corrections in validation research. *Journal of Applied Psychology, 88*(3), 570–7.

Ones, D. S., Viswesvaran, C. & Dilchert, S. (2005a). Cognitive ability in personnel selection decisions. In O. V. A. Evers & N. Anderson (eds.), *Handbook of Selection*, pp. 143–73. Oxford: Blackwell.

   (2005b). Personality at work: raising awareness and correcting misconceptions. *Human Performance, 18*, 389–404.

Ones, D. S., Viswesvaran, C. & Reiss, A. D. (1996). Role of social desirability in personality testing for personnel selection: the red herring. *Journal of Applied Psychology, 81*(6), 660–79.

Ones, D. S., Viswesvaran, C. & Schmidt, F. L. (1993). Meta-analysis of integrity test validities: findings and implications for personnel selection and theories of job performance. *Journal of Applied Psychology Monograph, 78*, 679–703.

Oosthuizen, S. (1990). Graphology as predictor of academic achievement. *Perceptual and Motor Skills*, *71*, 715–21.

Organ, D. W. & Ryan, K. (1995). A meta-analytic review of attitudinal and dispositional predictors of organizational citizenship behavior. *Personnel Psychology*, special issue: *Theory and Literature*, *48*(4), 775–802.

Orr, J. M., Sackett, P. R. & Mercer, M. (1996). The role of prescribed and nonprescribed behaviors in estimating the dollar value of performance. *Journal of Applied Psychology*, *74*, 34–40.

Oswald, F. L., Schmitt, N., Kim, B. H., Ramsay, L. J. & Gillespie, M. A. (2004). Developing a biodata measure and situational judgment inventory as predictors of college student performance. *Journal of Applied Psychology*, *89*(2), 187–207.

Paul, R. J. & Townsend, J. B. (1995). Shape up or ship out? Employment discrimination against the overweight. *Employee Responsibilities & Rights Journal*, *8*, 133–45.

Paulus, D. & Williams, K. (2002). The dark triad of personality. *Journal of Research in Personality*, *36*, 556–63.

Paunonen, S. V. (1984). Optimizing the validity of personality assessments: the importance of aggregation and item content. *Journal of Research in Personality*, *18*(4), 411–31.

Paunonen, S. V., Jackson, D. N. & Oberman, S. M. (1987). Personnel selection decisions: effects of applicant personality and the letter of reference. *Organizational Behavior and Human Decision Processes*, *40*(1), 96–114.

Pearlman, K., Schmidt, F. L. & Hunter, J. E. (1980). Validity generalization results for tests used to predict job proficiency and training success in clerical occupations. *Journal of Applied Psychology*, *65*, 373–406.

Peres, S. H. & Garcia, J. R. (1962). Validity and dimensions of descriptive adjectives used in reference letters for engineering applicants. *Personnel Psychology*, *15*(3), 279–86.

Perkins, D. N. (1981). *The Minds Best Work*. Cambridge, MA: Harvard University Press.

Peretti, F. & Negro, G. (2007). Mixing genres and matching people: a study in innovation and team composition in Hollywood. *Journal of Organizational Behaviour*, special issue: *Paradoxes of Creativity: Managerial and Organizational Challenges in the Cultural Economy*, *28*(5), 563–86.

Pervin, L. A. (1989). Persons, situations, interactions: the history of a controversy and a discussion of theoretical models. *Academy of Management Review*, special issue: *Theory Development Forum*, *14*(3), 350–60.

Pervin, L. A. & Rubin, D. B. (1967). Student dissatisfaction with college and the college dropout: a transactional approach. *Journal of Social Psychology*, *72*(2), 285–95.

Peterson, J. B. & Carson, S. (2000). Latent inhibition and openness to experience in a high-achieving student population. *Personality and Individual Differences*, *28*(2), 323–32.

Peterson, C. & Seligman, M. E. P. (2004). Social intelligence. In *Character Strengths and Virtues: A Handbook and Classification*, pp. 337–53. Washington, DC: American Psychological Association; New York: Oxford University Press.

Petrides, K. V., Chamorro-Premuzic, T., Frederickson, N. & Furnham, A. (2005). Explaining individual differences in scholastic behaviour and achievement. *British Journal of Educational Psychology*, *75*(2), 239–55.

Petrides, K. V. & Furnham, A. (2001). Trait emotional intelligence: psychometric investigation with reference to established trait taxonomies. *European Journal of Personality*, *15*(6), 425–48.

Phares, E. (1984). *Introduction to Personality*. London: Charles E. Merrill.

Phul, R. M. & Brownell, K. D. (2003). Psychosocial origins of obesity stigma: toward changing a powerful and pervasive bias. *Obesity Reviews*, *4*, 213–27.

Pingitoire, R., Dugoni, R., Tindale, S. & Spring, B. (1994). Bias against overweight job applicants in a simulated employment interview. *Journal of Applied Psychology*, *79*, 909–17.

Plomin, R. (2001). The genetics of *g* in human and mouse. *Nature Reviews Neuroscience*, *2*, 136–41.

Ployhart, R. E., Weekley, J. A., Holtz, B. C. & Kemp, C. (2003). Web-based and paper-and-pencil testing of applicants in a proctored setting: are personality, biodata and situational judgment tests comparable? *Personnel Psychology*, *56*(3), 733–52.

Porter, M. E. (1990). *The Competitive Advantage of Nations*. New York: Free Press.

Posthuma, R., Morgeson, F. & Campion, M. (2002). Beyond employment interview validity: a comprehensive narrative review of recent research and trends over time. *Personnel Psychology*, *55*, 1–65.

Prien, E. P. (1977). The function of job analysis in content validation. *Personnel Psychology*, *30*(2), 167–74.

Probst, T. M., Stewart, S. M., Gruys, M. L. & Tierney, B. W. (2007). Productivity, counterproductivity and creativity: the ups and downs of job insecurity. *Journal of Occupational and Organizational Psychology*, *80*(3), 479–97.

Proyer, R. T. & Häusler, J. (2007). Assessing behaviour in standardised settings: the role of objective personality tests. *International Journal of Clinical and Health Psychology*, *7*(2), 537–46.

Rafaeli, A. & Klimoski, R. J. (1983). Predicting sales success through handwriting analysis: an evaluation of the effects of training and handwriting sample content. *Journal of Applied Psychology*, *68*, 212–17.

Raven, J. C. (1938). *Progressive Matrices: A Perceptual Test of Intelligence*. London: H. K. Lewis.

Raven, J. C., Court, J. H. & Raven, J. (1998). *Manual for Raven's Progressive Matrices and Vocabulary Scales (Section 3)*. Oxford: Oxford Psychologist Press.

Redding, S. G. & Wong, G. Y. Y. (1986). The psychology of Chinese organisation behaviour. In M. H. Bond (ed.), *The Psychology of Chinese People*. Hong Kong: Oxford University Press.

Ree, M. J. (2003). Review of assessing business potential: a biodata approach. *Personnel Psychology*, *56*(2), 505–7.

Ree, M. J., Carretta, T. R. & Teachout, M. S. (1995). Role of ability and prior job knowledge in complex training performance. *Journal of Applied Psychology*, *80*, 721–30.

Ree, M. J. & Earles, J. A. (1991a). Predicting training success: not much more than *g*. *Personnel Psychology*, *44*, 321–32.

  (1991b). The stability of g across different methods of estimation. *Intelligence*, *15*, 271–8.

  (1992). Intelligence is the best predictor of job performance. *Current Directions in Psychological Science*, *1*, 86–9.

Ree, M. J., Earles, J. A. & Teachout, M. (1994). Predicting job performance: not much more than g. *Journal of Applied Psychology*, *79*, 518–24.

Reeve, C. L., Meyer, R. D. & Bonaccio, S. (2006). Intelligence-personality associations reconsidered: the importance of distinguishing between general and narrow dimensions of intelligence. *Intelligence*, *34*, 387–402.

Register, C.A. & Williams, D. R. (1990). Wage effects of obesity among young workers. *Social Sciences Quarterly*, *71*, 130–41.

Reilly, R. R. & Chao, G. R. (1982). Validity and fairness of some alternative employee selection procedures. *Personnel Psychology*, *35*(1), 1–62.

Renzulli, J. S. (1978). What makes giftedness? Reexamining a definition. *Phi Delta Kappan*, *60*, 180–4.

   (1986). The three ring conception of giftedness: a developmental model for creative productivity. In R. J. Sternberg & J. E. Davidson (eds.), *Conceptions of Giftedness*, pp. 53–92. New York: Cambridge University Press.

Rhodes, M. (1961/1987). An analysis of creativity: the role of ability, cue consistency, and active processing. *Creativity Research Journal*, *9*, 9–23.

Richards, R. L. (1976). A comparison of selected Guilford and Wallach-Kogan creative thinking tests in conjunction with measures of intelligence. *Journal of Creative Behavior*, *10*, 151–64.

Richardson, B., Henry & Co., Inc. (1963). *Test of Supervisory Judgment*. Washington, DC: Richardson, Bellows & Henry.

Rickards, T. & de Cock, C. (1999). Understanding organizational creativity: toward a multi-paradigmatic approach. In M. A. Runco (ed.), *Creativity Research Handbook*, vol. 2. Cresskill, NJ: Hampton Press.

Robertson, I. T. & Smith, M. (2001). Personnel selection. *Journal of Occupational and Organizational Psychology*, *74*(4), 441–72.

Robinson, D. L. (1997). Age differences, cerebral arousability, and human intelligence. *Personality and Individual Differences*, *23*(4), 601–18.

Robinson, S. L. & Bennett, R. J. (1995). A typology of deviant workplace behaviors: a multidimensional scaling study. *Academy of Management Journal*, *38*, 555–72.

Roehling, M. V. (1999). Weight-based discrimination in employment: psychological and legal aspects. *Personnel Psychology*, *52*, 969–1017.

Rogers, C. R. (1980). *A Way of Being*. Boston: Houghton Mifflin.

Rosenthal, D. A. & Lines, R. (1978). Handwriting as a correlate of extraversion. *Journal of Personality Assessment*. *42*(2), 44–8.

Rosse, J. G., Stecher, M. D., Miller, J. L. & Levin, R. A. (1998). The impact of response distortion on preemployment personality testing and hiring decisions. *Journal of Applied Psychology*, *83*(4), 634–44.

Roth, P. L., BeVier, C. A., Switzer, F. S., III & Schippmann, J. S. (1996). Meta-analyzing the relationship between grades and job performance. *Journal of Applied Psychology*, *81*(5), 548–56.

Roth, P. L. & Bobko, P. (2000). College grade point average as a personnel selection device: ethnic group differences and potential adverse impact. *Journal of Applied Psychology*, *85*(3), 399–406.

Roth, P. L. & Clarke, R. L. (1998). Meta-analyzing the relation between grades and salary. *Journal of Vocational Behavior*, *53*(3), 386–400.

Roth, P., Van Iddekinge, C., Huffcutt, A., Eidson, C. & Schmit, M. (2005). Personality saturation in structured interviews. *International Journal of Selection and Assessment*, *13*, 261–73.

Rothblum, E. D., Brand, P. A., Miller, C. T. & Oetken, H. A. (1990). The relationship between obesity, employment discrimination, and employment-related victimisation. *Journal of Vocational Behavior*, *37*, 251–66.

Rothblum, E. D., Miller, C. T. & Gorbutt, B. (1988). Stereotypes of obese female job applicants. *International Journal of Eating Disorders*, *7*, 277–83.

Runco, M. A. (1986). Divergent thinking and creative performance in gifted and non-gifted children. *Educational and Psychological Measurement*, *46*, 375–84.

(1998). *Creativity Research Handbook*, vol. 1. Cresskill, NJ: Hampton Press.

(2003a). *Creativity Research Handbook*, vol. 2. Cresskill, NJ: Hampton Press.

(2003b). *Creativity Research Handbook*, vol. 3. Cresskill, NJ: Hampton Press.

(2004). Creativity. *Annual Review of Psychology*, *55*, 657–87.

Runco, M. A. & Charles, R. (1993). Judgments of originality and appropriateness as predictors of creativity. *Personality and Individual Differences*, *15*, 537–46.

Ruzzene, M. & Noller, P. (1986). Feedback, motivation and reaction to personality interpretation that differ in favourability and accuracy. *Journal of Personality and Social Psychology*, *51*, 1293–8.

Ryan, A. M., Ployhart, R. M. & Friedel, L. (1998). Using personality testing to reduce adverse impact: a cautionary note. *Journal of Applied Psychology*, *82*(2), 298–307.

Ryan, A. M. & Sackett, P. R. (1987). A survey of individual assessment practices by I/O psychologists. *Personnel Psychology*, *40*(3), 455–88.

Ryckman, R. M. & Rodda, W. C. (1971). Locus of control and initial task experience as determinants of confidence changes in a chance situation. *Journal of Personality and Social Psychology*, *18*(1), 116–19.

Rynes, S. L. & Gerhart, B. (1990). Interviewer assessments of applicant 'fit': an exploratory investigation. *Personnel Psychology*, *43*(1), 13–35.

Rynes, S. L., Orlitzky, M. O. & Bretz, R. D. Jr (1997). Experienced hiring versus college recruiting: practices and emerging trends. *Personnel Psychology*, *50*(2), 309–39.

Sachs, G. (1999). *Die Akte Astrologie*, revised edn. Munich: Goldmann. [English translation: *The Astrology File*. London: Orion, 1999.]

Sackett, P. R., Burris, L. R. & Callahan, C. (1989). Integrity testing for personnel selection: an update. *Personnel Psychology*, *42*, 491–529.

Sackett, P. R., Burris, L. R. & Ryan, A. M. (1989). Coaching and practice effects in personnel selection. In C. C. I. Robertson (ed.), *International Review of Industrial and Organizational Psychology*, pp. 145–83. New York: Wiley.

Sackett, P. R. & Lievens, F. (2008). Personnel selection. *Annual Review of Psychology*, *59*, 419–50.

Sackett, P. R., Zedeck, S. & Fogli, L. (1988). Relations between measures of typical and maximum job performance. *Journal of Applied Psychology*, *73*, 482–86.

Sala, F. (2002). *Emotional Competence Inventory: Technical Manual*. Boston, MA: McClelland Center for Research and Innovation, Hay Group.

Salgado, J. F. (1997). The five-factor model of personality and job performance in the European Community. *Journal of Applied Psychology*, *82*, 30–43.

(1998). Big Five personality dimensions and job performance in army and civil occupations: a European perspective. *Human Performance*, *11*(2–3), 271–88.

Salgado, J. F. & Anderson, N. (2002). Cognitive and GMA testing in the European Community: issues and evidence. *Human Performance*, *15*, 75–96.

Salgado, J. F., Anderson, N., Moscoso, S., Bertua, C. & De Fruyt, F. (2003a). International validity generalization of GMA and cognitive abilities: a European Community meta-analysis. *Personnel Psychology*, *56*, 573–605.

Salgado, J. F., Anderson, N., Moscoso, S., Bertua, C., De Fruyt, F. & Rolland, J. P. (2003b). A meta-analytic study of general mental ability validity for different occupations in the European Community. *Journal of Applied Psychology*, *88*, 1068–81.

Salovey, P. & Mayer, J. D. (1989). Emotional intelligence. *Imagination, Cognition and Personality*, *9*(3), 185–211.

Salovey, P., Mayer, J. D., Goldman, S. L., Turvey, C. & Palfai, T. P. (1995). Emotional attention, clarity, and repair: exploring emotional intelligence using the Trait Meta-Mood Scale. In J. W. Pennebaker (ed.), *Emotion, Disclosure, and Health*, pp. 125–54. Washington, DC: American Psychological Association.

Samson, G. E., Graue, M. E., Weinstein, T. & Walberg, H. J. (1984). Academic and occupational performance: a quantitative synthesis. *American Educational Research Journal*, *21*(2), 311–21.

Santacreu, J., Rubio, V. c. J. & Hernandez, J. M. (2006). The objective assessment of personality: Cattells's T-data revisited and more. *Psychology Science*, *48*(1), 53–68.

Schein, V. E. (2001). A global look at psychological barriers to women's progress in management. *Journal of Social Issues*, *57*, 675–88.

Schmidt, F. L. (2002). The role of general cognitive ability and job performance: why there cannot be a debate. *Human Performance*, *15*, 187–210.

Schmidt, F. L., Gast-Rosenberg, I. & Hunter, J. E. (1980). Validity generalization for computer programmers. *Journal of Applied Psychology*, *65*, 643–61.

Schmidt, F. L. & Hunter, J. E. (1998). The validity and utility of selection methods in personnel psychology: practical and theoretical implications of 85 years of research findings. *Psychological Bulletin*, *124*, 262–74.

(2000). Select on intelligence. In E. A. Locke (ed.), *Handbook of Principles of Organisational Behaviour*, pp. 3–14. Oxford: Blackwell.

(2004). General mental ability in the world of work: occupational attainment and job performance. *Journal of Personality and Social Psychology*, *86*, 162–73.

Schmidt, F. L., Hunter, J. E., McKenzie, R. C. & Muldrow, T. W. (1979). Impact of valid selection procedures on work-force productivity. *Journal of Applied Psychology*, *64*, 609–26.

Schmidt, F. L., Hunter, J. E., Outerbridge, A. N. & Goff, S. (1988). The joint relation of experience and ability with job performance: a test of three hypotheses. *Journal of Applied Psychology*, *73*, 46–57.

Schmidt, F. L., Ones, D. S. & Hunter, J. E. (1992). Personnel selection. *Annual Review of Psychology*, *43*, 627–70.

Schmidt, F. & Rader, M. (1999). Exploring the boundary conditions for interview validity. *Personnel Psychology*, *52*, 445–65.

Schmidt, F. & Zimmerman, R. (2004). A counter intuitive hypothesis about employment interview validity and some supportive evidence. *Journal of Applied Psychology*, *89*, 553–61.

Schmitt, N., Gooding, R. Z., Noe, R. A. & Kirsch, M. (1984). Meta analyses of validity studies published between 1964 and 1982 and the investigation of study characteristics. *Personnel Psychology*, *37*, 407–22.

Schmitt, N., Jennings, D. & Toney, R. (1999). Can we develop measures of hypothetical constructs? *Human Resource Management Review*, *9*(2), 169–83.

Schmitt, N. & Kunce, C. (2002). The effects of required elaboration of answers to biodata questions. *Personnel Psychology*, *55*(3), 569–87.

Schmitt, N., Oswald, F. L., Kim, B. H., Gillespie, M. A., Ramsay, L. J. & Yoo, T.-Y. (2003). Impact of elaboration on socially desirable responding and the validity of biodata measures. *Journal of Applied Psychology*, *88*(6), 979–88.

Schneider, B. & Schmitt, N. (1986). *Staffing Organizations*, 2nd edn. Glenview, IL: Scott Foresman.

Schoenfeldt, L. F. & Brush, D. H. (1975). Patterns of college grades across curricular areas: some implications for GPA as a criterion. *American Educational Research Journal*, *12*(3), 313–21.

Schoppe, K. J. (1975). *Verbaler Kreativitätstest. Ein Verfahren zur Erfassung verbal-produktiver Kreativitätsmerkmale*. Göttingen, Toronto, Zürich: Hogrefe.

Schrader, A. D. & Osburn, H. G. (1977). Biodata faking: effects of induced subtlety and position specificity. *Personnel Psychology*, *30*(3), 395–404.

Schubert, D. S. (1973). Intelligence as necessary but not sufficient for creativity. *Journal of Genetic Psychology*, *122*, 45–47.

Schuler, H. (1993). Social validity of selection situations. In H. Schuler, J. Farr & M. Smith (eds.), *Personnel Selection and Assessment*, pp. 11–26. Hillsdale, NJ: Erlbaum.

Secord, P. (1965). Facial features and inference processes in interpersonal perception. In R. Taguiri & L Petrullo (eds.), *Person Perception and Interpersonal Behavior*, pp. 300–15. Stanford, CA: Stanford University Press.

Shackleton, V. & Newell, S. (1994). European management selection methods: a comparison of five countries. *International Journal of Selection and Assessment*, *2*, 91–102.

Shamir, B. (1991). The charismatic relationship: alternative explanations and predictions. *Leadership Quarterly*, *2*, 81–104.

Sharpe, R. (2000, November 20). As leaders, women rule: new studies find that female managers outshine their male counterparts in almost every measure. Business Week. Retrieved 15 December 2000 from www.businessweek.com/common_frames?ca.htm?/2000/00_47?b3708145.htm.

Shavinina, L. (2004). Explaining high abilities of Nobel laureates. *High Ability Studies*, *15*, 243–54.

Sheldon, W. (1940). *The Varieties of Human Physique*. New York: Harper.

Shouksmith, G. (1973). *Intelligence, Creativity and Cognitive Style*. London: Angus and Robertson.

Silversthorne, C. (2001). Leadership effectiveness and personality: a cross cultural evaluation. *Personality and Individual Differences*, *30*, 303–9.

Simner, M. L. & Goffin, R. D. (2003). A position statement by the International Grapho-nomics Society on the use of graphology in personnel selection testing. *International Journal of Testing*, *3*(4), 353–64.

Simon, H. A. & Chase, W. (1973). Skill in chess. *American Science*, *61*, 394–403.

Simonton, D. K. (1986). Presidential personality: biographical use of the Gough adjective check list. *Journal of Personality and Social Psychology*, *51*, 149–60.

(1987). *Why Presidents Succeed: A Political Psychology of Leadership*. New Haven, CT: Yale University Press.

(1994). *Greatness: What Makes History and Why*. New York: Guilford.

(2004). *Creativity in Science: Chance, Logic, Genius, and Zeitgeist*. New York: Cambridge University Press.

SIOP (2003). *Principles for the Validation and Use of Personnel Selection Procedures*, 4th edn. College Park, MD: Society for Industrial and Organizational Psychology.

Sisco, H. & Reilly, R. R. (2007). Development and validation of a biodata inventory as an alternative method to measurement of the five-factor model of personality. *Social Science Journal*, *44*(2), 383–9.

Slora, K. B. (1989). An empirical approach to determining employee deviance rates. *Journal of Business and Psychology*, *4*, 199–219.

Smith, K. L., Michael, W. B. & Hocevar, D. (1990). Performance on creativity measures with examination-taking instructions intended to induce high or low levels of test anxiety. *Creativity Research Journal*, *3*, 265–80.

Smith, M. & Robertson, I. (1989). *Advances in Selection and Assessment*. Chichester: Wiley.

Smith, W. J., Albright, L. E. & Glennon, J. R. (1961). The prediction of research competence and creativity from personal history. *Journal of Applied Psychology*, *45*(1), 59–62.

Smithers, A. G. & Cooper, H. J. (1978). Personality and season of birth. *Journal of Social Psychology*, *105*, 237–41.

Snyder, C. & Clair, M. (1977). Does insecurity breed acceptance? *Journal of Consulting and Clinical Psychology*, *45*, 843–50.

Sosik, J. J., Kahai, S. S. & Avolio, B. J. (1998). Transformational leadership and dimensions of creativity: motivating idea generation in computer-mediated groups. *Creativity Research Journal*, *11*, 111–21.

Spangler, W., House, R. & Palrecha, R. (2004). Personality and leadership. In B. Schneider & D. Smith (eds.), *Personality and Organisation*, pp. 251–90. New York: Maliwah.

Spearman, C. E. (1904). 'General intelligence', objectively determined and measured. *American Journal of Psychology*, *15*, 201–93.

(1930). Disturbers of tetrad differences: scales. *Journal of Educational Psychology*, *21*, 559–73.

(1938). Measurement of intelligence. *Scientia Milano*, *64*, 75–82.

Spector, P. (2006). *Industrial and Organisational Psychology*. Chichester: Wiley.

Spinks, R., Arndt, S., Caspers, K., Yucuis, R., McKirgan, L. W., Pfalzgraf, C. *et al.* (2007). School achievement strongly predicts midlife IQ. *Intelligence*, *35*(6), 563–7.

Spranger, W. D. & House, R. J. (1991). Presidential effectiveness and the leadership motive profile. *Journal of Personality and Social Psychology*, *60*, 439–55.

Sprecher, T. B. (1959). A study of engineers' criteria for creativity. *Journal of Applied Psychology, 43*(2), 141–8.

Spreitzer, G., McCall, M. & Mahoney, R. (1997). Early identification of international executive potential. *Journal of Applied Psychology, 82,* 6–29.

Stagner, R. (1948). The gullibility of personnel managers. *Personnel Psychology, 50,* 145–9.

Stajkovic, A. D. & Luthans, F. (1998). Self-efficacy and work-related performance: a meta-analysis. *Psychological Bulletin, 124,* 240–61.

Sternberg, R. J. (1985a). Natural, unnatural, and supernatural concepts. *Cognitive Psychology, 14,* 451–88.

   (1985b). Implicit theories of intelligence, creativity, and wisdom. *Journal of Personality and Social Psychology, 49,* 607–27.

(ed.) (1999). *Handbook of Creativity.* New York: Cambridge University Press.

Sternberg, R. J., Forsythe, G. B., Hedlund, J., Horvath, J. A., Wagner, R. K., Williams, W. M. *et al.* (2000). *Practical Intelligence in Everyday Life.* New York: Cambridge University Press.

Sternberg, R. J. & Gastel, J. (1989). Coping with novelty in human intelligence: an empirical investigation. *Intelligence, 13,* 187–97.

Sternberg, R. J. & Horvath, J. A. (1999). *Tacit Knowledge in Professional Practice: Researcher and Practitioner Perspectives.* Mahwah, NJ: Erlbaum.

Sternberg, R. J. & Lubart, T. I. (1995). *Defying the Crowd: Cultivating Creativity in a Culture of Conformity.* New York: Free Press.

   (1996). Investing in creativity. *American Psychologist, 51,* 677–88.

Sternberg, R. J. & O'Hara, L. A. (2000). Intelligence and creativity. In R. J. Sternberg (ed.), *Handbook of Intelligence,* pp. 611–30. New York: Cambridge University Press.

Sternberg, R. J. & Wagner, R. K. (1993). The g-ocentric view of intelligence and job performance is wrong. *Current Directions in Psychological Science, 2*(1), 1–5.

Stogdill, R. M. (1948). Personal factors associated with leadership: a survey of the literature. *Journal of Psychology, 25,* 35–71.

   (1974). *Handbook of Leadership.* New York: Free Press.

Stokes, G. S. & Cooper, L. A. (2001). Content/construct approaches in life history form development for selection. *International Journal of Selection and Assessment, 9*(1–2), 138–51.

Stokes, G. S., Mumford, M. D. & Owens, W. A. (1994). *Biodata Handbook: Theory, Research, and Use of Biographical Information in Selection and Performance Prediction.* Palo Alto, CA: Consulting Psychologists Press.

Stokes, G. S. & Searcy, C. A. (1999). Specification of scales in biodata form development: rational vs. empirical and global vs. specific. *International Journal of Selection and Assessment,* special issue: *Background Data and Autobiographical Memory, 7*(2), 72–85.

Strenze, T. (2007). Intelligence and socioeconomic success: a meta-analytic review of longitudinal research. *Intelligence, 35*(5), 401–26.

Strich, T. M. & Secord, P. F. (1956). Interaction effects in the perception of faces. *Journal of Personality, 24,* 270–84.

Strong, E. K., Jr (1955). *Vocational Interests 18 Years after College.* Minneapolis, MN: University of Minnesota Press.

Sue-Chan, C. & Lathan, G. (2004). The situational interview as a predictor of academic and team performance. *International Journal of Selection and Assessment*, *12*, 312–20.

Sulloway, F. (1996). *Born to Rebel*. New York: Pantheon.

Swami, V. & Furnham, A. (2008). *The Psychology of Physical Attractiveness*. London: Routledge.

Swann, W. B. (1987). Identity negotiation: where two roads meet. *Journal of Personality and Social Psychology*, *53*(6), 1038–51.

Taylor, P. & Small, B. (2002). Asking applicants what they would do versus what they did do: a meta-analysis comparison of situational and past behaviour employment interview questions. *Journal of Occupational and Organisational Psychology*, *15*, 277–94.

Terpstra, D. E. & Rozell, E. J. (1997). Why some potentially effective staffing practices are seldom used. *Public Personnel Management*, *26*(4), 483–95.

Tett, R. P., Jackson, D. N. & Rothstein, M. (1991). Personality measures as predictors of job performance: a meta-analytic review. *Personnel Psychology*, *44*, 703–42.

Tett, R. P., Jackson, D. N., Rothstein, M. & Reddon, J. R. (1994). Meta-analysis of personality-job performance relations: a reply to Ones, Mount, Barrick, and Hunter (1994). *Personnel Psychology*, *47*(1), 157–72.

Tett, R. P. & Palmer, C. A. (1997). The validity of handwriting elements in relation to self-report personality trait measures. *Personality and Individual Differences*, *22*, 11–18.

Thorndike, E. L. (1903). The influence of selection. In *Educational Psychology*, pp. 94–6. New York: Lemcke & Buechner.

Thorndike, R. L. (1986). The role of general ability in prediction. *Journal of Vocational Behavior*, *29*, 332–9.

Thorndike, R. L. & Stein, S. (1937). An evaluation of the attempts to measure social intelligence. *Psychological Bulletin*, *34*(5), 275–85.

Toops, H. A. & Pintner, R. (1919). Educational differences among tradesmen. *Journal of Applied Psychology*, *3*(1), 33–49.

Torrance, E. P. (1963). Creativity. In F. W. Hubbard (ed.), *What Research Says to the Teacher*, no. 28. Washington, DC: Department of Classroom Teachers American Educational Research Association of the National Education Association.

(1966). *Torrance Tests of Creative Thinking: Norms-Technical Manual*. Lexington, MA: Ginn.

(1974). *Torrance Tests of Creative Thinking*. Lexington, MA: Ginn.

(1975). Sociodrama as a creative problem solving approach to studying the future. *Journal of Creative Behavior*, *9*, 182–95.

(1979). *The Search for Satori and Creativity*. Buffalo, NY: Bearly.

Tracey, T. J. & Rounds, J. B. (1992). Evaluating the RIASEC circumplex using high-point codes. *Journal of Vocational Behavior*, special issue: *Career Decision Making and Career Indecision*, *41*(3), 295–311.

Tucker, M. F., Cline, V. B. & Schmitt, J. R. (1967). Prediction of creativity and other performance measures from biographical information among pharmaceutical scientists. *Journal of Applied Psychology*, *51*(2), 131–8.

Turner, N., Barling, J., Epitropaki, O., Butcher, V. & Milner, C. (2002). Transformational leadership and moral reasoning. *Journal of Applied Psychology*, 87, 304–39.

Twine, R. (2002). Physiognomy, phrenology and the temporality of the body. *Body and Society*, 8, 67–88.

Upmanyu, V. V., Bhardwaj, S. & Singh, S. (1996). Word-association emotional indicators: associations with anxiety, psychoticism, neuroticism, extraversion, and creativity. *Journal of Social Psychology*, 36, 521–9.

US Department of Labor (1999). *Testing and Assessment: An Employer's Guide to Good Practices*. Washington, DC: Labor, Employment and Training Administration.

Van Der See, K., Bakker, A. & Bakker, P. (2002). Why are structured interviews so rarely used in personnel selection? *Journal of Applied Psychology*, 87, 176–84.

van Engen, M. L. (2001). Gender and leadership: a contextual perspective. Doctoral dissertation, Tilburg University.

Van Iddelange, C., Raymark, P. & Roth, P. (2005). Assessing personality with a structured employment interview. *Journal of Applied Psychology*, 90, 536–52.

Van Iddelange, C., Sayer, C., Burnfield, J. & Heffner, T. (2006). The variability of criterion-related validity estimates among interviewers and interview panels. *International Journal of Selection and Assessment*, 14, 193–205.

Van Rooij, J. J. F. (1994). Introversion-extraversion: astrology versus psychology. *Personality and Individual Differences*, 16, 985–8.

(1999). Self-concept in terms of astrological sun-sign traits. *Psychological Reports*, 84, 541–6.

Van Rooy, D. & Viswesvaran, C. (2004). Emotional intelligence: a meta-analytic investigation of predictive validity and nomological net. *Journal of Vocational Behaviour*, 65, 71–95.

Vardi, Y. & Weitz, E. (2004). *Misbehavior in Organizations: Theory, Research, and Management*. Hillsdale, NJ: Erlbaum.

Vasilopoulos, N. L., Cucina, J. M. & McElreath, J. M. (2005). Do warnings of response verification moderate the relationship between personality and cognitive ability? *Journal of Applied Psychology*, 90, 306–22.

Verive, J. M. & McDaniel, M. A. (1996). Short-term memory tests in personnel selection: low adverse impact and high validity. *Intelligence*, 23, 15–32.

Vernon, P. E. (1971). Effects of administration and scoring on divergent thinking tests. *British Journal of Educational Psychology*, 41, 245–57.

Vestewig, R., Santee, A. & Moss, M. (1976). Validity and student acceptance of a graphoanalytic approach to personality. *Journal of Personality Assessment*, 40(6), 592–8.

Villanova, P., Bernardin, H. J., Johnson, D. L. & Dahmus, S. A. (1994). The validity of a measure of job compatibility in the prediction of job performance and turnover of motion picture theater personnel. *Personnel Psychology*, 47(1), 73–90.

Vinchur, A. J., Schippman, J. S., Switzer, F. A. I. & Roth, P. L. (1998). A meta-analytic review of predictors of job performance for salespeople. *Journal of Applied Psychology*, 83, 586–97.

Vinson, G. A., Connelly, B. S. & Ones, D. S. (2007). Relationships between personality and organisation switching: implications for utility estimates. *International Journal of Selection and Assessment*, 15, 118–33.

Viswesvaran, C. & Ones, D. S. (1999). Meta-Analysis of fakability estimates: implications for personality measurement. *Educational and Psychological Measurement, 54,* 197–210.

(2000). Measurement error in 'Big Five Factors' personality assessment: reliability generalization across studies and measures. *Educational and Psychological Assessment, 60*(2), 224–35.

(2002). Agreements and disagreements on the role of general mental ability (GMA) in industrial, work, and organizational psychology. *Human Performance, 15,* 211–31.

Viswesvaran, C., Ones, D. S. & Hough, L. M. (2001). Do impression management scales in personality inventories predict managerial job performance ratings? *International Journal of Selection and Assessment, 9*(4), 277–89.

Von Eye, A., Lösel, F. & Mayzer, R. (2003). Is it all written in the stars? A methodological commentary on Sachs' astrology monograph and re-analyses of his data on crime statistics. *Psychology Science, 45,* 78–91.

Wagner, R. (1949). The employment interview: a critical summary. *Personnel Psychology, 2,* 17–46.

Waldman, D. A. & Avolio, B. J. (1991). Race effects in performance evaluations: controlling for ability, education, and experience. *Journal of Applied Psychology, 76,* 897–901.

Wallach, M. A. (1970). Creativity. In P. Mussen (ed.), *Carmichael's Handbook of Child Psychology,* pp. 1211–72. New York: Wiley.

Watson, D., Clark, L. A. & Tellegen, A. (1988). Development and validation of brief measures of positive and negative affect: the PANAS scales. *Journal of Personality and Social Psychology, 54*(6), 1063–70.

Watson, P. R. (1993). Benefits of graphology. *Professional Manager,* May, 4.

Wechsler, D. (1939). *The Measurement of Adult Intelligence.* Baltimore: Williams & Wilkins.

(2002). *WAIS-III/WMS-III Technical Manual: Updated.* San Antonio, TX: Psychological Corporation.

Weekley, J. A. & Jones, C. (1997). Video-based situational testing. *Personnel Psychology, 50*(1), 25–49.

Weisberg, R. W. & Alba, J. W. (1981). An examination of the alleged role of 'fixation' in the solution of several 'insight' problems. *Journal of Experimental Psychology: General, 110,* 169–92.

Wells, S. R. (1866). *New Physiognomy; or Signs of Character, as Manifested through Temperament and External Forms.* New York: Fowler & Wells.

Welsh, J. R., Watson, T. W. & Ree, M. J. (1990). *Armed Services Vocational Aptitude Battery (ASVAB): Predicting Military Criteria from General and Specific Abilities.* Brooks Air Force Base, TX: Air Force Human Resources Laboratory.

Wernimont, P. F. (1962). Reevaluation of a weighted application blank for office personnel. *Journal of Applied Psychology, 46*(6), 417–19.

Wernimont, P. F. & Campbell, J. P. (1968). Signs, samples, and criteria. *Journal of Applied Psychology, 52*(5), 372–6.

White, J. L., Moffitt, T. E. & Silva, P. A. (1989). A prospective replication of the protective effects of IQ in subjects at high risk for juvenile delinquency. *Journal of Consulting and Clinical Psychology, 57,* 719–24.

Whiteside, R. L. (1974). *Face Language*. New York: Fell.

Wiesner, W. & Cronshaw, S. (1988). The validity of the employment interview. *Journal of Occupational Psychology, 61*(4), 275–90.

Wilk, S. L., Desmarais, L. B. & Sackett, P. R. (1995). Gravitation to jobs commensurate with ability: longitudinal and cross-sectional tests. *Journal of Applied Psychology, 80*, 79–85.

Wilk, S. L. & Sackett, P. R. (1996). Longitudinal analysis of ability-job complexity fit and job change. *Personnel Psychology, 49*, 937–67.

Wilson, N. A. B. (1948). The work of the Civil Service Selection Board. *Occupational Psychology, 22*, 204–12.

Wimbush, J. C. & Dalton, D. R. (1997). Base rate for employee theft: convergence of multiple methods. *Journal of Applied Psychology, 82*(5), 756–63.

Winter, D. G. (1973). Leader appeal, leader performance, and the motive profiles of leaders and followers: a study of American presidents and elections. *Journal of Personality and Social Psychology, 52*, 196–202.

Witt, L. A. & Ferris, G. R. (2003). Social skill as moderator of the conscientiousness-performance relationship: convergent results across four studies. *Journal of Applied Psychology, 88*(5), 809–21.

Wonderlic, E. F. (1992). *Manual for the Wonderlic Personnel Test & Scholastic Level Exam II*. Libertyville, IL: Wonderlic Personnel Test Inc.

Woody, C. & Claridge, G. S. (1977). Psychoticism and thinking. *British Journal of Social and Clinical Psychology, 16*, 241–8.

Yerkes, R. M. (ed.) (1921). *Psychological Examining in the US Army: Memoirs of the National Academy of Sciences. Psychological Examining in the US Army*, vol. 15. Washington, DC: Government Printing Office.

Yerkes, R. M. & Dodson, J. D. (1908). The relation of strength of stimulus to rapidity of habit formation. *Journal of Comparative Neurology & Psychology, 18*, 459–82.

Yik, M. S. M., Russell, J. A. & Barrett, L. F. (1999). Structure of self-reported current affect: integration and beyond. *Journal of Personality and Social Psychology, 77*(3), 600–19.

Yukl, G. (1998). *Leadership in Organisations*. Upper Saddle River, NJ: Prentice Hall.

Yukl, G. & Van Fleet, D. D. (1992). Theory and research on leadership in organisations. In M. D. Dunnette & I. M. Hough (eds.), *Handbook of Industrial and Organisational Psychology*, vol. 3, pp. 147–97. Palo Alto, CA: Consulting Psychologists Press.

Zaccaro, S. J. (2007). Trait-based perspectives of leadership. *American Psychologist*, special issue: *Leadership, 62*(1), 6–16.

Zaccaro, S. J., Kemp, C. & Bader, P. (2004). Leader traits and attributes. In J. Antonakis, A. T. Cianciolo & R. J. Sternberg (eds.), *The Nature of Leadership*, pp. 101–24. Thousand Oaks, CA: Sage.

Zebrowitz, L. A., Voinescu, L. & Collins, M. A. (1996). 'Wide-eyed' and 'crooked-faced': determinants of perceived and real honesty across the life span. *Personality and Social Psychology Bulletin, 22*, 1258–69.

Zebrowitz-McArthur, L. & Berry, D. S. (1987). Cross-cultural agreement in perceptions of babyfaced adults. *Journal of Cross-Cultural Psychology, 18*, 165–92.

Zhou, J. (2003). When the presence of creative coworkers is related to creativity: role of supervisor close monitoring, developmental feedback, and creative personality. *Journal of Applied Psychology*, *88*(3), 413–22.

Zyphur, M. J., Bradley, J. C., Landis, R. S. & Thoresen, C. J. (2008). The effects of cognitive ability and conscientiousness on performance over time: a censored latent growth model. *Human Performance*, *21*(1), 1–27.

Index